Artur <u>L</u>ondon

→The Confession

TRANSLATED BY ALASTAIR HAMILTON

William Morrow and Company, Inc.

 NEW YORK   1970

364.1310924

0424

Printed in the United States of America.

Library of Congress Catalog Card Number 70-136267

To my companions in misfortune who were executed although innocent or who died in prison.

To all the innocent victims of the trials.

To all those friends, known and unknown, who fought and who gave their lives in the hope of achieving a better world.

To all those who carry on the struggle to restore humanity to socialism.

Contents

Czechoslovakians involved in the 'Slansky trial'

LONDON, ARTUR: Born in Ostrava, Silesia, now a part of Czechoslovakia, in 1915; became a Communist by the age of 14; enlisted in the International Brigades to fight against Franco in Spain in 1936; worked for the underground in France until deported to Mauthausen in 1942; repatriated to France in 1945; left for Switzerland in 1947 to obtain medicine for tuberculosis contracted in Mauthausen; received aid from the Unitarian Service Committee headed by Noel Field; returned to Czechoslovakia in 1948 and in February 1949 agreed to be an Under-Secretary of Foreign affairs, a position also held by VAVRO HAJDU. Both appeared as defendants in the Slansky trial.

GOTTWALD, KLEMENT: Prime Minister under Czechoslovakian President Benes and head of the Communist Party; organized the Czech coup of 25 February 1948, forming a new cabinet in which the Communists held fifty per cent of the positions; became President of Czechoslovakia after the general elections of 10 June 1948, with ANTON ZAPOTOCKY as Prime Minister; died 14 March 1953; succeeded by Zapotocky.

CLEMENTIS, VLADIMIR: Became Deputy Minister of Foreign Affairs under JAN MASARYK as a result of the 'Czech coup' of 25 February 1948; after the general elections of 10 June 1948 made Minister of Foreign Affairs in Zapotocky's cabinet; relieved of this post in March 1950 and arrested at the end of January 1951 to appear as a defendant in the Slansky trial.

SIROKY, VILIAM: Became Deputy Premier under Zapotocky after the 10 June 1948 general elections; succeeded Vladimir Clementis as Minister of Foreign Affairs in March 1950; became Prime Minister, replacing Zapotocky, after Gottwald's death.

SLANSKY, RUDOLPH: Secretary General of the Czech Communist Party until that post was abolished, 7 September 1951; then made Deputy Premier, Siroky's old position, until arrested on 27 November 1951.

SLING, OTTO: Secretary of the regional committee of the Czech Communist Party for the Brno district; arrested in November 1950, first of the arrests leading directly to the Slansky trial although EUGEN LÖBL, Under-Secretary of Foreign Trade, was arrested 14 November 1949. Both appeared as defendants in the Slansky trial.

GEMINDER, BEDRICH: Head of the department of international relations of the Central Committee of the Czech Communist Party. Arrested during 1951 and appeared as a defendant in the Slansky trial.

ZAVODSKY, OSVALD: Minister of State Security until his arrest in January 1951; tried and executed in one of the trials following the Slansky trial.

Other defendants in the 'Slansky trial'

FISCHL, OTTO: Deputy Minister of Finance.

FRANK, JOSEF: Assistant Secretary General of the Communist Party of Czechoslovakia.

FREJKA, LUDVIK: Director of the Economic Section of the Chancellery of the President.

MARGOLIUS, RUDOLPH: Deputy Minister of External Commerce.

REICIN, BEDRICH: Deputy Minister of National Defense.

SIMONE, ANDRE: Foreign editor of the newspaper *Rude Pravo*.

SVAB, KAREL: Deputy Minister of National Security.

Other Important Figures outside Czechoslovakia

BERIA, LAVRENTI: Leading Communist in the Soviet Party; placed in charge of two ministries, Internal Affairs and State Security, in 1946; responsible for the purge trials of Rajk, Kostov, and Slansky, as well as those that followed these major trials in the satellite countries; executed on 23 December 1953, along with six associates.

FIELD, NOEL: Member of the United States State Department who, during World War II, worked for United States Intelligence; directed the Unitarian Service Committee from its head office in

Geneva from November 1942; disappeared in Prague on 12 May 1949 and imprisoned in Hungary until his release in 1954. His brother, HERMANN FIELD disappeared in Warsaw on 22 August 1949, following a trip to Prague in search of Noel; held in prison in Poland until his release in 1954.

KOSTOV, TRAICHO: Leading Communist in the Bulgarian Party; dismissed as Deputy Premier on 15 April 1949; tried in Sofia 7–14 December 1949; the only one of the ten defendants to plead not guilty; sentenced to death and executed on 16 December 1949.

RAKOSI, MATYAS: Leader of the Communist Party in Hungary from 1945 when he obtained the post of Deputy. Premier; made Premier in August 1952; succeeded by IMRE NAGY on 4 July 1953.

RAJK, LASZLO: Leading Communist in the Hungarian government; first Minister of the Interior and then Foreign Minister until 15 May 1949 when, after general elections, he was dropped from the cabinet; arrested 19 June 1949 along with TIBOR SZÖNYI, head of the Communist Party cadres section, and LAZAR BRANKOV, counsellor of the Yugoslav embassy in Budapest; tried 16 September 1949 and executed 15 October 1949.

Chronology of Events Relevant to the 'Slansky trial'

June 1947: Announcement of the Marshall Plan which Czechoslovakia decided to accept, but Stalin insisted she refuse.

25 February 1948: President of Czechoslovakia, Benes, gave way to Communist demands and accepted the new cabinet proposed by Prime Minister Gottwald, in which the Communists, by then the largest party, held fifty per cent of the positions; so called 'Czech coup' in which the Communists gained control of the country.

10 June 1948: After general elections Benes resigned; Gottwald became President; Zapotocky, Prime Minister; Clementis, Minister of Foreign affairs; and Siroky, Deputy Premier.

June 1948, U.S.S.R.: The Cominform officially condemned Yugoslavia, expelling it from their ranks; Tito, formerly Stalin's favourite, was branded as the enemy within the party for having shown political and economic independence from the U.S.S.R.

February 1949: Artur London made Under-Secretary of Foreign Affairs.

IN CZECHOSLOVAKIA	IN OTHER COMMUNIST COUNTRIES
12 May 1949: Disappearance of Noel Field in Prague from where he was taken to a Hungarian prison.	
	15 May 1949, Hungary: General elections leading to a reorganization of the Cabinet from which the Communist, Laszlo Rajk, was dropped as Foreign Minister.
	22 August, 1949, Poland: Disappearance of Hermann Field from Warsaw airport.
	16–24 September 1949, Hungary: 'Rajk trial'. Eight defendants, all prominent officials who pleaded guilty to various charges of Trotskyism, espionage for the West, conspiring to overthrow the government, Titoism and bourgeois nationalism, as well as individual political experiences. On this score, former Foreign Minister Laszlo Rajk and Tibor Szönyi, were made to describe their dealings with Noel Field who was 'identified' in court as a leader of the American espionage service working for Allen Dulles who had been head of the Office of Strategic Services (O.S.S.). Rajk had been helped to escape from le Vernet internment camp in France by

IN CZECHOSLOVAKIA	IN OTHER COMMUNIST COUNTRIES
	Noel Field and Szönyi had received O.S.S. and Unitarian Service Committee money from him during the war.
	15 October 1949, Hungary: Rajk, Szönyi and Szalai, Szönyi's deputy, executed.
24 November 1949: Arrest of Eugen Löbl, one of the three defendants in the Slansky trial who was not executed.	
	7–14 December, Bulgaria: 'Kostov trial'. Traicho Kostov, former Deputy Premier, along with ten other leading political figures, accused of Trotskyism, espionage for the West (Noel Field's name was mentioned as in the Rajk trial), plotting to overthrow the government with the help of Yugoslavia, Titoism, and bourgeois nationalism; Kostov pleaded not guilty throughout the trial but before his execution, retracted his statement and 'admitted' to the crimes. The ten other defendents pleaded guilty and were sentenced to imprisonments of varying lengths.
	16 December 1949, Bulgaria: Kostov executed.

15 March 1950: Vladimir Clementis dismissed as Minister of Foreign Affairs, succeeded by Viliam Siroky.

November 1950: Arrest of Otto Sling, a regional Secretary of the Czech Communist Party.

28 January 1951: Arrest of Artur London, Under-Secretary of Foreign Affairs. Also arrested at the end of January 1951 were Vladimir Clementis, former Minister of Foreign Affairs, and Osvald Zavodsky, Minister of State Security.

16 February 1951: Arrest of Karel Svab, Under-Secretary of National Security.

7 September 1951: Slansky relieved of his post as Secretary General of the Party, and made Deputy Premier.

23 November 1951: Arrest of Slansky.

20–27 November 1952: 'Slansky trial'. Fourteen defendants, all leading Communists, and many former volunteers in the International Brigades, were accused of Trotskyism, Titoism, espionage for the West with the intent to overthrow the government, and Zionism, making the Slansky trial the first of the Stalinist 'show trials' in a satellite country in which antisemitism played a role. (Eleven of the fourteen were Jewish.) The main defendant, Rudolph Slansky, former Secretary General of the Party and Deputy Premier, was accused of organizing the conspiracy of which the other thirteen were members. All fourteen pleaded guilty to all the crimes which for some, among them Artur London, included espionage dealings with Noel and Hermann Field, Americans who had been used for the same purpose in the Kostov trial, having originally been 'identified' as 'spies' in the Rajk trial.

3 December 1952: Execution of eleven of the fourteen defendants in the Slansky trial. (Artur London, Eugen Löbl, and Vavro Hadju were sentenced to life imprisonment.)

5 March 1953, U.S.S.R.: Death of Stalin; succeeded by Malenkov.

14 March 1953: Death of President Klement Gottwald.

4 July 1953, Hungary: Imre Nagy succeeds Matyas Rakosi as Prime Minister of Hungary.

23 December 1953, U.S.S.R.: Execution of Lavrenti Beria, formerly head of the Ministry of the Interior and State Security, along with six of his associates.

25 October 1954, Poland: Release and rehabilitation of Hermann Field by the Polish government.

17 November 1954, Hungary: Release and rehabilitation of Noel and Mrs Field by the Hungarian government.

2 February 1956: Release of Artur London.

14 February 1956 U.S.S.R.: Twentieth Party Congress of the Communist Party of the Soviet Union at which Khrushchev, then First Party Secretary, denounced Stalin and the work of Beria and his men.

29 March 1956, Hungary: Posthumous rehabilitation of Laszlo

IN CZECHOSLOVAKIA	IN OTHER COMMUNIST COUNTRIES
	Rajk by the Hungarian government.
14 April 1956: Formal announcement made by Prime Minister Siroky that Artur London had been released.	14 April 1956, Bulgaria: Posthumous rehabilitation of Traicho Kostov, and release and rehabilitation of the other ten defendants in the Kostov trial.
	March 1958, U.S.S.R.: Khrushchev made Premier of the Soviet Union.
April 1963: Penal rehabilitation of all fourteen defendants in the Slansky trial.	
1 May 1968: Full rehabilitation and exoneration of all fourteen defendants in the Slansky trial.	
31 May 1968: Soviet troops enter Czechoslovakia.	
3 August 1968: Withdrawal of Soviet troops from Czechoslovakia.	
20 August 1968: Invasion and seizure of Czechoslovakia by troops of the Soviet Union, Hungary, Bulgaria, Poland and East Germany.	

Compiled by the Editor

'What do you expect me to see when I look in the mirror? This empty world, like a hastily deserted room with a torn book on the floor, with everything torn. . .What has become of that nineteenth-century universe where we paid in sous and crossed every frontier where we liked and as we liked? It was to no avail to see the clouds on the horizon, to prophesy disaster. Who, living in his own home, could imagine what it would all lead to – the broken doors, the exasperation, those poor objects which we thought were ours? And we stood there, terrified or rebellious, hanging on to those values which we had never questioned, still finding the strength to survive in our old trust.'

LOUIS ARAGON
La Mise à mort

Part One

Koldeje

One

I could stand it no longer. I felt hunted ever since my friends
Pavlik and Feigl had been arrested and even more nervous after
the disappearance of the American, Noel Field, who was
mentioned as a spy at the famous Rajk trial in Hungary. Pavlik
and Feigl I had known in Paris from French Resistance days;
Noel Field I had met later on in Switzerland, and yet it would be
so easy to account for my dealings with all three of them. I had,
in fact, been interrogated at length and assumed that all suspicion of me had thereby been dispelled until I observed that I
was again being shadowed and in such an obvious way that
several of my friends had noticed it too. I later discovered that
the State Security had even asked my chauffeur for a full report
on all my movements.

Finally, that Sunday in January 1951, I decided to ask Ossik
to help me. Ossik – Osvald Zavodsky, the Head of Czech State
Security – had been a friend of mine since the days of the
Spanish Civil War and later in the French Resistance. We had
even been in Mauthausen concentration camp together. But for
some months I had felt that he had been avoiding me. I had
the impression that he was unable to resist the wave of suspicion
sweeping through the Party and the country. And yet our
common past should have been some guarantee for me.

Ossik, like many other state officials, lived in one of the large
buildings opposite the Ministry of the Interior. But first I
called on Oskar Vales who also worked for the Security Services,
another friend from Spanish Civil War days. He was someone I
could trust, a broadminded man, who was not tainted by his
work. As soon as he heard what was happening to me, he

offered to accompany me to Ossik's in order to demand an explanation.

In Ossik's apartment Vales and I found two other friends, Tonda Svoboda and Otto Hromadko. They too seemed anxious. Ossik himself had gone to fetch Josef Pavel who lived on the floor above. There we were, six veterans of the Spanish Civil War, volunteers in the International Brigades, but the pleasure and enthusiasm of recalling Teruel, Madrid, Casa de Campo, Albacete were absent. Now, all we could talk about were the events in our own country, Czechoslovakia. The arrests: first Sling, another veteran from Spain and a member of the Central Committee of the Communist Party, and then others. According to our friend Pavel these arrests were nothing to what was to come. We in Czechoslovakia were soon to be having our own Rajk trial.

Indeed, some weeks earlier Pavel had been removed from his post as Under-Secretary of the Interior. First he was put in charge of the border guards, and then sent to study at the central school of the Party. Svoboda, too, no longer directed the military department of the Central Committee but had been sent to the Military Academy to take a 'finishing' course. Of my five friends only Oskar Vales and Ossik still retained their original jobs, and as for myself, I wanted to leave the Ministry of Foreign Affairs where I had been an Under-Secretary since February 1949. Pavel actually seemed quite contented with his new life, and, as we discussed these changes, he said, 'We were lucky to have been able to supply the factual reports on the former volunteers in the International Brigades which we sent to the Party. That precaution may have saved us a lot of trouble and spared our old comrades from these new purges.'

Ossik then asked me if there was any news. He seemed startled to hear that though he, as head of State Security, had for a short time managed to prevent my being followed, the shadowing had now resumed. He paced the room nervously: 'Are you sure you're right? What makes you think they are cars from Security?'

I went to the window, showed him the car parked in the street, and handed him the slip of paper on which I had noted the numbers of all the cars following me over the last few days. He gazed at it in silence.

I told the others what had happened to me – except for Oskar Vales none of them knew about it, and none of them took it particularly seriously. Tonda Svoboda made a few jokes about the 'cops' while Hromadko, alluding to Ossik's position as Head of Security, remarked: 'The shoemaker's wife is always the worst shod!' Pavel alone remained silent. He was clearly uneasy and after a while he said to Ossik: 'If he's still being trailed after your personal intervention it's bad. You must check on where these orders are coming from. And if they're coming from the people I think, watch out, it might be very dangerous.'

I was astonished to hear him say this because I had no idea which 'people' he was thinking about. Ossik became increasingly ill at ease. The conversation foundered. Pavel left, and was soon followed by the others. I departed in my turn and drove home slowly, my eye on the Security car in my driving mirror. It was exasperating – as though they had nothing better to do!

Later in the afternoon, I decided to go to the Foreign Ministry for some newspapers. I was still being followed, so this time I changed my mind and went back to see Ossik.

He was alone, and looked none too pleased to see me when he opened the door. Before I could tell him why I had come he asked if I had been followed again. He paled when I told him I had, turned off the light and went to the window to look at the car parked in the street.

'I'm fed up with this business!' I burst out. 'What do they want now? Haven't I answered all your questions about Field? Haven't I given you a detailed report on all my dealings with him? You can easily find out if I'm lying. I'm not such an idiot. I know perfectly well that Field is in prison in Hungary. Why don't you face me with him if you don't believe me?'

At that stage I had no idea that the Security Services could make anyone admit anything, about himself or about anyone else.

He did not try to stop me, but seemed to look straight through me. Although I had come to ask him for help he was as scared and helpless as I was, as though, in spite of his position, he had no idea of what was going on.

He walked round the dark room more and more nervously. What light there was came from a street lamp. He talked incoherently and I was unable to follow his line of thought. He was afraid, he no longer tried to hide it, and all he could do was to promise to look into my case, to keep me posted.

I left him, and as he said goodbye he asked me to drive off slowly so that he could make sure that the car parked behind mine was from Security. But obviously he was now convinced that I was being followed, and, indeed, the black car immediately drove after me. This time I was frightened. Why was I followed night and day by Security cars despite formal orders given by the head of State Security?

And what about Ossik's confusion and helplessness? I couldn't understand it, and this, on top of the constant anxiety which I now felt, was what scared me most.

I hurried home, eager to be near my family, to get away from my gloomy thoughts. Talking to my wife and her parents, watching my children, usually made me more relaxed, but today nothing worked. I had the feeling that everything would end in disaster. What would become of them all, foreigners, who could not even speak the language?

On Monday morning another car followed me when I left for the Ministry. But at midday, that evening, the next day, there was nothing. The week went by without my being followed and I grew a little calmer, although I could never completely rid myself of anxiety. I worked as hard as I could – ever since I had been watched I tried to devote the maximum amount of effort to every one of my tasks, because I knew that the slightest mistake on my part could be interpreted as a deliberate act of hostility.

Ossik spoke to me on the telephone and from his voice I could tell he was relieved to hear I was no longer being followed. I too tried to reassure myself, but to no avail. I decided to talk to my superior again, Siroky, who had been Minister of Foreign Affairs since March 1950 when Vladimir Clementis had been superseded. I would tell him what was going on and then I would resign once and for all.

Siroky knew me well, for we had worked together in Paris in 1939 and 1940, and had seen each other every day for almost a year. He knew that I had successfully and conscientiously carried out all the most difficult tasks with which the Delegation of the Czech Communist Party in France – of which he was a member – had entrusted me. He also knew my whole family, who had always received him with open arms. He was aware of the trouble I had been having ever since the previous year. And he knew that when I was staying in Switzerland in 1947 to cure my relapse of tuberculosis brought on by my deportation to Mauthausen I had met Noel Field and, through him, managed to obtain help from the Unitarian Service which he directed. It was also Siroky who had introduced me to Pavlik and Feigl in Paris in 1939. Finally, he knew that once I had become aware of the suspicion with which the State Security regarded me, I had asked the Party leaders to relieve me of my post as Under-Secretary because I no longer felt that I inspired the confidence necessary for the job.

Siroky's recent behaviour towards me had not been what I had hoped, but I was sure that we could settle the matter, that he would see my point and accept my resignation. Now that I had made up my mind I felt better.

Then I realized that I hadn't seen Siroky for two weeks. He no longer organized the usual meetings with the Under-Secretaries. My colleagues were summoned individually to his office to discuss current affairs, while I had been told by his secretary that he was too busy to see me and that I had to give him my report through her. I told her to tell the Minister how surprised I was, but it was no use, so I then asked her to get him to grant me an appointment for personal reasons. I was put off from day to day. Then, on Saturday, when I told myself that it would never take place, Siroky's secretary told me that he would see me first thing on Monday morning.

I was not to keep the appointment, and Siroky must have already known it.

Two

We had now reached that fatal Sunday, 28 January 1951. Tonda Havel was at the house, a former farm labourer whom I had met through Otto Hromadko. He had joined the Party in 1933, and was now the administrator of a state farm. Havel had practical experience of the soil instead of a diploma, but he was constantly at odds with local and regional authorities who mechanically applied orders from above, even though common sense should have told them that the natural conditions would prevent their experiments from working. According to him, totally incompetent individuals had jobs about which they knew absolutely nothing. In short, he was in Prague to meet Smrkovsky, the general director of state farms and forests. They had been in the Communist Youth together before the war, and I promised Havel to arrange an appointment for him on Monday. He was thrilled; at last Smrkovsky would hear him and solve his problems.

My wife was finishing the novel *Far From Moscow*. 'Every communist should read it,' she said, 'and so should you.' Lise had retained all the freshness of her youth. Whenever she was enthusiastic about something she wanted everyone around her to share her views. She put her heart into everything she did. Ready for any sacrifice for her friends, she was severe and intransigent about her duty as a communist. She had complete faith in her ideal and total confidence in the Party and the USSR.

For her the basic principles of militancy were simply – 'Whoever has doubts about the Party is no longer a communist,' and 'Truth always triumphs.' She was sure that our present troubles would soon be over. 'What have we to fear if our conscience is clean?' she would ask me.

I hesitated to tell her of my fear and anxiety, but in whom could I confide if not in her?

After lunch I had to drive Havel to Otto Hromadko's so I went into the garden where my wife was playing with the children. I watched Lise hugging Michel in the folds of her blue cape, while Gérard ran round them in circles. I didn't want to leave them and I asked her to come with the children for a drive. I felt that she wanted to come, but Gérard said: 'You promised to play with me today. I don't want to go.' She smiled at me. 'I promised, so hurry back.' I kissed her and left them. This was the last I saw of my wife and children before my arrest.

I was so used to being shadowed that I automatically checked in my driving mirror, but noticed with relief that I was not being followed today either.

I drove past the Castle. The city emerged from a violet mist, the tarnished red, the old bronze and gold of the roofs glimmering. In the streets the passers-by were huddled in warm winter clothes. Suddenly, in the driving-mirror, I noticed a Tatra, one of the cars which had followed me in the past. I had an unpleasant sensation, and told Havel to take the car's number. I made several detours and asked him whether the car was still following us. 'Yes, it's behind us. What's going on?'

'The communists are going through a difficult period, some important events have been happening and must be cleared up in the Party's interest. But it'll sort itself out.'

I don't think he knew what I was talking about and he said nothing.

I drove past a group of people and recognized Dora Kleinova pushing her son's pram. I had met her in Spain where she was working as a doctor in the International Brigades, and then in France during the war, in the Czech-speaking group of the

Main d'Oeuvre Immigré, the central section of the French Communist Party in charge of the immigrant labourers. Arrested in Paris and deported to Auschwitz, she returned to Czechoslovakia on her way to Poland, her native country. But after the pogrom at Kielce, she decided to settle in Prague where she had studied medicine. It was here that she met Gisèle who was with her today, the wife of the writer Egon Erwin Kisch.

They smiled at me and I waved to them. I knew that they too had been in trouble recently, for they had also known Field. But while I thought their problems were over, I felt that I was rushing to my doom.

Havel couldn't understand how an old communist like me, a veteran of the Spanish Civil War and a Resistance fighter, could be the object of suspicion. He was indignant. I told him that I had been implicated in an obscure business, the issue of which remained uncertain in spite of my innocence. As we were talking we came to Otto Hromadko's house in the Valentinska, a little street behind the old Parliament building. Havel said goodbye, and for a minute I wanted to go in with him, but I thought better of it as I didn't want to compromise him.

The Security car drew up behind me; at the end of the street another car of the same make was parked with three men inside it. I drove off without even realizing which road I was taking. I wanted to see Ossik again, but on the way I decided to telephone him first. I had no idea that he, Oskar Vales and some others had been arrested the day before. I went to the Ministry.

As I entered the building the two cars stopped next to mine. Deciding not to ring Ossik but to go straight to his apartment, I said a few words to the porter and got back into my car. The two cars continued to follow me. Again I changed my mind. I would go home first and tell Lise what was happening and then go to Ossik's.

After three hundred yards, as I was entering the lane behind the Tuscan Palace, one of the cars overtook me and stopped dead in front of me. Six armed men rushed up, pulled me off my seat, handcuffed me and threw me into the first car, which drove off at full speed. I struggled, and demanded to know who they were, but they blindfolded me and shouted: 'Shut up! No point in asking questions! You'll know who we are soon enough!'

They were not arresting me, they were kidnapping me. It was like detective stories which I had always thought exaggerated, but now I was involved in one myself, in broad daylight, in a residential area of Prague. I even thought some subversive organization was behind it, for there had been recent rumours that the western powers had sent armed gangs into the country and that shots had been exchanged with men from Security.

I protested again, and told them to show me their papers. 'Shut up! You've nothing to ask!'

The car drove through the town. I heard trams and cars passing us, and we stopped several times. The men were whispering. One of them got out and then came back. More whispering, and off we drove. I had the impression that we were driving round in a circle and the whole thing became more agonizing.

Finally one of the men started up the car and said: 'We can go in in twenty minutes.'

On we drove. The noises diminished and then the tyres creaked on gravel. Hands seized me, pulled me out of the car and pushed me down a passage. We went up and down flights of stairs, and along corridors. After we had turned in every direction, my eyes were unbandaged, my handcuffs removed, and I found myself in a small bare room, with no window, lit by a tiny bulb burning in a corner above a table. The rest of the room was in darkness.

I was made to undress and put on some dungarees with no buttons and a pair of shapeless slippers. I asked to see a Party official immediately, but my demand was greeted with insults and threats. The few objects of value which I had on me were

removed and I had to sign for them. As for my Darex coupons*
which I put on the table – about 1,200 crowns – one of my
kidnappers took them and hurried to the door. Another ran
after him. 'Where are you going with all that? Leave them on
the table.' I later discovered that all these things were stolen
from me.

I was again blindfolded with a cloth tied so tight that I was
stifled. I went down more corridors, up and down stairs, bump-
ing into walls. Finally the bandage was torn from my head.
I was in a cell, with a mattress and two folded blankets in the
corner. Before the door was closed I received an order: 'You
are not allowed to sit down. Walk!'

This arrest was the worst ordeal of my life. The moment I
had been handcuffed the images of twenty-two years in the
Party filed through my mind, comrades – dead and alive – with
whom I had fought in Czechoslovakia, in Spain, in France, in
prisons and Nazi concentration camps, their confidence and
their affection which I had never betrayed, my family which
had performed so many sacrifices for the Party, my parents-in-
law, my wife and children who were even now vainly awaiting
my return.

Alone in my cell I was in despair, but at the same time,
paradoxically, I felt a certain relief. After more than a year of
being suspected, after the anxiety that had turned me into a
hunted animal, I was at last to know what I was accused of and
I would be able to defend myself. Everything would be cleared
up. It was in the Party's interest. I clung to this hope in spite of
the barbarous way I had been arrested. I stopped walking for a
second – I felt so tired – but the door opened noisily. Two
guards seized hold of me, shook me and knocked my head
against the wall, 'to set my ideas in order' they said, and told me
they would repeat the treatment if I had another lapse of
memory. The two guards were in uniform with a five-pointed

* Coupons corresponding to the equivalent sum of western currency
which enabled the bearer to purchase in special shops where Czech
crowns were not accepted.

red star on their caps. There was no longer any doubt: I was definitely in the hands of State Security.

Night had fallen and no light shone through the opaque glass window. I wondered where I was. Was this the notorious Ruzyn prison near the Prague airfield, of which there had recently been talk? The sound of aeroplanes close by seemed to confirm this supposition. And yet I had no doubt that I would soon be able to see one of the Party officials. Maybe Siroky, who knew my past and present work, or Kopriva, Minister of State Security, who could clarify the Field business in which he knew I had only been accidentally involved. I was sure my arrest had created a scandal. After all, I was Under-Secretary of Foreign Affairs and my colleagues would undoubtedly intervene on my behalf.

I thought about my family. I tried to imagine what they were doing in that moment. They must first have thought I had stopped for a chat with my friends, but then started to worry. Lise might have tried to telephone everywhere to be sure that I had not met with an accident, but by this time she must have been informed of what had happened to me. What did they tell her?

How sorry I was not to have been able to go home. Havel's visit meant that I hadn't been able to talk to Lise since the night before.

I heard the dull noise of an object being placed on the floor. It was soup time. I had so many prisons behind me, from Ostrava in the early thirties to La Santé, Poissy, Blois, in France during the occupation, and in each one soup time was always accompanied by the sound of bowls, the grinding of a trolley, the noise of clogs and the shouts of the warders. Here all was silent. Outside my cell I only heard muffled steps and whispers.

I imagined a long corridor, lined with doors, and assumed that this silence was part of Security methods. I had always believed that these methods must be strict to be efficient, but that they should be more humane than in the prisons of the bourgeois. I still had no idea of what was in store for me. But the steps did not stop outside my door. There was to be no bowl for me, but it didn't matter much since I would have been incapable of swallowing anything. I couldn't imagine that I would also be tortured by hunger! For the time being my main torment was the thought of the ghastly night my family must be spending.

Three

At last I was allowed to lie down on my mattress, and I lay staring at the electric light. My cell hardly differed from the ones I had been in almost twenty years before, except that then I had had an iron bed, while now my mattress was on the ground.

I thought again about my wife and family. I had often told Lise about the suspicion surrounding me; I had told her I was being watched and shadowed, and had tried in vain to make an appointment with the Party Secretariat and, more recently, with Siroky. But I had played down my fear. I thought that she felt lost and helpless, regretting her job as a journalist.

There had been that telephone call in the middle of the night in November. Lise had answered, half asleep, and a drunken voice on the other end of the line had said: 'Ah, you're the Frenchwoman. . . . Your husband will be hanged one of these days.'

'Who's speaking?' Lise had asked, but all she heard was laughter, the laughter of several drunken men. 'Pay no attention,' she told me. 'Just a bunch of thugs.'

As the hours passed my mind started to wander, and my anxiety increased. I thought of the oppressive atmosphere in Moscow when we were there from 1935 to 1937, of the men who had vanished from one day to the next, leaving no trace. In our international groups it was unthinkable to ask questions, for disappearances could also mean that people had returned to their country for underground work. I once mentioned it to

Jiri Drtina, my secretary in the Ministry of Foreign Affairs, who was asking me about my youth and my stay in the Soviet Union. 'And what happened to all those people?'

We only saw one of them again, a Polish woman called Marthe, who had studied in France before going to work in the USSR where she was adopted by the French colony. She had disappeared at the beginning of 1937 and nobody had ever mentioned her name. We saw her in Paris again in 1945 shortly after our return from concentration camp. Lise had asked her: 'Were you in camp too?'

Of course Lise meant the Nazi camps, but Marthe burst into tears: 'Yes, I was in a camp, but in Siberia. A very hard camp. But don't let's talk about that,' she had added. 'It was a black page of our past, but it's all over now.'

Lise and I had often discussed Marthe. Our three years in prison in occupied France and in concentration camps were nothing to what Marthe had endured; to fall fighting the enemy can never be compared to banishment by one's own people. We tried to account for these mistakes, to justify them by the discipline imposed by a struggle as pitiless as our own, but we never mentioned our doubts.

I thought of my youth, of when I was fourteen, when I threw myself into the battle for the revolution. The Communist Youth was really young. We were boys during the First World War and had lived through the difficult years which followed it. At home there had been unemployment, misery and a brutal struggle between the workers and the forces of repression, while abroad there was fascism in Italy, and a succession of reactionary regimes in Poland, Bulgaria and Hungary. There had been the Sacco-Vanzetti case, which my father told me about, and I marched at his side through the streets of Ostrava to protest against the legal murder which America was about to commit.

A militant member of the Communist Youth and the Communist Party, the authorities had chosen me, despite my age – I was only sixteen – to work in the antimilitarist organization, as a tribute to my loyalty and courage, indispensable qualities for a task which was considered so important at the time. Every communist felt that the main duty of the working class and of the Party was to protect the first socialist power. Hence the need to campaign against imperialist war within the armies of the capitalist countries, and to teach the young soldiers the importance of peace and revolutionary defeatism.

I was working at the time – it was 1931 – with a couple of political émigrés who had escaped to Czechoslovakia after the fall of the Hungarian Commune. After their years of service, the Party had given them the trickiest jobs to perform. I had to hide the propaganda material in my house, and give it to the groups who were to distribute it in the barracks and the trains of soldiers coming home on leave.

First I had to fetch the pamphlets from the underground printing press, then hide them in my father's study or under my brother Oscar's bed in our tiny flat. My father saw what I was doing and must have realized that it was illegal material, but he said nothing. On 1 August 1931 an 'International Day of Mourning for the War' had been declared, and to prepare for the demonstration I handed out packets to comrades whom I did not know.

While this was going on one of our neighbours telephoned me at work to warn me that the police had raided our flat and had confiscated the pamphlets. I just had time to inform a comrade in the Communist Youth who was working as a decorator in the same store as I was, and to tell him to warn the local Party secretariat before the house detective – a retired policeman – asked me to make a delivery. I looked at him ironically and said: 'I was waiting for this delivery.' He never left my side as I changed my clothes and went out by the staff exit where two policemen were waiting for me. 'Follow us quietly,' they said, 'otherwise we shall have to handcuff you.'

I was interrogated at length at the police station. They asked me from whom I had received the material and to whom I was giving it, but no matter how they questioned me or hit me

I never told them anything. When they faced me with the comrade who had caused my arrest I pretended not to recognize him, and always insisted that neither my father nor my brother knew what I was doing and that I myself was unaware of the content and destination of the material I had hidden.

I was simply obeying the Party's instructions, 'Never speak to the enemy.' So the efforts of the police to discover an adult culprit failed, and as a minor I could not be convicted. Nevertheless I was sent to the local prison in Ostrava, put in solitary confinement in the minors' quarter, and charged with endangering the security of the Republic. There I started worrying about my parents. But I stuck to all I had said before the examining magistrate and he had to release me.

Owing to my conduct nobody had been questioned apart from myself and the antimilitarist organization could safely continue its work. But my imprisonment had marked me. The hours, the weeks never ended . . . and then there was the hunger. Though I was only sixteen, nothing could weaken my morale or my determination to pursue the struggle.

I spent further periods in the Ostrava prison and police station. Eighteen months later, in January 1933, I was again interned in the minors' quarter of the local jail for the same reasons as before. Twice a week I was taken to the prison school where I was taught civics by a peevish old gentleman. But this was a change after solitary confinement, and we were lent books which relieved the boredom somewhat, although they were supposed to be edifying and were intended to convert us to respect of the established order.

One day the head warder of my floor asked me whether I was Robert London's nephew. When I told him I was, he said he often played cards with my uncle, in the café in the evening, and seemed surprised that so decent a man should have such a rascal of a nephew. Nevertheless, this discovery entitled me to a double ration of beans or split peas, all we were ever given to eat, and I was so hungry that this was a real blessing.

On another occasion I was made to share my cell with a young gypsy who had been arrested for vagrancy. To begin with I was pleased to have company, but we soon quarrelled about cleaning the cell. We were supposed to take it in turn twice a week, but my fellow prisoner was so negligent that the floor remained covered with dirt. The head warder – the one who played cards with my uncle – put the blame on me and used to beat me as hard as he could. After this I found my neighbour unbearable, always bragging about his pickpocketing and his good luck, so I asked to go back to solitary confinement. How long ago that all seemed.

It was still night, and at regular intervals I heard the spy-hole open. Then the wintry sky of dirty grey loomed through the window. What time was it? A blackbird sang. Lise couldn't have got much sleep either, and I wondered what she was thinking about.

I waited for the day to begin. Who could tell? Maybe I would see a representative of the Party who would give me some hope. At last the prison awoke. My door opened and a warder told me to fold my blankets and start walking. Again I had to wait, uncertain, anxious and humiliated.

I must have been walking for hours when the door opened and a warder holding a notebook shouted at me: 'What are your requests and complaints?' I started to speak: 'When can I see . . .' but he interrupted me at once: 'Stand to attention! You don't have a name here, only a number.' I forget the number he gave me when I arrived.

I continued to pace from one wall to the other. At midday I ate my first bowl of soup, but I was not allowed to sit down. The light was already fading when they came for me, blindfolded me and pushed me down stairs and corridors. After a while my blindfold was removed and I saw I was in an underground cell with no skylight. My surprise and anxiety were short lived, however, for I was given some clothes which I exchanged for my prison uniform. At last I would know what was going on!

But I was bitterly disappointed when the door closed again.

I walked round the cell, in the dark, for a long time, blinded periodically by the bright light of a naked bulb. Not only did it light up when the warder opened the spy-hole but it sometimes flashed on and off for ten minutes at a time, which was really unbearable.

I have no idea how many hours elapsed before they came for me again. Instead of the cloth which they had hitherto bandaged round my eyes I was given a sort of mask in the form of a motorcyclist's goggles, two patches of black material replacing the glass. At least that meant I could breathe more easily. Then I was handcuffed again – and this time I was to remain hand-cuffed for almost a month.

We walked into the open air and I had to get into a car, a guard on either side of me. All these conspiratorial manners intrigued me more and more. Where were we going? I was so eager to arrive that I almost forgot my anxiety.

The noises of the town grew fainter, and we were soon driving at full speed in the country. At first I tried to make out where we were, but I soon gave up. There was no point in asking my guards, who wouldn't open their mouths until our arrival. Finally the car stopped and I was led through a maze of stair-cases and corridors. I was later to discover that I was in the Koldeje castle, about fifteen kilometres from Prague. It had first served as a summer residence for Klement Gottwald, before he was elected President of the Republic. Since then it had been requisitioned by the State Security and was used for professional and political training courses.

I was shoved against a wall, my tie and belt pulled off, and the handcuffs tightened behind my back, the steel cutting into my flesh. I was then forced into a room where my mask was removed and I was again ordered to walk up and down. The room was feebly illuminated by a naked bulb in the middle of the ceiling, and thick planks of wood were nailed to the window. This was not a normal prison, and the room was entirely empty. A coarse spy-hole had been cut in an ordinary door. I went up to the window to try to see through the splits between the planks, but I could see nothing; the planks were nailed together too closely. A kick against the door made me jump and the same voice as before ordered me to keep walking.

It was four yards from the wall to the door. The spy-hole was constantly being opened, and from time to time I could hear a short whisper behind the door. It was very cold, and I walked faster to keep warm. The handcuffs had cut into my wrists and my swollen hands were numb and frozen.

This second night lasted an eternity. The sound of footsteps echoed in other cells. Others were going through the same hell as myself. But who were they? I walked, from wall to wall, deep in my thoughts, and if I stopped an anonymous voice immediately repeated the order. So I knew that, behind the spy-hole, eyes were always watching me.

The guards came for me, put my mask on, and, after another walk through the maze, I found myself in a heated room. When my mask was removed I was blinded by the crude light of a small projector concentrated on my face, leaving the rest of the room in darkness. A voice with a strong Ukrainian or Russian accent said: 'You are here for a very serious reason. The Party ordered your arrest and told us to interrogate you. I repeat that the matter is very serious indeed, a matter of international espionage and treason against the Soviet Union and the peoples' democracies. Your duty is to help us get to the truth. You are not the only person to have been arrested. Other important people have been implicated in the same business. You cannot count on anybody's assistance. You have been in the Party a long time and I appeal to you to help the Soviet Union and our Party. Have you anything to say?'

I listened in amazement. Who could this be? A Russian? I later discovered that it was Janousek who had lived in the USSR and had been working in the Ministry of the Interior for several years until he was fired by Ossik Zavodsky on account of the brutality of his methods – he was known to have tortured certain culprits during interrogations. He was said to be a drug addict and he nursed a fierce grudge against his former employer and all of us who were now in his hands. After losing his job he had been chosen by the Soviet advisers to work in the special branch of the Security which they had created.

As I gradually grew accustomed to the dazzling light I distinguished two figures next to the man who was speaking to me. 'Have you anything to say about Field,' he asked, 'and about the hostile activities of the volunteers in the International Brigades?' I replied that despite the shock of my arrest and the conditions of my imprisonment I was relieved to find myself face to face with someone who, in the name of the Party, was going to clear up my position. I had constantly demanded to be heard by the Party and was ready to answer any questions.

The same voice interrupted me: 'Very well, then we'll draw up a report.' He turned to one of the figures and ordered: 'Go ahead!' and then to the second one: 'Write!'

I heard the sound of a sheet of paper being placed in a typewriter and another voice which asked me: 'When did you enter the American intelligence services directed by Allen Dulles? Who recruited you, and where? And with whom have you collaborated?'

I was stunned. They hadn't summoned me to explain anything. Not only was I accused, but I was also declared guilty! 'Never. Nowhere. By nobody!' I shouted, and protested against the inanity of these accusations. I later discovered that I was being interrogated by Major Smola, who had been put in charge of investigating the activity of the former volunteers in the International Brigades. The first voice, Janousek's, screamed: 'Shut up! I'm warning you that this business is going to have serious consequences. We have all the proof we need. We shall use methods that may surprise you but which will make you confess anything we like. Your life depends on us. Either you decide to redeem yourself by a full confession, or you insist on remaining an enemy of the Soviet Union and the Party until the gallows. So start by answering the questions you have just been asked.'

I continued to protest, so Janousek called a warder and

dismissed me: 'Think about it in your cell. And if you don't reach the right conclusions you'll regret it.'

The mask was again put over my face, and then I was placed in the cell and ordered to keep walking. I was terrified. Once more I thought of my past.

Four

Paris was cloaked in white to welcome our convoy of prisoners, evacuated from Mauthausen by the International Red Cross. This repatriation during the war was only for natives of the western countries, but the leaders of the clandestine resistance movement in the camp had decided to include the foreigners arrested on French soil. Thus Zavodsky and I returned to Paris together, where we found Laco Holdos, another veteran from Spain, who had returned from Buchenwald the day before by aeroplane.

It was snowing on 1 May 1945 when we marched in the immense procession from the Place de la Republique to the Place de la Nation, together with a few dozen comrades who, like ourselves, had returned from concentration camps. Paris greeted us as the first men to return from the death camps. We were pathetically thin. People wept when they saw us. Men, women and children came up to us, some of them showing us photographs: 'Did you know my father . . . my husband . . . my son . . . my brother?' For them we represented hope, but we knew how feeble that hope was. So few of us were to survive. We didn't dare tell the truth, that truth so atrocious that it was incredible. But it was not long before we heard voices, the voices of those who had helped the purveyors of the concentration camps: 'and why is it that you – and only you – should have returned?'

And to think that I should soon hear this question in the prisons of my own country.

I could at last meet my son who had been born two years earlier in the prison of La Roquette. I was to see my daughter, a big girl aged seven, and my parents-in-law. But Lise was not there. We had no news of her. Every day we went to the Hôtel Lutétia which had been turned into a reception centre for the prisoners to consult the lists of survivors. She finally came back at the end of May.

Some of our old comrades had managed to survive the tortures and the hardships and had taken part in the battle for the liberation of Paris. They were now preparing to return to Prague. For me the problem was different: my wife was a militant member of the French Communist Party, and she had just been elected National Secretary of the Union de Femmes Françaises, whose press department she directed. André Marty, who still had some say in the Party administration, suggested that I should return to my country, but that my wife should remain in France. This solution seemed to me inhuman and unacceptable.

I can still remember the conversation we had with Maurice Thorez at dinner with the Ricols, my in-laws. 'André's view is wrong. The problem was badly put. We aren't internationalists for nothing. You've been in France for a long time, you've fought in the Party, you fought in the Resistance, you have numerous comrades and friends, and your family is here. Why go back if you can work here as a communist just as well?'

And when Jeannette Veermersch said something about the bonds with one's home country and every man's desire to end his days there, Maurice smiled and said: 'Ask old Ricol if he wants to go back to Aragon. He left it because of the misery there. His home is where he could work and live, where he could feed his family. That's how we should understand the words of Marx and Engels at the end of the Communist Manifesto: 'The proletariat has no fatherland, it only has fetters to lose. Workers of the world, unite!'

The Party Secretariat suggested I remain in France where I would be put in charge of the political section of the Main d'Oeuvre Immigré, the Party organization in charge of imigrant labourers. My compatriots understood my position and had nothing against my choosing France as my second country. We even discussed this when I returned to Prague in April 1946 to accompany Jacques Duclos, the French representative at the Eighth Congress of the Czech Communist Party. Slansky, the Secretary General of the Czech Party, had initially tried to persuade me to return and work in the Party Cadre Department, but he soon saw my reasons for remaining in France.

It was in the spring of 1946, in Paris, at the Conference of Ministers of Foreign Affairs in preparation for the Peace Conference, that I again met Clementis, then Secretary of State for Czechoslovakian Foreign Affairs, and that I first became acquainted with the Minister, Jan Masaryk, and with Vavro Hajdu, who was one day to share my fate. A man of great intelligence and culture, Vavro was an expert on the German problem.

Shortly afterwards, in the second half of 1946, in Paris, the Czech Information Bureau was founded and the Franco-Czech friendship newspaper, *Parellèle* 50, was started. At the request of Clementis and Kopecky, the Minister of Information and Culture, I agreed to become political director. To begin with I did the job without pay and later I was put on the local staff.

At the beginning of 1947 I had a bad relapse of tuberculosis, with both lungs affected. Because I required doses of streptomycin which were unavailable in France at the time, I had to leave for Switzerland in order to obtain the necessary treatment.

As I was unable to pay for my cure, Clementis and Kopecky, when they heard about it, immediately gave orders that I be attached to the regular staff of the Ministry of Culture and receive my salary in Switzerland. These formalities took some time, however, because my appointment to the Ministry had to be approved by the Prime Minister's Staff Commission and the currency had to be transferred by the State Bank.

While waiting for these problems to be solved I gratefully accepted the hospitality of my friends Jean and Ninon Vincent who were already putting up my son Gérard while he recovered from an infection contracted in prison. Who would then have thought that this stay in Switzerland would one day be considered a crime? Since I received neither a salary nor a grant, the French Communist Party allowed my friend on the Main d'Oeuvre Immigré, Hervé-Kaminsky, to get me temporary assistance from the Unitarian Service, an American welfare organization which had helped antifascist and Jewish refugees during the war. The resthouses which the organization owned in France – in Savoy and near Hendaye – had been put at the disposal of prisoners returning from concentration camps, and a large number of Spanish Republicans had also received assistance from it – particularly wounded soldiers who were being looked after in a hospital near Toulouse.

That was how I met Noel Field, an American citizen, living in Geneva, who acted as European director of the Unitarian Service. I had a letter of introduction to him from his assistant in France, Herta Empi, and he agreed to help me for a short period. Three months later, when I finally received my salary from Josef Sup, the Czech cultural attaché in Geneva, I told him that I no longer needed his assistance, but said how touched I had been by all he had done for me.

My relapse was extremely serious and I only escaped the thoracoplasty which my doctor had suggested thanks to the insistence of a French surgeon.

In the course of 1948 my health improved. I was drawing my salary from the Czech Ministry of Foreign Affairs, and Clementis, now the new Minister, wanted me to act as first councillor at the embassy in Paris on the staff of the new ambassador, Hoffmeister. Things turned out differently, however. A campaign was launched against me in the Swiss press, immediately after what was known in the West as the 'Czech coup'. Attacks against my country were rampant, and some journalists, obviously basing their information on what they had heard from Czech émigrés, thought that instead of coming to Switzerland for a cure I was there to form a liaison between the French

Communist Party and the Swiss Labour Party. Normally such an assertion would have seemed ridiculous to everyone, particularly since I was openly staying with Jean Vincent, one of the secretaries of the Swiss party.

But my detractors went further. According to them I was no less than the Grey Eminence of the Cominform* for France and had also been the Comintern† agent in Spain – not André Marty and Palmiro Togliatti, but myself, then a twenty-two-year-old volunteer, had represented the Comintern in Spain!

But at the time of the rift with Tito's Yugoslavia the cold war was raging. This stupid campaign against me which would not have stood up to any serious examination resulted in my being refused a prolongation of my residence permit in Switzerland, and worse still, made the French government delay their approval of my diplomatic post. So I had to return to Prague at the end of 1948.

There, two years later, liars of the same stamp, but working for an opposite cause, were to accuse me of being an agent of the French Second Bureau and a spy in the American intelligence service. Twenty years after that the Neo-Stalinists, who never believe in smoke without a fire, were to regard me with suspicion, while the others, who had not forgotten or learned anything either, believed my loyalty to Moscow to be the only reason for my escaping the gallows. And in the meantime, in the prison of Ruzyn, my interrogators regarded the fact that I returned alive from Mauthausen as proof of my guilt.

I only returned to Prague in order to await the French visa, but since it had still not arrived by February 1949 the Party offered me the post of Under-Secretary of Foreign Affairs. I therefore decided to settle in Prague, where my family then joined me.

Hardly had we settled down, hardly had I had time to adapt myself to my new job, than the rumour of Rajk's arrest in Hungary spread through the city. Meanwhile Noel Field had

* Bureau of Information of Communist Parties and workers.
† Communist International.

disappeared while travelling in Czechoslovakia, and it was rumoured that he was connected with the men arrested along with Rajk. At the Ministry I was able to follow the continuous exchange of notes about him between the American and the Czech governments.

When I heard the news I went straight to Bedrich Geminder, who was in charge of the International Section of the Central Committee and followed the activity of the communists in the Ministry of Foreign Affairs. I wanted to tell him about my dealings with Field, but he suggested I inform the Cadre Department which was then directed by Kopriva, Svab and my friend Zavodsky who dealt with security problems within the Party. First I told them verbally and then I wrote a report about the matter. I believed the whole business to be over.

But I was wrong. Shortly afterwards five friends of mine were arrested because of Field: Pavlik and his wife, Feigl, his wife Vlasta Vesela, and Alice Kohnova, whom I knew very well.

Svab questioned me at the Central Committee. 'It's strange that all the people who have been arrested should mention you,' he told me, and I was amazed to see that he behaved more like a policeman than a comrade. That was why I insisted that my personal dealings with Field should be investigated once and for all by the Cadre Department. 'You'll see what will come of it,' he said, with no trace of friendship.

Suspicion towards me was now to increase until my arrest. Everything I said or did was regarded as suspicious.

In August 1949 Kavel Svab, who dealt with security problems within the Party, told me that Field's wife was in Prague. Wanting to know what had become of her husband, she had asked to see me on several occasions, but had been told that I was away on holiday. On her insistence, however, the Party Secretariat granted her an interview. I met her in the Paris Hotel. She wept as she told me about her husband's life and the sacrifices he had made for the communist cause, but there was nothing I could do. I went straight back to the Central Commitee in order to tell Svab about the meeting, and he asked me to send him a written report. I refused. 'No, give me a typist, I want to dictate this report immediately, while I can still remember everything. That'll save your finding contradictions with the recording of our conversation which you can't have failed to make at the hotel.'

Svab smiled at me. 'It would be interesting to know how you found out about these things.'

A month later, in September 1949, the Rajk trial took place. Three facts increased my anxiety. First, Field was presented as a major spy playing a leading part in the American intelligence service against the peoples' democracies. The Unitarian Service was henceforth described as a centre of espionage and a recruiting office for American agents.

Second, Szöny, who was in charge of the cadres of the Central Committee of the Hungarian Communist Party and who had been condemned to death at the Rajk trial, admitted that he and other members of his group had received money from Field in Switzerland. He claimed that the receipt he gave Field was used as a means of blackmailing him into becoming an American agent. Szöny also said that Field and American Intelligence had a secret organization in Czechoslovakia of which Pavlik was a member. Then the Yugoslav Brankov, who was sentenced to life imprisonment, said, in his turn, that, according to Rankovitch, the Yugoslav Minister of the Interior, the supposed agents were working even better in Czechoslovakia than in Hungary.

Third, Rajk, himself a former volunteer in the International Brigades who had been interned in France, confessed that the majority of the veterans from Spain were under the Trotskyist influence of the Yugoslavs; that the French Second Bureau, together with the Gestapo and the American intelligence services, had found numerous agents among them; and that during the war the Gestapo had undertaken to repatriate those volunteers who agreed to serve as German agents.

As one of the national directors of the Main d'Oeuvre Immigré, I had personally seen to the repatriation of many volunteers, some of whom were Yugoslavs, so that they could fight against their collaborationist governments or against the Germans in occupation. I did this on the instructions provided by the Communist International and by the leaders of the French Communist Party. I decided to talk again, to Geminder who was in charge of the International Section of the Czech Party's Central Committee, and to persuade him to have my case reviewed as soon as possible by the Party. Nothing happened so I asked him to arrange for me to meet Slansky, the Party Secretary General. I rang him every day. 'He's terribly busy,' I was told at last, and from his confusion and awkwardness I realized that Slansky had refused, 'but he'll call you himself as soon as he can.' Slansky never could.

When Jacques Duclos came to Prague I told him everything: didn't he know about what the Main d'Oeuvre Immigré had done during the war? Hadn't he been directing the underground movement? He admitted that he was as worried as I was by Rajk's statement about the repatriation of the volunteers, but said we shouldn't let minor issues blind us.

Five

The Czech delegation to the United Nations in the autumn of 1949 was led by Clementis. In his absence Siroky, the Vice-Premier, temporarily replaced him at the Ministry of Foreign Affairs. We had worked together in the past, and since he had known about my activities in France I decided to tell him about my troubles. I hoped he would help me, but, as I now realize, his attitude towards me changed from that moment on. He became reserved and distant.

I then received another blow. One of our diplomats in Switzerland who had known Field sent me an unsealed letter which he asked me to pass on to the Party's Central Committee. It was his duty, he wrote, to inform the Party that he had sent some letters of Noel Field, who had been revealed as a spy in the Rajk trial, in the diplomatic pouch *on my orders*. It was true that when Field's wife had visited Prague that spring she had brought with her some letters for Noel Field's friends, Gisèle Kisch and Dora Kleinova, as well as a card for me in which he congratulated me on my appointment to the Ministry of Foreign Affairs. I accordingly mentioned this fact to Svab and Zadovsky in Security, and passed the letter on to the Central Committee with a denial. Shortly afterwards, my friend and colleague Vavro Hajdu told me that the diplomat who had sent me the unsealed letter had been summoned to Prague. As this order should have gone through my department I told Siroky of my surprise that it had been carried out without my knowledge, since the affair concerned me personally. He replied coldly that he had acted as he thought best.

A few days later I was summoned to the Ministry of the Interior by an anonymous telephone call but the caller refused to say why I was to appear. I then underwent an intensive interrogation by three inspectors from State Security which lasted from eight in the morning to nine at night. At my request they confronted me with the diplomat and his wife. He immediately withdrew the accusation, showing considerable surprise because, he said, 'I admitted several days ago that I had been mistaken.' The whole interrogation had been entirely pointless. I realized that the State Security was deliberately acting against me, but I could not see why.

A captain from State Security, who arrived at the end of the morning, had interrupted several times to calm the interrogators. Then, after taking them aside, he asked me to admit in writing that I had been careless in my dealings with Field. I later discovered that it was my friend Ossik Zavodsky, then head of the Security Services of the Ministry of the Interior, who had sent the captain to help me and prevent my being arrested. I was increasingly mystified by these concepts and methods of the Party. I had applied in good faith to the Secretariat of the Cadre Department to have my case investigated and settled so that I could prove my political loyalty. As a result I was interrogated as a suspect by the Security Services.

I told Siroky, who was Acting Minister of Foreign Affairs, about my interrogation, the confrontation and the withdrawal of the charge against me. It was then that I first asked him to relieve me of my post as Under-Secretary as long as my case remained unsettled. Three days later he told me that Kopriva, Minister of State Security, refused to accept my resignation since the Party had nothing against me. I insisted, but Siroky confirmed the refusal and told me that I would soon be seeing Kopriva, who would settle all my problems. The meeting was put off on various pretexts and never took place. Geminder, head of the Foreign Section of the Party's Central Committee, thought it equally futile to discuss these matters with me, since I 'had been cleared'.

I knew this to be untrue. They had taken their time to see the diplomat and settle everything for him, and in the Ministry Siroky's distrust of me was obvious. It had been suggested that I go to Paris to meet Clementis on his return from the United Nations, but at the last moment Siroky refused on a feeble pretext.

At the same time several people who had known Noel Field or his brother Herman, who had himself disappeared in Poland, had also been arrested. Then, on 5 January 1950, a few days after Clementis returned to Prague and resumed his duties at the Ministry of Foreign Affairs, his Secretary General, Théo Florin, was arrested in the street on his way to work. Clementis tried in vain to find out why Florin had been arrested and what had happened to him. Even the Minister of the Interior, Vaclav Nosek, said that he knew nothing of the matter. When Clementis told me and my colleague, Vavro Hajdu, of this we were astounded; how could the Security Services act without the knowledge of the Minister who directed them? As a last resort Clementis asked Slansky and President Gottwald to help him find out the truth. Three days later Gottwald informed him on the telephone that his secretary's arrest had nothing to do with politics and that his case would soon be settled.

A week later I witnessed an extraordinary scene. I entered the Minister's office with Vavro Hajdu. Clementis had not heard us knock and was standing by the window, cautiously raising the curtain and looking out into the street. He was nervous and worried. He told us that an additional group of men from the Security Services had been added to his body-guard that morning, and that they were now in the corridor and the anteroom of his office. Their orders were to 'watch him' night and day. When he asked his colleague Nosek why he was being watched, Nosek told him that the same measures had been taken against himself. According to the State Security officials they were intended to provide greater protection for certain ministers whose lives had been threatened by foreign agents. Nosek said this in good faith. He himself had been threatened with arrest as head of communist emigration in London during the war, and it was probably Klement Gottwald who had saved him.

But this did little to reassure Clementis. Florin's arrest now had another meaning for him: he felt it was directed against him-self, in connection with the campaign which had been launched in the western press during his stay in New York. It was then rumoured that he would be arrested on his return to Prague, but Gottwald, President of the Republic and Party Chairman, who had always shown the greatest confidence in him, wrote to him confirming his friendship and allowed his wife Ludmilla to join him in New York. After his return from America, although he remained on excellent terms with Gottwald, he was never-theless aware of some plot being hatched against him. This he attributed to the Secretariat rather than to Gottwald.

He justified his fears by reminding me about André Simone.*

* A well-known journalist in France who had written for Emile Buré's *L'Ordre* before the war. He wrote a book entitled *Les hommes qui ont trahi la France*.

He too had enjoyed the confidence of the Party leaders and of Gottwald, and had fallen into disgrace overnight. Clementis told me how it happened. During the Peace Conference in Paris in the autumn of 1946, Molotov, who was then Soviet Minister of Foreign Affairs, had scornfully asked Slansky about André Simone in Gottwald's presence. 'What's that globe-trotter doing here?' Slansky passed this remark on to the other leaders of the Political Bureau in Prague, and shortly afterwards André Simone was relieved of his post as foreign policy editor of the *Rude Pravo*, the main voice of the Communist Party. He was soon obliged to write his articles and to broadcast under a pseudonym.

Clementis's fears confirmed my own. At the beginning of February two commissions of the Central Committee, one of which I was a member, and another of which Clementis and I were members, stopped their meetings in such a way that it was perfectly obvious that their intention was to get rid of us.

On 13 March 1950 Clementis called me into his office. He had just returned from the Hradcany Castle and told me that Gottwald had asked him to resign in view of his incompetent cadre policy. I heard this with astonishment. 'Did Gottwald give concrete examples?' Clementis shook his head. 'That means my work is also implicated, since we've been working together in this department for a year!' Clementis shrugged his shoulders helplessly. I was extremely worried, the more so because the reason given, which also concerned me, seemed a mere pretext. I asked him whether, in his discussion with Gottwald, any mention had been made of his political stand in 1939 against the Finnish war, the German-Soviet Pact, and the occupation of White Russia and the Ukraine by the Red Army. Clementis replied that this had not been mentioned but agreed that it might be a reason.

I told him about the difficulties which I was having and of my dealings with Noel Field. I also told him that whatever was held against him would be held against me. Two days later, at a directors' meeting attended by the Under-Secretaries, Clementis and Viliam Siroky, Clementis's resignation and Siroky's permanent appointment as Minister of Foreign Affairs were officially announced.

The day after this meeting Siroky asked for me.

'How could you collaborate with Clementis for over a year and sanction his incompetent cadre policy?' he said, accusingly.

When I asked him for details and concrete examples, he replied that the entire cadre policy had been bad and that I had my share of the responsibility. So Siroky's arrival in the Ministry of Foreign Affairs entailed no improvement in my situation.

I saw Clementis several times since he continued to live in the Ministry apartment, while his new flat was being decorated by the Ministry of the Interior. I had become particularly sensitive to the police methods in use so I concluded that security agents were installing microphones in his apartment to increase surveillance. When I saw him for the last time we merely hinted at it; he had the same suspicions as I.

The only person in the Ministry of Foreign Affairs whom I could now rely on was Vavro Hajdu. His extreme professional competence, his knowledge and his experience, were of great assistance to me in my new job as Under-Secretary, especially since I had returned to Prague after fifteen years' absence and had never worked in a government office before. Ever since February 1948 my Ministry had been in a particularly difficult situation. In addition to the current problems – the numerous defections of diplomats who 'chose freedom' – I found an atmosphere of intrigue and corruption. Besides, our services were infiltrated by Security officials who encouraged denunciations, fermented suspicion and distrust, and led systematic campaigns against the excessive number of Jews or intellectuals in the Ministry. Complications in our work were always presented as deliberate acts of sabotage on the part of those employees.

In spite of my own precarious position I never hesitated to combat this unhealthy phenomenon. I even forbade the employees of the State Security to enter the Ministry building and told the departmental heads to give only documentary information to those who asked for it – a measure directed primarily against the staff of the Ministry of the Interior – if the demands were not made through the normal channels. This often led to serious clashes with officials from the Ministry of the Interior although initially I had the support of Clementis, Geminder, and even of Siroky and Gottwald.

In June 1950 I discovered that the Central Control Commission of the Party and the Security Services had asked several Ministry employees about me. My desk was searched and once I even found that the drawers had been forced. It was at this stage that I started to notice cars which followed me, or parked all night near my home. My telephone was tapped, and calls came through with no response at the other end of the line. When I had problems to discuss with Party officials I was only allowed to see subordinates, and at meetings and receptions they always tried to avoid me.

And then the Field business cropped up again in the German Democratic Republic. Several Party functionaries and civil servants whom I had known in Spain or France were penalized for having been in contact with him, and at a reception at the Castle, Svab, a little the worse for drink, came up to me and said: 'Your dossier is swelling. Have you seen what's going on in Germany? That business isn't over with here either!'

It was strange, after Svab's cruel treatment of me, that both he and I would soon be in the same prison. After using him, *they* decided to sacrifice him too.

I started to develop a true persecution complex; I saw suspicion in every eye, allusions in every phrase. My old friend Ossik, who had helped me to begin with, now avoided me and seemed frightened himself. Leopold Hoffman, Head of the President's bodyguard, a veteran from Spain who was soon to join us, also told me of a conversation he had had with Ossik on their way back from a reception: 'We, the former volunteers in the International Brigades who remained in the West during the war, will soon have some difficulty in explaining who we really are!'

This was at the end of December, when Kopriva asked me, under the vow of secrecy, about Zavodsky's alleged betrayals during the war.

At the Ministry the atmosphere was unbearable. Despite the care I devoted to my work it was soon the object of attacks.

There was the Treister affair: a letter from the Party Committee of the Ministry of the Interior told their opposite number in the Ministry of Foreign Affairs that I should be questioned about my refusal to employ a man named Treister who had been arrested and charged with espionage.* Treister had been recommended to us by Josef Frank, the Secretary of the Central Committee of the Party, and by Arnost Tauber, who was then Minister Plenipotentiary in Berne and who had known him very well in Buchenwald. The only reason why our Cadre Department had not taken him was that Treister, who was of Polish origin, had only recently obtained Czech nationality.

This had all happened over a year ago. It was now being produced to 'prove' that I was responsible for Treister's subsequently being employed by the Ministry of the Interior in view of the fact that I had not informed the Ministry of our refusal to take him on. The Party organization in the Ministry of the Interior also demanded that I should be penalized and that they should be kept informed of the consequences of the matter. What should have been a joke became of state importance. And yet my arguments made nonsense of their whole fabrication.

Was I Under-Secretary of Foreign Affairs or was I obliged to account for my work to the Minister of Foreign Affairs or to

* This accusation turned out to be false. Treister was rehabilitated in 1956.

the Minister of the Interior? Should I have asked a fortune teller about where Treister was going to search for a job? Should a circular be sent to every office in the Republic every time my department refused to employ someone?

The Party Committee of the Ministry was ordered to question me. This suggested a deliberate intent to increase the suspicion surrounding me. The State Security put me through another interrogation and tried for hours on end to prove that I was responsible for a 'spy' having been employed by the Ministry of the Interior.

The net was closing in on me. At the end of November 1950 a leading member of the French Communist Party visited me on his way to Moscow and told me confidentially that the Field affair was far from over, that it had had repercussions in every country, and that in France the Main d'Oeuvre Immigré was deeply implicated. As I accompanied him to his hotel I tried to show him how absurd these suspicions towards the Main d'Oeuvre Immigré were, since Jacques Duclos himself had been in direct control of its activities throughout the war.

Then there was a further warning. Our Minister Plenipotentiary in a Scandinavian country, M—, was staying in Prague in January 1951 on the invitation of the State Security who had summoned him back to help them unmask the 'criminal' activities of Sling, the Party district secretary of the Brno Party (a region of central Czechoslovakia) who was already under arrest. In his day M— had held an important position in Brno, and Sling had dismissed him for incompetence. As compensation, however, Gottwald himself had given him the diplomatic post he now held.

Four days after these discussions M— gave Siroky a report against me, containing the most fanciful accusations. He claimed that the Foreign Ministry was full of criminals of Sling's stamp, like London, and denounced others who were part of my 'group'!

Siroky put Cernik, my subordinate, in charge of the investigation – naturally forbidding him to mention it to anyone – but

Cernik, convinced of the absurdity of these accusations, took no notice and told me. I had no doubt that this denunciation had been made by M— at the instigation of the Security Services.

A vacuum was forming round me and my family. Even Geminder, who, like me, was from Ostrava on the Czechoslovakian–German border, tried in spite of our long standing friendship to avoid us. Until then he had always been delighted to join us when we entertained friends from France, Italy or Spain, but now, on one pretext or another, he refused our invitations.

One day Lise visited the wife of Gregor, the Minister of Foreign Trade. As she was leaving, the chauffeur, who had waited for her, told her that Slansky's wife had left through the back door just before she arrived. My wife asked Vera Gregorova the reasons for this sudden departure, which she quite rightly took as an insult. Vera Gregorova, who was most annoyed about the incident, asked if she could tell Slansky's wife what Lise had just said; Lise insisted that she should, and added that she herself was going to ask for the explanation of such an insulting attitude on the first occasion available.

Lise now knew that this departure was a refusal to meet her: one doesn't meet the wife of a man who is about to be arrested!

I felt abandoned by the Party and tried once more to get an appointment with some official. Slansky, Secretary-General of the Party, Geminder and Köhler,who had by now replaced Kopriva as director of the Cadre Department of the Central Committee, would not see me, and Siroky, as I have said, made every excuse to avoid me. I spent sleepless nights.

As I recalled all these methods which had been used against me for almost two years, starting with the Party Secretariat's refusal to hear me and ending with my arrest, it seemed obvious that a plan had been devised to demoralize me systematically, to increase my anxiety and despair. Everything had been done to break me, make me feel hunted, to make me fall into the trap set by the men determined to ruin me.

Six

My thoughts were interrupted by the sound of the door. A border guard in field uniform, wearing a fur cap with a red star, stood in the doorway pointing a machine-gun at me. Another guard put a steaming bowl on the floor and took off my handcuffs. What a relief. But no sooner had he done so than my hands were again chained, this time in front of me, and the two men left without saying a word.

I was thirsty and terribly cold. I looked in perplexity at the bowl at my feet. A few minutes went by. Doors slammed and I heard the sound of empty bowls being collected; I realized that I would have neither a spoon nor would my hands be freed to eat. I knelt down and raised the bowl to my lips with difficulty. But how could I eat? I tried to suck up the pieces of vegetable, but at that moment the door opened. 'Give me that,' said the warder, seizing my bowl. 'And start walking again.'

Now that my hands were chained in front of me I walked more easily. What time was it? Fatigue made every step harder. The warder had already come in twice to beat me because I had paused for breath. What could I do other than obey, yield, give proof of my good will and display a conciliatory attitude?

The pain in my shoulders and back was piercing. The incapacity to stretch my arms gave me such unbearable cramps that I could hardly think. Without my vest, my jersey or my coat I was frozen. When the food was next passed round I wouldn't stand helplessly before my bowl, but would try and eat in spite of my handcuffs. Again I heard the sound of doors and bowls, but nothing before my cell. I tried to believe that my turn had not yet come! But I was soon in no doubt: I heard the bowls being collected again: I had been deliberately omitted.

I went on walking. I had had nothing to eat or drink since the day before. The dawn of a new day was visible between the planks. I could stand it no longer and lay on the ground, but a brutal voice immediately ordered me to keep walking. When I refused to obey the warder opened the door and shouted threats at me. I refused to get up, and told him that he had no right to treat a man, and particularly an innocent man, in such a way. He called another warder who started insulting and beating me: 'You won't behave as an enemy here! Either you obey our orders or you'll be punished!'

I started walking again, painfully, until they came for me that evening to blindfold me and take me to another building.

My hands were again chained behind my back, and my mask removed. This time I was standing in front of a new man, of medium height, thick set, and elegantly dressed. I later discovered that he was an unsuccessful lawyer from Prague, S—, who had offered to work for Security. He was in charge of my interrogation.*

I expected him to ask me precise questions, which would enable me to give him precise answers and defend myself. Nothing of the kind happened. All I heard, throughout that night, were insults and the same words, repeated over and over again: 'Admit who you are, confess your crimes, men like you have a name, say what it is.'

I couldn't understand the sense of the questions. Who was I? I was Artur London. I had nothing to confess.

My interrogator was beside himself with anger. He seized me by the collar of my jacket and hammered my head against the wall: 'Admit who you are, confess your crimes, men like you have a name, say what it is.'

I thought I was dealing with a lunatic and I was determined to remain calm.

But now the interrogator took it out on my family. When he described them as a 'nest of enemies', I observed that this nest of enemies contained a member of the Political Bureau of the French Communist Party, my brother-in-law. He shouted

* After the examining magistrates had been relinquished for this sort of work in 1950, they were replaced by men from Security who questioned the prisoner from his arrest to his trial. These men were known as *référauts* which has been translated as 'interrogator'

louder than ever: 'You're all enemies. Your brother-in-law too. We know what he's up to. He can't do a thing for you. You can't count on anyone.'

The questioning, a hysterical monologue, went on all night. It was almost daybreak when the interrogator called a warder to take me back to my cell. I was about to leave the room when I turned back to him and said: 'You must have found a packet of dollars in my safe at the Ministry. Before you indulge your imagination I should tell you that these dollars belong to the World Peace Committee, and were given me by my sister-in-law, Fernande Guyot, the administrative secretary of the Committee, so that I should look after them for ten days while she went to the mountains on holiday.'

The interrogator looked at me, disconcerted. He told the warder to watch me and left the room. When he returned he asked me to repeat my statement about the dollars, and typed out a note. He looked like a dog whose bone had been removed. I had just given him fine proof of my venality.

When I was taken back to my cell I could see light through my mask. All along the corridors I heard doors open and close: empty bowls were being picked up, and once more I was too late. Though I was cold and hungry I had to continue my walk.

I thought of the interrogator's words. How could I let the outside world know that I was innocent? In all the prisons I had been in so far, the prisoners' laundry was sent to their families who washed and returned it. I had to tell my wife I was innocent. As I went up to the window I saw a loose nail which I tore out and I forced one of the celluloid stiffeners out of my shirt collar. Since my hands were chained in front of me I moved with difficulty. And yet, in the brief intervals when the spy-hole was closed, I managed to scratch, letter by letter, on the stiffener: 'I am innocent.' That I could trust Lise, who had had experience in methods of secrecy during the occupation, to find my message, calmed me somewhat.

But the shirt and the message were never to reach her. They disappeared in the prison clothes' shop. I was cold, and my hunger gave me stomach cramps. I still did not fully register what I had experienced, seen, and heard. I knocked at the door and asked for a sanitary bucket. The warder refused to take my handcuffs off, pointed his machine-gun at me, and I had to relieve myself like that, standing up. It was appallingly humiliating and I was so clumsy with my hands chained. I felt more debased than an animal.

They came for me late that morning. My mask was again put on, and I was pushed along, knocking my head against the planks. I remained in the dark for some time while several people whispered behind my back. Finally I heard a door open: I was brutally pushed round, my mask was torn off, and I was thrown against a wall. Four men were standing in front of me, one of whom, Major Smola, was in civilian dress. He seized me by the throat and shouted with hatred:

'We'll get rid of you and your filthy race! You're all the same! Not everything Hitler did was right, but he destroyed the Jews, and he was right about that. Too many of you escaped the gas chamber. We'll finish what he started.'

And stamping his foot on the ground he added: 'We'll bury you and your filthy race ten yards deep.'

These words were uttered by a man who wore the Party badge in his buttonhole, before three other men, in uniform, who tacitly agreed. What did this anti-Semitism, this pogrom spirit, have in common with Marx, Lenin and the Party? This was the first time in my adult life that I was insulted because I was a Jew and was held to be a criminal because of my race, and that by a man from the State Security of a Socialist country, a member of the Communist Party. Was it possible that the mentality of the SS had arisen in our own ranks? This was the mentality of the men who shot my brother Jean in 1941, who deported my mother, my sister Juliette and her husband, and dozens of members of my family to Auschwitz and sent them to the gas chamber. I had concealed my race from the Nazis, should I do the same thing in my own socialist country?

Smola hurled me into a corner. 'You're going to talk. You're going to confess. We know everything. You're not the only one here. Your friends who protected you are here too and they've talked. Look . . .' He showed me a tray containing several cards. 'You've all been expelled from the Party. You've been rejected like vermin. Look . . .' There were Ossik Zavodsky's Party card, Vales's, mine and several others. 'And the ones which are missing,' he added, 'are being collected. You're to answer these comrades' questions.' He pointed at the men in uniform. 'Your only chance to save your skin is to talk faster than the others.'

At this he left the room. The others sat behind a table. I knew one of them. I had seen him at the Ministry of Foreign Affairs, where he had come on several occasions to discuss problems regarding the Ministry of the Interior, and I had had various disagreements with him about the interference of the Security Services in matters which concerned me. He now sat before me, as an inquisitor, but he was the only one whose eyes were not full of hatred.

'Last Sunday your Trotskyist group of veterans from the International Brigades held a secret meeting at Zavodsky's. You knew you had been discovered and had your backs to the wall. How did you decide to get away?'

How could they suspect my visit to Zavodsky on Sunday and my chance meeting with my other friends of being a conspiracy? They seemed to know about our conversations. What did that mean? And above all, how could they give such a distorted interpretation to our meeting? I was not allowed to speak. Questions were being asked from every side, questions which did not even demand an answer. My three inquisitors shouted names of veterans from the Spanish Civil War – some of whom I had not seen since 1939 – the names of volunteers of various nationalities, among others the Poles, Rwal and Winkler, who had disappeared in Moscow; the Hungarians Rajk and Baneth; the Yugoslavs Copik and Daptchevitch, and the Soviet journalist Koltzov. They questioned me about others, whom they accused of organizing Trotskyist meetings in Paris and Prague.

What were they driving at? Every time I tried to answer or to refute something they interrupted me, shouted, yelled the most monstrous accusations. They screamed out names of towns – Paris, Marseilles, Barcelona, Albacete – they mentioned my meetings with so and so, but gave no details.

They knew about our life and our struggles, so what did they want? We were all proud of our past. 'Confess your crimes,' they shouted at me continuously. 'You must tell us, it's your only chance of saving your skins. The others confess, so you must do as they do, otherwise you've had it. You've had it anyway. You're all here. You won't succeed in overthrowing our regime. We never let our corn grow too high, we cut it in time.'

I continued to defend myself, passionately. 'Ask me precise questions, I've nothing to hide. I want to explain, let me explain.' But it was no good.

One of the three men went out. The interrogation continued, but more calmly. The two others asked further questions about the International Brigades. They took sheets from a large pile of papers on the table: 'What do you know about so and so?' I tried to remember, but they never gave me time. 'We know he deserted.' Another had behaved badly in the French camps. Another had criticized the Party and showed oppositional or Trotskyist tendencies. So and so had been considered suspicious or hostile by the Spanish Communist Party or by his division ...

But what material did they have? As they interrogated me, as they showed me sheets of paper, I realized that those were reports drawn up in Spain on the volunteers by the Party organizations of every company, battalion and brigade. They were formulated in the heat of the moment, and were often intransigent, dogmatic, written under fire, in the trenches, during battle. Their severity was due to the gravity of the moment.

Not all the volunteers were saints; some of them were cowards and intriguers: the latter soon revealed themselves. And who could claim not to have had moments of weakness in battle? I know some who left the front in terror at their first experience of fighting. But the same men later proved themselves highly courageous. Later, during years of underground work in France, Czechoslovakia or the Czech army in England, most of the volunteers behaved like determined and valid warriors. But the interrogators only retained the negative content of these documents. Of course the 'Cadre reports', to use Party jargon, had to give strict verdicts on the possible defects of the fighters, while their qualities were generally known. But these were political, not police records. They belonged to the Central Committee, not here. Who had given them to the State Security? The Party? Why? I remembered how we had contributed to these reports. We had been conditioned by the political education we had received, by the implacable rigour of the Bolsheviks, and we had been determined to keep our commitment to the cause of the Spanish people pure. We had been at pains to emphasize every shadow and error. And this was what became of our intransigence towards ourselves! Everything became petty and dirty. Everything was turned against us.

The door suddenly opened and Smola threw another bundle of papers onto the table. He seized me by the collar and shouted: 'Here it all is! Zavodsky's confessed everything. There's nothing you can tell us. All you have left to do is make a confession and complete his statements. We know about your activities against the Party. Your activities in Marseilles. Your collaboration with the Americans. Your contacts with Field. It's all there. Now you admit it!'

In the passages he read me I recognized certain conversations I had had with Zavodsky. They couldn't have made it all up! But everything we did or thought was described as Trotskyist, as acts of hostility to the Party, as sabotage. Our meetings were invariably presented as conspiracies. Had we formed a Trotskyist group years ago which carried out activities against the Party?

I shook my head. 'No, that's not true. If some of the facts you mention are true your interpretation and conclusions are wrong. I don't believe you when you say that Zavodsky wrote things of this kind.'

Smola slapped me and knocked my head against the wall.

'No, it isn't true, it isn't true!'

'You know his writing, so look at this signature. Is it or is it not Zavodsky's?'

He showed me the sheets and at the bottom of each was Zavodsky's signature. I knew it too well to be mistaken. Smola then showed me another page headed 'My activity for the FBI in Marseilles', in which Zavodsky told how, as a Trotskyist, he established contact with certain agents.

'But it's all untrue. It's not possible.' All I could do was to repeat those words. I was amazed, flabbergasted. I couldn't understand a thing. I went on repeating: 'It's not true.'

Then Smola gave me a sheet of the manuscript. 'You know your accomplice's writing. Read his written confessions and compare them to what I told you.'

It was indeed Zavodsky's writing, but he had written a pack of lies, imaginary stories which contained – and this was the worst of it – some half-truths. He reported our conversations and activities, but his interpretation was the product of fantasy. It would take us all to the gallows! How had Ossik Zavodsky been able to write something so blatantly false, he of all people? I had known him in Spain and in France during the occupation to be a loyal man and an exemplary soldier.

I could see him that day in Paris when I told him of the importance of armed resistance against the Germans. It was in 1941 and he and Alik Neuer had been proposed as members of the OS, the Special Organization, a nucleus of the FTPF.* Two weeks later Hervé-Kaminsky, another member of the national triangle of the Main d'Oeuvre Immigré, told me of Ossik's difficulties in adapting himself to his new activities. I was to mention it to him. Ossik had been delighted to see me again and told me about his problem. His military superior had given

---

* Les Francs-Tireurs et Partisans Français, the left-wing group of the armed French partisans.

him certain specific duties to fulfil, but when Zavodsky asked him for a weapon the other man told him, in accordance with his instructions, that he must win the weapon from the enemy. How, in the middle of Paris, could he overpower and disarm a German officer? In order to give him some confidence I told him how Neuer, with the help of some chemists, had fabricated some archaic and primitive incendiary bombs. We discussed it at length and when he left me I felt he was ready for anything.

He captured his first weapon a few days later. He had noticed that when the German officers went to the barber's shop they usually hung their belt and pistol on the clothes' hook before sitting down. One day the opportunity presented itself: he went into the barber's as a German officer was being shaved, seized the revolver and fled. He told me, laughing, that if his pursuer had come too close he would have fired his first shot that day.

Zavodsky rapidly became an experienced soldier and took part in the riskiest military operations. In the autumn of 1942, with two other Czechs, he had joined in an attack on a German hotel in the Rue d'Alésia which had resulted in about thirty dead and wounded German officers.

Why, therefore, had Zavodsky, who was in a better position than anyone in State Security, agreed to write such monstrosities? He was well aware of the consequences of these statements for himself, for me and for the others.

Smola left the room with an interrogator, and I found myself alone with the man I had met in the Ministry. He looked at me for a moment.

'You're in a nasty mess. What they said wasn't a joke. Zavodsky has confessed. He was arrested on Saturday, twenty-four hours before you. He made his first confessions half an hour after his arrival. The thirty pages you've just seen were written that same night. Since then he's written and goes on writing more of them. His statements will cost you your life and you only have one means of escape – to confess everything. I have no interest in all this and none to harm you. You always behaved well towards me in the past and if I can give you a piece of advice, it's to confess. You must believe me. You must confess, and quicker than the others. Otherwise, you, their leader in France, won't have a chance of escaping.'

'But what Zavodsky's written isn't true!' I said. 'Nobody can take his confessions seriously. There is evidence, there are the official documents. The others will deny them just like me. Everything can be checked. You only have to ask the witnesses in the French Communist Party and the other resistance organizations.'

'You can't do a thing against these confessions. The others have also started to confess. And those who haven't will do so sooner or later. Believe me, everybody confesses here. And remember one thing: only Zavodsky's confessions will be taken into consideration, both because they are against you, and because he was your accomplice.

'Look,' he said, and picked up Zavodsky's confessions, 'look how they're written. To start with he admits his own crimes: "I spied for the Americans in order to overthrow the regime. . . . In this hostile activity I was directed by Artur London." Don't you realize that this will be convincing enough for the court? A man accuses himself of the worst crimes and then adds that he committed them on your orders. Who will they believe? You or Zavodsky? You can be sure that nobody will believe you.'

He was talking calmly, almost gently.

'But it isn't true! I can't say I'm guilty of crimes I didn't commit.'

'What do the confessions matter? Why do you think Zavodsky confessed? Why did he confess things that can cost him his life? He's no fool and he knows our department. He knows what these confessions mean. He's worked long enough in the Security Services. He was head of them until yesterday, don't forget that. So why do you think he did this? Because he wants to save his skin. He knows there's only one thing to do here: confess, confess as quickly as possible and as completely as possible. Think about that!'

I leaned against the wall. My head was spinning, I was terribly tired and every part of my body ached. I had agonizing cramps in my arms and shoulders, and I looked at the little room next door, its door ajar. It was a bathroom. Nothing about this place was like a prison, it was more like an apartment. Where was I? In whose hands was I, in what trap?

I was thirsty and asked for some water. The man raised a glass to my mouth, for my chained hands were too stiff. He went on talking, trying to make me see reason. At that moment the other two interrogators came back, and Smola shouted out, when he heard how amicably he was addressing me:

'He's not a comrade, but a criminal unmasked by the Party. He's a traitor, a man due for the gallows. Your interrogation must be as severe as possible.'

Coming up to me he seized me again by the throat and shouted: 'You are forbidden to mention the Party here. You are forbidden to mention the name of any of our comrades directing the Party. You are a traitor who has nothing in common with the Party. The Party had you arrested. Otherwise why would you, Zavodsky, and so many others be here? We'll use every method to reveal your treason, the filth in which you and your friends are wallowing, to the Party and the people.'

The interrogation continued. Statements by other volunteers from the International Brigades were read out, confirming what Zavodsky had written. They accused themselves and me. And in every one of them there was an element of truth, either deformed or tendentiously interpreted, mixed with blatant lies.

I was more and more worried by Zavodsky's 'confessions' and the statements I heard. The interrogators continuously repeated to me:

'Do you think the Party would have ordered your arrest if all this were untrue, as you claim?'

I began to wonder about the times when I was out of touch with my comrades – when they were in the internment camps in France and Africa, or in exile in London, or even in Czechoslovakia while I was in Paris – whether they had been ensnared by the enemy.

The interrogators provided a mass of details on their enemy activity which was entirely new to me. My bewilderment increased when they said such things as:

'You didn't realize whom you were dealing with. They hoodwinked you. The only way to prove your honesty is to tell all you know.'

I tried to explain, but I soon realized that the interrogators distorted my answers in the same way that all the things I read had been distorted.

Seven

To start with we did all we could to aid the Party by replying to every question in detail. We wanted to help the Party see things clearly, just as we wanted to see clearly into ourselves and others. We wanted to know why we were there, what unknown mistake we had made. The years of struggle and discipline, all our past education, had taught us that the Party was never wrong, that the USSR was always right. We were prepared to criticize ourselves, to admit that we had made involuntary mistakes in our work which may have harmed the Party.

And then we saw that the men from Security turned not one or some, but all our answers, inside out like a glove, that they distorted their very substance. The result was that each of our acts and thoughts became a crime. Not once did these men want to discover the truth. All they wanted to do was to make a culprit of the man in their hands.

We felt that we were alone, abandoned by everybody: by the Party, our friends and comrades. We knew that for everyone outside – even for our own families – we were probably guilty, since the Party had decided on our arrest. I knew all that from experience. I had myself reacted like that during the trials in Moscow, Budapest and Sofia. For what sincere and honest communist – even a relative of the man whom the Party had arrested – could avoid doubt? How could he conceive that the Party – which he had always placed above everything – could resort to illegal procedures, to monstrous acts intended to make innocent men confess? But what should he confess and why? These two questions obsessed us. We could find no answers, for there were none.

At one point the interrogator whom I knew was called out of the room. I was never to see him again. I was now questioned by one interrogator at a time. He asked me about my dealings with Field, my work in France and in the Ministry. These questions were always deceptive – attempts to make me feel guilty, to disorientate and disarm me, to confuse me.

Gradually the violence of the first part of the interrogation decreased. The interrogator read me passages from Zavodsky's statement, told me about him, Vales and Pavel. He told me so many things that I was finally incapable of telling truth from lies, because everything was based on half-truths. For example, the interrogators claimed that Pavel had entered the service of the Gestapo in the internment camp at Vernet, that Vales had started to work for the Secret Service in England during the war. . . . When I refused to believe these accusations they gave me a mass of details. According to them Pavel was in the following position: he could either be repatriated in the German Protektorat of Bohemia and Moravia (where he would have been tried and almost certainly sentenced to death), or he could remain in a French camp and be deported to Africa on the condition that he undertook to work for the Gestapo as soon as he was released.

The interrogator also gave me details about Zavodsky's alleged betrayal after his arrest in France in 1942. First I told him what I had told Kopriva, that when we returned from the Nazi camps we had heard about the interrogation of Zavodsky by the Special Anti-Terrorist Brigade in Paris; although he had been tortured Zavodsky had refused to give way. The interrogator then read passages from Zavodsky's 'confessions', which said something to this effect: 'Arrested in Paris in 1942 I betrayed several comrades of mine to the Gestapo; they were subsequently arrested and deported to Germany, and some of them never returned. It was because of my agreement to spy for the Gestapo that I was not tried and sentenced to death. It was on the orders of the OSD (*Oberste Sicherheitsdienst*) that I was only deported to Mauthausen . . .

'When I heard that London was an agent for Field and when I had proof that he was the leading resident agent of the American Intelligence Services in Czechoslovakia, I did what I could to prevent this information from being circulated. I prevented London's arrest because I knew that he knew about my betrayal to the Gestapo and was protecting me. His arrest would have entailed my own and that of other members of our Trotskyist group of veteran volunteers from Spain.'

The interrogator then picked up some other sheets of paper and read me further statements, without telling me who made them, and then the slanderous reports of two veterans from Spain, N— and M—, made several months before our arrest. Each one of them, in great detail, told of Zavodsky's betrayal; he was even held responsible for the arrest and death of a girl who had worked with him in the Resistance.

I was later shown Nekvasil's report after his arrest, in which he confirmed these facts and also wrote: 'London knew about Zavodsky's betrayal to the Gestapo and had even seen the reports of Zavodsky's interrogations where this betrayal was evident. London told me about these facts when he returned from Mauthausen. We met in the Café des Deux-Magots in Saint-Germain-des-Prés and it was there that he showed me the report. I told him that we should immediately inform the Party. But he replied that we should leave the matter for the time being, that he would see to it later himself.'

Thereupon the interrogator told me that these 'confessions' constituted proof that I had known of Zavodsky's betrayal and that I had kept it a secret to protect my own espionage activities.

These 'confessions' were to have appalling consequences in our trial for they were one of the chief proofs which the Security Services held of our guilt and my complicity with Zavodsky.

And yet it was perfectly easy to reconstruct what had happened. Why had they not checked with the French Communist Party, as I had suggested at the beginning? It would have been so easy to disprove this terrible charge immediately if they had wanted to.

After my liberation in 1956 I told Lise about the accusations against Zavodsky. I told her to get in touch with 'Zavodsky's young victim' when she first went to France. This was Régine Ickovic, the sister of our friend Salomon. I wanted to provide the Party Rehabilitation Commission with additional proof of the falsity of the Security's charges in order to get the Party to rehabilitate the veterans from Spain who were still in prison, and those who had been released but had not received the honour due to them.

The first lie was that Régine had been killed after her arrest. But Lise had to check the rest of the charge. So she told Régine that her Resistance comrades had asked her about details of her arrest and interrogation. Régine, thinking that her own conduct was being questioned, said: 'Nobody denounced me. I was caught after my superior, a Rumanian comrade in the MOI, had been arrested. He was to give me an identity card at our next meeting and when he was searched the card was found and that was how the police got to me.'

'Were you faced with your comrades after your arrest?'

'Yes, with my boss. Poor man, they had beaten him so much that his face was hardly human. I denied that I knew him, so they beat me and finally showed me my identity card with my photograph, so there was no denying anything . . .'

'Were you confronted with Zavodsky too?'

'No, never. You can ask him.' She had no idea of what had happened to Ossik. 'He'll tell you that we met after our return from the camps; he came up to me, embraced me and congratulated me on my behaviour with the police. "You did very well."' he said. '"You knew how not to talk."'

And once again she told Lise to get Zavodsky to confirm what she had said. Then they drew up a report which I gave the Rehabilitation Committee in 1956 and which finally destroyed the accusation made against Zavodsky, the last of us to be executed, in March 1954, after a reprieve had been refused.

Until dawn the interrogator went on reading me further reports and denunciations against other members of the Brigade, without telling me who had made them. The same psychological pressure was always used to persuade me that I had been hoodwinked by my comrades, that they had taken advantage of my good faith, and that that was how I found myself in a network of spies and Trotskyists. This theme prevailed until the arrival of the next interrogator, who, after consulting his colleagues' notes, started to accuse all the volunteers of demoralization and treason.

And yet no more than ten per cent of the volunteers from Spain had ever broken under the strain – a remarkably low percentage in view of the conditions which we endured. Besides, throughout the whole of the Spanish Civil War our volunteers were never left to themselves. They remained under the supervision of the military and political leadership of the Brigades and under the aegis of the Spanish Communist Party. Nothing important could take place among them without the immediate knowledge of the Party leaders in Prague who then took all decisions regarding them.

Now the statements of the bad elements, who had been rapidly unmasked by us in Spain or in the French internment camps, were being used against us. They were called good communists, victims of our Trotskyist gang. It is easy to imagine the ease with which the Security men persuaded them to lie about us, the satisfaction with which they got their own back and established a new moral virginity for themselves.

These men attacked Josef Pavel, the commander of the Dimitrov battalion of the International Brigades, with special bitterness. He was a worker who had come to Spain from Moscow where he had attended the Lenin School. Energetic, competent and courageous, he had rapidly imposed himself as a leader on the men in his unit. Even in Spain certain demoralized soldiers had slandered him in order to undermine his authority, and went so far as to accuse him of having instigated the execution of a Czech volunteer. I had been told of this matter by Petr Klivar and Jan Cerny, who was responsible to the Czech Cadre Department at the base of the International Brigades in Albacete. The man had been executed as the result of a mutinous act on the Front in extremely serious military conditions.

A detailed investigation had been held by the superior military and political authorities, and Pavel had never been implicated; on the contrary, he had even been promoted at the beginning of 1939. These same men had later written slanderous slogans against Pavel in the French internment camps: 'Pavel, murderer!' Most of them belonged to the 'Compania de Oro', a refuge of demoralized deserters, some of whom had become police spies in the camp and had therefore been generally ostracized.

Sitting in front of his typewriter the interrogator began to draw up a report based on what we had all written on Pavel's initiative after the Rajk trial in order to clear up the misleading statements made about the volunteers in Spain. I repeated that this was a political report, addressed to the Cadre Department of the Central Committee and, as such, could not be used in a police investigation.

It was now midday on Wednesday. Since my arrest seventy hours earlier I had only eaten once and drunk the glass of water given me by the compassionate interrogator. At last the door opened and I was given a bowl of soup with a spoon. I was allowed to sit down, and although I had some difficulty in eating, with my hands chained, my fingers numb, I managed somehow. But the respite was brief. Soon I was again standing in my corner, and the interrogation continued late into Thursday night.

Then, with my mask on, I was taken to another cell. I had not slept since my arrest. I looked round me and saw that the room was completely empty, with not even a mattress. It was icy cold. 'You can lie down,' shouted the warder. I curled up on the floor in a corner and immediately fell into a heavy sleep. When I was awakened I felt I had only just dropped off. The grey light of dawn filtered through the splits between the planks. I couldn't have slept for more than two hours. The warder brought me a bucket, a rag, and ordered me to wash the cell. I asked him to remove my handcuffs, but he refused. I had to scrub the cell and ring out the rag with my hands chained. My wrists and my hands, swollen by the handcuffs, were agonizingly painful; they were more like bloated purple chunks of flesh than hands, and I almost screamed with pain. No sooner had I finished than the warder took off my handcuffs to tie my hands behind my back and ordered me to start walking again.

Eight

On Friday morning I was masked as usual, taken out of my cell, and led along endless corridors and down interminable flights of stairs, until I started to breathe an icy, humid air which smelt of must. Finally my mask was removed and, as the door slammed, a voice shouted: 'Walk!'

I was in a cellar, or rather a hole with two walls of brick and two of clay and coarse fencing. I barely had four square yards at my disposal. Dampness oozed from the walls and my clothes were instantly wet through. Icicles hung from the ceiling and the floor was muddy. I walked. Or rather, I paced round like an animal in a cage. What was this new device?

For a moment I thought of throwing myself on the ground,

where two planks lay over the mud, and of refusing to walk. But I remembered what an interrogator had once told me: 'Every day we send a report to the Party about the results of the investigation and the behaviour of the accused. You can be sure that what we have written about you is not in your favour: your refusal to confess proves that you are a hardened criminal.'

I was determined not to give them any excuse for saying that I was rebellious.

In this hole I had no feeling of time. It was as though life had stopped, were it not for occasional blows on the planks of the nearby cells and the monotonous orders: 'Walk, you must walk.'

So I was not alone in this cellar, which, to judge from the echo, must have been vast. There were other jails, like mine. Every quarter of an hour a warder knocked on my door and I had to stand to attention in front of the spy-hole and answer in a low voice: 'Prisoner Number . . . Present!'

I tried to recognize my neighbours by their voices, but it was no good. I could only hear a feeble murmur, the sound of doors opening and closing, steps coming nearer or fading into the distance. There was no way of telling night from day.

I moved with ever greater difficulty and felt intensely tired. My whole body was in pain. Unable to stand it any more, I fell down. A few seconds later I heard furious kicks against the door and an anonymous voice which shouted: 'Get up! Walk, walk!' I lay where I was. The door was thrown open and two warders lifted me by the armpits and knocked my head against the wall. 'You must obey. You must do as we say.' I refused because I could no longer move. A third rushed in with a bucket of freezing water, and, seizing my head, he plunged my face into it. 'You're awake now,' said the other two. 'You must keep on walking, or else we'll repeat what we've just done. We'll use other methods if you remain so stubborn.'

They left me and I resumed my hallucinatory walk. At one point I heard voices behind the door, mocking me, insulting me and my family. I took no notice and after a while they stopped.

I have no idea how long I went on walking round in circles, my body a well of pain. I could hardly keep my eyes open and gradually everything I saw faded, as behind a veil. I banged into some planks and ended up on the floor. Hands seized me again. Warders kicked me in the ribs, stripped me to the waist, and sprayed me with cold water. That was how they kept me awake, and they did it several times a day as long as I was there. I staggered forward, sleeping on my feet. I awoke crashing into the walls. I walked, dreamt, heard voices. I could no longer distinguish what was real from what was imaginary.

Long afterwards, on Sunday night (I found it out a little later when I saw the calendar on my inquisitor's desk) I heard a voice ask in Slovakian: 'What have you done?' I didn't understand at first, I was simply aware of a presence behind the spy-hole, but then I heard some gentle knocks and went to the door. The voice whispered 'What have you done?'

'Nothing, I'm innocent, I have no idea why I'm here. I can't understand what they want, I'm innocent. I'm not allowed to eat, drink or sleep. I don't know what's going on.'

The voice continued: 'We're not allowed to give you anything to eat or drink. What have you done to deserve this? You're the only one. I'll bring you something to drink.'

Thirst is a worse torture than hunger. I thought I was feverish. I felt sharp pains in my lungs and breathed with difficulty, as a result of my pleurisy. The Monday before my pneumothorax was to have been insufflated, but Dr Dymer had waited for me in vain.*

After what seemed an eternity the door opened gently, and before me I saw a young guard in uniform, a fur 'chapka' with a star on his head. He held a bottle of water, raised it to my mouth and patiently let me drink it. 'Don't tell anyone or I'll be punished,' he told me. 'You'll probably be called in a few

* Dr Dymer was a specialist in lung diseases. When he saw that I had not kept my appointment he made inquiries about me and tried to continue his cure, but this cost him dear and he was officially boycotted.

hours, and then you can ask for something to eat and drink.'
He left at once and closed the door.

This charitable act renewed my confidence. All was not lost,
even here! I dragged myself round, exhausted, until they came
to carry me off for another interrogation. I walked blindly
down stairs and corridors, although I was hardly able to climb
from one floor to the other. I was out of breath and panted, on
the verge of collapse, but strong arms seized me, pushed and
dragged me.

The bandage was removed from my eyes. I found myself in
front of a man I had never seen before. He made me stand in a
corner and gazed at me for a while. 'What's the matter? You
don't look well.'

'I have been here a week' – I had just seen the calendar on
his table – 'and I have hardly had anything to eat or drink. I
have only slept two hours. I have just spent three nights and
three days in a cellar where I had to walk the whole time.
You're committing a crime. You don't have the right to use
such methods. I'm innocent. Ask me what you like, but let me
answer normally and please write down my answers as I give
them to you. I want to see a Party representative.'

The man pretended to be surprised. 'What, you've had
nothing to eat or drink, you haven't slept? We must do something about that. It must be the warders' fault.'

This sinister game, which consisted in putting the blame on
the warders, was frequently repeated in the future, but the
night before, from the young Slovak, I had proof that the orders
were given by the Security men and that the warders were only
carrying them out. How many more weeks of sleeplessness,
harassing marches, privation of food and water, was I still to
experience? How many uninterrupted interrogations lasting for
days and nights?

The interrogator removed my handcuffs and chained my arms
in front of me. He went out and I heard him give an order. A
few seconds later I was brought a bowl full of a warm liquid
and a piece of bread. I literally pounced on it.

The interrogator was talking:

'With regard to your request to see a Party representative I must remind you that I and my colleagues represent the Party here. The Party has ordered us to interrogate you, to keep them informed of your behaviour, your acceptance or refusal to help us elucidate the serious problems facing us. You must therefore consider yourself in the presence of the Party. I can't be any clearer than that! You must confess, and you must help the Party.'

The interrogators replaced one another at regular intervals and I remained on my feet. Before leaving the room each one typed out a note for his successor, probably to inform him of the course of the interrogation. The new interrogator would read it before asking me the same questions.

As they wrote out my statements about such and such a volunteer the interrogators systematically omitted anything that might seem in my favour, and I refused to sign the reports.

At one point Smola came into the room and said: 'So that's that. They've just brought him along.' And turning to me: 'I mean your friend Laco Holdos.* He was the only one missing, and now you're all here! Your whole group is in the bag. Now we know who you veterans from Spain really are. You know what happened in Hungary. But you don't know what happened in Poland, in Germany. Your group isn't an isolated case. All the International Brigades are implicated.'

An interminable time elapsed. I fell onto my knees several times, and the interrogator had to drag me to the bathroom and plunge my head into the sink. The questioning would resume, without my getting anything to eat. From time to time, as my tongue became so numb that I could barely speak, the man would give me a glass of water.

Questions, and more questions. Some of them reminded me

* After being Vice-President of the Slovak National Council, Laco Holdos was Secretary of State of Cultural Affairs in Slovakia until his arrest on 2 February 1951.

of the Rajk trial and I exclaimed: 'But those are the questions that Rajk was asked!'

'You seem to know a great deal about the Rajk trial, Mr London. And indeed, you are implicated in the same conspiracy. It is up to us to act as the Hungarians have done. Don't imagine that we don't know what you were up to behind the Pyrenees! They didn't hide you when you were in Spain any more than the Alps hid you in Switzerland. We're not alone in this, either. The Soviet intelligence services are helping us. We have learned from their experience of the Moscow trials and the purges in the Bolshevik Party. Their intelligence services have given us a full idea of your activities in Spain, France and Switzerland.'

This was a shock. So the Soviets were behind it all, and it was their intelligence services which were providing information. It must have been to them that Pavel was alluding in his conversation with Zavodsky the Sunday before my arrest. I knew that the Russians worked in Prague as advisers, because the Ministry of Foreign Affairs had been told to provide the 'Soviet experts' with special food tickets and other privileges reserved for the diplomatic corps, and we had refused to facilitate these acquisitions. But the presence of Soviet 'advisers' in the key sectors seemed as natural as it did to receive assistance from the elder sister of socialism, so I was far from suspecting the part they were playing in the Security apparatus.

I remembered the doubts I had had about some of the charges in the Rajk trial. So the same men who had been behind the Rajk trial were now at work here. All these thoughts ran through my head, but I had no time to go into them because I had to reply continuously to the questions which succeeded each other at a maddening rate.

'You can't deny having known Rajk!'

They questioned me at length about the Bulgarian volunteers, and my friendship with those Yugoslavs who had remained loyal to Tito.

When I collapsed my head was again plunged into the basin and the ordeal resumed: interrogations accompanied by blows and insults, threats to my family, threats to arrest my wife. I replied mechanically, no longer knowing what I was saying, unable to tell one interrogator from another.

I no longer knew the day of the week or the date; I started to talk different languages; I was amazed to hear myself questioned in Spanish, French, Russian and German, and I jumped from one language to another.

At one point I was no longer talking to the interrogator, but to my friend Wagner. We were in Moscow in 1936 during the great purges. He was working in Comintern and came to see me in my little room in the Soruznaya.* He was depressed and demoralized, having just lost his job because some detail, relation to a distant episode when he was living in Manchuria, was found to be incorrect in the new *curriculum vitae* which he had filled in – at least his tenth *curriculum vitae* in the last few years. His father, who had worked in the railways under the Tsars, had been posted to Manchuria, where he lived with his family, and Wagner had been a militant member of the Chinese Communist Party. He subsequently worked for the Comintern as a liaison agent with Canton, Shanghai and the other large Communist centres, and smuggled members of the Korean Communist Party across the borders. When his position became too dangerous in Manchuria he returned to Moscow.

His chief had been arrested during the last Comintern purge, and Wagner's numerous *curricula vitae* had again been examined. The slight differences, he told me, had been underlined in red and black pencil, and he had lost his job, his identity papers, his Party card and his room in the Lux Hotel where most of the Comintern employees were living. In this dilemma he had come to see me and I tried to cheer him up. He was a well known and highly respected figure, I told him, and everything would turn out all right.

---

* A small hotel in Gorky Street, near the Lux Hotel, which provided rooms for members of the Communist Youth International, under the protection of Secours Rouge, employees in foreign-language publishing firms, etc.

There he was, in the room where I was being interrogated, his head drooping, despair in his eyes. We were talking and I said: 'Sleep in my bed. You can stay with me and eat with me. You can easily get to my room, nobody will know you're there. Don't worry. They'll never drop someone like you, and while they're clearing things up they'll have to give you a job and somewhere to live.'

And then we were joined by another Czech, who had introduced me to Wagner. He only had one arm, and had just finished a journalists' course in Kharkov. Now he was waiting to leave for Czechoslovakia, where he was to direct the Party paper in a district near the Carpathians. At the time we had long discussions about the attempt on Kirov's life, the arrests, the Zinoviev and Kamenev trials, and the purges raging through the Youth International and the Comintern.

We were all together and I couldn't understand why the interrogator was interrupting our conversation. Why was he shouting 'Talk Czech! Talk Czech! What are you muddling up?' What did he want? He hadn't been in Moscow with us and why was he talking about Spain and the Spanish? I hadn't yet been to Spain. Anyhow, what was he doing here? How did he know me? Why was he shaking me and dragging me off to the bathroom to plunge my head in water?

'Look what they're doing,' I told Wagner, 'they've gone mad.' I so wanted to be able to talk to my friends, but they wouldn't let me. They went on asking questions, more questions, Spain, the Spanish. . . . But I was in Moscow, with my friends, and I was telling them that I intended to volunteer for the International Brigades. Why was this man jumping ahead in time? I heard him shout, but I couldn't make out what he was saying.

Someone said: 'You're going insane. You're making no sense.'

I was blindfolded and again led to the cellar. When my eyes were free I saw my new jail, a little larger than the last one, and in the middle was a sort of drainpipe which periodically emitted a nauseous, dark liquid which flowed over the floor.

My feet were deep in muck. The warder repeated the order: 'Walk!' I lurched forward like a sleepwalker, eyes unable to distinguish the walls. I collapsed and all round me I saw enormous cobwebs closing in on me. I tried to fend off huge black hairy tarantulas which were attacking me, but a sort of black and white grid was always coming down between my hands and the insects. I got up, but I could no longer judge distance. I again crashed into the walls, and then blacked out totally.

I was vaguely aware of the door opening and a voice saying: 'Leave him there, we'll come for him in a minute.' My clothes were dripping with water. I was dragged onto the planks nailed in a corner of my cell, and then carried somewhere, into the open air, where I had a beautiful vision. I thought I was in Monte-Carlo (a place I had never been) on a beach lit by thousands of bonfires. Warships, a whole fleet of them, were moored off the shore. Fireworks were let off and an orchestra played soft Viennese waltzes. Then the ships at anchor fired their guns. . . . And I regained consciousness. I was lying on the floor, but the light filtering between the planks showed that it was day. How long had I slept? Four or five hours? I received another bowl of soup and a piece of bread.

In the afternoon the interrogation resumed. The calendar on the interrogator's desk showed me the day of the week. It was Friday. Another week had passed. I had hardly eaten or slept at all. I was always on my feet, my hands chained, submitting to constant questioning.

The interrogators became increasingly violent. Now two or three of them questioned me at a time, and when they punched me or knocked my head against the wall they blindfolded me first. Why? To prevent me seeing which of the three was hitting me. Or just to bewilder me?

Two of them suddenly seized and dragged me blindfolded into the corridors. I went downstairs and found myself in the open air. A rope or a scarf with a slipknot was placed round my neck and I was pulled along like a dog on a leash. I was choking but they went on pulling me. 'Go on!' They made me run, and I felt soft earth under my feet. I fell but they pulled me up by tugging at the knot. 'Go on! Walk!' I walked. 'And now run!' I collapsed.

Finally two powerful arms seized me and I was forced down some steps. From the icy air and the smell of must I could tell I was in the cellar again. A voice insulted me in Russian: 'You bastard, you Trotskyist bandit! You started your filthy Trostkyist job in the USSR. Admit it! Who were your accomplices? We'll shoot you as a Trotskyist.' But it was not a Russian who was talking. The voice had a Czech accent.

I replied: 'I'm not a Trotskyist and I never have been. You won't make me say things which aren't true.'

Someone punched me, and the insults continued in Russian. Then I was again dragged off to be interrogated. Every time I denied something I was punched, and when I fell the interrogators pulled me up and continued to hit me and question me. At last they removed my mask, but I couldn't see a thing, the room was spinning round me, and I only had one wish: to sleep!

That night Smola came into the room. He spoke calmly and tried to coax me. 'It is quite obvious, Mr London, that the top echelons of the French Communist Party were full of enemies. Their policy after the defeat proves this and it would be much to your credit if you could help us reveal who they were. It would also provide you with an opportunity to make up for your crimes. You do want to help the Party and the USSR, don't you? Or have you sunk so low that you still refuse to collaborate?'

He now appealed to my Party spirit and my loyalty towards the Soviet Union, and to my conscience as a communist to obtain from me what he could not obtain by physical and moral pressure.

After these three days and nights of uninterrupted interrogation I had hallucinations; I heard voices, Lise's voice and the children's, in the corridor; I spoke to imaginary people, and started to rave. I collapsed several times, and fell asleep. Smola then thought he could gain a point and force a signature out of me. He typed out a report on the political errors of the French Communist Party, but in spite of the state I was in I protested against the way he had formulated it and made him agree to certain changes. 'I have made some mistakes in my work which resulted from errors committed by the leaders of the French Party. I had dealings with Alice Kohnova, Vlasta Vesela, Pavlik and Feigl, who have already been convicted for their contact with Field (except for Vlasta Vesela who committed suicide at Ruzyn during the trial); I accepted money from imperialist American agents for the Party's underground work.' (That was how the money we received from Feigl at the beginning of the occupation was interpreted by the Security Services.)

I can no longer remember the exact wording of these statements, because of my physical condition at the time, but I was ready to sign anything for five minutes' sleep.

Proud of what he considered his victory Smola immediately had me taken back to my cell where I was allowed to sleep for a few hours. The next day, when the interrogation resumed, my first concern was to cancel my signature of the day before, which I said had been extorted from me while I was virtually unconscious.

Smola was livid: 'So you think this report is a confession? It wouldn't even serve as a self-criticism at the meeting of a Party cell. What the hell are we going to do with your statement? You're only beginning to speak, and you will speak!'

The interrogations succeeded one another, becoming increasingly violent. My physical condition due to lack of sleep, hunger and thirst was deplorable, and yet everyone knew I was very ill. As soon as I was arrested I told them that I was having medical treatment and that it was essential my pneumothorax be insufflated. But they refused to let me be treated. 'You'll be looked after when you've admitted that you're a Trotskyist and a spy!' was the only answer I could get.

By wearing handcuffs the whole time my hands had turned

into huge, agonizing chunks of flesh. I was still questioned standing up and the interrogators followed each other regularly. Sometimes two or three of them deafened me with questions and insults. From time to time I was led into a completely bare cell or cellar. The only difference was that my hands were no longer chained behind my back, but always in front of me so that the warder would not have to undo the handcuffs and put them on again when I relieved myself in his presence. If he was at all compassionate he would help me pull up my trousers.

My bowl was put on the ground and since I couldn't use my hands I knelt down and tried to eat, but with great difficulty. The use of these methods which aim at destroying a man's dignity is radically opposed to socialist morality. They are medieval, fascist methods, and as I was subjected to them I felt degraded and humiliated. And yet I wanted to live! I cancelled my first signature, and I was determined to stand firm, even if they killed me. I had to fight, for myself, for my past, for my friends: I owed it to my comrades and my family.

Nine

There was neither day nor night, only noises – steps in nearby rooms, sobs, women's voices, blows on the doors, the order 'Walk!', or the sound of someone being dragged along.

During the interrogations I knew that the night had ended when the interrogator started to yawn and stretch. Towards dawn there was a hushed atmosphere and I felt I was living outside time, in unreality. This nightmarish world obeyed certain laws, and from time to time the door opened and the interrogator was brought a snack which he devoured before my eyes. There were also moments when even the interrogators lost their hold and had no idea of what was going on.

I represented a period about which they knew nothing and which they couldn't help admiring:

'When did you first meet Oskar Vales?'

'When he was on leave, in Barcelona.'

'It's not surprising that men like him, who have always been anarchists, should have been traitors. In Spain he even deserted his unit of the International Brigades.'

'Yes, he left his regular unit to volunteer for a far more dangerous mission. He was like a character in Hemingway's *For Whom the Bell Tolls*. With volunteers of every nationality he crossed the fascist lines to perform acts of sabotage in enemy territory. One day, in 1938, his guerrilla group was sent fifteen kilometres behind the lines, in the Tremp sector, where it was to raid the headquarters of a fascist division.'

I told how, that night, they had approached the building on the outskirts of a village. Some of them had to get inside it while the others had to lay some mines to blow it up. Vales was in the group covering the others to ensure their retreat. The night was very clear and the guerrillas lay in a ditch a few yards from the sentry post. When a sentry, who had just spotted Vales's men, was about to sound the alarm, the attack started. The sentry and some of the staff officers were killed, an officer was captured, and the guerrillas managed to bring their prisoner to the Republican lines without losing a man.

The interrogator listened to my account, astonished. For him the man sitting opposite him and the men I was talking about had been arrested on the Party's orders and were therefore enemies.

I realized that some of the interrogators believed that by behaving towards us as they did they were fulfilling an 'honourable duty', they were helping the Party to show us up. They were trained and brought up to believe that any method was good which could extract confessions from Party enemies. The methods they used, the setting, the moral and physical pressure, the provocations, seemed normal and legitimate to them.

Many of the interrogators were new recruits; some had been picked in the factories, and they were the products of the rapid and summary training provided in 'their department'. How could men who were not basically evil become such blind and docile instruments? I realized that for them the Party was an abstract idea, not a vital organization for which they felt responsible. It was represented by their superiors and the Soviet advisers, or by anyone who stood above it. Their orders were sacred, unquestionable. Such a mentality necessarily led to complacency, to the concept that they themselves were supermen with the right to pry into everything and everybody in the Party and the country.

When he relieved his colleagues and continued the interrogation the new interrogator received his slip of paper containing one or two questions and the answer he was to obtain. Each interrogator knew only one aspect of the elaborate charges formulated against us by his chiefs. He had to obtain a confession on this point whatever the price. Then he was given another point, and so on.

If the low level of political education which characterized them showed that they were novices, some were positively primitive and stupid. It was often impossible to make them understand the most elementary things about the struggle of the clandestine Communist Parties and their policy of a national front.

'Why did you remain in contact with the Czech consulate in Marseilles run by Benes's men after the occupation of France? Why didn't you apply to the Soviet Embassy in Vichy for money for your underground activities?'

When I told him about the national front of Czech émigrés in France, which included Benes's men, communists, and independent individuals, the interrogator saw it as a renunciation of communist principles: 'How could communists collaborate with Benes? Are you taking us for idiots?'

Another one flew into a rage when I told him about the FTPF in Paris. 'You're not going to make me believe that the partisans could function in towns, still less in Paris. They only existed in the country and the woods.'

'There is no such thing as a group of three or five partisans or an isolated attempt. How dare you tell such lies? Operations organized in the heart of Paris in broad daylight! Do you think you can get away with telling us such incredible stories?'

Another interrogator simply questioned the value of armed resistance in a western country, because 'all that counted in the war was the Red Army which would have obtained the same results with or without the resistance movements.'

Still other interrogators couldn't understand why the French Communist Party did not come to power after the Anglo-American landing in Normandy. As far as they were concerned any man who had travelled in the west was suspicious, a potential spy. They demanded such absurd confessions as 'In France the Main d'Oeuvre Immigré is the leading branch of the Fourth International in Europe.' In spite of explanations which they could easily have obtained from the French Party about the meaning of the letters MOI (Main d'Oeuvre Immigré) they insisted on interpreting them as the Nazis had done before them: Mouvement Ouvrier International (International Workers' Movement).

There is nothing worse than to find oneself helpless and alone before stupidity and blindness, for hours, days, months on end. The interrogators remained deaf to every argument, to the most obvious proof. I could only assume that the use of these men by 'the Security organization for which we are working' was intentional because they could be manoeuvred like robots. This was a guarantee that even the most convincing arguments used by the defendant would slide off the shell of their ignorance and make no impression on the concept of the 'confessions' which they had been ordered to obtain from 'their client'. Their blinkers allowed them to see no further than from the Ruzyn prison to Dejvice.*

Only gradually in the course of the interrogations did their organization emerge, and this was how it was formed:

Each group of interrogators had a chief who was usually a

* The quarter of Prague where the central office of State Security was located.

captain or a major. Lieutenant-Colonel Doubek coordinated the activities of each group, and it was he who was in contact with the Ministry of Security. The group leaders did not merely follow instructions like the interrogators. They managed the interrogations more intelligently and cunningly, and their view of the accused was broader. They were the docile and obedient instruments of the Soviet advisers who instructed them personally, and they therefore knew part of their masters' 'construction'. It was to contribute to this 'construction' that they used the interrogators.

In addition, this is what I was told after my rehabilitation in 1956 by Alois Samec, a former volunteer from Spain who had initially collaborated with the Soviet advisers working for State Security:

'The Russian advisers arrived in Czechoslovakia in the autumn of 1949, soon after the Rajk trial. They said that we must have had some form of conspiracy against the state in our country, and that the enemies who wanted to overthrow the socialist regime had infiltrated every branch of the Party and the government.

'According to the instructions they gave us we arrested individuals who "might" have been acting against the state because of their jobs or their contacts. Only later did we look for evidence.

'One of the Soviet advisers, Borissov, ordered me to give him a copy of each report signed by the accused after the interrogations. When I pointed out that the Secretary-General of the Party already received a copy of these reports he reprimanded me sharply and told me not to question his instructions.

'I also had dealings with other Soviet advisers, notably with Likhache and Smirno, who were gathering compromising information about everybody, particularly politicians in the highest places, including Slansky and Gottwald.

'They increased their power by exploiting the trust of the Party leaders who regarded them as a guarantee of highly qualified and just security work. Gottwald took their advice on every important case. They instigated most of the main measures taken by the Ministry of Security and they took advantage of this to use methods practised in the USSR. With increasing frequency the Security staff took their orders straight from the Soviet advisers – particularly from the ones working in the investigation bureau – instead of through the normal channels.

'As soon as they arrived they began to infiltrate every branch of Security with "confidential agents" who were wholly devoted to them. This was how they managed to create a parallel police force under their own command in the heart of State Security, where they were supposed to occupy an official function.'

In Ruzyn, during my twenty-two months of detention which ended in my trial, I became aware, at my daily interrogations, of the presence of these 'confidential agents' recruited by the advisers, not only among the group leaders but also among the interrogators themselves. They carried out special orders given them by their chiefs, and on several occasions I noticed some antagonism between the official organization and the secret one created by the Soviet advisers.

For example, one day Kohoutek came in and took my interrogator aside. He whispered to him – but I managed to catch their conversation – that the boss (Doubek) wanted the reports of a name which I couldn't hear, in order to hand them over to the Minister (Kopriva). 'You must remove from the file . . .' here again I missed a few words, 'and put it all back when the file is returned to you.'

Thereupon the interrogator produced a file and removed a bundle of papers which he locked in a drawer. Fifteen minutes later, when Doubek called for so and so's file (this time he showed the interrogator a scrap of paper with the name written on it) he was given the expurgated dossier. When Doubek returned it, the interrogator replaced the original sheets. 'Is everything all right?' Kohoutek asked a little later. 'Did he say anything?'

Two or three days before my trial, in the middle of November 1952, Kohoutek rushed into the room and said to the interrogator: 'Give me all the reports of the men who have to appear. The Minister Rais has come to see them.' (This meant, incidentally, that the Minister of Justice was only informed about the reports drawn up by the accused two days before their actual trial!) But it so happened that these reports were not intended to be read by the Minister, and I saw Kohoutek and my interrogator search feverishly in each file for pages which they piled together and locked in a drawer: these pages contained those parts of the interrogations which referred to the Minister of Justice, Stefan Rais, himself. The 'confessions' proved his contacts with the centre of the conspiracy against the state, and since he was not only Minister of Justice, but also of Jewish origin, it was necessary to hold the material against him in reserve.

Then in the central prison of Leopoldov, where I was transferred in 1954, I saw the Soviet advisers' confidential agents doing the same sort of thing. They came to question one of my fellow prisoners, Oldrich Cerny, who had been convicted for Trotskyism, in order to make him confess the 'war crimes' committed by the President himself, Antonin Zapotocky. Indeed, Zapotocky had committed the unforgivable mistake of having been deported to Sachsenhausen and of having fought in the Resistance. The advisers tried to extort from Cerny the same 'evidence' against the President as that which had served to convict others in our trial.

Besides, in Ruzyn all the important reports were translated into Russian and this was the version which counted. The advisers made the necessary changes and corrections before passing them on to the group leaders whose job it was to force the defendant to sign them.

This system enabled the advisers not only to follow the interrogations step by step but also to establish the direction the 'confessions' were taking, and to organize a form of competition between each group, and between each interrogator within the group. The permanent aim was that 'each report should constitute an admission of guilt.' But this aim was broad and allowed every zealot full liberty to employ the method he preferred. So the best of them obtained the 'best confessions' quicker, and pleased their 'real chiefs' most. It was not only a question of obtaining the 'confessions' but also of adding a remarkable personal contribution. Our interrogators bragged about their formulations between themselves with as much vanity as bad poets.

I became aware of this almost immediately, at the beginning of April. While Smola was questioning me, an interrogator rushed into the room brandishing a piece of paper. He was radiant. 'It's going splendidly,' he told Smola. 'He's breaking. Look how I've put it. This gives us all we need.' And before leaving he gave Major Smola a copy so that he could appreciate the text. As he left he repeated: 'Oh yes! It really is going well!'

Half an hour later Smola, infuriated by my constant denials, seized me by the collar and shook me violently. Suddenly he showed me the passage with which the interrogator was so pleased, and I saw it was from the proceedings of my friend Tonda Svoboda's questioning. To one question they made him answer: 'That's all I have to say about the activity of the Trotskyist group of former volunteers in the Brigades during their stay in Paris.' What the interrogator was so proud of was his own introduction of the phrase 'Trotskyist group', which merely served to enrage Smola still more, since he had failed to score a similar point from me.

Later, when I protested to Kohoutek, who had succeeded Smola, about the use he was making of the phrase 'Trotskyist group' to designate the veterans from Spain, he replied cynically: 'That's nothing. In future reports I shall be referring to a Trotskyist espionage organization and you'll be obliged to accept that. Don't think you won't!'

It became more and more obvious that the interrogations

were being aimed against the former volunteers in the International Brigades, and that there was a basic prejudice against all the veterans, who were considered, without exception, as spies and dangerous elements. As for those of us who had been arrested, we were Trotskyists, Party enemies, agents of the French Second Bureau, the Gestapo and other foreign intelligence services. The name of every veteran on a report was now accompanied by adjectives like 'demoralized', 'Trotskyist', and so on. Later the word 'volunteer' alone became the equivalent of the most pejorative terms. Each conversation, each incident implicating a volunteer, even the most normal and harmless ones, took the form of a conspiracy against the state, an enemy act.

There was the same prejudice against the volunteers as there had been against the Jews, a distorted attitude which was again expressed in 1953 in a circular addressed to all government offices by the National Security. The volunteers were identified as members of the German Protektorat police and armed forces in Bohemia and Moravia and of Hlinka's fascist Slovak guards. The International Brigades were simply put on the same level as the units which had fought against the Red Army from 1918 to 1922 and against the Soviet Republic in Hungary in 1919.

This attitude covered all the members of the Brigades; no one was spared. I was therefore interrogated at length about a dinner Pavel, Svoboda, Zavodsky, Vales, myself and others had had in Prague in 1950 with Luigi Longo, who was now Secretary General of the Italian Communist Party and had been Inspector General of the International Brigades in Spain. The same applied to my dealings with Edo D'Onofrio, a Senator and leading member of the Italian Communist Party, who visited me every time he passed through Prague.

I was also asked about a meal I organized for my friend the Bulgarian Minister Dimo Ditchev, when he came to Czechoslovakia, wanting to see some of the volunteers he had known in Spain. The meal had also been attended by my brother-in-law, Raymond Guyot, a member of the Political Bureau of the

French Communist Party, and his wife, who were passing through Prague. The interrogator literally jumped out of his chair when he heard this. He passed me on to another interrogator, saying that he had to see some 'friends' about a very urgent matter. When he returned he slapped me repeatedly to make me confess that I had organized this meal in order to enable Guyot to construct an 'espionage network in Europe' with the Bulgarian Minister Ditchev's help.

Ten

Spain: against the mud which they churned up day after day, I tried, when they left me alone, to reconstruct our Spain, the Spain which remained in my heart.

Since the political amnesty proclaimed in Czechoslovakia in spring 1936 did not affect me, I volunteered for the International Brigades in November when the fighting was raging in Madrid. I was still in Moscow and I had to wait for the KIM's* authorization to leave. It was in March that a comrade from the Czech department suddenly told me that I was to leave an hour later. She told me to study my false passport and the numerous visas which had been stamped on its pages since I had deposited it with them on my arrival. I set off immediately, travelling by train to Malmö, and from there, by ferry, to Copenhagen, and thence to Isberg. Once on the boat to Antwerp I felt at last that the road to Spain was clear.

In Paris, at the Gare du Nord, bewildered by the crowd, I heard someone calling 'Gérard! Gérard!'† My wife's parents had come to meet me. They had never seen me, but recognized me from a photograph which Lise had given them. I spent two weeks with my parents-in-law in the 20th Arrondissement, near

* The Communist Youth International

† After 1934 all my friends and comrades called me by this Christian name.

the Père-Lachaise cemetery. My father-in-law showed me round the capital on foot, obstinately refusing to take the underground. 'If you want to get to know a town,' he said, 'there's nothing like a pair of legs!' Thanks to him I really got to know and to love the streets of Paris.

When the day of departure at last arrived I went to a café at the appointed time and a comrade came to fetch me. He took me to a hotel where I remained for twenty-four hours before catching my train. The man in charge of the convoy told me that a number of other volunteers, most of whom had come from Austria, were sitting in other compartments, and, since I knew several languages, he asked me to help him keep in touch with them.

In my compartment there were some veterans from the Schutzbund* who had fought against fascism in the barricades in Vienna in February 1934 and had fled to the USSR after their defeat; and in addition to the Germans, the convoy included Bulgarians, a few Yugoslavs, Englishmen and Americans.

We reached Perpignan with no difficulty, and that same evening we were driven out into the country. The night was fine and cool, and against the black sky we could see the outline of the Pyrenees. The guide, a French mountaineer, was waiting for us. We walked in single file, myself behind the guide, acting as interpreter, and we wore espadrilles so that we could climb more easily and silently.

Crossing over the high mountains was exhausting: the Pyrenees deserved their reputation. We went through the thick mist which clung to the peaks, and we were soon enveloped in a luminous grey haze. Day was dawning and we watched a magical play of colours which heralded our first day in Spain. We stopped for the last time in a wood, where we waited to run across a meadow between two border patrols.

All went well. We arrived, out of breath and worn out, at a small wood cabin topped by a column of smoke pink under the

---

* An armed organization of the Austrian Socialist Party.

first rays of the sun. Four men came out, their fists raised: 'Salud camaradas!' At last we were in Spain.

The road now descended, but I was too weak to walk. The Spanish comrades had to carry me on a stretcher formed by their rifles, and that was how I reached the fortress of Figueras, the first assembly point of the volunteers.

It was also via Figueras that I was to leave Spain at the end of the war in February 1939. The Cadre Department of the Spanish Communist Party had sent four of us, a Bulgarian, an Englishman, an Italian and myself, to Lagostera where a new International Brigade was being formed. Our job was to set up the Party organization, while Pavel was in charge of forming the military unit. Until then he had commanded the Dimitrov battalion which ranked as one of the best, and now, in spite of his exhaustion after a long night's march from La Garriga, he was worrying about being in time for the rear-guard battles. As Pavel was leaving Hromadko came into the room where we were sitting. His hands in his pockets, a mischievous smile on his lips, he was as debonnaire as ever and took no notice of the bombardment which had suddenly begun. Later, when we helped him escape from a convoy to Germany in Paris in 1941, his spirits were just as high and he threw himself into the fray until the Liberation of Paris.

We were supposed to hold a meeting that evening but the situation had deteriorated. The Italian motorized divisions had broken through the Front and were about to invade the village. We could already hear rifle shots and machine-gun fire. Pavel said he had ordered the brigade to take up its position on the way out of the village, and that was where I came across Tonda Svoboda, near the church, picking the best positions for his company of machine-gunners to cover our retreat. He was a fine figure in his uniform, his hair almost completely white, and one could feel the power he had over his men. He showed us the way to Gerona where André Marty was expecting us the next morning.

We reached Gerona at dawn, after numerous difficulties, only to discover that Marty had already left. At the local Party headquarters the man on duty took us for deserters, but fortunately Marty's liaison courier vouched for us. We were to return to Figueras and join him there, but the town was under the worst bombardment of the war.

A few days later, towards 9 February 1939, when the fascist armies were a few miles from the French frontier, the Cadre Department of the Central Committee of the Spanish Communist Party made out a list of the political and military cadres of every nationality, even the volunteers from the Soviet Union, in order to help them reach Paris and thence return to their respective countries. The Czech list consisted of about twenty names including those of Pavel, Hoffman, Knezl, Hromadko, Stefka, Svoboda, Neuer, Grünbaum. Couriers were dispatched to tell them where to meet, behind La Junquera. The Republican army, which was already out of action, was concentrated on a thin strip along the French frontier, and the units of General Lister and General Modesto covered the retreat, but in the confusion we could only establish contact with some of our men.

André Marty ordered me to get in touch with the Central Committee of the Spanish Communist Party, which was constantly on the move in order to avoid a surprise attack from the motorized fascist units or from the Fifth Column. I had to find out in what order the last units of the Republican army were going to cross the border, and tell Ercoli* to join André Marty. A motorcyclist was put at my disposal and we had to cross an area already infiltrated by the Fascists and the scene of rearguard action. In the end I got hold of Mije, a member of the Political Bureau of the Spanish Communist Party, and accomplished part of my mission, since Ercoli had already left.

Just as I was about to leave I realized that my motorcyclist had disappeared: he had been too scared to face the same road

* The pseudonym of Palmiro Togliatti, who was then one of the secretaries of the Communist International and its delegate in Republican Spain.

back and had headed straight for the frontier. I was sixteen kilometres from La Junquera, and had to return on foot, in the wave of refugees and soldiers in retreat. When we arrived at the crossroads nobody took the road to La Junquera. 'Figueras has already fallen,' they all said. 'They must have reached La Junquera by now!'

What was I to do? If it was a false rumour – and there had been so many recently – and if I failed to appear, it could look like desertion. So I decided to head for La Junquera, occasionally stopping to hear the sound of distant cannon. I paused before entering the hamlets and villages, but they were all empty. I knocked on doors and windows, but nobody opened, although there were noises which suggested that the inhabitants had locked themselves in. Alone on the highway I was terrified of encountering an enemy patrol.

The Fascist reconnaissance planes flew low, but there was no point in hiding whenever they passed. My only hope of escape was to advance as fast as possible. Then I saw some figures in the distance, and went up to them, my heart in my boots. But they were our men, political prisoners who had been released from the prisons of Barcelona: anarchists and members of the POUM, all fleeing from Franco's forces. They said we must move still faster for the Fascists were only a few miles off.

It was nightfall when I reached the little house behind La Junquera where André Marty was expecting me. He was standing in the road, a large bandage round his head, exhausted, and almost mad with anxiety. He shouted insults at me for being late. He was surrounded by volunteers of every nationality who had not been evacuated. At one moment he ordered us to send back the soldiers making for the French border and only let civilians pass, at another he threatened to have us shot if we stopped the military trucks.

That night he called me and told me that all the Czechs were already at the border. 'It's your turn to go now,' he said. 'Anyhow, we'll all be leaving tonight or, at the latest, tomorrow morning. You must leave together with Rol Tanguy and a

German comrade, and you'll be crossing the police cordons in a car with two French deputies, your brother-in-law, who's just arrived, and Jean Cathelas.'

This was the only time I ever met Cathelas who was guillotined in 1942 in the Santé prison under the German occupation. It was to Rol Tanguy and General Leclerc that General von Choltitz, in command of the German garrison in Paris, surrendered on 24 August 1944, and I don't know what happened to my German comrade.

We started off towards the border on foot; it was only a few miles away. We destroyed our Brigade papers, dismounted our weapons, and threw the various parts into the ravine at our feet.

At the border the guards searched all the soldiers, and on each side of the road lay heaps of arms, but they didn't ask us anything since we were in civilian dress. To every civilian who asked how to get to Toulouse, Marseilles or Bordeaux the guards answered invariably, 'The main road on the left,' which led to the improvised camps of Argelès and Saint-Cyprien.

Our group crossed the border without any difficulty and we reached the village where the large car, a deputy's rosette on the windscreen, was waiting for us. The German comrade and I rode in the back, curled up on the floor. We passed several control points and the two deputies showed their Assembly cards. We got to Perpignan, and the next day the car drove us to Tarascon where we took the train to Paris.

Eleven

One night, as he was sipping his coffee, the interrogator told me he had received orders to work night and day on our case in order to provide material for the Central Committee which was to meet in the course of the month. Comrade Gottwald was to justify the arrest of the volunteers in the International Brigades before the Party and the country.

So, using Ossik Zavodsky's 'confessions', false statements and denunciations, the leaders of the Security division wanted to get the Central Committee to approve their theory that Czechoslovakia was menaced by a Trotskyist plot fomented by former volunteers from the International Brigades!

Gottwald did indeed make a speech to the Central Committee on 22 February 1951:

'After the fall of Republican Spain many volunteers in the Brigade were interned in France. They lived in appalling conditions and were subjected to pressure and blackmail first from the French and American espionage services, and later by the Germans and others. Thus, by taking advantage of the poor moral and physical condition of the volunteers, these services managed to enlist a number of them as agents. Those enlisted by the Americans and the French were in the direct service of the western imperialists while those enlisted by the German Gestapo were, like all the Gestapo agents, transferred to the American espionage services after the defeat of Hitler's Germany.'

At that very moment I, and others like me, were fighting to prove our innocence. But we had already been condemned and the Party's attitude was fully exploited by the Security with disastrous consequences for us. The determination of the interrogators now knew no bounds.

The formulations devised by the State Security in the sinister castle of Koldeje came back on us after passing through the Central Committee. Gottwald's words now constituted incontestable proof of our guilt and justified all the methods used by the interrogators. The Party sanctioned them, and it was by torturing us that they were to prove their devotion to the Party.

Although I was questioned in a number of different rooms, I never saw daylight. I remember this whole world drenched in the subdued or blinding light of electric bulbs.

Every time an interrogation was interrupted I was either sent to another room or led back to the cellar in order to prepare for the next one. It was no advantage to be in a room with a dry floor and a mattress in a corner, for I had to unroll the mattress with my chained hands, and, before leaving, roll it up and wash the floor. The pain actually made me miss the damp cellar. Day after day, my handcuffs seemed to grow tighter and my wrists and my hands swelled to bursting point.

The memory of those handcuffs haunts me to this day and I still occasionally rub my wrists. The position of my arms gave me cramps in my shoulders and spine, while my benumbed arms were dragged down by the weight of the chains.

When I fell asleep while pacing round my cell I crashed into the wall, and when the shock brought me to my senses I could no longer tell fact from fiction. A fantastic and terrifying world pursued me everywhere. It must have been something like *delirium tremens*. When I fell to the ground from exhaustion and pain I was doused with cold water, and forced to do exercises in my cell.

Even the meals which I longingly awaited were torture. The bowl, steaming in the icy air, was always put on the ground – there was neither a table nor a stool – and I had to lap up my food on all fours. Man has none of an animal's resources so when the bowls were taken away mine was almost full, and my hunger increased my hallucinations.

Eventually the interrogations became less confused, the violence and pressure gradually assumed a definite direction. I realized that I was designated first with Pavel, and then alone, as the leader of the demoralized Trotskyist group of volunteers in the International Brigades. But only later were these tactics explained to me.

In 1953, a few months after my trial and sentence, I found myself in the office of one of the interrogators who had formerly questioned me. 'Don't believe, Mr London,' he told me, 'that you had been chosen as the leader of the group of volunteers from the start. You had been away from Czechoslovakia for many years. You only returned in 1948 and that was a handicap. At first we tried to make Pavel, and then Holdos the leader, but that was not entirely satisfactory. Then we picked on you because you had spent a long time in the West, and there, as here, you were in a responsible position. You were responsible for the volunteers in France. You had had dealings with Field and had numerous acquaintances on an international level. And besides, you were of Jewish origin. So you had all the qualities we required.'

I was still only at the beginning of my ordeal. As I paced round my cells I tried to set my ideas in order, but I always came up against the same obstacles. How could a man like Gottwald condemn hundreds of men who had not hesitated to obey the Party's orders and leave their homes, their jobs, their loves, to fight on the fronts of Madrid and Aragon, determined to defend their own countries by fighting for Spain? How could the Party pronounce itself on the basis of police distortions without looking for any evidence? Why did it not hear us before taking a decision? How could it leave its basic obligations to its members to be performed by State Security? The most superficial investigation would have immediately shown up the absurdity of the charges against us. And why were Soviet advisers behind the interrogators, manipulating them like puppets?

I was unable to unravel the confusion in my mind, and nothing is worse than being unable to understand what is happening to you.

Once again I was led away blindfolded. To the cellar? No, instead of the damp must I smelt pure fresh air. I breathed it in avidly: we were outside. I was pushed into a car. I never ceased asking myself questions as we drove along: where were we going? was I going to be released?

The car stopped. I climbed some stairs, and went down long corridors. Then, when my bandage was removed, I saw that I was in a normal prison cell. The door closed behind me and a voice said: 'You can lie down.' The order was unnecessary, for I collapsed in a corner and immediately fell asleep. Two men kicked me awake and one of them removed the handcuffs which I had worn night and day for over a month. The relief at having free arms, at being able to move my fingers and to stretch, was indescribable. From then on I was only to have my hands chained behind my back once a week, when I was shaved in my cell.

I put on a pair of dungarees, and some heavy felt slippers with rough inner soles which cut into my feet. I did not realize that the handcuffs were to be replaced by a new torment.

And once again I was ordered to walk. I felt pains in my feet almost immediately. I was walking on razor blades and my feet rapidly started to swell. But after the hell I had been through the fact that I was in a normal prison gave me some hope. My case was going to be cleared up, I was going to know where I was and why I was there, what was going to happen to me, and even, perhaps, something about my family.

I received a steaming bowl and a piece of bread, and I was allowed, as an exception, to sit on a stool and eat it.

A little later I was again blindfolded and led to another room. I was facing Smola. He looked at me for a moment: 'If you had a mirror you wouldn't recognize yourself.' I had no doubt that my appearance had changed, what with a month's growth of beard, my face dirty, thin, emaciated by weeks of hunger, thirst and lack of sleep.

He added: 'Today is 1 March. You are in a State Security prison. We are going to start your interrogation from the beginning. The Party has told us to deal with your case and others like it. Every day we inform the Party of your behaviour towards us during the investigation. You only have one way of redeeming yourself: confess all you know about yourself and the others.'

'I am quite prepared to answer all the questions you ask, but on one condition: that the report gives an exact account of my answers, and not the distortions you have so far provided.'

'Your life is at stake. Think well about the attitude you intend to take. By opposing us you oppose the Party. Now go back to your cell.'

So it was 1 March. I had spent over a month in Koldeje!

Twelve

I was sure that my wife was moving heaven and earth to find out what had become of me and obtain some explanation.

Later she herself told me what had happened after my arrest:

'We waited for you all afternoon. I was hurt by your absence since you had promised to come back as soon as possible. Towards dinner time I tried ringing your friends to find out where you were. I rang the Hromadkos three times, but there was no answer. I called Zavodsky. His wife answered in a sad, subdued voice. "Have you seen Gérard this afternoon?" "No, he hasn't been here, and anyhow Ossik's away."

'I called several other of your friends but none of them had seen you. We were just about to go in to dinner when I heard a car draw up outside the door. I thought it was you, but when I opened the door four young men rushed in, pushing me inside the house: "We've come to search."

'"Who said you could? Show me your warrant?"'

'They didn't have one so I wouldn't let them into the drawing room, and told them I was going to telephone immediately to Slansky and the Minister of Security. They wouldn't allow me to telephone, but after a brief conversation they decided to send a man to headquarters. While they waited for him the others sat on a sofa in the hall.

'My parents were with me and their grief upset me deeply. I persuaded my mother, who felt ill because of the shock, to go to bed, while my father remained with me. Although he couldn't understand what was going on, he stood by me courageously.

'In the meantime Françoise had come back. I told her the men had been sent by her father from the Ministry. She suspected nothing and went up to bed.

'My father paced up and down in the drawing room, while Michel ran from one chair to another, muttering: "Papa – papa." He went up to the young men, who now looked embarrassed, and clung to their knees, laughing. I offered them some coffee and explained that my father was a Spanish miner and an old member of the French Communist Party. I felt that they were impressed by our attitude, because they became politer and tried to make themselves unobtrusive.

'Three hours later another car drew up and another gang of thugs rushed in. There were at least five of them. One of them, who appeared to be the chief, showed me a piece of paper and without giving me time to read it pushed past me and gave orders to search. This lasted most of the night. I managed to make them be silent in the room of the children, who barely opened their eyes and went back to sleep as soon as they heard my voice. They also searched my parents' room from top to bottom, and my mother wept silently in bed. "You're behaving no better than the Nazi police who came to arrest me and my husband in 1942," I told them.

The second gang left with a case full of documents and family papers. The three younger ones remained in the drawing room, and my father and I spent a sleepless night in their company. I tried to get them to explain, but they clearly knew absolutely nothing and were simply carrying out orders.

'The next morning a man from Security came for his colleagues in a car. Before leaving he told me not to mention what had happened to anyone and to go to work as usual.

'The Ministry car came for me at the normal time to take me to work. The chauffeur looked uneasy but didn't ask any questions, and before leaving I rang Siroky on the direct line to the Ministries and the Central Committee, told him about your arrest and asked if I could see him at once. He gave me an appointment for the next morning.

'I saw him in his office. He seemed very embarrassed and said that nobody had been more surprised than he by what had happened. I told him that you had been uneasy recently, demoralized by the atmosphere of suspicion which surrounded you, and I asked him why he had refused to see you when you tried to hand him your resignation and ask for his help. He pretended to be amazed. "Did he try to see me? I didn't know that." He told me that he had made inquiries about you after my call and that I wasn't to take things so seriously. You hadn't been arrested, but merely isolated in order to clear up certain problems in the utmost secrecy. They needed your help in some way to unravel certain complicated matters connected with the Party. I told him you were to have had your pneumothorax insufflated the day before, but he assured me you were being looked after. In the end he told me the car and the chauffeur were at my disposal as always. So after this meeting I felt more optimistic. As I left him I passed Hajdu's office. Hajdu was waiting for me, and looked very upset by your absence. He asked me what was going on. I repeated what Siroky had said, and he sighed with relief. He tried to comfort me and told me that he would do anything he could for me.

'I went to my office every day. On Wednesday another chauffeur in an old Skoda came for me, saying that the Ministry had sent him to replace your driver. I had no doubt that he was a detective, but that didn't matter much. He accompanied me everywhere for over two months until the day when he told me that the Party Committee of the Ministry had expelled you . . .'

After her meeting with Siroky Lise had written to the Party Directing Committee. I was only to see a copy of the letter after my rehabilitation. It was dated 30 January 1951, and ran as follows:

To the Party Secretariat
Dear Comrades,
At the moment I am going through one of the hardest ordeals of my life – and my life has not been easy. I have been a member of the Party and the Communist Youth since 1931 and I have always enjoyed the Party's confidence. You have my *curriculum vitae* in the Cadre Department and I am not going to repeat it here.

Last Sunday two groups of agents from the National Security searched our house. They behaved as though they were dealing with enemies of the regime, with fascists. I told them my husband did not have an office at home – and indeed, he never worked here so as not to have to transport his files to the Ministry. So all they found were personal papers, my children's and my parents' belongings – correspondence, articles, documents, packets of letters I received from my husband during the war when we were both in prison in France, letters which we had then sent to my parents who had carefully kept them. The case full of papers and documents which the Security agents took away with them belonged to me and to my parents, except for a few identity cards and papers of my husband's.

At the same time I discovered to my distress that my husband had been arrested. Comrade Siroky, whom I saw at the Ministry yesterday, said that I shouldn't use this word – but all the appearances pointed to it.

I say 'to my distress'. How could I not be distressed to see my husband, in whom I have absolute trust, undergo such an ordeal: isn't the worst thing that can happen to a communist to think that his Party no longer trusts him?

But I confidently await an explanation of this misunderstanding. I've lived with Gérard for over fifteen years. Together we have faced the hardest trials and he has always behaved like a true communist – during the Spanish Civil War, under German occupation in France, in prisons and concentration camps.

Wherever he has fought and worked he has not only enjoyed the full trust of the Party, but also the affection of all his comrades. I have absolute faith in his political integrity, in his loyalty to the Party which has been the centre of his life. I speak about my husband simply and objectively. I am not blinded by love. I judge him as a communist, aware of his qualities and defects.

Comrade Siroky told me that although Gérard had not been arrested he is placed in isolation to help clarify some serious and important problems.

I have been in the Party too long not to realize that it has the right to know everything about its members, that, at any moment, it can demand explanations about their life and actions. Nobody in the Party is an exception to this rule, and if Gérard can help I see that it is his duty to do so.

But I cannot approve of your methods. Nothing in our behaviour justified such treatment. I can assure you that I wouldn't have objected if comrades had asked me if they could check on our belongings. But these methods are frankly inadmissible.

When, two years ago, Gérard had to provide Security with explanations about his chance contacts with Field during his stay in a Swiss sanatorium, the Cadre Department never deigned to discuss this matter with him thoroughly and to elucidate it once and for all. I believe that to be a mistake. If the Party has the right to know all about its cadres, it is also bound to study and to judge every case. Gérard suffered considerably from the Party's attitude towards him.

I am certain that he too is confident and courageous, that he is trying to clear up any matter that remains obscure. Here again he will act like a conscientious communist and will not let himself be discouraged by the methods used against us.

I must also add, however, that, despite my demands to meet some official in the Security Services, I find myself up against a wall.

It is therefore only my complete trust in Gérard which has dictated my decision to hide what I am experiencing from everyone, from my colleagues and friends, because I am sure that my husband will soon return and I believe these matters should not be overpublicized in order not to harm the Party. And I beg the Directing Committee to take all the measures necessary to elucidate this business as soon as possible.

Communist greetings.

Lise Ricol-London.

Only after my release did I find, amongst the papers returned to me, a letter which my wife and daughter had written for my birthday, four days after my arrest, and which I had never received.

1 February, 10 o'clock.
Darling Gérard,

Today is your birthday and I am sure you have been thinking about us as constantly as we have about you. I miss you very much but I am awaiting your return confidently. I am confident because I am a communist and I trust you. 'One can't burn truth or drown it in a well,' says an old Russian proverb. The truth always triumphs, especially in the Party.

Darling Gérard, can you feel how close you are to me in my thoughts? I never stop thinking of you, but I am not unduly upset. I play with my children and work. I have complete trust in you and in the Party. Of course I would rather not have undergone this painful ordeal, but when one is an old communist, as we are, one must face difficulties with courage and fight to sort them out.

That, darling Gérard, is what I wanted to tell you this evening. I am waiting patiently. I love you.

Your Lise.

Prague, 1 February 1951.

Darling Daddy,

This is to wish you a happy birthday and say how much I think of you when you're away. I am very happy to be able to say that for your birthday I got good marks at school and I soon hope to get my pioneer's scarf. And I think how pleased you'll be when you see me come home wearing the scarf which you always wanted to see round my neck. Gérard also had good marks. He says, 'When Daddy comes home he'll be proud of me and will let me go to the USSR to learn my job.' We often think of you, and today more than usual. We sat down to dinner sighing. We all thought: 'If only Daddy were here ... ' Mummy told us you'll be back in a week and that we'd celebrate your birthday then. We're on holiday from today and we're all very happy. Michel can play football and climb on the chair. Mummy has cut his hair so that he looks like a little girl. ... To-morrow I'll go and see the film *A Great Citizen* with Pepe which is about life in Kirov. At school my teachers have become very strict, and one can no longer whisper to one's neighbours. Mummy has just finished reading *Far from Moscow* and I'm going to start it. I'm now ending *The Life of Oleg Kochevoi* who was the commissar of the Young Guard. I hope you're keeping as well as we are.

Your loving daughter,

Francoise.

Part Two

Ruzyn

One

Nobody ever told me the name of the prison I was in. From the constant roar of aeroplane engines I gathered that I was again in Ruzyn, the prison near the Prague airport. That was my only landmark. I was to spend twenty-seven months in complete isolation, seeing only warders and interrogators. When led from my cell to the room where I was interrogated I was always blindfolded with a knotted towel.

My cell was small and narrow. A double window with thick panes was opened a few minutes every day to air it, while I was made to stand at the other end. When I was not ordered to face the wall I could see two poplars against the sky. Later, after I had been transferred to another cell in the new building, I was not even able to see these trees, for the ventilation was such that the windows did not have to be opened.

I almost feel nostalgic when I remember the first cell. It was a refuge for me between interrogations; I could hear noises from outside: distant voices, dogs barking, birds singing. Sometimes I heard a funeral march because my cell must have looked onto the Ruzyn cemetery. There was a narrow wooden table and two stools chained to the wall, a mattress, and latrines in the corner. I learned how to tell the time from the angle of the sun's rays and the shadows, and I gradually managed to identify all the prison noises. Once again I was in solitary confinement but never before had it been like this. When I was allowed to sleep, the mattress had to be facing the spy-hole. The light was on all night and shone in my eyes. It was very cold. The dungarees I was wearing offered me no protection and in the evenings, before going to sleep, I had to fold them carefully and put them on the stool; if the warder decided they were badly folded he would wake me up any number of times to make me fold them again.

To the left of my cell was another cell whose inmates rapidly succeeded each other. I realized this because they tried to contact me by tapping Morse code or the alphabet used by the revolutionaries in the Tsarist prisons. I only knew the latter, and could therefore only answer certain calls, which were always anonymous. I never gave away my name since I never knew to whom I was talking. Twice the warder discovered me doing this: as a punishment I had to strip, and he sprayed me with cold water, made me do physical exercises and fold and unfold my mattress several times.

Sometimes I heard violent blows against the neighbouring door, screams, the hurried steps of the warders, sounds of a struggle, then a body being dragged along the corridor and stifled groans. A few seconds later the door was opened again and my neighbour was brought back. From the words whispered by the warders I understood that they had put him in a strait-jacket and gagged him to give him a cold shower. Some prisoners were to keep the straitjacket on for twenty-four or even for forty-eight hours, and I was soon to become acquainted myself with this sinister dungeon.

I received no mail and knew nothing of what was going on outside. I was constantly alone with my thoughts. Every morning the warder appeared for a report with his eternal: 'Requests and complaints'. I automatically repeated the same request: 'I want to write to the Central Committee. I want an interview with a Party representative.'

Although food was more regular here than at Koldeje I was always tortured by hunger, for the rations were minute. One night, seeing the ravenous looks I aimed at his sandwich, an interrogator said to me: 'So you're hungry are you? Well then, confess! After that you'll get your full rations.' In spite of a violent argument he offered me a piece of bread – he was a compatriot of mine from Ostrava.

The worst part was not being allowed to sleep, having to

stand during the questioning, and the exhausting marches round the cell.

The prison woke up early, between five and six o'clock. We then had to get up, fold our blankets, roll up our mattresses, clean our cells and wash. And then start walking again.

At the beginning of my stay in Ruzyn the interrogations went on day and night. They started in the morning and only ended the next day, between four and five o'clock. While the interrogator rested I was taken back to my cell where I had to walk until they came for me again. Sometimes, after making me walk all day, they came for me in the evening and the interrogation went on until morning. Then, when day broke, without being able to sleep for a second, I had to continue my hallucinatory march.

When I was allowed to sleep for the four hours to which I was theoretically 'entitled' those hours were a fresh torment. I had to lie on my back, my hands alongside my body outside the blankets. If I turned round or put an arm under the covers the warder woke me up at once, made me get up, fold my bed, and do squatting exercises with my arms outstretched. He made me undress and sprayed me with cold water, and ordered me to walk. Only then could I go back to bed.

This would happen up to three or four times in a row. If not to me to a fellow prisoner, and the warders' shouts and kicks against his door would wake me up. In practice these four theoretical hours were reduced to a mere hour or two.

As I was often interrogated for eighteen or twenty hours on end I was sometimes allowed to sleep in the mornings. The interrogation which started the day before towards nine o'clock in the evening ended at four in the morning. By the time I had returned to my cell, made my bed and undressed it was half past four. I fell asleep. At half past five the alarm for the whole prison rang. So I too had to get up, wash, clean my cell, wait for the warder to bring the soap which I then had to return to him together with the bowl, the towel and the toothbrush. At a quarter to seven I went to sleep again. But I was constantly interrupted: at a quarter past seven a warder came to open the window to air the cell; at half past seven another one came for the daily report; at a quarter to eight the first one came back to shut the window. At eight I had to get up and at nine the interrogation resumed.

Other times I came back from the interrogation at eight in the morning, and had to see to the daily drudges. I went to bed at nine, I was woken up several times and at half past eleven I had to get up. I received my food, and again had to start walking, then the interrogation and so on . . .

For a long period I walked round my cell all day. At night I made my bed and went to sleep, more dead than alive, but no sooner had I closed my eyes than the warder shook me awake and took me off to the interrogation. One or two hours later I was taken back to my cell, fell asleep again to be woken up shortly afterwards and led back to the interrogation. And so on all night.

This lack of sleep for weeks and months on end accounts for the moments of insanity and the hallucinations which I experienced. I was no longer in control of my senses, I thought I was going mad and would fall into a state of total sottishness and apathy, moving like an automaton.

I had been arrested several times during the First Republic, and then in France under the occupation. I had been interrogated by the Special Anti-terrorist Brigades in Paris notorious for their brutality. I had known the worst Nazi concentration camps, Neue Bremme, and Mauthausen, but the insults, the threats, the blows, hunger and thirst were child's play when compared to systematic lack of sleep, this infernal torture which voids man of every thought and turns him into an animal dominated by his instinct for self-preservation.

Every physical and moral torture was carried to an extreme. I had been forced to walk continuously in the Gestapo punishment camp of Neue Bremme near Sarrebruck, before being deported to the extermination camp of Mauthausen. But there it had only lasted twenty-six days, while here it went on for months, and was made all the worse by my having to keep my arms to my sides, level with my trouser seams.

After a few hours' march, thanks to the slippers which I was given on my arrival and which were changed as soon as the soles got too soft, my feet were covered with blisters; a few days later my feet and legs were as swollen as if I had elephantiasis. The skin round my toenails burst, and the blisters became suppurating wounds. I could no longer get the slippers on. I walked barefoot, and was brutally taken to task for it. In the end this became as ghastly as the handcuffs.

One day, as I was walking barefoot, the warder was startled by the sight of my deformed feet exuding water and pus. He called a doctor who, after examining me for a few seconds, gave me some diuretics, saying that I didn't urinate enough. After six months my feet were in such a state that the interrogator who was questioning me, as a great favour, let me sit down for a few minutes.

Initially I was not allowed to see a doctor despite my requests. I spat blood for two days running, and when, towards the end of March, I was taken to the Bulovka hospital to have my pneumothorax insufflated Major Smola told me: 'Don't think we're doing this for your health. No, no. We're only doing it to be able to take you to the gallows alive.'

The doctor established that my pneumothorax had collapsed. He tried to fill it out but only partially succeeded. The lower part of my lung had caved in, and he diagnosed pleurisy with discharge.

The interrogations increased. At the end of my stay in Koldeje, the Security Services concentrated on making me the leader of a 'Trotskyist group of volunteers in the International Brigades' and the head of the Trotskyist conspiracy in Czechoslovakia. Each new interrogation brought me fresh charges.

I was presented with more 'confessions' extorted from fellow-prisoners – from Zavodsky, Dora Kleinova, Svoboda, Holdos, Hromadko, Pavlik, Feigl, Spirk, Nekvasil and others. Each confession contained charges more terrible than the last, as well as half-truths which confused the issue, and downright lies. I later discovered that the report containing Vales's 'confessions' had been entirely made up by the interrogators. He didn't even know about it.

Dozens of statements were also collected against us from outside by the Security and the Party Organizations. The Party's call – that everyone who had known us should help reveal the traitors – released the wave of hysteria and collective psychosis necessary for the preparation of our trial.

Every day I saw the pile of letters denouncing me on the interrogator's desk grow larger. He showed them to me happily, to increase my bewilderment and prove that I would get away with nothing. Numerous letter writers, influenced by the articles and speeches made by the Party leaders ostracizing us, interpreted normal facts as crimes. Some of them wanted to raise their credit in the Party's eyes, others acted out of fear. Many of them wrote things which they were later to regret or for which they tried to find excuses. Without suspecting it they were serving the Security Services. Whether or not these denunciations were made in good faith their consequences were the same for us. Other individuals made up whatever our accusers liked, and assured their careers and their future.

Important figures in embassies or in Party organizations, even if they hardly knew me, invented the most extraordinary stories. Some did it to disassociate themselves from me and guarantee their own safety, while others were themselves arrested, under the pretext of acknowledging receipt of their reports; the Security Services had decided that their personality fitted into their idea of the 'plot' and that they too could make some useful 'confessions'.

Most of the letters were addressed to the Central Committee of the Party. Some of them were read to me, and others I saw myself. In one of them a member of the Cadre Department had noted in the margin: 'for the attention of the Minister Kopriva', and another hand had added 'for Comrade Doubek'.

All this time I could still not get the Party to hear me. I felt totally helpless. The interrogators refused to draw up a report with my replies; instead they wrote daily reports for the Party in which they interpreted my refusal to sign the 'confessions' as the attitude of a hardened criminal.

When, after the trial, I met Vavro Hajdu – who had been arrested some time after myself – he told me of the conversation he had had with Siroky about my arrest. To his question: 'How is Gérard taking things?' Siroky simply replied: 'Very badly. He has the wrong attitude.' This wrong attitude was to proclaim my innocence.

I was beginning to become aware of the interrogators' impatience. At Koldeje one of them had already told me they were working night and day on my case. This had originally been to enable the Central Committee to make a statement about our arrest, but now it was so that our group should be tried as soon as possible, because a public trial had become 'politically necessary'. I was told that this trial should take place in May or June, and they repeated that 'the political situation requires the denunciation of your criminal activity.' Smola added details: 'It will be a large trial before the Supreme Court. Your gang will be shown up before our working classes. You know what that means for you? The Supreme Court won't have much mercy.'

As I still refused to sign my 'confessions' I was now threatened with a trial *in camera*. 'You'll pay for it with your head, for even if you don't confess, the pile of material we possess, and the number of witnesses against you, are enough to have you condemned. Our reports alone are enough,' said Smola, and another interrogator told me: 'We'll inform the prosecutor and the court. We'll be there when you're tried and we'll be the ones who address the Judge and the jury. Your sentence will be whatever we ask. *Our* attitude towards you at your trial will be determined by *your* attitude towards us now.'

So they could have me tried *in camera* – and nobody would know I was innocent! This threat was more terrible than all the others. But it didn't have its full effect on me because even if my hopes diminished day by day I still refused to believe that I would never be able to explain myself. It was inconceivable that the Party could have an interest in covering up such crimes and because it was inconceivable I held my ground. I had now been caught up in this infernal machine for four months.

Two

The ringleaders of Ruzyn were past masters in the art of arousing guilt in the prisoners. They exploited the fact that the victim was telling them his life story like a Catholic to his confessor, and they constantly searched for some error on his part, some reservation towards the Party which could once have caused a misunderstanding, in this way 'deducing' facts that could later be held against him. The ringleaders could then find the weakness which served their purpose, and they kept it in mind for the future. They manipulated subjectivity and objectivity solely to get their victim to admit that he was guilty; they had experience, and they had time. They worked at a distance, through an intermediary. The man in their trap only became aware of their existence by cross-checking. And this mystery surrounding them served to increase their authority, their power, and the anxiety of their victims. These ringleaders were the Soviet advisers.

Kierkegaard admirably described the sort of thing I felt: 'The individual becomes guilty not because he is guilty but because of his anxiety about being thought guilty.'

This feeling of guilt which potentially exists in every individual, even in daily life, is inherent in the human conscience. Who has not blushed when the schoolmaster told the perpetrator of a prank to own up? Who has not sensed a certain anxiety when crossing a frontier, even if he had nothing to hide, at the mere sight of a customs officer in uniform? Who has not asked himself: 'What have I done?' when a policeman comes up to him in the street? Of all the comrades arrested during our underground work, who had not thought: 'If only I had followed the instructions closer . . . . If I hadn't been to see my wife or my mother . . . . If I hadn't been back to my lodgings . . . . If . . . If . . . . If . . . .'

In our life as militant communists the practice of self-criticism, our very effort to be perfect, led us to look in ourselves for the responsibility for our mistakes. We had been brought up with this discipline without ever suspecting that Stalinist methods – the so-called personality cult – would turn it into a form of religion.

If we reacted like that when we were free, if we automatically felt this sense of guilt before the Party, how could we believe in our innocence after our arrest which had been ordered by the Party, sometimes by its President, and by these 'Soviet advisers'?

I myself experienced the efficiency of this Security weapon, and if today I can analyse its mechanism, I obviously could not do so at the time. I simply accepted it. 'Every action, every fact,' they told me, 'must be judged objectively in the reports. Its subjective side will be appreciated later.' This meant that since I had known Field and since Field had been denounced as a spy in the Rajk trial, I had to admit my 'objective' responsibility for this friendship even if, 'subjectively', I had been unaware of Field's activities at the time. Since my comrades of the International Brigades had signed confessions in which they admitted their guilt of various crimes against the state, I was 'objectively guilty', since I was their superior. Day after day, night after night, this refrain of objective guilt was repeated.

I was questioned about a ministerial meeting which had taken place in 1949 in Clementis's office, with Dolansky, the Vice-Premier, Kabes, the Minister of Finance, and Gregor, the Minister of Foreign Trade. Following a request from the government of Pakistan the four ministers decided to send a certain Havlicek there as an industrial adviser. They knew that Havlicek was not a supporter of our regime but they hoped that he would obtain some orders for our industry. I was told by

Clementis to arrange for Havlicek's departure, which I did, although I never saw Havlicek in my life.

Had he 'chosen freedom' or what? I was now accused of having sent to Pakistan an unreliable individual, 'objectively' an enemy. The subjective side – that I was only carrying out an order from the Ministry – was not mentioned in the report. All that was mentioned was the 'objectivity': I was 'objectively' guilty of sending an enemy to Pakistan.

'You were responsible for the Cadre Department at the Ministry of Foreign Affairs when Brotan was sent to Switzerland and Kratochvil to India. Both refused to return to Czechoslovakia when they were recalled by the Ministry. So they betrayed! You can't deny sending traitors abroad. And what does one call a cadre policy which consists of sending traitors abroad? Objectively it's a policy of sabotage and treason.'

The interrogators also claimed that any information – even if it had been taken from articles published in the Party paper, *Rude Pravo* – communicated to a foreigner – even if he were a communist – constituted an act of espionage according to our laws.

'The conversations you had with your French guests in your house – and who told you there were no agents among them? – concerned the situation of our country. So "objectively" these conversations smack of espionage.'

In Ruzyn one of the interrogators gave me brilliant proof of what a crime of espionage was:

'We know that Field did not present himself to you as a spy. That's not how those people work. He asked you for certain information which you gave him: the address of the radio building in Prague and the name of the director, Lastovicka; the address of the department of cultural relations of the Ministry of Information and Culture and the name of the director of this department, Adolf Hoffmeister. You told him you were editor of the Parisian weekly *Parallèle 50*. All this to a man who has been proved a spy. Objectively these are acts of collaboration with a spy and that's how our laws regard your attitude.'

And he continued:

'You knew Field?'

'Yes.'

'You had dealings with him?'

'Yes.'

'Was Field revealed to be an American spy in the Rajk trial?'

'Yes.'

'What do we call consistent dealings with a spy? Espionage. Don't we? He who has dealings with a spy is a spy himself, isn't he? Why are you afraid of words? Someone who makes bread is a baker . . . '

I defended myself against such a distorted interpretation of facts, saying that the information I gave Field was known to everyone: he could have found the addresses in the Prague telephone directory. So the interrogator replied:

'If a soldier tells you that the calibre of his gun is 7.92 that's espionage, even if a detailed description of the gun was printed the day before in the papers.'

Nothing could escape a similar interpretation. Once the accused had been made to admit their guilt 'objectively' there was a change of tone. And after this 'confession' the interrogators started to write not only that they were enemies 'objectively' but also 'subjectively'.

'You yourself said and admitted that you had dealings with Titoists, and with the spy Field, that you undermined the cadre policy in the Ministry of Foreign Affairs. You can't claim that this was all fortuitous. You're not a fool. If you did this it's because you're a traitor, because you wanted to damage the Party and the government.'

Every event and act in a man's life was susceptible to these distortions – everyone could be made into a traitor, a spy, a saboteur, a Trotskyist. Each honest and loyal activity in and for the Party became suspicious or hostile.

The mere repetition of this kind of 'objective' proof was

enough to drive you mad, especially since the Soviet advisers revealed themselves by their abominable questions which betrayed a total ignorance of conditions of life in the West and by their refusal to understand either these or previous political situations. Everything we had done was judged in the light of the immediate international situation, according to the political standards in force at that moment in the USSR. That was how my friendship with Field was regarded. If I had met a Yugoslav communist in 1937 in Spain the interrogators wrote that 'before the war I had already been in contact with the Titoist X.'

One of the directors of Ruzyn, the confidential agent of the Soviet advisers, told me: 'We must see the events and activities of the past in the light of events of today and not in their context at the time, otherwise we could never hold a trial and the Party needs a trial.'

From time to time they applied different tactics: 'Since the Party says you and your group are guilty you must admit you are guilty.' Or: 'As an old and disciplined Party member you must bow to the Party's verdict and confess as the Party demands.'

Doubek, the head of Ruzyn, put the same idea in more 'poetical' terms: 'The only way of proving your loyalty towards the Party is to adapt yourself to its *present* means of judging *past* events. You only have to imagine that the Party is on the other bank, and it's up to you to jump into the water and swim over to it. You mustn't be afraid of cold water. And in any case, the Party always wins. If you agree to act in the interests of the Party we promise to take your behaviour into account.'

To these arguments I replied: 'But if I'm a good Party member what am I doing here? If I'm a Trotskyist enemy, as you claim, how can you appeal to my feelings as a good communist?'

In the end you asked yourself: When am I helping the Party? When I deny something untrue? The interrogators say no. When I confess to crimes which I haven't committed? They say yes. But you, a communist, know perfectly well that lies can never constitute the foundations of a socialist society. On the contrary, communism means honesty, truth, freedom.

I thought over these problems and I always came up against the motive which induced Ossik Zavodsky to 'confess' whatever they wanted him to confess, and to write out his own confession the day he arrived. The most appalling pressure might have been exerted on him to prove that I was a spy and that I could carry out my activities and avoid arrest under his protection, despite all he knew about me and all our past conversations. But this did not explain so rapid and total a submission.

Had the injustice and absurdity of his alleged betrayal to the Gestapo broken him? But even this was not enough. Only now was I beginning to understand what the interrogator had meant at Koldeje when he said that Zavodsky knew the Security Services. He knew about the service directed by the Soviet advisers. I thought about Pavel Kavan's remark that all these things were happening over Zavodsky's head when I complained about being followed. He can't have had any illusions about the Soviet advisers. He knew that, sooner or later, as in the Moscow trials, their victims 'start to confess', and he preferred to take the lead. Was it because he knew more about it than we did that he yielded so soon?

One night Major Smola, who was interrogating me, was called to the telephone. He left me in the corridor, blindfolded, under the supervision of the interrogator working in the room next door, who stood in the doorway to watch me. As I stood there I heard a whispered conversation and recognized Zavodsky's voice: 'Who's in the corridor?'

'London.'

There was a pause, and then Zavodsky said: 'How tired he must be!'

The interrogator told him I was only getting what I deserved, that I was too thick-skinned and that my fate was assured. Zavodsky then asked him what would happen to *him*.

The interrogator answered: 'You'll probably be sent to a

state farm or somewhere isolated for four or five years, as long as it takes to forget about the whole business.'

During a subsequent interrogation, when Smola was producing other 'statements' made by Zavodsky against me, I screamed at him: 'You extorted all these lies out of Zavodsky by promising . . . ' and I told him what I had overheard in the corridor. That day I was furious and told him what I thought of his methods and lies. Smola flew into a rage and left the room, probably to scold the interrogator who had spoken to Zavodsky.

Later, after my rehabilitation, I met this interrogator and when I asked him about Zavodsky's 'confessions' he told me that for two months he had been personally ordered by Kopriva, the Security Minister, to treat Zavodsky with special regard, like a comrade. Two months later, with no explanation, this order was revoked.

The 'confessions' of the others were extorted by inhuman methods and under the pressure of Zavodsky's 'confessions'. The new ones were supposed to confirm what Zavodsky had said, but also to provide new elements which could increase the pressure on me. Long passages from the reports were read out to me, and some of them were cleverly formulated. For example, Svoboda was made to say that he had discussed the Czech army, its firing capacity, etc. in front of me, and that London *could* therefore 'transmit this information to the western imperialists as a Trotskyist agent'.

In this 'confession' the word *could* answered the interrogator's Machiavellian question: 'Could he transmit them?'

'Yes, he could.'

This then became proof that I had done so, in view of my 'dealings with Field'.

To fill the gaps during the years I had spent outside Czechoslovakia, they made Zavodsky 'confess' that he had written to me about the group's activities, thereby giving me the information which I required for spying. It was also in writing that I had given him my orders. Svoboda was made to 'confess' that

Zavodsky directed his enemy activities, but that, 'since he knew he was corresponding with me', he realized that I was directing the group through Zavodsky.

Pavel was forced to say that in 1944 I gave him orders in France to carry on his 'enemy' activity in Czechoslovakia. When I replied: 'How could I have done this since I was deported to Mauthausen in 1944?' Kohoutek, who had succeeded Smola, said: 'That just shows you how everyone is turning against you. They're like wolves, ready to tear you to pieces.'

For that was the Security's last weapon.

Diabolically, they turned one man against another. They fanned up personal dislikes and old rancour. They mystified us: 'So and so said this about you.'

'He can't have said that, the bastard!'

'He said some even worse things, and you, poor fool, you're trying to let him get off.'

This was how they obtained the most defamatory evidence.

The pressure on me was increased: 'These are the people who were under you. Their personality gives an even better idea of of their leader's character.'

What had become of the solidarity which had united the political prisoners in the Nazi and bourgeois prisons, one of the most important elements in their courageous and heroic attitude towards the police, the judges and the executioners?

I saw myself in the yard of the sinister medieval prison of Poissy in September 1943 together with eighty other political prisoners, all serving heavy sentences. Detachments of Vichyite and German police, armed to the teeth, were waiting for us at the gates, and we all thought we would be shot as hostages. We sang the 'Marseillaise' and the 'Internationale', we shouted *Vive la France! Vive de Gaulle! Vive l'Armée rouge! Vive Stalin!* and soon all the other political prisoners in their cells joined us.

Suddenly I heard my name: 'Gérard! Gérard!' I looked up at the men clinging to the bars of the windows over the yard and I recognized Laco who was waving to me. I went nearer and waved back: 'Goodbye Laco!' He was crying and shouted: 'I want to go with you, I want to die with you!' Those were our bonds of fraternity and loyalty unto death. But what had become of us here? The prisoners whose mutilated statements, whose false and slanderous 'confessions', were shown us, accusing us of every crime, were no longer fellow warriors but a bunch of rats.

Every day my file swelled with a new 'charge', and every day the interrogators accused me of a worse 'crime':

'Your espionage activity did not start with Noel Field in 1947. You were already a spy in Spain. The proof . . . '

This was how it was formulated:

'London enabled the International Commission of the League of Nations to enter the camps of the Czech volunteers and talk to them individually, and get them to fill in questionnaires . . . . That was how he spied on an international scale.'

I remembered those autumn days in 1938 when, at the suggestion of the Spanish Republican Government, the League of Nations decided to withdraw all the foreign forces from Spain. In order to check that this was being carried out by both sides an International Commission visited Fascist and Republican territory.

The volunteers were withdrawn from the fronts and concentrated in repatriation camps in Catalonia.

After registering them – by nationality – the members of the Commission had the right to interview each volunteer, with no witnesses. The main problem was to know where the volunteer was to be repatriated. This applied above all to men from countries with a Fascist regime, who might have been imprisoned on their return.

I was working as an instructor of the Central Committee of the Spanish Communist Party with the Czech volunteers and in this capacity I had received a visit from a former officer in the Brigades, another Czech called Smrcka, who was then acting as interpreter for the International Commission. He wanted to tell us that during their interviews with the members of the

Commission some of the volunteers had ingenuously indicated the channel they had used to come to Spain, and had given the names of the people working in the Aid Committees for Republican Spain who had helped to recruit them and organize their departure. Some of them had even given this information in their questionnaires.

In view of the situation in Czechoslovakia after Munich this was particularly serious. Most of our comrades had said that they wanted to return home and continue the struggle against Hitler who already occupied the Sudetenland and was preparing to devour the rest of Czechoslovakia.

Thanks to Smrcka, however, we managed to withdraw these questionnaires and persuaded our comrades to fill in new ones without giving away any detail which might harm the antifascist and communist fighters in Czechoslovakia.

My contact with Smrcka, who had been invaluable to the anti-Fascist International and to our Party, was here used as evidence that I had spied 'for the League of Nations' International Commission and collaborated with the spy Smrcka'.

Smrcka, a regular army officer who had come to Spain to fight with the International Brigades, had been appointed liaison officer at the headquarters of the 15th Brigade. Some people suspected him of working for the Czech intelligence services – and he may well have been. In any case, he was on good terms with the Czech consul in Barcelona. On the other hand his attitude in the Brigades was irreproachable. He knew how to talk to his men and was extremely popular among the soldiers. His exceptional physical courage commanded admiration and respect. After his Brigade had attacked some Fascist positions the political commissar lay wounded a few yards from the enemy trench. Every attempt to carry him back to our lines had failed, for the Fascists opened fire every time someone tried to get near him. Smrcka volunteered to fetch him, crawled up and brought him back at the risk of his own life. He himself had been wounded seven times and had lost an eye.

Shortly before the end of the war Smrcka left Spain for France, and in 1941 some Czech comrades said he had been seen in Belgium. He had tried to escape, after the German invasion, by embarking secretly on a ship bound for the Argentine, but when he reached his destination he had been refused admission and sent back back to Belgium on the same ship. After the war we discovered that he had been executed by the Gestapo in 1943.

The interrogators ridiculed my explanations. 'So you spied in Spain with your accomplice Smrcka. But that's not all: from that moment you started to collaborate with Field and the American intelligence services . . . '

I had never heard of Field before my friend Hervé gave me a letter for him in Paris 1947 just before my departure for Switzerland, but day and night one interrogator after the other tried to make me 'confess' that I had been 'richly rewarded by Field after my return from Spain for the excellent work performed there for the CIA . . . '. They claimed that Field had been a member of the League of Nations' Commission.

And there was now a new charge. I was Tito's agent. Since I had worked with the representative of the Yugoslav Communist Party in 1939 and 1940 and since this representative was none other than Kidric, who was now a Minister in his own country and described by the Soviets as 'one of the leaders of the Titoist clique', my Titoist betrayal was fully confirmed, even if I had then visited Kidric in order to provide Sverma and Siroky, the leaders of the Czech Communist Party in France, with false passports.

But this was another matter, part of my activity in the MOI and the conclusions the Soviet advisers and the interrogators were to draw from it.

Three

In spite of the inhuman treatment inflicted on me and my state of physical debilitation, I continued to hold my ground before the interrogators.

Smola threatened me: 'Don't think you're going to wear us down. We've got enough interrogators to replace the ones you wear down! We won't stop interrogating you until we've obtained your confession or else we'll kill you like a rat!'

One afternoon Smola had me brought into his office, and opened before my eyes a packet of cheese and small rolls. He took two bottles of beer out of the cupboard and started eating. I tried not to watch his jaws. 'Are you thirsty?' he asked me. 'Do you want a drink?'

I didn't say a word. I thought he was teasing me, but he handed me a glass of beer.

'Here.'

I took it, hesitantly, and then swallowed it in one gulp. He told me to sit down and gave me a roll with two slices of cheese.

'Eat it.'

Although his attitude surprised me I started eating.

'If you confess, Mr London,' he said, 'I promise to write a letter immediately to the Central Committee with your help. The Party will take your excellent past into account. It will give you the chance to escape from the position you are now in. Think of Marker and Leo Bauer in East Germany. They were as implicated as yourself in the Field business, but they were not arrested, only penalized. The same will happen to you if you confess and thereby prove your loyalty to the Party. Have you decided to confess?'

My mouth full, I replied, 'I've got nothing to confess since I'm not guilty.'

He jumped out of his chair, rushed round the table and seized me by the collar and by my hair, squeezing my neck. He shook my head to make me spit out what was in my mouth. 'You bastard!' he shouted. 'That's what you want! To have a meal, but not to confess!'

'I've got nothing to confess. I've asked you to face me with Field several times. He's in prison in Hungary so that's perfectly easy.'

Ever since my transfer from Koldeje to Ruzyn on 1 March, every day, at the morning report, I had asked permission to write a letter to the Central Committee or to the Party President, Gottwald. I repeated the request to the interrogators and to Major Smola who replied each time: 'The Party will say the same as us. We're the Party! You're a criminal. The Party has nothing to say to you. Only if you prove your wish to repent by confessing your crimes and your espionage will the Party hear you!'

Nevertheless, I continued to make the same request. Finally, on 3 April, I was led into a room where I found myself face to face with Kopriva, Minister of Security. Smola and Doubek, the head of Ruzyn, were both there.

'What's all this?' shouted Kopriva. 'You still refuse to talk? How long are you going to keep this up?'

'Ever since my arrest I have asked to write a report replying to all the questions you have asked me, but I cannot accept these half-truths.'

Kopriva was furious. 'You must confess on whose orders you distributed your Trotskyist agents over Europe.'

'I don't understand what you mean. I've only done what the Party told me to do.'

He interrupted me, yelling: 'You repeated to Zadovsky that I had questioned you about him.'

I wanted to explain myself but he wouldn't let me.

'You're lying as you have always lied! We'll liquidate you, with or without your confessions. We'll be able to trick you in court, you can be sure of that.'

And he ordered me back to my cell.

As I reached the door I turned back to him: 'At least let me send my family and my children the money I had on me when you arrested me.'

'Only when you've confessed,' he screamed.

Back in his office, Smola was delighted. 'Well, you've had your meeting with the Party. You'd been warned. Did the Minister say anything different from what I told you?'

He concluded: 'And now you'll be put in the punishment cell.'

'Why?'

' Because you were insolent to the Minister and dared to make a request before confessing.'

I was put in a cell without blankets or mattress. I had guessed correctly: it was the cell that had been next to mine.

I walked in pitch darkness, blinded at regular intervals by a bare light each time the spy-hole was opened. I decided it was all senseless. I stopped and lay on the ground. The warder ordered me to get up. I refused. A second warder threw a bucket of water over me. I didn't budge. They tried to pull me to my feet, but I fell back like a stuffed doll. They threatened me with a straitjacket, but I remained motionless. One of them went out and I heard noises outside the door. He had probably gone for orders. Then the second one went out, the voices faded into the distance, and I remained on the ground, shivering in my wet dungarees.

This meeting with Kopriva, a member of the Political Bureau of the Party and Minister of Security, marked the end of all my hopes. I was now sure that the leaders of the Party had decided on my sentence. I was isolated, weak and helpless before the 'representatives' of this Party to which I had devoted my life, of this regime which I had assisted through years of struggle and sacrifice. My feeling of helplessness and pain grew boundless when it became evident that behind the Security men torturing me there were the Party leaders. How was such a thing possible? Where was the truth? Where was the Party?

I realized that the words and threats of the interrogators were true and that the trial they threatened me with was going to take place in any event. I no longer had anything to cling to: I was lost.

I remembered my wife's words after the Rajk trial: 'It must be terrible for a communist suddenly to discover, from one day to the next, that she had lived with and had children from a man who turned out to be a traitor.' This time it was I who was to be the traitor in everyone's eyes – even in my wife's.

The day of my meeting with Kopriva was the birthday of my son Gérard. He was born on 3 April 1943 in the prison of La Petite-Roquette in Paris.

'This morning at six o'clock you had a son,' Odette Duguet, who had been arrested with my wife, wrote to me. 'You should have heard him scream! Lise is fine. She was very brave and always thought about you. They've just been carried on a stretcher to Baudelocque.'

I knew from our lawyer, Maître Bossin, that my wife wanted to give birth in the prison although it was against the rules: but she had good reasons for it.

Three weeks earlier she had had pains and the prison doctor diagnosed the beginning of labour. She had immediately been driven away in an ambulance guarded by policemen, with an escort of motorcyclists. The head of the Anti-terrorist Brigade and his men were waiting for her at the hospital door. While the doctor was visiting her, as she lay on the surgical couch, they insulted and threatened her, exploiting her weakness to extort information which they had never been able to get out of her.

She had then been put in a little barred room where two policemen watched her the whole time, one sitting next to her bed, the other in the corridor. Her labour suddenly stopped, and my wife begged the prison doctor to dismiss her and let her return to the prison, where she felt freer and where there was at least some solidarity. This happened twice – the ambulance, the police, the motorcyclists – to Baudelocque and back.

The third time she felt pains she didn't tell the prison doctor, but with the complicity of her comrades she decided to have the child at La Roquette. Her friend Odette managed to get a bed next to her in the infirmary and some common prisoners smuggled some sheets and towels out of the linen closet to put on her bed. The child was born at dawn on Saturday, 3 April, when the nuns were at mass. On their return they called the doctor, who arrived just in time to cut the umbilical cord.

Lise had hoped to be able to stay there with her child, among sympathetic companions and the old nun, Soeur Sainte-Croix de l'Enfant Jésus, who guarded the infirmary and was so fond of her that she wept whenever Lise was taken away. It was a Saturday – visiting day – and that afternoon Lise was to see her parents and our daughter. She thought she would be able to show them her son, but she couldn't, for she was rushed off to the maternity ward and placed under guard.

On 15 April she was taken with her child to the prison of Fresnes. In the large, cold entry hall she watched helplessly as the nurse who had accompanied her undressed the baby to take the garments back to the maternity ward. She took him on her knees, naked except for the band of gauze round his waist.

This was one of the worst moments of her imprisonment. She had hidden the details from me, as she had of all the other ordeals she endured. The letters she wrote to me were gay, confident and optimistic – never a complaint, while every night she dreamt of how she would behave when she mounted the scaffold.

I too was a prisoner in the Santé at the time and death was our daily companion: but how fine and rich our life was then.

My wife and I had been arrested on 12 August 1942 after falling into a police trap. My wife had been wanted by the Anti-terrorist Brigade ever since the great patriotic demonstration had taken place on 1 August in the Avenue d'Orléans, near Denfert-Rochereau.

All the walls of Paris were covered with those red notices of the *Kommandantur* informing the Parisians of what would happen to partisans caught with weapons on them and of the reprisals which would be carried out against their families.

Madeleine Marzin and members of the FTPF, who had been arrested shortly after a demonstration in the Rue de Buci, had just been sentenced to death, and tanks patrolled the main streets of Paris to intimidate the population.

It was in this atmosphere that, on 1 August, hundreds of women moblized by the women's committees of the Paris region, of which my wife was one of the leaders, assembled at the appointed place. Masses of housewives were queuing in front of the Félix Potin department store at the corner of the Rue Daguerre and the Avenue d'Orléans, and the pavements were crowded with people. The partisans in charge of security were at their posts.

At exactly three o'clock my wife climbed onto a counter and harangued the crowd, appealing to the armed struggle against the invaders and begging them not to work for the German war machine. Tracts rained onto the people and the 'Marseillaise' was sung. Two policemen with pistols in their hands tried to get hold of Lise, but she broke away. The partisans covered her flight, killing two policemen and a German officer who fired on the crowd. Two demonstrators were wounded and one killed. The witnesses commented: 'They're real Amazons.'

The demonstration had a great effect in France, where Fernand de Brinon* ranted against 'the shrew of the Rue Daguerre', a description that was then repeated by the whole of the collaborationist press, while the demonstration was mentioned in several broadcasts on Radio-London and Radio-Moscow.

After our arrest we spent ten days in the hands of the notorious Special Brigade. The interrogations were carried out day and night. My wife stood her ground before the inspectors; far from denying anything she prided herself on having taken part in the demonstration. 'I've done nothing but my duty as a Frenchwoman. . . . I don't regret what I've done and assume full responsibility for it. On the other hand the people arrested with

---

* Pétain's Ambassador in Paris.

me had nothing to do with it. My father and my husband know nothing about my activity.'

Her old father, Frédéric Ricol, had indeed been arrested after us and held as a hostage to increase the pressure on my wife. When he was faced with her, he pretended to be surprised to find 'these things' out about his daughter, and as he protested his good faith in his curious Franco-Spanish he winked at Lise to keep her spirits up.

I myself said nothing. My real identity had been discovered after my fingerprints had been checked, but all that was established was that I was living under a false identity. However much they punched and slapped me, the police discovered nothing about my underground work or about my having volunteered for the International Brigades in Spain; I claimed that I had fled to France after the German entry into Prague.

Not a single name or piece of information could they extract from us which would have enabled them to trace the people responsible for the demonstration and proceed to further arrests. My wife, who had taken everything on herself, was charged with the sole responsibility for the *affaire de la rue Daguerre*, with murder, attempted murder, conspiracy, communist and terrorist activity.

Before leaving the Special Brigade for the Police Station we heard about Madeleine Marzin's escape during her transfer to the Central prison of Rennes, after her sentence had been commuted to hard labour for life. When my wife showed how pleased she was, an inspector told her: 'That doesn't make things much better for you. Now you don't stand a chance of surviving.' But when she arrived at the prison she realized she was expecting a baby, and when she was tried by a State Tribunal on 16 July 1942, almost a year later, she escaped death thanks to the birth of our son who was more than three months old at the time of the verdict. She got off with forced labour for life. I myself had been sentenced two months earlier to ten years' forced labour, listed as a hostage, and was later deported to Germany.

But then I had been surrounded by comrades, I had the Party, I had hope, and I was proud of what I did. Now I had nothing but boundless despair.

It was at this moment that I decided to commit suicide, rather than be hanged as a traitor. But it was difficult to kill oneself in Ruzyn, as difficult as it was to reveal the truth. Captain Kohoutek once told me: 'If we didn't take precautions most people here would try to kill themselves.'

So I chose the only possibility which offered itself to me: to die of hunger without letting anyone notice, because if it was discovered that a prisoner was on hunger strike he was fed by force. I hoped that several days' privation would hasten my tubercular relapse, and kill me sooner. Pretending to be constipated, I twice asked for laxatives to weaken myself and for eighteen days I had nothing but water to drink.

I threw away my food carefully in order not to be found out; but one day I almost gave myself away. Unable to resist the 'good' smell of the soup I threw the whole thing into the latrines. A little later the warder looked through the spy-hole and rushed in: 'What have you done with your food? You haven't had time to eat it, but your bowl is already empty!' He looked at the latrines but could see nothing abnormal. I'd pulled the plug. So he left the cell, reassured.

I got visibly thinner. The third day I felt a fever coming on and my thirst increased. I tried to drink as little as possible to abbreviate my martyrdom, and yet I was forced to ask for water during the interrogations because my tongue would no longer move: it stuck to my palate, filling my mouth like an alien body. My words were unintelligible. I was afraid the interrogators suspected something, because they looked at me curiously. In the end they gave me as much to drink as I liked. I always had a bottle of water at my feet, which I constantly drained in order to survive the interrogations. I had become so thin that my trousers were falling down and I felt terribly weak and dizzy. My lips were parched and split; my veins stood out like thick ropes on my arms and hands. In the middle of the day I would dream of a waterfall in the corner of the cell – fizzy water mixed with raspberry syrup giving out an intoxicating scent which obsessed me.

On the eighteenth day of my hunger strike I was asked about Milan Reiman, one of the Prime Minister's collaborators, arrested for dealings with Field. The interrogator told me: 'His suicide in prison proves that he had a dirty conscience.' This remark reminded me of a speech made by Kopriva, the Security Minister, at a meeting of the Central Committee in February 1950 when he used exactly the same words to explain Reiman's suicide. The same would happen to me. Instead of saving my honour as a man and a communist by escaping trial and a defamatory sentence by suicide, this would confirm to the Party and the world that I had 'a dirty conscience'.

So I decided to continue eating in order to sustain my strength for the day when I faced the court, denounced the criminal methods of State Security and affirmed my innocence. In spite of my lamentable state of health, this decision to hold firm gave me strength to live and to carry on fighting.

But now that I had decided to live the first meal I ate made me violently sick. Was this the result of the two purges I had taken on the fourth and sixth days of my hunger strike which were only taking effect now? Or was it the result of bad food after my long fast? The fact was that this time I really thought I would die.

The interrogators were very concerned about my physical state, fearing that I would escape them. It was essential that they retain their main card, so they informed Smola who came to see me during an interrogation. He too seemed surprised. 'What's happening to you?' he asked. 'You look odd. Your head looks as though it's on the end of a stick.'

They then decided to submit me to a medical visit, and even the prison doctor, Sommer, who was well known for his insensitivity to the prisoners' sufferings, had difficulty in hiding his amazement. I had lost about thirty pounds. He immediately ordered me a course of calcium injections, and from then on I received my normal ration in addition to the supplement to which I was entitled as a sufferer from tuberculosis.

I provocatively told Smola and his interrogators about my attempt to commit suicide, and said that if I gave up it was to prevent its being interpreted as an admission of guilt.

'You bastard!' shouted Smola. 'Your children may be starving while you throw your food away.' He threatened me with reprisals if I ever tried again, and on several occasions had me X-rayed after my meals to make sure that I had eaten.

I was again accompanied by a nurse and a new interrogator to the hospital to have my pneumothorax insufflated. The doctor examined me and anxiously asked me about my health. He had difficulty in insufflating and had to try three times. Finally he and the nurse withdrew into the next-door room where they had a long talk.

On my journey back the interrogator forgot to blindfold me, as he had done on my way to the hospital in the centre of Prague. We were driving towards Ruzyn, which confirmed my suspicions. I knew the way, for I had driven along these streets every morning on my way to the Ministry, and I knew that we would soon be passing in front of my house.

Then suddenly I saw my father-in-law at the end of Lomena Street, bent, exhausted-looking, pushing the pram together with little Michel. Michel's large black eyes were wide open, and he trotted along with a serious expression. It was a fleeting but poignant sight, and I burst into tears. When the interrogator asked me what the matter was I could hardly speak, and when he realized I had just seen my son he too was moved. He gave me a cigarette and tried to calm me; then he blindfolded me. saying: 'I should have done this earlier for your sake.'

The interrogations continued and my treatment, which had improved for a few days, again deteriorated. But I fought on.

To the interrogator from Ostrava I shouted: 'You may hang me but you won't catch me with your methods. There was a Yejov who had a lot of comrades shot, but he ended up by paying for it with his skin. The day will come when the instigators of what's going on now will pay too.' In my fury I went as far as to mention Kopriva whom I had cursed ever since my meeting with him on 3 April. Every day now Major Smola and his interrogators threatened me with death. 'You'll definitely be hanged,' they said. 'Before you die show your children that you have atoned by admitting your mistakes!'

On 1 May I was allowed to write a short letter to my wife, for the first time since my arrest. My main concern was to reassure her that she was not the wife of a traitor or a spy. But Smola sent this letter back to me and it was torn up before my eyes. I had to limit myself to matters of health and the family.

The interrogator who gave me these instructions added: 'It is we who will decide whether or not you are a spy and a traitor. You won't even be able to speak to your wife in court. If you don't change your tune you'll be tried *in camera*. Your family won't be able to attend the trial. There'll only be two of our men. They'll inform your wife about your case and your sentence.'

They had foreseen everything. I wrote to Lise as the men sentenced to death in the Gestapo prisons must have written their last letter, without knowing whether it would ever arrive.

Darling Lise, we exchanged our first kiss over sixteen years ago. Every day I think of that moment and all the time that has passed since and revealed to me your pure, strong love. The future of our children and parents is now in your hands. It may be better if all of you return to France. That's your country, and you'll be able to find a better job there. With the help of your brother and sister you'll manage to support the family. Maybe someone from the Party could advise you. Personally I think this the best solution. But it's so difficult for me to advise you here. I hope to see you soon, my darling. My love to you all.

A little later Smola showed me a letter from my wife. He hid the writing, only allowing me to see the signature and one sentence: 'Of course it's not easy to keep six people, but I'll manage with the help of the Party.' And he told me that my wife had repudiated me and asked for a divorce. So I had lost not only the Party, but my wife and children. As I continued to fight I was rejected by everyone I loved.

I was led to believe this for a long time. Only after my confessions was I given the letters from my wife and children, and there again I discovered how long I had been deceived.

Five

After the Spanish Civil War I became the representative of the Czech volunteers at the International Aid Committee for Republican Spain, in agreement with the Central Committee of the French Communist Party and with Bruno Köhler who was the mandatory of the Czech Communist Party in France. I had also been asked to take over the political leadership of the Czech-speaking group of the MOI.

When foreign labourers flocked to fill the gaps in industry and agriculture left by the Great War after 1918, the French Communist Party and the trade unions decided to organize them in order to defend their own interests and to make sure that they would not be used against the French proletariat. Hence the MOI. The rise of fascism in Europe added numerous political emigrants to the organization, while the veterans from Spain confirmed its anti-fascist spirit.

This was the situation when I was appointed one of the leaders. The MOI provided a solid basis both for underground resistance and for an armed struggle. In spring 1939, after our country had been totally occupied by Hitler, Viliam Siroky and Jan Sverma joined the delegation of the Czech Party in France, and it became my duty to help them.

Towards July Clementis arrived from Moscow. He was on his way to join the Slovak emigrants in the United States but he was arrested together with other refugees by the French police in September 1939. On his release he was mobilized in the Czech army in France and hence evacuated to England after the defeat in June 1940.

In October my wife obtained a flat for Jan Sverma in the block where we lived in Ivry. The flat was in the name of my brother-in-law who was in the army.

It was then that the Czech delegation was called back to Moscow by Gottwald and we had to obtain false passports for them, exit and transit visas, which I got through Kidric, the representative of the Yugoslav Communist Party in Paris.

Sverma was the first to leave for Moscow at the end of the year. I was never to see him again. On my return from Mauthausen I heard that he had been killed in 1944 during the Slovak insurrection in which had he fought with Slansky.

Siroky left in March 1940. I went to fetch him in his hotel in the Rue du Cardinal-Lemoine where he was playing chess with our friend Erwin Polak, a member of the Czech Youth and one of the directors of the KIM. Although I tried to hurry him our taxi arrived at the station at the last moment. As I was paying the fare Erwin and Siroky rushed towards the train and I saw Siroky board it just as it was leaving the station.

When he joined me again Erwin told me that, as the result of a last minute change in time-table, Siroky was on the train for Switzerland and not for Italy. The ticket collector told him of his mistake in Dijon, and he returned the next day in a vile mood. He left the day after and, this time, reached Moscow with no difficulty. But today his friend Erwin Polak, who had become the Bratislava Party Secretary in 1950, was in the cell next to mine in Ruzyn prison.

As for Köhler, he was supposed to leave earlier, but when he and his wife received their passports he refused to use them because he found a flaw in them. Siroky thought I should give him new ones, maintaining that if a man was afraid he automatically got caught at the border, although the passports which Köhler turned down were later given to Ackerman, one of the leaders of the German Communist Party, who travelled to Moscow with his wife perfectly safely. But the loss of time cost

Köhler dear. He was arrested and interned by the French police before the new passport was ready.

Today Siroky was Vice-Premier, Minister for Foreign Affairs, and President of the Slovak Communist Party, and Köhler had replaced Kopriva as director of the Cadre Department of the Central Committee. When I was questioned about my former activities with the delegation of the Czech Communist Party in France, activities which they had directed themselves and which facilitated not only their work but also their life in Paris, I wondered how those two men managed to keep a clear conscience. How could they remain silent and approve of our executioners?

I was charged with joining the Czech army in France, and yet Sverma, Siroky and Köhler had been the first to join and had told the others to do the same. Most of the volunteers from the Brigades followed their instructions, and soon had an enormous influence over their comrades because of their experience and determination.

Laco Holdos became their military chief. After the defeat, he had single-handedly assembled a dozen leaders of the volunteers in the fields near the Sigean – Portel road, in order to decide on their action in the future.

In view of the defeat and the occupation of part of France by the Nazi armies they had decided to set up a clandestine movement, hiding among the local population and the mass of their compatriots living in France. They had also arranged for several of their comrades to return to Czechoslovakia where they would carry on the fight. The instructions which I gave to Laco Holdos confirmed these decisions.

It was natural that the Czech emigrant leaders in France should be veterans from Spain and that several of them should have assumed important responsibilities on a national level, in the MOI, the FTP, or the TA.*

The government of Vichy refused to demobilize the two hun-

* A Resistance group within the occupying armies.

dred volunteers from the Brigades and decided to send them to internment camps and later to hand them over to Hitler.

In the confusion at Agde, Laco Holdos procured a number of blank demobilization papers, and arranged for the illegal demobilization of the volunteers, while those who were in the greatest danger were given new identities which were later to be invaluable in the underground. The Czech group of the MOI subsequently obtained further demobilization papers and service certificates from Paris for the other language groups in the French Resistance. But here, in Ruzyn, my friend Laco was charged with theft for doing this.

I have written enough for the reader to guess what our inter-rogators made of all this resistance activity, particularly since our relations with the Yugoslav volunteers and emigrants were excellent and further improved by the fact that we could under-standard each other's language.

One of the jobs incumbent on the Czech group of the MOI was to facilitate the escape of the former volunteers in the Bri-gades who were still interned – the invalids and those listed by the Vichy government as dangerous communists.

We had two ways of doing this: either we organized their escape or we arranged for them to leave legally by giving them a visa for a foreign country. Such a visa enabled the holder to leave the camp and live for a certain period in the free zone. By so doing he could join one of the underground groups.

The leaders of the Marseilles group successfully organized the escape of a number of invalids from the camp of Argelès, whence they were secretly conveyed to Paris. According to their physical condition they either remained in France, where they fought in the Resistance, or volunteered to return to Czechoslovakia.

The French Communist Party ordered the various language groups to draw up a list of invalids and political cadres so that they could obtain an emigration visa for the USSR. The Czech list was handed to the Soviet Ambassador at Vichy by Laco Holdos, and I myself gave a copy of it to the leaders of the French Communist Party.

This was the Ruzyn version of what happened:

'By applying orders received from the American intelligence services, London tried to send part of his "Trotskyist" group of volunteers to the USSR under cover of the leaders of the French Communist Party by requesting Soviet visas for the invalids and cadres from the Brigades.'

The leaders in Marseilles remained in contact with the comrades interned at Vernet. From Paris we dispatched illegal material and orders from the French Communist Party in the double bottoms of cases full of clothes.

This was how we told Pavel to get a visa for Mexico, a country which accepted Spanish republicans and volunteers in the Brigades, while the leaders in Marseilles were to support his request at the Mexican legation.

According to Ruzyn, 'I wanted to send Pavel to Mexico to establish contact with the Fourth International.'

'How dare you deny spying in France during the war for the American intelligence services, the YMCA, and its agents Lowry and Dubina? What was the YMCA? A cover organization for the American intelligence services... Your accomplices from the Marseilles group all admit having received funds from the YMCA. You were their leader, you've admitted it. So why go on denying that you were leading a group of spies?'

After 1939 the Czech Consulate in Marseilles had remained in touch with the Czech government in London from which it received instructions and the financial means to carry them out. This is how Marseilles became the centre of Czech emigration in France. After the defeat and the partitioning of the country the consulate had become an Aid Committee for Czech citizens in France. It provided them with money, helped them get work, solved their material problems and procured emigration visas for those who wanted to go elsewhere.

During a three-day visit to Marseilles in the autumn of 1940 Laco Holdos told me that the group of former volunteers received money from the Aid Committee. I found this quite normal. Indeed, if the money came both from the London government and from the Aid Committee functioning under the aegis of the YMCA how could the acceptance of this money by our comrades constitute a crime against the Party, the crime of espionage with which we were now charged? Wasn't it perfectly normal that they should receive assistance like all the other refugees?

At this time France had capitulated and the German troops were encamped on French soil. Nobody in his right mind speculated on the 'alleged' contacts of the YMCA with American imperialism. We simply thought of the best way to continue the fight against Hitler, with new methods adapted to the new conditions. The main enemy was Nazi Germany, its armies in occupation, the collaborationist government of Vichy and not the future reactionary America of Allen Dulles and MacCarthy.

It was in vain that I explained all these things ten or twenty times over: they remained the 'basic proof of the espionage activities of the Trotskyist group of former volunteers in the Brigades during the war in France'.

After December 1940 the volunteers concentrated in the Marseilles region had started to get to Paris. They appeared with a password in the two flats of our loyal comrades Nelly Stefkova and Vera Hromadkova. When we thought they were ready to leave they applied to the German employment bureau which recruited labour for the Reich. The papers we gave them were excellent, and the only test they had to go through before being assumed was the medical examination.

From Germany, our comrades were to return to the Protektorat at the first opportunity, and once there they had to get into contact with the Party, or, if that failed, to search for isolated communists amongst themselves, anti-fascists and patriots, and organize acts of sabotage against the occupants on their own until they could join a group of partisans.

If our comrades found it impossible to get to the Protektorat they were to return to France on their first regular leave, where they joined the FTPF.

By the beginning of 1941 nearly all the Czech communists

from the Marseilles group had returned home this way. They sent us a postcard saying they had safely ended their journey, and from then on we had no further contact with them.

At the same time the Slovak Repatriation Commission was set up in Paris, and provided us with another opportunity to repatriate our Slovak comrades as well as the volunteers who were still interned.

They easily reached Bratislava together with the numerous Slovak economic emigrants residing in France who were repatriated with their families, and we also managed to send Czechs, Hungarians, Rumanians and Yugoslavs home with Slovak papers. It was much easier for them to reach their country from Slovakia than from France. Some of our Slovak comrades were of Jewish origin. The Party made no difference between Jews and non-Jews; and the Jews themselves asked to return. Had we refused them permission, they would have felt hurt and humilated; but of course we took still greater precautions where they were concerned.

Now the men who had greeted me at Koldeje with antisemitic remarks, regretting that Hitler had not accomplished his task of exterminating the Jews, pretended to be good disciples and accused me of repatriating Jews to Slovakia and sending them to their death.

We told those of our comrades who were still interned at Vernet to apply to the German employment bureau which was represented in the camps. We then had to arrange for them to escape on their way to Germany and incorporate them in the underground. The first of these convoys passed through Paris at the end of May 1941 and was quartered at the Tourelles barracks. We managed to get all our Czech comrades out – they included Neuer, Hromadko, Stern, Bukacek, Klecan and many others – as well as Rumanians, Hungarians and Yugoslavs, about forty in all. Most of them left France by the routes I have mentioned, while the others joined the French Resistance.

I did not realize that that would earn me the basest charge of all.

Six

After five months of questioning I realized that not even the greatest heroism at the time of the French Resistance would now save us from the interrogators. They slandered Sirotek who was scalped by the Gestapo, Vejrosta who swallowed cyanide, Kuna, Honek, Formanek, Marsalek, who were all beheaded, and Grünbaum who fell in the rising of the Warsaw ghetto.

Then came the most disgusting charge of all. Because I had assisted in the repatriation of volunteers, the interrogators deduced that I 'had handed the Central Committee of the clandestine Czech Communist Party over to the Gestapo with Fucik and Jan Cerny at the head'.

I had known Fucik and Cerny well during my stay in Moscow in the thirties. Fucik, bearded, as sunburnt as an explorer, was just back from a long expedition in Central Asia where he had gathered material for some brilliant reports on the Soviet Union. During the evenings we spent together I had the privilege of hearing him recount his impressions.

Cerny and I had been on a delegation to Gorky on 1 May 1935, and to the autonomous Chouvach republic whose communist youth organization had sponsored the Czech one. I was to see him again in Spain in 1938. First he was political commissar for the Dimitrov battalion and he had been badly wounded in the lung. After his convalescence he became responsible for the Czech Cadre Department at Albacete. For several months we had shared the same flat with him and Klivar, who then represented the Party in Spain, and we met again in Barcelona towards the end of the war. Cerny had gone to Belgium, and had then returned to Czechoslovakia on his own.

I was accused of betraying them through Klecan, one of the volunteers interned at Vernet. A former youth leader in the mining area of Kladno, he had been a brave soldier but we regarded him as undisciplined and ordered him not to get directly into touch with the Party but to create his own resistance movement. We recorded this order in our report to the clandestine Central Committee on the comrades we were repatriating. But it was obviously up to the Party to make up its own mind and Cerny, who had known Klecan in Spain, let him join the Central Committee. Together with Cerny and Fucik, Klecan had been caught by the Gestapo, and in his book, *Written Under the Gallows*, Fucik wrote that Klecan had spoken under torture.

These were the facts: but in their 'confessions' and 'statements' my fellow prisoners said that they had heard me order Klecan to hand over the party leaders – those I had forbidden him to contact – to the Gestapo.

Smola went a little further. 'You are guilty of the arrest of the Czech and Slovak volunteers whom you repatriated. You knowingly sent them to their death.' And for this too he had the necessary 'evidence'. Nothing surprised me any more. I was now guilty of the death of hundreds of Jews in France. This charge was originally based on the orders of the collaborationist French police obliging the Jews to register at their local police stations. At that time the Party did not have a technical organization capable of providing all our Jewish comrades with shelter and false papers. To gain time and allow the comrades who were generally known to be Jews to keep within the law until they received a new identity, the Party leaders advised them either to register or to leave for the free zone.

At that point there was only a Jewish census. Subsequently the technical organization of the Party gave false papers to all the Jewish comrades in the Party and the Resistance. So, when they had to wear the yellow star a few months later, all our Jewish fighters had gone underground or did so immediately.

The fact that I had given these orders to Jewish comrades was now distorted. I had sent 'hundreds of Jews to their death', and, as always, this interpretation rested on Zavodsky's 'confessions' and the 'statements' extorted from Stefka and other witnesses of this period.

The Security accused me of having tried to betray Siroky to

the French police. His mistake at the station was considered a crime of mine: 'Your attempt to hand over Siroky to the French police by knowingly making him board the wrong train proves that you have been working for the French police since 1940.'

It was in vain that I tried to prove that if that had been Erwin Polak's or my intention we would not have awaited the day of his departure but would have had him arrested in Paris. Nor would we have chosen a train leaving for Switzerland, a neutral country where nothing could happen to him. Besides, he had taken the right train a few days later.

But Ruzyn was deaf to logic, to proof; its only preoccupation was to use every half-truth to make its fabrication look likely.

As I said, Bruno Köhler and his wife were interned in France at the beginning of 1940. At the time of the defeat they were free in Toulouse and then went to Portugal to get their American visas which Alice Kohnova, who was today in the same prison as ourselves, was to procure for them.

Before the departure of Köhler and his wife from Portugal to Moscow via the United States and Japan the leaders of the French Communist Party thought of sending me to Lisbon to bring them back to France where their Soviet visas awaited them at the Soviet Embassy in Vichy. But the difficulties and risks of such a journey made the Party renounce this idea, and through a comrade emigrating to the United States via Portugal I arranged for Köhler to receive 10,000 francs (a sum which entailed a considerable sacrifice for our group), a few products of our underground press, a report on our activities and the proposal of the leaders of the French Communist Party. In the reply he sent me shortly afterwards he refused to return to France. From Portugal, and later from the United States, Köhler twice invited me to emigrate to the USSR, but I refused, for my job was to continue the fight in France where I already occupied an important position in the Resistance.

The Köhler affair earned me new charges: I was not only responsible for his and his wife's arrest in Paris after providing them with 'unusable' passports but also for trying to make them return to Paris where I could hand them over to the Gestapo.

So in Ruzyn I was an agent of the French police and the Gestapo.

One of the 'proofs' for the first charge was that 'the general intelligence services of the Paris police had a list of all the former volunteers in the internment camps.'

I asked : why did the French police arrest me in 1942 instead of continuing to use me as an agent in the French Communist Party especially in view of the responsible position I held? 'The police wanted to keep you for more important tasks after the war when the people's democracy would be installed in Czechoslovakia. To make you seem a martyr and to increase your prestige and your credit, they preferred not to use you to begin with and to have you arrested in 1942. But at the same time they made sure that you survived.'

This was always the way the Security interpreted my evacuation from Mauthausen at the end of April 1945 in an International Red Cross convoy. 'Hundreds of documents,' claimed the interrogators, 'prove that there were contacts between the German and American intelligence services even during the war. That's why it was easy for the Americans to arrange for your escape from Mauthausen, through the Gestapo, in one of the Red Cross convoys. Their purpose was to get you back to France as soon as possible to enable you to resume your collaboration with their services against our Republic.'

'My return to France in a Red Cross convoy,' I replied, 'was decided on by the secret international Committee of the camp.'

'What proves that they too were not Gestapo agents?' asked the interrogator, unperturbed.

To all my arguments – the bad treatment I received after my arrest in Paris and in prison, my classification as a hostage, my deportation to Neue Bremme and Mauthausen, my subsequent illness and my activity in the clandestine Resistance organization in the prisons and the camps, there was only one answer: 'The mere fact that you, a Jew, returned alive, is sufficient proof of your guilt and *therefore* proves us right.'

There is no point in listing all the crimes I was accused of. I felt crushed by a pyramid of lies. Night and day, experts worked on me to make me the leader of the Trotskyist conspiracy which they had been asked to invent.

I discovered that Ruzyn practised several degrees of interrogation according to the role assigned to the man who was to be placed on the chess-board of the future trial. Later, after the trial, from my conversations with the survivors, I was to establish the following hierarchy: the leader, the accomplices, the confederates and the witnesses. The 'treatment' deteriorated according to this hierarchy, and also according to whether it was to be a large public trial or a small one. I was therefore entitled to the worst treatment.

The interrogators tried to obtain from my fellow defendants, as well as from other prisoners outside the group and from free witnesses, statements corroborating the part which they assigned to me. So that these charges should seem more convincing, and constitute irrefutable evidence against me, the leader, my fellow prisoners had to start by admitting their 'own' guilt.

If the Security failed to obtain these results quickly enough they tried to extort statements against me. To do this the interrogators claimed that the Party had every proof that the man against whom the statements were required was a dangerous enemy. By making these statements the prisoners were assisting the Party and this would be in their favour when their own fate was decided upon.

These arguments were very efficient. Comrades started to believe that they had been duped by the 'leader of the group', and that he was the cause of their present misfortune. If each one were sure of his own innocence, he soon doubted that of the others, and found reasons for providing evidence against them.

The interrogators also promised not to hold against them any statements they would make against the 'leader' which might be compromising for themselves. 'The Party will take into account your good faith and your statements will only be used in the course of the investigation.'

Obviously those who let themselves be taken in by these arguments discovered too late that none of their statements had been forgotten and that they were to be tried all the same. The Security never let its victims escape. It used the men it had broken physically and morally, not to mention the ones it had convinced. I have already spoken of the guilt complex which I developed myself. Later, in the Leopoldov prison, I was to meet comrades who, even after their sentence and their farcical trial, considered themselves guilty. One of them said: 'I may have deserved a maximum of six years, but eighteen seems really unjust.' Another said: 'Objectively we were Trotskyists and potential enemies if only because of our contacts during the war . . .' Most of these obsessions stemmed from carelessness or real mistakes but had nothing to do with our trials – some of them had not realized that they had been followed when they were working in the underground, others had been arrested with a list of names on them, or had made a political assessment different from that of the party. . . . But guilt had become a psychosis. And in his speech at the Twentieth Party Congress Khrushchev was to refer to those comrades who had been in prison for eight, ten or fifteen years and who then had to be convinced that they were innocent.

A friend of mine told me, after our rehabilitation, that he had refused his signature, denied his own name for weeks and months, because he thought it was a test to see whether he really was capable of occupying the important post he had held before his arrest in the State Security. 'And when they put me in the punishment cell,' he told me laughing, 'I rubbed my hands, thinking: this is the last ordeal. Today's Tuesday, they'll let me go on Friday. So I've only got three more days.' It was only in court that he heard himself rewarded with twenty-two years in prison and realized that it had not been a test.

Seven

'Do you think you will continue to deny for much longer?' a new interrogator asked me one day. 'You are one of the most hardened and determined enemies that we have ever had. While the others have already made honourable amends before the Party by admitting their crimes, you persist in your cynical attitude. Take Holdos for example: by confessing he has shown that he still has a spark of true communism in him, and that we only have to blow on it to revive it. You have already exhausted a number of interrogators. When you've exhausted the two who are interrogating you at present, they will be relieved by others. We'll see who gets tired first. A man like Radek lasted three months. After that he confessed everything. You have resisted for four months. Do you think that'll go on much longer? You have nothing to gain by waiting. Your crimes are so vast that one rope won't be enough. You'll need at least four!'

Always the same threats. The mere mention of Radek . . . so I was right. This remark confirmed the contacts between the interrogators and the Soviet advisers, who were the only ones who could know about Radek's behaviour before his trial.

Now the interrogators were harping on a theme which had already been raised at Koldeje in my first interrogations. The most appalling and insulting charges were levelled at the leaders of the French Communist Party and their policy during the war. Every means of intimidation, punches and blows, were used to extort from me compromising statements against them. They were alleged to have sustained a leading nucleus of European Trotskyism in the heart of the Party throughout the war – the MOI, a branch of the Fourth International, a mass of Zionists whose three leaders were Jews. The Gestapo and the information services had their men in the Party leadership and that was why the order had been given to repatriate the Trotskyist members of the International Brigades and other Party enemies.

When I replied that Jacques Duclos had personally followed and controlled the work of the MOI, the interrogator told me: 'What does that prove? Svermova was also a Party Secretary. Where is she now? In the same hole as you and for the same reason: she's an old enemy.'

I was interrogated about Duclos' assistant during 1940, Maurice Tréand. The interrogators wanted me to say that he had been one of the leaders of European Trotskyism in France and a Gestapo agent. They wanted to transform the errors of the beginning of the occupation in France, like the attempt to have *L'Humanité* issued legally, into deliberate complicity with the Nazis. It was sheer lunacy!

The attack against the French Communist Party and its leaders persisted through May and June. They wanted me to 'confess' at all costs that my wife's brother-in-law, Raymond Guyot, was an agent of the Intelligence Service; that it was under the aegis of this organization that he was parachuted into France during the German occupation, that he knew about my Trotskyist activity which he had covered up and aided; and that he was the head of an espionage network in Europe. Major Smola, who led these interrogations in the most brutal way, claimed that 'our Soviet friends possess all the material concerning these facts, that their intelligence services have revealed everything,' and he was acting in their name.

He also showed me 'statements' by some of my fellow prisoners against Raymond Guyot and Jacques Duclos to this effect and he told me calmly: 'Wait for a change of regime in France and you'll see what will happen to your brother-in-law and the likes of him.'

I am still unable to see the point of these attacks against the French Communist Party. They were inspired neither by the men of Ruzyn nor the ringleaders. The initiative must have come from higher up, directly from Beria. This was proved by the fact that the Soviet advisers ordered the interrogators to combine the charges against the French Communists with those against Desider Fried, who had been a leader of the Communist

Youth and in the Direct Committee of the Czech Communist Party in the late twenties. I was amazed when they asked me about him, and tried to make me confess that the source of my criminal political deviations – anarchism, Trotskyism, anti-Sovietism – was the bad influence which Fried had had on me. They wanted me to say that he had been eliminated from the Party leadership in 1929 for gross political deviations. That was ridiculous. I was fourteen when he left Prague for Moscow, where he had become a Comintern instructor for France under the pseudonym of Clément. Personally I had only met him two or three times in Moscow in 1935 during the year of the Seventh Comintern Congress. On the other hand it was at this period that Maurice Thorez mentioned him to me for the first time – 'your compatriot' as he said, affectionately and respectfully. After my rehabilitation, when I was taking a cure in the south of France in February 1964, Thorez spoke of him nostalgically. He told me that Clément deserved the recognition of the French workers' movement for the part he had played in working out the policy which enabled the French Communist Party to take a leading part in French politics.

Why was I questioned about Fried? He had left Czecho-slovakia over twenty years ago and had been shot in Belgium during the occupation in mysterious circumstances. The charges against him, now that he was dead, which had been extorted from the accused, had nothing to do with the fabrications concerning Czechoslovakia. In view of the fact that hardly anyone in the country knew what had happened to him, his implication in the trial could only mean an attack on the French Party itself and against the leaders who had worked together with him . . .

This is what two defendants at our trial were made to say about Fried. The prosecutor asked Geminder: 'Did you subscribe to the hostile line of these enemy elements?'

Geminder: 'Yes, I collaborated closely with these men accused of having had a bourgeois past. In 1929 I made friends with Alois Neurath who was revealed as a Trotskyist and expelled from the Party. Subsequently, in 1927, I met Desider Fried and remained on good terms with this man who was expelled from the leadership of the Czech Communist Party in 1929 for his gross political deviations and his hostile attitude towards the Party.'

Prosecutor: 'So your bourgeois capitalist past and your contact with enemy elements in the Czech Communist Party prevented you from becoming a true communist?'

Germinder: 'That's right . . .'

The second defendant to mention Fried was Reïcin:

Reïcin: 'In the autumn of 1929, with other members of the Central Committee of the Comsomol (Communist Youth) I subscribed to the attitude of Fried's extreme left Trotskyist faction which opposed the new direction Gottwald was giving to the Central Committee . . .'

My wife and I had many friends in France. When they came to Prague they enjoyed seeing us, and we had visitors nearly every week. I tried vainly to explain to the interrogators that all these visitors were members of the Central Committee of the Communist Party or well known militant members of mass organizations: they claimed that my house in Prague was a haven of Trotskyists and spies from the Second Bureau and accused my wife of serving as a liaison agent with me.

Now, almost every day, they threatened to arrest her unless I confessed, while Major Smola even told me that she had already done so.

The interrogators attacked my wife violently. They asked me about colleagues of hers whom I did not know. They mentioned names of mysterious people who, they claimed, were in touch with her. During one interrogation, in a little room in which I was standing near the interrogators' desk, I managed to read some papers heaped on it and realized they were reports on my wife from the Ministry of Security. So she was constantly being watched. I was also presented with declarations extorted from some of my fellow prisoners against her. They accused her of having played an active part in our 'Trotskyist group' and slandered her in other ways. One of my comrades even 'admitted' having been her lover.

When I met him later at Leopoldov he told me why he had made this confession. When he was interrogated about my wife he said he had known her in Paris. When Lise came to Prague in 1948 she had been to visit him in his office at the Central Committee building. That was just when the Cominform resolution concerning Yugoslavia had been published. My wife, leaning on my friend's shoulder, was listening to him translating the text, when an employee of the Central Committee came in to give him a file. My friend introduced him to Lise, and it was on the basis of this man's denunciation that the interrogators put the following question: 'Since she was leaning on your shoulder you must have been on intimate terms with her.' 'No, not intimate, very friendly.' 'Was she or was she not leaning on your shoulder?' 'Yes.' 'So that proves that you were on intimate terms. That's the word in the dictionary.' 'All right, call it intimate.'

And by a new distortion she became 'his mistress' in the report.

I was also told that Svab had said she was Geminder's mistress.

At Ruzyn the prisoners were frequently interrogated about 'intimate' subjects, both to accentuate the moral pressure on them by increasing their guilt complex and to make them appear to have loose morals.

And they generally yielded easily on such matters which gave them some respite and enabled them to recuperate their energy to defend themselves against capital charges.

At one point, for example, a good dozen of the accused 'confessed' to have been the lovers of a girl who subsequently turned out to be a virgin.

Everything served as a pretext to compromise my wife. She was thus accused of having known Hilda Synkova, a deputy of Prague, who had committed suicide in the summer of 1950. The Security interpreted her death as the proof of some activity against the Party which was about to be discovered.

Hilda Synkova was an intelligent woman, energetic and humane, and it was she who looked after my wife in Ravensbruck at the beginning of 1944. Hilda frequently talked to my wife about her husband Otto Synek and his brother, Viktor, both members of the first Central Committee of the clandestine Czech Communist Party who had been tortured to death by the Nazis. She said: 'The worst part will be when we're free. That's when we'll feel the void.'

When we moved to Prague they continued to see each other. Hilda committed suicide in the summer of 1950 after a nervous breakdown. The day before her death she had come to see us and ask our advice about her nomination as Under-Secretary of Public Health. She had seemed depressed. At the time there were difficulties between the Directing Committee of the Party and the Prague Committee of which she was one of the secretaries. She had recalled the comradeship among the communists before the war, and complained that this had now given way to indifference and suspicion, that the leaders had become a closed sect cut off from the Party and the people.

My wife was heartbroken when she killed herself. And now this was considered a crime. I understood nothing, but then there was nothing to understand in this factory of forgeries and lies.

The welter of accusations, the systematic attempts to extort compromising charges against the French Communist Party and some of its leaders, convinced me that this was not the initiative of Smola or the interrogators, who were far too primitive to work out such a plan, but a line premeditated by the ringleaders of the apparatus to which the Party had surrendered us.

How else could one account for the fact that the Security should take precedence not only over our own Party but also over a foreign party like the French one? The objects of these charges had been known, checked, or even ordered by the leadership of the two parties. Here, for example, is a passage from Svoboda's 'confessions': 'After our return from France in 1945 we hoodwinked Slansky by pretending to be good communists, and concealing our Trotskyist activity.' I can see why Svoboda was forced to make this 'confession' which added a touch of realism to our imaginary conspiracy, but how could Slansky allow it? He knew about our past in Spain and France; why did he not react?

When I mentioned the names of Slansky, Gottwald, Siroky, Geminder, Kopecky, or Köhler, there came the indignant reply: 'A criminal like you has no right to pronounce the venerated name of Slansky!'

But if Slansky's or Gottwald's names were so venerated, how could activities undertaken on their personal orders be considered criminal? There were diplomatic nominations, for example. Or should we believe that the Party had deliberately chosen to sacrifice us? This would explain Siroky's attitude when I was arrested, and that of Kopriva at our meeting. . . . But why and by whom had we been selected as victims? None of us had ever been in any faction. We were all loyal, disciplined Party members. And again I realized that the State Security, under the Soviet advisers, took precedence over the Party, and that the interrogators used the cadre files to compose their charges against us.

When you think you are the victim of a judicial error or an intrigue you can find the strength to fight, but here you realized that the Party had decided on your fall and that your future had been settled mechanically. You were crushed by your very helplessness. The illusion that there was some recourse, some sort of justice, would have sustained me, but there was not even that.

Eight

Once again I heard my cell door slam behind me, and I automatically started walking. Overcoming the pain in my feet I tried to walk faster in order to keep warm, for although it was the end of June I still felt cold. The interrogators were in their shirt sleeves and I was shivering.

A sepulchral silence reigned in the prison, only interrupted by the sound of the spy-holes opening and the furtive whispers of the warders.

I tried to visualize my friends in similar cells, tortured by the same thoughts, the victims of the same despair. I imagined what this unjust imprisonment, these inhuman and criminal methods, had made of them, how they must have hated and cursed their lives. They joined the Party in the hope of a fairer, more fraternal life, and they had continually fought for that until the day when . . .

I imagined them trying, like myself, to flee from the present into their memories, those treasures which belong to us alone and which nobody can steal from us.

Four steps to the wall, half turn, four steps to the other wall. The cracks in the walls gradually adopted human aspects. To start with I intentionally tried to reconstruct the features of my comrades in battle. But then the cracks broadened out until they could walk through them. First their faces appeared, smiling at me, and then their bodies. They were there next to me, crowding into my cell, walking with me and talking to me.

Did our battle and our goal retain their value? We compared them to what the prison's inquisitors were doing to me and my fellow defendants. They shook their heads. Just as you couldn't escape from your past where you were constantly seeking refuge, you couldn't reject your life with all the courage, struggles and friendships which it contained . . .

So, between interrogations my cell became an asylum where I met my companions. I must have talked aloud for my door opened and an angry warder said: 'Stop telling that nonsense to the walls!' One of them even made a report on my strange behaviour.

And yet, in spite of my obsessions, it was with joy that I returned to my comrades. . . . For example, I saw myself with the comrades whom I had lived with in Moscow, in my room in the

Soyuznaya. There were usually twelve of us, but when they added some extra beds, up to eighteen men slept in that room. What discussions we had, on every problem, every country, on the world revolutionary movement and the state of things in Russia . . .

Together with Dimitrov and Kolarov, Boris had taken part in the insurrection of Sofia in September 1923, and had served ten years in prison as a result. Alberto came from an Italian prison and interpreted for José and Ramon, although he was unable to follow their quick chatter when they told us about the battle of the Asturias.

Every language was spoken in room 18 – we had two Chinese comrades who had been tortured by Chiang Kai-Shek's jailors; there was a mysterious, silent Korean, and my Polish friend whom Lise and her friends maliciously nicknamed 'Secotine'.

Sleep was a sin. We went out at night, sometimes at one or two o'clock in the morning, when the blizzards blew in the streets of Moscow. We walked across the Red Square with clouds of dry snow swirling up, and watched the shadows of the past, visualizing scenes of the great October Revolution.

We were excited by the idea of treading the soil of the metropolis of the Revolution, of standing in the square where Lenin had harangued the crowds and where the victors of Denikin, Kolchak, Wrangel, Petlioura and the interventionists of all the capitalist states, had marched.

We were living in an extraordinarily stimulating period. The revolution was so close and there was fighting all over the world – barricades in Austria, riots in France, rebellions in the Asturias in Spain. We were full of faith and optimism: tomorrow the revolution would be everywhere!

Erna, the wife of my friend Erwin Polak, looked at me kindly as she did when I went into her room in the Soyuznaya in which, once a week, she entertained our little colony of Czech youth. She drifted out of the left part of the wall, the screen of my memories. Round her were assembled Bruncliko, who was to be executed by the Nazis, Heinz, parachuted into Czechoslovakia

during the war and beheaded, Schönherz, hanged in Budapest
by Horthy's fascists, Krejzl, killed in a concentration camp. . . .
And now Erna was looking at me sadly. Just as she was going
to join Erwin in France she had been arrested by the Gestapo
in Prague, deported to Austria with her daughter and gassed . . .

Amongst my Bulgarian friends I saw Pavlov, the leader of the
Divisionario battalion. We had spent a whole night at Tortosa
in a cave a hundred and fifty yards from the fascist positions
on the other bank of the Ebro, drinking wine, and he told about
his ten years in prison in Bulgaria after the fights of 1923.

Then there was Wiesner, a young Bessarabian political re-
fugee in Czechoslovakia, who later worked in the world Youth
Committee for Peace in Paris. He came then to Valencia in
Spain, and I remember our conversations with Lise in the Plaza
Emilio Castellar, during nights so bright that it was possible to
read the paper by the light of the moon and the stars. We
dreamed aloud of our future and the revolutionary future of
humanity, when our ideal would triumph.

I saw him again on the Catalan front and then lost track of
him. He had been evacuated from Vernet, where he was interned, to Djelfa in North Africa, with other members of the
International Brigades, and had then been repatriated in the
USSR after the liberation of Algeria. Bessarabia had become
part of the Soviet Union and two years later I heard he had died
a heroic death fighting the Japanese with the Red Army.

Why did Winkler (K. Cichocti) now appear with that tense
expression he had the last time I saw him in Spain? He was a
Polish aristocrat, one of the founder members of the Polish
Communist Party, and we nicknamed him 'the baron'. He was
recalled by Moscow, and left reluctantly at the time when the
Comintern was dissolving the Polish Communist Party. He had
come to say goodbye to us in Valencia and had a premonition
that nothing good was in store for him. But nevertheless, he, like
a number of other Polish Communists, went off to face the fate
awaiting him . . .

After the German entry into Paris we often met Poulmarch,

our neighbour at Ivry, and Pierre Rigaud, both of whom were shot among the fifty hostages at Châteaubriant.

Even Oskar Grossmann appeared, my Austrian friend from Moscow, who died in Lyons after the Gestapo had tortured him, and Paula, the young Austrian whose baby was eighteen months old when she killed herself after having been arrested and tortured by Pétain's police in Lyons. She had given away an address, thinking the flat was already empty – but her comrades had been caught.

I now saw our arrival at Mauthausen on 26 March 1944. Our convoy of fifty prisoners came from Neue Bremme, and for four days we had had nothing to eat or drink. We were exhausted when, after a forced march of six kilometres, we saw the dark mass of a fortress whose high towers and sinister walls stood out against a sky of slate. The snow flakes whirled round, the wind screamed on this high plateau known as the Austrian Siberia. We stood to attention near the gate-way opposite the yard for several hours. The icy Alpine wind tore through us. When day dawned we saw the first prisoners, and suddenly, as if in an hallucination, I thought I recognized an old friend in a group of three convicts who bared their heads as they passed an SS man. Despite his shorn head I recognized Gabler, whom I had seen a few years earlier in Moscow where he represented the Communist Austrian Youth at the KIM. We had been great friends and when he passed me a second time, he still had the same frank face, his slight squint increasing his mischievous expression. . . . I thought I would never see him again for I had been told the Nazis had beheaded him in Vienna.

I stared at him to try and attract his attention, but he passed our group three times without seeing me. A few hours later, in the quarantine block, a nineteen-year-old Spaniard, Constante, after asking me two or three questions, realized that I was a volunteer from the International Brigades. He was the first person in Mauthausen to display communist solidarity and fraternity. Despite his youth, he was a 'veteran': he had been deported in 1940. Thanks to him I managed to establish contact that very day with comrades of different nationalities.

The next day he brought Gabler to me. In the weeks that followed we recalled all the comrades we had known together. He spoke at length about his wife Herta whom I also knew well and of whom he had long been without news. He told me he had been parachuted into Austria to take up his post in the leadership of the clandestine Austrian Communist Party, and he had then been deported without trial: he hoped the war would end before he was tried. Together we helped to create the clandestine International resistance and solidarity committee which he directed until his transfer to Vienna, where he was at last tried. He knew he was going to die, but he left us serenely. When we embraced for the last time we did not say a word. . . . I followed him with my eyes until he vanished between the two SS men who took him to the gate of the camp. Shortly afterwards his execution in Vienna was confirmed . . .

On the evening of my arrival I met Leopold Hoffman, who had been one of the first volunteers from the Brigades in France to return to Czechoslovakia despite the dangers involved. In Prague he had fought against the Nazis and had subsequently been deported here. Owing to his courage my compatriots chose him as one of the leaders of their clandestine national committee. After Gabler's execution and my serious illness which caused my transfer to the *Revier* in September 1944 the leadership of the International Committee was reorganized. Hoffman replaced me, while Gabler was succeeded by Razola, an intelligent and courageous Spanish comrade of whom I was very fond. I now saw myself in Block 5, the camp hospital. My brother-in-law was lying a few yards away from me with bad gangrene. Razola and Hoffman came to see me every day to bring me news or food which they had somehow procured.

Of all my encounters at Mauthausen one of the most poignant was with Conrad. Originally from my home town he had left Ostrava to become an instructor in the KIM. I had lost sight of him in 1937 and it was now in 1944 that I saw him again.

One day two prisoners from the Bunker – the camp prison – were led into the yard by some SS men. I recognized him at once, and I was to see him twice more in identical circumstances. We exchanged friendly glances at a distance, smiled and waved discreetly. He was not to witness the liberation of the camp, but was shot by the SS in the Bunker a few days earlier.

So many men sacrificed their lives to our cause. Was it now betraying us? Was the revolution only great in its moment of birth?

Nine

The key suddenly turned in the lock, and the warder gave me a towel to put round my face. I had hoped to be left in peace until food time, but my illusion was short-lived. Today, Friday, we were getting gruel, which at least was hot, and I thought it would assuage my hunger and above all keep me warm.

When we got to the barred door of the corridor the warder released me and another hand seized me. The hand was familiar, but it was not my interrogator's. I tried to guess whose it was and to which office I was being led. Then I realized it was Smola from the way he pushed me against the wall as he opened the door.

When the towel was removed I saw him sitting behind his desk. Very calmly he said to me: 'We are going to write a report about Fritz Runge. There is no point in my saying that you must tell us all you know about him.'

I was flabbergasted. Hitherto he had always re'used to write a report on me, so why should he write one on Runge, who was one of the employees in the press agency of the Ministry of Foreign Affairs? And then this calm, polite voice. What was he hiding?

Smola began the interrogation: to start with details about Runge's life. And then, how had I met him? He wrote everything down. It all seemed normal, and I replied conscientiously and precisely. But now Smola read out the text he had just typed. It began: 'He collaborated for many years with the press agency of the Communist International...' All were false statements and I interrupted: 'I'll never sign this report.'

Smola lost his temper, started to hit me, and, seizing me by the shoulders, knocked my head against the wall, until he saw me spit blood. He then seemed rather worried and made me wash in the basin and clean the patches of blood on my dungarees. The next day the same thing happened. It was the last time I was interrogated by Major Smola. He had failed to make me 'confess', and this was the sixth month of my detention.

Smola was in his fifties, with greying temples, an undershot jaw, and grey metallic eyes. He was fanatical and violent. When he tried to be gentle, appealing to my feelings as a communist, I soon realized he was reciting a part. And yet that was the only occasion when he was not a mere machine for obtaining confessions. The rest of the time he never betrayed a personal opinion and remained deaf to all that was not in accordance with his instructions.

I had such an aversion for this obtuse and cruel man that if he had continued to interrogate me I think I would have refused to sign until my dying day, if only to stand up to him until the end.

I was now transferred to Captain Kohoutek's group, and as a welcome he said: 'You've liquidated a good dozen interrogators. We've decided to question you from the very beginning. We're in no hurry. We have enough interrogators to replace each other even if it takes over a year. You'll confess all we want sooner or later. We're far from having used all our methods, and you can imagine what's in store for you.'

Kohoutek was the exact opposite of Smola, a little younger, in his forties and putting on weight, but dressed with elegance, whether in uniform or civilian dress. He had something of the professional salesman, indifferent to the quality of the goods which did not fit into his transaction. He was never coarse or brutal, either in words or acts, and showed no animosity, going as far as to ask polite questions about my state of mind, my health and my family.

I soon realized that he did not believe in his work and that he interpreted things with a crude cynicism. In his eyes the whole thing was a political step: the Party had to eradicate the faults and errors undermining it. That was the point of the trial. At the same time it would enable the Party to make a leap forward by getting rid of certain categories of men in power.

It was unlikely that Kohoutek envisaged an actual physical elimination. The elimination was to be political. That must have been how he justified what he was doing. 'If you had stayed in France,' he told me, 'you would have remained a militant Party member of great value in a capitalist country. But men like you, with your past, your ideas, your concepts, your international contacts are not made for countries in the process of constructing socialism. We must get rid of you. When the difficult moment is over the Party may revise your case and give you a living, although you will not, of course, be able to play a part in politics.'

But Kohoutek had several arrows to his bow. He could be both gentle and tough. He really was like a cat playing with a mouse – with him, as he said, 'the roundabout began.' The interrogations lasted twenty or twenty-one hours on end, and, as usual, I had to stand throughout. Back in my cell I was not allowed to lie down, let alone to sleep. After over five months' inhuman treatment Kohoutek's roundabout finished me.

But what affected me most was his cynicism, the glimpse he gave me of a political operation set up at my expense.

I later discovered that Kohoutek had been the police commissioner in charge of the anti-communist repressions in my home town of Ostrava. So he continued the same work against the same people under two regimes.

Hitherto I had counted on the trial of the 'enemy group of former Trotskyist volunteers in the International Brigades' which Smola and his interrogators had fixed for May or June.

I tried to assemble all my strength to establish my innocence on this occasion and to reveal the criminal methods which the Security had used against us. I was convinced that most of the comrades who knew of our activities would not let themselves be hoodwinked, that they would insist on an explanation and would not allow us to be convicted – for it would be their own conviction too.

Besides, this trial would have marked the end of the abject and degraded existence which I had been forced to lead for almost six months and which was gradually turning me into an animal. But now that the time was approaching Kohoutek no longer mentioned the trial. The worst thing was to know that nothing would help and that was what I now knew.

Every day I was threatened with a trial *in camera* which would end with the gallows. That would mean silent execution and the perpetual stigma of a traitor, with no hope of the truth ever being discovered.

Should I accept such a death by denying until the end? Who could agree to die like that? Only when a man gives his life to a great cause which he has chosen does his sacrifice have some sense.

But for the man who remains alive there is a hope, however feeble, because, deep within himself, he continues to believe that things cannot remain like that forever and that one day his innocence and the truth will be revealed.

My dilemma was appalling: before the war I had been interrogated by the Czech police and tried in Czech courts; during the occupation I had been questioned by the special Antiterrorist Brigade and tried in the French courts; I had also experienced German concentration camps. But here I was in my own country, in the people's democratic republic of Czechoslovakia. The men before me acted in the name of the Party and the Soviet Union. It is easy to fight someone you know is your enemy. In the class war and the battle against the Nazi occupants, heroism was natural. In my youth, in Spain, in the underground, before the police, in the prisons and concentration camps, I had always been brave and had never hesitated before danger, and this was how I had earned the confidence and affection of all my comrades.

But I was here at the behest of my Party and a member of the Political Bureau had told me 'We'll liquidate you with or without your confessions.' How can one fight against such a foe? Each one of my gestures or refusals to 'confess' was interpreted as the continuation of my struggle against the Party, as the attitude of a hardened enemy who refused to make honourable amends by confessing even after his arrest. In such conditions, it is not only impossible for a communist to prove his innocence but it presents him with a grotesque conscience problem: if you agree to 'confess', in the Party's eyes you enter the path of your redemption. But if you refuse to sign because you are innocent you are a hardened culprit who must be mercilessly liquidated.

Kohoutek knew how to play on my feelings of loyalty towards the Party as he did on the guilt I had felt ever since Field had been revealed as a spy during the Rajk trial, merely because I had known him and had accepted money from him. He argued: 'Mr London: You know that Szöny has been condemned to death as a spy in the Rajk trial. He only received 300 Swiss francs from Field. How much did you receive?'

He encircled me with his syllogisms: 'Someone who bakes bread is a baker. You were at the head of a group of men who admit their Trotskyist activity. So what are you objectively? You are responsible for a group of Trotskyists. And who is responsible for a group of Trotskyists? A Trotskyist himself.'

'Don't be naive,' he continued. 'You've seen the confessions of Zavodsky, Svoboda, Holdos, Dora Kleinova, Hromadko, the incontestable evidence of Nekvasil and Stefka as well as the heap of letters we have received denouncing you. Even if you haven't done anything yourself your fellow prisoners have confessed that they were guilty of horrible activity in the most important branches of the state: the Party, Security, the Army. They all admit that you were responsible for them. You can't deny that yourself. So the crimes which they have committed fall back on you even if you are not guilty subjectively. Your only way out, and your duty, is to appeal to the mercy of the Party. So far you have had the attitude of a hardened enemy: now you must change that.'

'Your only way out . . .' I was exhausted physically, but above all Kohoutek exhausted me mentally. He had trapped me in a political operation and had removed from me every hope of being able to fight. Maybe either he or the ringleaders calculated that it was by removing the point of my resistance that they would undermine it, rather than by trying to break it. I could really see no way out. When you realize that every effort is pointless exhaustion gets the better of you. I began to think that my obstinacy was uselessly prolonging my ordeal.

One day in July I agreed to sign my first 'confession': 'Since the former volunteers in the International Brigades admit to having been Trotskyists and traitors, the fact that I was their leader puts me on the same level as them.

'Since Field is a spy and I was in contact with him, I am objectively guilty . . .'

Ten

My wife had continued to write to me. Even at the time of our mutual arrest in 1942, when the examining magistrate had forbidden us to correspond, she had persisted. After a month the magistrate had given in and I had received all her letters. This time it was after my first 'confession' that I received the letter from which Smola had read me an extract, and two others.

4 May 1951.

Gérard, I received your letter yesterday and read it over several times to try and find an answer between the lines to all the questions which I have been asking myself since you left the house on 28 January. How we waited for you! Every time we heard a car we thought it was you. But days, weeks, months went by and you didn't return.

I had such confidence in you, Gérard, is it possible that you did not deserve it? I love you Gérard, but you know that I am primarily a communist. In spite of the pain I will know how to tear you out of my heart if I discover you are unworthy.

I weep as I write to you and no one knows as well as you how much I have loved you and how much I love you now. But I can only live in peace with my conscience.

I always hoped, until I received your letters, that you would return to us rehabilitated and that our life would resume where it had left off. But your letter seems a product of despair. I can't resign myself to abandoning all hope. But when it's all explained, when I see things clearly, it'll be easier.

I see you are worried about our material necessities. Of course it's not easy to keep six people, but I manage with the help of the Party. Because if you are guilty, Gérard, our children and parents have nothing to do with it and will not bear the consequences. I mean from the material point of view. Morally, as you can imagine, it is different. My parents have suffered and continue to suffer as much as myself. The thought that you – the person we love most – were unworthy to belong to the great communist family torments us.

I still work and write and look after the children. I read a lot, to try and fill in my time as much as possible and not yield to the obsessive thoughts which haunt me.

Mummy and Daddy are tired, but I'm lucky to have them here. I don't know what I'd do without them. We're still in the same house but we're going to move soon.

Finally, Gérard, I want to remind you of Jan Huss's words: 'The truth will triumph.' If you are innocent, fight, struggle to prove it! Otherwise it is right that you should pay for your crimes.

Send us your news. Love from the three children and from me, Gérard darling.

End of May, 1951.

Darling Gérard, my first letter may have seemed hard to you, but how can I explain what I feel? I await your reply impatiently but nothing ever comes from you. I hope it will confirm everything I feel; it is impossible that you have committed acts hostile to the Party or your country. I won't believe it because otherwise what would the sixteen years of our life together mean? I think I am aware of both your qualities and your faults, and I cannot have lived with an evil man without knowing it.

Your letter upset me because it was so sad and hopeless. But it was also so full of your love and care for us, and you wouldn't have dared write us such a letter if you felt guilty. You know our loyalty to the Party and that we could forgive you anything except betrayal.

I try to see clearly but I am surrounded by darkness. And everywhere I look I see your frank face, your kind eyes, your affectionate smile. I can hear your voice saying: 'Don't mistrust me, Lise!' I don't mistrust you, Gérard, but I also have faith in the Party, and if the Party has authorized such measures I know there must be some justification. But I hope everything will clear up and that you will return. Above all don't worry about our material situation. With Mummy's capacity for saving we'll always get through. Think only of clearing up your own problems and of proving your innocence. I believe in you. Be brave. You owe it both to us and the Party.

I love you, Gérard. And if you love me too you'll find the strength to make truth triumph, and I believe that can only be in your favour. That's true, isn't it? Your Lise.

June 15, 1951.

Darling Gérard, we have already moved into the new flat at Dyrinka, Prague 19. From our windows we can see the whole city. I like it here, amongst our furniture from Ivry which reminds me of the past, when we were happy. You'll soon come back, I'm sure.

Behind the house there's a little garden and in front there's a square which reminds me of the village. I'm not sorry we moved. I feel more at home here than at Stresovice. The children will soon be coming home on holiday. Françoise still goes to her old school, which she refuses to leave. Little Gérard goes to school near home. The children are very well. Although Michel was ill for a week he's better now. The move exhausted Mummy. I'm in good health. Gérard, I'm sure things will sort themselves out for you and that you'll soon be back. It can't be otherwise. After July I'm going to work in a factory.

Above all don't worry about us, Gérard, we're all well and we await you with complete confidence. Why haven't you written since 1 May? Please write to us. If only you knew how impatiently we await your news.

We're very worried about your health. All our love. Lise.

When I read these three letters I was all the more amazed that Smola had hoodwinked me. From the passage which he read me from Lise's letter I concluded that she had repudiated me. I knew of her candid faith in the Party, and above all I realized that I had been guilty towards her. The day of my arrest I had decided to tell her all my fears and now I had no more doubts about how the Security would distort my failure to tell Lise everything. They would force her to admit that if I had lied to her on a personal level I could also have done so on a political one.

But Lise stood by me bravely. She showed complete trust in me and even if she had hesitated for a sentence in her first letter, she had now recovered her confidence.

Despite her difficult situation as a foreigner with a whole family to support she never thought of abandoning me in order to protect her parents and her children. On the contrary, she encouraged me. She reassured me about our family so that I could concentrate on clearing up my own problems concerning the Party and my work. This belief that we would soon meet again was her way of saying: 'Fight on, hold firm, I'm with you!'

I later discovered the true conditions of her life which she depicted so lightly in her letter – the bitter struggle to keep our family.

And these letters were given me now that I had signed my first 'confession'. I imagined the dreadful shock she must feel on discovering that she had waited in vain, the tragedy it would represent for her and her family. Her whole life would be scarred by it, in this country where she was already treated like a pariah. Never had I felt so close to Lise. I regretted not having been shot as a hostage; I regretted having survived Mauthausen. The present disasters would have been avoided and she would have retained a pure image of our love forever, and pride in her husband, the father of her children. I reproached myself bitterly for having caused their misfortune, for not having sent them to France as soon as I realized that my difficulties could end in catastrophe.

The fact that she should have made my children – who still believed I was in the hospital – add a few lines to her letters was further proof of her confidence in the future. She hid the ghastly truth from them in order to preserve the image of their father whom they would soon see again.

And then her naïvety, her complete faith in the Party's spirit of justice and equity. This was the first break between her communist concept of unlimited confidence in the Party which can never be wrong and the concept I was obtaining after six months in prison. I was becoming aware of the puerility of unconditional faith in the abstract idea of the Party. You can have confidence in the Party when you think of it as it should be, that is to say as the emanation of a mass of communists, but you can no longer trust it when it is a narrow, bureaucratic organization which abuses the loyalty, confidence and sacrifices of its members in order to drag them down a perverted path which has nothing in common with the ideals and programme of true communism.

Now my only concern was to persuade Lise to leave for France with her parents and children. There she would find a healthy world, sheltered from the reprisals and filth which the support she gave me in adversity, the love which transpired from every word she wrote me, would almost certainly entail.

Amongst her own people, in her country, with her comrades and friends, the pain she would have in hearing of my condemnation would be easier to support.

On 19 July 1951, I wrote to her:

Darling Lise, I received your last letters and you cannot imagine how happy they made me, and how pleased I am to be able to answer them. I am in good health and receive medical attention. All I miss is liberty, you and the family. These three things are everything to me. I am less worried about you now, but I can imagine the moral and material situation into which I have forced you.

Ever since the first day of my arrest I have been thinking about you. Never in my life have I felt closer to you. And never have I loved you as much as I do now, in spite of my bad behaviour towards you.

Why did I act as I did? I can no longer account for it today. It was the result of demoralization, and you can imagine my remorse and my regrets.

Can you please forget or try not to think of my error? If you knew how well I remember our flat in Ivry where we were so happy and where nothing overshadowed our love . . .

I had decided to tell you everything and ask your forgiveness. I had been ashamed of myself for so long and could hardly look you in the face. And when I saw you in the garden on Sunday I intended to get rid of Havel and to come back as quickly as possible to tell you all. But my arrest prevented me.

How will you manage in the factory? You can't do any manual labour and your health is weak. You should return to France where you have friends and with the help of your sister and brother it would be easier for you, your parents and the children to survive the hard period ahead of you. Think of this, Lise. All my love to you, the children and your parents.

22 July, 1951.

Darling Gérard, a letter from you after so many long months! I am so pleased to know you are in good health, but I was sorry to read your confession. It would all have been so easy and simple if you had confided in me. I could have helped you; I was your comrade as much as your wife.

You ask me to forget or at least not to think about it. That's difficult for me with my character. But I fully forgive the harm you did me, Gérard. As far as I am concerned I can forgive you everything, but I cannot do so as far as the Party is concerned. I always hope that you have not committed any grave error and that your demoralization was limited to searching for distractions outside your home.

You ask me to go back to France. But, Gérard, this depends on you: I will only go if I discover that I can no longer honourably regard you as my husband.

God, Gérard, how stupid and sad it all is.

My parents cried when I read them your note. How brave they are, but it's hard for them.

I have to work in a factory in Karlin, 'Autorenova', which specializes in repairing the electric parts of car and aeroplane engines. The work is interesting and only demands skill. I have it and manual labour does not frighten me, so don't worry about me. On the other hand work will take me away from home and my obsessions.

Goodbye, Gérard, my parents and the children send their love and I hope we will soon resume our previous existence together, because I love you.

I felt that Lise was searching in each of my letters for the slightest hint which would justify her trust in me and her hope in our future. But I had to prepare her for the sinister drama which was soon to take place, give her to understand that I was lost, make her think I was guilty. Otherwise she would refuse to leave me and I wanted her and the whole family to be far away.

On 7 August I could write to her again:

Never doubt my love for you, Lise, and believe me when I say that I have always loved you and still love you.

Otherwise, Lise, your trust is not justified. I am guilty and I must pay for it. It is my duty to tell you so, so that you can face the consequences for yourself and for our family. I no longer want to lie, so I am starting by telling you the painful truth. I know it will make you suffer considerably. But the sooner you look things in the face the better. I know how brave and strong you are and that every decision you take will be right. Believe me, every word I write to you tears out a piece of myself, a piece of my life which was so happy with you. I am courageous, but my courage would not be enough without my love for you. That's why my first duty is to tell you the truth. Write to me, Lise, and tell me what you intend to do.

You will now understand why I asked you to return to France. Do you think I would otherwise have been able to imagine life without you, without the children and your parents?

In spite of this Lise stood by me and wrote me two more letters:

9 August 1951.

Darling Gérard, I received your letter the day before yesterday and read it several times. Your way of putting the problem is not very clear but I want to be more so because there must be no misunderstanding about a matter on which our future relationship and my life depends.

Gérard, you say you have committed mistakes for which you must pay. But I cannot understand the importance of these mistakes. I cannot take a decision according to my honour as a communist until I know exactly what they are. Stalin has taught us that man is the most precious capital that exists and that if a man is drowning we must help him out of the water, not desert him.

Every communist must make a mistake in his lifetime and must pay for it, but life goes on and he has a chance to atone and advance if he learns his lesson from his mistakes. If that is your case, Gérard, I would still agree to help you, and this attitude of mine seems compatible with my duties as a communist.

If you were a traitor there would be nothing to discuss. One doesn't talk to traitors, one spits in their faces. My position on that score is clear.

I have confidence in man. I know he has some good in him and that I won't be losing my time especially after the ordeal we have endured, which I am sure will bear fruit.

There, Gérard, that is what I wanted to say about this basic problem.

Apart from this I enjoy my work. I learned the job in six days when it should have taken a month. The old foreman says that I am skilful, very skilful. I am pleased with myself and the time is now passing much faster. Françoise and Gérard are in the country. My parents are well and Michel gets sweeter every day. I hope I can still say I love you, Gérard.

Prague, 12 August 1951.

Gérard, today is Sunday, 12 August. Can you remember what this date means for us? Nine years ago we were arrested in Paris and three years of separation began. How splendid that all seems to me in comparison with the sad period we are going through today. And yet, as we exchanged that long kiss in the car taking us to the police station, I thought it was our last farewell. I now think it may have been better had it been so. My pregnancy in prison, my labour in the infirmary of La Roquette awaiting the death penalty, and my deportation which separated me from my little Gérard, the idea that I would never see you again were painful but seem so easy compared to the present ordeal.

I am waiting for your reply to my last letter, a reply which must tell me whether the errors you have committed can be atoned for or whether they mean that you are forever lost to the Party and myself.

Gérard, you can't have betrayed me in this point too, you can't have acted criminally against the Party, your life's ideal. It would be too ghastly. But it isn't possible! And I live in hope that one day you will have paid for the faults you have committed in a period of demoralization and my children will again be proud of their father.

I repeat what I wrote in my last letter: I won't refuse to help you if these faults can be atoned for . . .

Last week I did more than 200 per cent of the norm imposed on us in the factory. For the next two weeks my work will be less interesting because my partner is on holiday and I shall have to do things like dismantling and cleaning. Anyhow, one has to dismantle everything before putting it together again . . . so let's be patient!

Goodbye, Gérard, I hope to hear from you soon. We all send our love, Lise.

End of August, 1951.

I am waiting for your reply impatiently, Gérard. I won't take a decision concerning my future until I know exactly how things stand with you. I remember a speech by Maurice Thorez at the Central Committee about the methods of leadership, criticism and self-criticism. He coined a good image: 'But when you criticize a comrade make sure that you don't crush him still more, but help him to see the roots of the evil and remedy it. When one washes a child one tries not to throw him down the drain with the dirty water.'

No, Gérard, I'm not throwing the child down the drain. Only his dirt has remained in the water which is going down the drain.

Of course if you had anything more than dirt, if you were a real pig, then I wouldn't say these things. I would repudiate you entirely because no water would ever clean you. And I would have nothing but the shame of having married a swine. But this has not yet been proved.

Good night, Gérard. It is ten o'clock and I'm sleepy. I have to get up at five tomorrow. My partner will be back and I shall start reassembling the magnetoes which will be more interesting . . .

I had no idea of the struggles Lise was having with the Party on my account and to support her family. I only found out about them after it was all over. They show the other side of what we were going through in Ruzyn – the Party leaders who dealt with our case, were forced to think about it and rub their noses in their methods because of Lise's simple faith in the Party and communism.

This is the letter she wrote to Slansky on 15 March 1951, six weeks after my arrest:

For twenty years, comrade Slansky, I have been proud to be a communist, and have always deserved the title. My father, who lives here with my mother, joined the Party in 1921. On several occasions Maurice Thorez mentioned him as an exemplary worker, honest and loyal to his class and the Party. If I say that, it's to make you understand how hard the ordeal we are going through is for us particularly since we still know nothing about Gérard and the reasons for his detention.

I realize, comrade Slansky, that, as Party Secretary, you are a very busy man, but I believe that in certain circumstances it is your duty to hear a Party member . . .

In March, Lise heard from her chauffeur-detective who followed her everywhere that during a plenary meeting of the Party organization at the Foreign Ministry, presided over by Viliam Siroky, a violent attack had been made against me. A few days later she wrote again to the Party Secretariat and to Bruno Köhler:

A comrade has told me that it was even suggested Gerard should be expelled from the Party. I tried to obtain the explanations to which I am entitled as his wife, as a communist and as the head of the family, for now I support six people, and according to the news I receive I shall decide about my future. But I have been unable to see either Comrade Slansky or Comrade Köhler. On the other hand some employees from the Ministry's housing department visited me to tell me we must move.

Don't you think, comrades, that before doing this you should have told me why you were doing it?

I am sorry to have to ask you this kind of question, but I am faced by very difficult material and financial problems.

Our money is blocked in the bank. Nobody will help me solve

this problem, but I must pay the rent and keep my family alive. Can't I draw the family allowance in my name? And am I not entitled to an allowance for my parents? You may think these questions importunate but I must solve these problems and believe me, this is not easy . . .

And to whom can I appeal if not to the Party? Don't forget how isolated we are here, and that makes our situation all the more difficult.

Until I have proof to the contrary I cannot admit that Gérard is a Party enemy. He may have made some mistakes in his work and come under evil influences. But I don't believe he is an enemy.

I beg you once again for an appointment and I hope you won't refuse it this time.

As a result of this letter my wife was summoned on 21 March by Bruno Köhler, the head of the Cadre Department of the Central Committee of the Party. She had known him very well ever since I worked with him in Paris in 1939 and 1940 and this is what she told me:

'He received me in his office but before we started talking his secretary opened the door to a tall well-built man with blue eyes who looked to me like a veteran from Spain.*

' "Have you got some more information?"

' "Yes, we get more every day."

'He handed Köhler a large envelope full of papers.

Köhler looked very excited and took his visitor into the far corner of the room where they whispered to each other. When the visitor left I asked Köhler:

' "What's happening to my husband?"

' "It doesn't look too good. He seems in it up to his neck. You saw the material that's just arrived, it's about him too and I receive piles of it every day."

' "But is he under arrest or not? If he is I have the right to know why, first as his wife and then as a Party member."

---

* Judging from the description this was Alois Samec, a veteran from Spain who was then in charge of gathering material against the other former volunteers. He collaborated with Soviet advisers.

'Köhler told me there was no charge against you, but that you were implicated in a whole lot of things and he didn't see how you would get away with it.

' "You can't say he behaved very well towards you. He was deserting you, he came home late . . ."

'And he started saying how sorry he was for me.

'This put my back up. "It's true he was late sometimes. But his morale was very low, and he was running away from himself. He may have had his weaknesses, like everyone. But I trust him. I love him and I know he loves me and his children. And then you're touching on a problem which only concerns the two of us! That can't be why the Party arrested him or, as Siroky said, "isolated him".

' "For the time being there is no charge against him. Siroky was right to talk of isolation. But I can give you some advice: leave as quickly as possible: go back to France with your children and your parents. Life is going to be too hard for you."

' "Leave? How could I? That would mean abandoning my husband. Worse still, it would mean condemning him. I have no reason to do that and I shall stay here. If you can prove that Gérard is an enemy, I'll reconsider my decision."

' "Think about it. This is a friend's advice. You're not alone, you have a family to keep. Believe me, it won't be easy. Besides, I'm afraid I must tell you that you will soon have to leave your job on the radio."

' "Why? What have I done wrong? I've just been told I was the best reporter because of the French broadcasts I did on the Peace Conference in Warsaw. I can't speak Czech properly so where else could I work?"

' "You can't go on working for the radio or any other government office. Your only hope is to get a job in a factory."

' "I'm not frightened of manual labour, but I have no experience. I would be far more use in a job I'm familiar with."

' "That's not the problem. This is how cases like yours are solved in the Soviet Union."

' "It's an odd way to do things. To start with, even if my

174

husband is guilty – and according to what you say it hasn't yet been proved – am I responsible for what he's done? Second, it seems rather strange to send someone to work in a factory to punish him or reeducate him. Is factory work considered forced labour? It's a pretty unpleasant definition for the working classes."

' "There's nothing I can do: I'm not the one who makes the decisions." And to gild the pill he added: "It wouldn't be so bad if you could be of some use in a factory, in a spinning-mill, for example.*

' "The work's not too bad there, and you've heard about the Filatov sisters, the famous Stakhanovists! You might become one too . . ."

'Again I turned the conversation on to you. I told him about the difficulties you had had in the last year, of your inability to get a hearing and settle your problems with the Party. I reminded him of the circumstances in which you had met Field, that the French Communist Party knew about the whole business and that it was easy to get to the root of the matter.

'I also told him that I could only account for your arrest as the possible result of a provocation by certain enemies camouflaged in the Security Ministry. In order to avoid attention themselves they started spreading rumours about the "London case" and confusing clear and easily controllable facts concerning you.

'I told him that I based this feeling on the fact that a Swiss paper had published an article on "the future trials in Czechoslovakia" asking the question: "Will London be the main defendant or the main witness?" in 1949 at the time when the Security was interrogating you about Noel Field. Didn't that prove that the whole matter was a provocation?

'Köhler advised me to write to Kopriva, and I did so the next morning, sending a copy of the letter to the Party Secretariat.'

* Since the spinning-mills were outside Prague, Köhler's suggestion gave some idea of what was in store for Lise: like the wives of many other prisoners she was to be sent away from Prague.

In this letter, dated 22 March 1951, my wife repeated the arguments she had used with Köhler the day before, especially with regard to the Field question. She ended by criticizing the Party's method:

After my husband had been interrogated at length by the State Security Services the problems seemed to have been clarified. But they still had to be settled with the Party. My husband told Geminder that he wanted his case to be examined by the Cadre Department and Geminder replied that Comrade Kopriva and he intended to discuss it with him the next day. But days and weeks went by without the Party settling the matter. My husband's position became increasingly difficult and he suffered accordingly.

He should of course have had enough energy to insist on a hearing, and to put his questions to the Party in view of his conviction that the Party was making a mistake by leaving it to the Security Services to investigate the case of an old Party member who occupied as important a position as he did. He thought that this way of doing things was in flagrant contradiction to a fair cadre policy . . .

I repeat what I told Comrade Bruno Köhler yesterday: my trust in Gérard is based on the fact that all his life everything he has done can be checked. The sixteen years we spent together have enabled me to verify his unimpeachable devotion to the Party in periods which were often very difficult, his great honesty, his courage and his loyalty . . .

I have one request to make to Comrade Kopriva. In view of my husband's ill health and the fact that I always fear he may have a relapse of tuberculosis, would it be possible for me to have some news about his state of health?

On 27 May the Foreign Ministry sent a lorry to move my family to the new flat where there was not even a cooking stove. My wife refused to move in these conditions, and sent away the truck drivers and the employees from the Ministry. The next day she wrote to Siroky:

From Paris we had only brought books, linen and the furniture in my room. We had to pay for the furniture which is now in our house with the money in my husband's bank account until the inventory was finished.

But this morning the employees from the Ministry informed me that I would not be allowed to take this furniture unless I paid for it cash down . . .

Do you think it normal that I should move with two old people and three children into an empty flat, without even a kitchen and with no possibility to furnish it since our money is blocked in the bank and I myself only receive my salary from the radio until the end of June . . .

I still don't know what you have against my husband; but I hope everything will be sorted out because the Party is there and I have faith in the Party. Personally I have no reason to doubt Gérard's honesty or innocence. But, as I told Comrade Köhler, whatever he has done neither his children, my parents nor myself should pay for him. I know that I have never forfeited the Party's trust and I carry my head high–as high as ever in this painful and difficult period we are going through.

So my wife had also been trying, day after day, to meet a Party leader. She had told the Party about all she knew and all hat shocked her ideal as a communist. None of the leaders could say 'they didn't know.' My wife's letters should have warned them. But Siroky, Köhler, Kopriva and the others wanted neither to hear nor to see anything.

Part Three

Charge of Conspiracy

One

As the long night was ending the interrogator suddenly said: 'Tell me about your past, your youth. Tell me about your life in general.'

At first I was surprised. How on earth could my life interest this interrogator in view of the image he wanted to give of me and the incredible charges he held against me? I suspected that he was tired and wanted to recover his strength by sidetracking me, but I was wrong. These were new tactics, a distortion and a caricature of the methods used by the heads of the Party cadres, who make people repeat their accounts of a certain period in order to catch them contradicting themselves. So for two weeks, day after day, for twenty hours on end, I had to tell the interrogator my life history, from my childhood to 28 January 1951, when two cars drove up to me and I was kidnapped in the middle of Prague. I had been in the hands of State Security for six months now, but I had not yet realized that I had entered a world of fastidious repetition, protocol, reports, paper work and signatures. I was not aware of the stage I had reached. It was an apprenticeship, in a way, my apprenticeship in an absurd, evasive, destructive activity – the fabrication of my confessions.

I started to tell my story. The man appeared not to be paying much attention. He drowsed, his eyes half closed, occasionally showing some interest and then lapsing back into his half sleep.

I plunged into my past. I did not talk to answer questions: I talked for myself, for Lise and my children, for my family, my comrades, my closest and dearest friends, as though, after all these months, I was at last allowed to explain myself with the help of my own life.

Of five brothers and sisters only two of us survived Hitler's massacres. My sister Flora, who lived in New York, had been concerned about my return to Czechoslovakia. 'When the hangings start in Prague, there'll be a gibbet for you,' she had written to me.

So when I talked about my family I knew I was one of two survivors, but a survivor who was himself doomed to die with only one last chance to justify himself.

My father, Émile, was the fifth of five children of a railway employee in Moravia under the Austro-Hungarian monarchy. Hard times soon drove the children away from home, and when I said this I searched for the sources of my later ideas. The first thing that I knew about my father's adult life was that he worked as a comrade in Vienna, where he had joined the Socialist Party. That was in the late 1890s. Subsequently he went to live in Switzerland and entered into contact with certain Russian political refugees. He frequented anarchist circles for which he had some sympathy, since he regarded them as more revolutionary than the Social Democrats. He respected Bakunin's physical courage and admired Kropotkin, though he did not share the basic anarchist ideology.

At the beginning of the century he set sail for America. Here he met two of his elder brothers and kept on good terms with the anarchist workers, although he had become an active member of the socialist groups.

America amazed him – a young country, making large strides with a fantastic future and an astonishing capacity for absorbing and amalgamating emigrants from all over the world.

After the yoke of the reactionary powers or the countless vexations and miseries of the ghettoes of old Europe, men like my father felt free, and determined to fight for their rights, when they arrived there. At this time there was a powerful socialist movement in the United States. My father soon learned English and studied the literature, poetry and history of the country. I remember that he used to recite poems by Whitman and passages from Paine and Jefferson to us. And he kept the complete works of his favourite poet, Heinrich Heine, in his little library.

He met my mother in New York after she had arrived with her sister from Slovakia. In the daytime she worked as a maid in a hotel, and at night in the kitchen of a large restaurant, where my father met her. He was unemployed as the result of a strike at the Ford Motor Works where he worked as an upholsterer, and had been temporarily taken on as a dishwasher. They got married in New York, and soon afterwards she gave birth to my sister Flora, who therefore had double nationality and managed much later to obtain an American passport after the German occupation of Ostrava in 1939. She left for the United States and thus escaped the Nazi concentration camps.

My parents returned to Czechoslovakia – although they often regretted it. America was to remain the great period of their lives. They were forever telling us stories about it, even if life had not always been easy for them there. And they always discussed important matters, which the children were not supposed to understand, in English. The language of their first love made them feel closer to each other.

When war was declared my father left for the front. My sister Flora and my brother Jean were already born. Oskar was born during the war and Juliette and I were conceived on leave.

My father was sent to the Russian front as a stretcher bearer. Because of a wound and his weak eyesight he was put to work as a male nurse in a hospital at the end of the war. At his first contact with Russian prisoners, for whom he organized manifestations of solidarity, he met Bolsheviks, became a violent supporter of the October Revolution and an ardent propagandist. He survived, although he had been blacklisted by the Austro-Hungarian army as a political suspect.

The war days were hard for us. There were already five children in 1916. My only memory of this period dates from shortly before the armistice when I was three and a half years old. One night my brother and I were lying next to each other with chicken pox, our hair shaved because of the lice, covered in scabs, and our grandfather, a railwayman, came to see us. He pulled three lumps of sugar for each of us out of his knapsack. It was the first time I had ever tasted something so good and I have always remembered the little white cubes, which we gnawed slowly to make them last.

The post-war period was not much easier. My father worked to feed seven mouths. It was a great deal for a small salary. We lived in a two-room flat with a tiny kitchen, in Ostrava, already an important industrial centre with dozens of coal mines, factories of coke and chemicals, and ironworks, some of which were among the largest in Europe.

After his return from the war my father devoted all his free time to politics. He often found himself at odds with his bosses and lost his job. Deciding to start up on his own, he rented a small workshop in the backyard of a nearby house. He thought he would be freer by becoming an artisan, and his political activity increased. He often addressed public meetings and wrote articles for the socialist press. It was the time when the Socialist Parties were arguing about joining the Third International and discussing the constitution of the Communist Parties. An old member of the socialist left, he was naturally one of the founders of the Communist Party in his home town and in the country.

Boycotted by the Jewish community, who considered him a traitor because he was an atheist and a militant member of anti-religious organizations, my father rarely found work. He repaired mattresses and workers' sofas, and most of his clients, who were in financial straits themselves, paid irregularly. At the end of each week my mother, grumbling and angry, was unable to make ends meet. My father's family considered him a fanatic who was ruining his family's reputation. With the exception of my uncle Zigmund to whom he was closest, his wealthier brothers were unwilling to help him, and were always moralizing before lending him the money he required to redeem his only sewing machine from the pawnbroker or the bailiff.

My father was the first person to tell me about Bebel,

Liebknecht, Rosa Luxemburg, the Spartacists, the Russian Bolsheviks, Lenin, Lunacharsky, Trotsky, John Reed, and the communes of Canton and Shanghai. It was through him that I first heard of the veterans of the American Socialist Party, like Tom Mooney, and it was with him that I took part in the first street demonstrations.

He made me read Heinrich Heine, and it was thanks to him that I joined the Communist Youth when I was thirteen and a half. I started working then because, in our family, only one child could study, and even for him there were many sacrifices. Our student was Oskar, a year older than I, who died at the age of twenty before ending his schooling.

My father was very popular in town and was known as 'the old Bolshevik'. Every evening, at our front door, a group of people – adversaries, socialists, communists – discussed the problems of the time with him.

Despite his activity my father had only twice been in trouble with the authorities – once during an open-air meeting when he had refused to take his hat off during the national anthem and had stated that he would only take it off for the 'Internationale', and the second time because of me. On a winter night in February 1932, towards two in the morning, the police burst into our flat to arrest me. When I was dressed I put on my father's coat instead of mine. But he said nothing. I had done so because I still had a number of tracts in my pockets and was being arrested for distributing them. When I had to empty my pockets in the police station the inspectors soon saw, from the incongruous objects which I produced, that the coat belonged to my father, and rushed back to our flat to get mine. But my father had got rid of all the compromising material after I had left. The police searched the house and found nothing. They tried to intimidate my father, but in vain.

I saw him for the last time in Moscow in the summer of 1935, after my brother Oskar's death. Since we did not know when he was arriving my wife and I were at an aviation meeting at the Tushino airport. We had to walk home, because there was no transport, and we found him asleep on a bench in the hall of our hotel. He had aged visibly, but his joy in seeing me and meeting my wife appeared in his smile. In order to visit us he had come on an organized trip. As we walked along the streets I had to answer thousands of eager questions about this world which he had only read about and imagined.

'Why, eighteen years after the revolution, in this sweltering heat, do people still wear felt boots? Why does orange juice cost a dollar in my Intourist Hotel?'

Often I had difficulty in answering his questions.

And he wanted to write everything down in his notebook – the rents, the salaries of the various categories of workers, the price of books and theatre tickets, the possibilities of education.

I can still see the young propagandist on the Birobidzhan stand* in the Maxim Gorky Culture Park, who was overwhelmed by my father's questions. 'What about this Birobidzhan? Communism doesn't recognize Judaism as a nationality and we are against emigration to Palestine, so why do the same thing here with Birobidzhan? And what are conditions like down there?'

In the end the young man begged my father to come back the next day when he would answer all his questions in writing. But my father was not satisfied.

He was conscientiously preparing a lecture to the Association of Friends of the Soviet Union upon his return to Ostrava. To tread the Red Square, to see Lenin in his mausoleum, to see the walls of the Kremlin with the tombs of the great revolutionaries, to see Moscow and breath the air of a country which had accomplished the first revolution, was a dream come true.

He had not liked everything. There were some things which he had not understood. But on the whole he was pleased. When he left us he was sad. When would we meet again? My wife was to see him once more when she stopped in Ostrava in 1936 on

* Birobidzhan was an autonomous region of the USSR where all the Jews were to be concentrated.

her way back to France. As for me, I never saw him, my mother, Jean, or Juliette again.

Two

There were not many of us in the Communist Youth from 1928 to 1933, but our determination made up for it. We were incredibly active. We did everything, distributed tracts, wrote on walls, pinned up notices. We took part in public meetings, sold papers, organized propaganda and demonstrations among the youth in the factories and the mines, recruited and formed other youth groups.

We once declared a hunger strike when twenty-five of us had been locked in the police station after a demonstration. And then, the day before the First of May, in the local prison, we had flown the red flag from the cell window. When we were freed at ten in the morning I was chosen by my comrades to address a rally of 20,000 people in their name.

I recalled the demonstrations and the police charges, when we were dispersed with whips and sabres, and the fascist meetings which we disrupted.

I can see us again, four young comrades led by our federal secretary to the Polish Consulate. After writing in blood on a sheet of paper: 'We will avenge our murdered Polish brothers,' we threw stones through the windows and hurled in our messages on the point of a dagger. That was after some strikers had been shot by the police in Poland; in those days we were passionate internationalists.

During the large strikes in my district the police opened fire and the wounded fell at my side. In the rebellious romanticism of our age, three of us had decided to reply to police terror by blowing up the police station. With cartridges given to us by the miners we made a minute bomb. We were about to carry our plan through, but one of my comrades had boasted about it, and the federal Party secretary heard of it. He soon called us to heel and warned us of the dangers of anarchy.

I recalled my activity in the leadership of the Communist Youth and the Youth of the Red Unions in the Ostrava district, the journey which I and a group of comrades made to Berlin in 1931, when we had to cross the frontier illegally, having failed to obtain passports.

That was the first of my clandestine visits to Germany. The Spartacus meeting we were to attend had been forbidden, so we went to Chemnitz in Saxony to take part in a demonstration against the ban. Uniformed members of the German Communist Party self-defence organization, the Antifaschistischer Kampfbund, protected us, for many of us, Swiss, Austrians, Italians, and Czechs, had entered the country without papers.

I also told the interrogator about the other secret visit to Germany I made shortly before Hitler came to power, in the autumn of 1932, to take part in the plebiscite, and the two border meetings between the trade unions when Germans, Poles and Czechs united against Nazism. I was then Secretary of the Youth of the Red Unions in the Ostrava district.

It was at the beginning of January 1933 that the police were tipped off and burst into a club where I was addressing some thirty young communists about revolutionary defeatism. I was arrested.

After three months' detention I was provisionally released on account of a hunger strike, large-scale demonstrations in my favour by the Communist Youth and the intervention of our deputy Kliment. I recalled how I later escaped from the police sent to arrest me for attempts to undermine the security of the Republic, and the decision of the Party Central Committee to send me into hiding in order to avoid another prison sentence.

That was how I found myself illegally in Prague. I was to assume the regional direction of the Youth of the Red Unions but at the time I was being hunted by the police. The Party and Union headquarters were constantly being searched and everyone had their papers checked near the workers' clubs. The identity papers I had been given would not have stood up to a serious examination, so it was decided that I be sent to Moscow.

One morning, towards nine o'clock, a comrade brought me a passport and some money and told me to get ready to leave at once. My route was through Poland, so I would have to pass Ostrava where I was well known. I told him this might be dangerous, but he retorted: 'You must follow closely all the instructions our organization gives you since it knows about journeys abroad. If you were to disobey and something happened because of it, you would be entirely responsible.'

An hour and a half later this same comrade caught me in the station where I was about to buy my ticket for Poland. At the last minute he had reported what I had said to a leader of the technical organization whom he had met by chance shortly after leaving me. On no account must I leave that way. He gave me another appointment at four o'clock. I had to go there with a case of my personal belongings and leave that very evening.

I met him in a café: he gave me a ticket for Berlin, the money for a ticket from Berlin to Moscow, and a Soviet visa. He told me to conceal it carefully, and only produce it at the Soviet border. I hid it in the peak of my cap and ran to the station. I had a Czech passport with a German name, Gerhard Baum. I looked a little old for this passport since I hadn't had time to shave, and the black beard aged me. In a few days I would be nineteen, but on the passport I was just seventeen.

The train crossed the winter landscape towards the German frontier. Sitting in my compartment I repeated my new identity to myself, what I would say if I were questioned and all the instructions I had received. Two passengers sitting opposite me, a man and a woman, looked at me curiously. We were nearing the last station before the border. They stood up and prepared to get out, still staring at me. I couldn't think why. Suddenly the man said:

'Aren't you getting out?'

'No, I'm going on.'

'Aren't you afraid?'

'Why should I be afraid?'

'But you're going to Germany. We're almost at the border.'

'I know. I'm going first to Berlin, and then still further.'

I then realized that my physical appearance, my cheeks darkened by three days' growth of beard, accentuated my semitic aspect. This was why they were so concerned and surprised about my going to Germany.

On the Czech side the passport control went smoothly, and on the German side the policemen were so busy searching a man whom they found in possession of some Socialist papers forbidden by the Nazis that they paid no attention to me. Late that night we reached Berlin. At every station we went through there were Nazi uniforms and Hitler greetings.

In Berlin I had to change stations and buy my ticket. The comrades at home obviously had no idea of the price of the ticket: it cost me all my money and I only had fifty pfennigs left. It was not enough for me to buy a postage stamp if I was in trouble, still less to send a telegram. I had no food with me, but I had no alternative: I must go on.

We crossed the Polish corridor in the morning and arrived at Koenigsberg. Nearly everyone got out, only a few passengers remaining in the carriage. We were approaching the Lithuanian border, and customs officers and men in civilian clothes boarded the train to check our passports and our luggage. The customs man asked me where I was going. According to my instructions I said I was going to Riga to see an aunt of mine who had paid for my journey.

'But you've got a ticket to Moscow.'

'Yes, because I'm also going to visit Moscow.'

He looked at me for a while and then called an officer, who was amazed to find my case almost empty. They went away and came back with two men in civilian dress who started to interrogate me. I told them the same thing. They wanted to know my aunt's address and I immediately told them what I had learnt in Prague – the address I got out of the Riga telephone directory at the post office. They questioned me about my father and what

I did. I replied with a mass of details: the journey was a reward for an exam which I passed at school. But what intrigued them most was why I was going to Moscow when my aunt lived in Riga and why I had bought my ticket in Berlin instead of in Riga. They obviously found my replies unsatisfactory and forced me to undress completely, making obscene and provocative observations which I pretended not to understand. They carefully searched my case, my shoes (including the soles and heels), the seams of my jacket. I started to be frightened. The whole thing must have looked rather odd, as I stood naked in the compartment with my cap on my head – and not one of them thought of searching it. They got out of the compartment at the border after shouting some unpleasant remarks, mingled with insults in Yiddish.

I sighed with relief and sank back into my seat, as I watched the landscape slip by. We were crossing a sad, monotonous country covered in a white carpet. I was in Lithuania. Suddenly the train seemed to be going at full speed. A little later, in the corridor, a passenger looked at me and said:

'You're smoking Czech cigarettes?'

He spoke Serbo-Croat. I told him I was Czech, like my cigarettes. He looked pleased, and sat in my compartment. He did not have any money and asked me for a cigarette, and, as he smoked, he told me he was Yugoslav, that he had worked in Czechoslovakia for some time, that he had then been to Canada but had been extradited for communist activities. He asked where I was going, and, as I had told everyone else, I said: 'Riga . . .'

We crossed the Latvian frontier with no difficulty and arrived at Riga. Determined to give my fellow passenger the slip, I got out with the other travellers and entered another carriage. That evening, at Daugavpils, I got into the carriage for Moscow which was at the end of the line.

When I entered the compartment the first person I saw was the Yugoslav. He looked at me in astonishment: 'But what are you doing here, you said you were going to Riga? And I saw you get out at Riga.' I muttered something, said I had made a mistake and had decided first to go to Moscow and then to see my aunt in Riga.

I had managed to take my visa out of my cap without anyone seeing it, and to put it in my passport. My first soldier in the Red Army, a tall fellow with a long winter coat which reached his ankles and a Boudienny cap with a red star on his head, asked for our passports. They had told me he would return my Soviet visa folded, as a sign that all was in order, and that I could continue my journey. And sure enough, after about a quarter of an hour, he gave me my folded slip of paper and saluted.

When my Yugoslav companion saw that, he started to talk excitedly. He repeated one word constantly: 'Comintern, Comintern!' I shrugged my shoulders: 'I don't know what you mean.' I really couldn't understand his lack of discretion. We reached Bugossovo in silence. There we had to change trains and have our luggage searched. I'd lost the keys of my case and my Yugoslav friend broke the locks in his enthusiasm, saying that we mustn't waste the Soviet soldiers' time.

I was to meet him a few days later on the staircase of the Comintern. He reproached me for not having told him the truth, and I was to see more of him in Moscow and, in 1937, at Albacete in Spain where he was a captain in the International Brigades. We reminisced with much amusement.

The journey had moved and impressed me, not only because it was my first long journey abroad, but because I was going to the Soviet Union, that country round which all my thoughts and political activity had been centred since my childhood. I was going to the country about which I had heard so much from my father, and from comrades who had worked or studied there, and from those who had gone there as tourists. I also knew and liked the USSR from what I had read and I was now going to know it and its people.

The cold, which had become extreme, hit me as I got out at the station in Moscow. My light Czech coat was not made for a Russian winter. I went to the waiting room where Mirko Krejzl, the representative of the Czech Communist Youth at the KIM, was to meet me. I looked curiously at the people around me, the soldiers in their various uniforms, and I tried to understand snatches of their conversation. After a time, when there was still no sign of Krejzl, I began to pace up and down. Then I saw two fellow passengers with their families. After hesitating an instant, they came towards me: 'Who are you waiting for?'

I told them that the person I was to meet at the station had not yet arrived. They said they were going to the buffet but would come back to see whether I was there a few minutes later and if nobody had come for me, would take me to the address I was making for.

I was slightly irritated, for I had been formally instructed to tell nobody where I was going. And yet, half an hour later, when I saw them come back, I was greatly relieved: I felt lost in the unknown crowd. They said they would take me to their house and give me something to eat.

There was a blizzard outside. One could just make out an enormous white square. Some thirty yards away an acetylene lamp, giving out a pale light, swung from a lamppost in the wind. Sleds hurried past to the sound of cries and whips. I gazed at them in astonishment. Those were the troikas I had imagined, with their gloved *izvoshicks* in their great cloaks and fur hats. The icy wind blew huge flakes in our faces. We got into a sled and, through the dark streets of Moscow, sped towards my new friends' flat. There, for the first time, I became acquainted with Russian kindness and hospitality. I did not feel a foreigner among this family, although I understood little of what they were saying. I ate a real Russian meal, with masses of *hors d'oeuvres* and vodka, and when it was time to leave I was almost sorry. The eldest daughter, who spoke a little German, said she would accompany me. 'Where should I take you?' she asked. Although I was annoyed at having to give away my destination I had no alternative: 'To the Comintern!' They looked surprised, but seemed to understand my discretion. We took a tram, changed twice and finally reached the Riding-School Square. She knew it was near there but did not know which building. She asked a sentry, but he shrugged his shoulders and replied: 'I've no idea!' We insisted, but he could only reply 'Nieznayou! I've no idea!'

We hesitated for a second and then, just behind the sentry we saw a plaque: 'Executive Committee of the Communist International.' I had reached my destination.

Three

In Moscow I could at last live a legend. Lenin's widow, Krupskaya, twice entertained us and talked at length about her husband and his comrades. We met the old Bolsheviks who had known Lenin, Trotsky, Kamenev, Martov, Plekhanov, who had been at the heart of the revolution in Leningrad, Moscow, Odessa and elsewhere; the German communists who had fought in the ranks of the Spartacists, next to Rosa Luxemburg and Karl Liebknecht, and the Italian communists who had fought with Gramsci against Mussolini.

In the corridors of the Comintern I saw Bela Kun, and spoke to men who had fought in the Hungarian Commune and the Bulgarian uprising of 1923. I saw and heard Manuilsky, so attractive and impressive with his mane of grey hair; and then the great figures of the international communist movement: Maurice Thorez, Marcel Cachin, Ercoli-Togliatti, La Pasionaria, José Diaz, Wilhelm Pieck, Browder, Pollit, Prestès and many others.

I heard Dimitrov's report at the Seventh Comintern Congress on the antifascist union of the working classes, and the account of Mao Tse Tung's and Chou Te's long march by the Chinese representative Van Min, who showed us their route on a huge map. I saw Gorky, and heard his death announced on the loud speakers when I was rowing on the Moskva with Lise. I spoke to the men who built Magnitogorsk, and Comsomolsk, and raved about the men who had turned Novossibirsk into a Siberian metropolis.

I followed enthusiastically the transformation of the mysterious regions which I had only known from the legends of Genghis Khan and Batushan. I heard the young Uzbeks talk of ancestral and religious traditions, of their land, where their caravans met the first tractors, and many women were still veiled although they worked in large textile factories. As for the revolutionary anniversaries, the burials of Kirov, Gorky, Ordjonikidze, I filed past with the crowd of Moscovites, and devoured our idol Stalin with my eyes. My heart beat faster when I saw him, and I was ecstatic when he appeared briefly at the Seventh Comintern Congress. When he gave interviews I thought the simple way he answered yes or no were marks of genius. Like the whole of the International Communist Movement I fervently cultivated his personality.

Day after day, I had to describe every detail of my life history. From one account to the next harmless or important recollections emerged from my memory and added further beads to the rosary of my life, this life which had come to such a miserable end. The interrogator had long ceased to listen. When I ended with the words: 'And on 28 January 1951, I was arrested,' he said, 'Start again.'

Twice, ten times, a hundred times. It was sheer lunacy. At first it enabled me to escape from my surroundings and forget my inquisitors. But after a few days I began to hate myself, my past, all that was part of my life, because to recall my life here, ceaselessly, before these obtuse individuals who could only blindly obey their orders, didn't even listen and only knew how to say 'Start again!' was to invite derision. It was as though they were spitting in my face. I already felt degraded, smelly, dirty and unkempt, with my hairy beard, and my trousers sliding down my hips, and now I was like a record repeating the same tune. It made you scream 'Enough!'

Who were these men? What had they to do with my past?

Why did I have to tell them about things which belonged only to me?

I now knew that they were trying to exhaust me, but even if I knew it, even if the interrogators showed that they weren't listening, my life was at stake. I was at stake. And not only did this process wear me down and humiliate me, but it devalued in my own eyes my whole life and made me accept additions, cuts, changes and the aspect of a traitor.

Besides, I soon had proof that when Kohoutek and his team really needed to consult my biography it never occurred to them to refer to my accounts, but to the *curriculum vitae* I wrote on my return to Czechoslovakia for the Central Committee.

Fortunately the ordeal ended before I gave in.

On occasion, when the interrogators dropped off to sleep, I had a few minutes' respite, provided I kept on making some noise, since the silence woke them up. I said the first thing that came into my head. I recited the alphabet or poetry, and one night an interrogator woke up and said: 'Repeat what you've just been saying about Holdos when you were in Strasbourg together.'

'But I've never been to Strasbourg, with or without Holdos!'

He was furious and told me to repeat what I'd just said.

I thought about my friend Laco Holdos. Our friendship had been forged by years of combat, from the battlefield to the concentration camps. Two weeks ago the interrogators had read me long extracts from his 'confessions'. What agony it must have been for such a good and honest man. Our friendship was turned into complicity in crime. And yet man has nothing nobler than friendship. It is in no way in contradiction with communist ethics.

The interrogator had gone back to sleep. I leaned against the wall, then crept up to a stool and sat down. I had started talking again in a monotonous voice, describing my surroundings: 'an iron cupboard in a corner, painted grey, with two doors, the key in the lock . . . '

The interrogator snored conscientiously. The door suddenly opened and Doubek came in. He saw me sitting down and saw the interrogator snoring. He shook him roughly and said: 'Send him back to his cell and come to my office!' This earned me a few hours sleep.

The next day the second interrogator shouted at me: 'You swine, because of you my colleague's been punished for eight days.' And then I had to start all over again: 'I was born on 1 February 1915, in Ostrava . . .' It was night time, silent and empty. Nothing had anything to do with me. It was all over and done with. I was now in another world where I didn't exist. I waited in the silence of the night, interrupted only by the cries and blows from the nearby rooms, and I waited for the grey dawn to appear through the window, the knock of the woodpecker and the morning concert of the birds.

'Are you waiting for the woodpecker?' asked the interrogator, as relieved as I was to see day break. He looked at his watch. I knew it was almost four o'clock, and he too could stand it no longer. A few minutes later he blindfolded me and in my cell I heard the sparrows and the blackbirds behind my windows. A new day of despair had begun.

Four

How could I have been so naive as to think that my inquisitors would be content with my 'confession' of guilt about the 'Trotskyist group' of former volunteers and my contacts with Field? I thought this would be enough for my trial, but I now knew it was just a spring to fling me further.

The interrogators increased their pressure on me to make me admit that I had not waited to be posted to France before starting my Trotskyist activity, but that I had already been a Trotskyist agent in Spain.

'Your Trotskyist convictions cannot have been spontaneous.

What better preparation was there than Spain? Admit that you were already a Trotskyist in Spain, because if you had been a good communist there, you would have remained one. And you can't claim to have been a good communist. You have admitted being responsible for a Trotskyist group in France and admitted having been in contact throughout the war with Pavlik who was revealed as a Trotskyist and an American agent in the Rajk trial . . .'

One day Kohoutek continued his interrogators' proof: 'It was not in Spain that you became a Trotskyist, but in the USSR.'

As he realized that no flight of fancy would make me admit this, he added cynically: 'That's what our Soviet friends think, so I'll have to add something to this effect in the report.'

He knew I had spent a few weeks in the Lux Hotel in Moscow during the first trials against Zinoviev and Kamenev in 1935. Several arrests had been made at that time, so he wrote: 'Even in Moscow I was staying in a hotel in which many Trotskyists were arrested.'

This statement seemed so stupid to me that I let it pass with a certain satisfaction. No responsible person reading these things could take them seriously, for, in the same years, from 1934 to 1937, and later still, no lesser personages than Gottwald, Slansky, Kopecky, Geminder and other Party leaders had lived in that same hotel. Did this prove that they were Trotskyists? I hoped that when they read these passages they would question the value of these 'confessions'.

For a while I tried to use these tactics to discredit the reports, because I believed – and this was what I was told every day – that my 'confessions' would be examined by a responsible organ of the Party, consisting of the most qualified comrades from the Political Bureau and the Secretariat.

One day, for example, I admitted that I was responsible for appointing Kratochvil Ambassador to New Delhi, Fischl to Berlin and other similar decisions which came directly from

Gottwald and the Minister. I told myself that it was impossible for Gottwald not to see through all this.

How could I have supposed that Köhler and Siroky would believe 'reports' in which I was charged with things done in France in 1939 and 1940 on their direct orders? I thought they would have the courage to admit this and therefore to refute such charges. But they didn't.

Every objective study of my 'confessions' should show that they were false admissions written under pressure. I hoped this would alert the Party and enable it to change its mind, but I was wrong. The Party leaders cannot be excused on the grounds that the larger the lie is, the more likely it is to be believed, because they knew full well that my 'confessions' were lies to which they had the key.

This, for example, is what Margolius was made to say at his trial:

The prosecutor: 'The investigation has also proved that you committed subversive acts by negotiating the commercial and political agreement with England in 1949.'

Margolius: 'Yes, I concluded this agreement in 1949 according to instructions received from Löbl. The harmful and subversive nature of this agreement lay chiefly in the fact that we were providing considerable advantages for the British capitalists.'

The prosecutor: 'In this agreement you also consented to pay old debts contracted before Munich.'

Margolius: 'At the end of the agreement of compensation I committed the Czech Republic to the payment of debts contracted before Munich and during the war, both by the pre-Munich government and by the émigré government in London. I also consented to pay private capitalists' debts guaranteed by the pre-Munich government. These debts were to be paid principally by the export of leather products and textiles made from imported raw materials which had been paid for in sterling. That meant that the products made from these raw materials were virtually given to Great Britain free . . .'

As Under-Secretary of Foreign Affairs I had been well

acquainted with all the details of this agreement and had read the various telegrams which passed between Margolius (through the Embassy in London), Gottwald, Dolansky, the Vice-Premier, and Gregor, the Minister of Foreign Trade. All the other under-secretaries in the Ministry of Foreign Affairs as well as numerous officials both from my ministry and the Ministry of Foreign Trade were also aware of what was going on.

In this case Margolius had merely carried out the orders received from Gottwald, Dolansky and Gregor to conclude the trade agreement in question with England. And yet these three men allowed the interrogators of Ruzyn and the Soviet advisers to term Margolius's arrangements as crimes, to convict him and sentence him to death without making the slightest attempt to resist.

Similar facts emerged from the charges brought against each of the fourteen defendants.

It was part of the Soviet advisers' tactics to describe as 'crimes' the tasks, treaties, agreements, and activities carried out by the leaders of the Party and the State or under their supervision. By making the defendants responsible for them they held a sword of Damocles over President Gottwald and the rest of them, turning them into frightened and docile instruments bound by perjury.

The interrogators were now trying to find the sources of my Trotskyism, and they established that 'I was originally an anarchist . . .' by using a part of the *curriculum vitae* which I wrote for the Central Committee after my return to Prague in 1948. It concerned my attempt to blow up the Ostrava police station with some comrades when I was sixteen. As I have already said, it never came off owing to the vigilance of the local Party secretary. But with this episode of my youth they constructed a true anarchist's past. I had really entered another world where nothing had the same meaning or the same value.

The combined efforts of Kohoutek and Doubek produced the following formulation, a masterful distortion of partial truth into a huge lie: 'My anarchist tendencies continued in Spain. I felt much closer to and had more respect for the anarchist leaders than those of my own party.'

When I objected Kohoutek and Doubek replied in chorus: 'In view of your anarchist activity in your youth you must have been an anarchist in Spain,' or 'When once one has professed anarchistic views, one keeps them all one's life. So admit that you felt closer to the anarchists than to the communists in Spain!'

And he added: 'Incidentally, this is a mere formality. Just to complete the picture of you. You can't be convicted on this basis because as far as our laws are concerned it is not a punishable crime.'

They knew that the main thing was to minimize the importance of the confessions they were trying to extort. Their last argument was this: 'Anyhow, this is just an administrative report. It's not meant for court.' According to them some reports were just for the files, so that one day there should be evidence that such and such a thing had been written. It was the kingdom of bureaucracy.

But from one administrative report to another the formulations gradually changed, twisted, lost their original meaning. It was no longer a matter of facts or truth, but merely of formulations, a world of scholastics and religious heresies. There were heretical formulations, too, and the purpose was to make the culprit proceed from confession to confession and end by permitting the formulations which really made him guilty. Thus the teams of Ruzyn, composed of cynical and primitive men, managed to wear down our resistance, by their mechanical obstinacy in repeating administrative reports day after day and 'improving' their formulation each time by rewriting it masses of times. You ceased fighting over a word because the rest of the sentence was devoid of meaning. And the word you allowed to pass entailed another phrase, another word which was suggested or imposed on you.

This was how they reconstructed my anarchist, Trotskyist

past, which could only lead to espionage according to the model of the Moscow trials.

There was a ground where this battle of formulations and distortions lost its innocence, and that was the ground of anti-semitism. Soon after my arrest, when I was confronted by a virulent, Nazi-type of antisemitism, I thought it was limited to a few individuals. The Security Services couldn't be expected to recruit saints for such a dirty job. But I now realized that even if this mentality only appeared sporadically during the inter-rogations, it was nevertheless a systematic line.

As soon as a new name cropped up the interrogators insisted on knowing whether or not it was Jewish. The clever ones put the question like this : 'What was his name before? Didn't he change his name in 1945?' If the person really was of Jewish origin the interrogators managed to fit him into a report on some excuse or another which often had nothing to do with the matters in question. And this name was inevitably accompanied by the ritual adjective 'Zionist'.

They were trying to collect the maximum number of Jews in their reports. When I mentioned two or three names, if there was one which 'sounded Jewish', this was the only one they noted. However primitive this system of repetition, it succeeded in giving the impression that the defendant was in contact solely with Jews, or at least with a considerable number of Jews.

And yet the word 'Jew' was never actually used. When, for example, I was questioned about Hajdu, the interrogator crudely asked me to say whether each of the names mentioned was that of a Jew. But when he wrote out his report he replaced 'Jew' by 'Zionist'. 'We are in the Security Services of a people's democracy. The word Jew is an insult. That's why we write "Zionist".'

I pointed out that Zionist had political implications, but he replied that this was not true and that he was following orders. 'Besides,' he added, 'the word Jew is also forbidden in the USSR. They say Hebrew.'

I said there was a difference between Hebrew and Zionist, but it was no good. He explained that Hebrew sounded bad in Czech and he had orders to write 'Zionist'. That was that.

Until the end, the term Zionist was applied to men and women who had nothing to do with Zionism. And when they drew up the reports for the court, the interrogators refused to make any changes. This subsequently turned into a witch hunt. The discriminatory measures against the Jews increased on the pretext that they were foreigners in Czechoslovakia, cosmopolitans and Zionists, more or less involved in espionage.

To begin with, the interrogators vied with each other in their antisemitism. One day I told one of them that I didn't see how it could be applied to the group of former volunteers which, apart from Vales and me, contained no Jews. He answered perfectly seriously: 'You forget their wives. They're all Jewish and that comes to the same thing.'

Ruzyn had a whole theory about this and I often heard it exposed by Kohoutek and the other interrogators. 'In a household it's the wife who rules the roost. If she's Aryan and her husband's a Jew he loses his original characteristics and becomes like his wife. That's your case, Mr London! But if an Aryan marries a Jewess he inevitably falls under her influence and becomes pro-semitic. This plays an important part in the present case because many of our compatriots who had emigrated to the West during the war returned with Jewish wives.

'Svoboda isn't a Jew. But his wife? She's a Bessarabian Jewess. Hromadko isn't a Jew, but his wife is! Zavodsky, Pavel and many others are all in the same situation. What does that prove? That where Jewry has not penetrated directly it has done so indirectly – by giving you Jewish wives.'

When my report was drawn up for the court and when they wrote 'Jewish nationality' (as they did for ten out of fourteen defendants) I asked an interrogator how they had reached this definition, particularly since my father and I were atheists. He replied by learnedly quoting Stalin on the problem of nationality, and concluded by saying that Stalin's five conditions of nationality corresponded to the definition of 'Jewish nationality'. Later the formulation became 'of Jewish origin' – I can't think why – and remained so in the records of the proceedings.

Five

My body and brain were crushed. It was like being in a mill. Round and round we went. The pyramid of my crimes rose. One man was not enough to support it, it needed a good half-dozen.

– Trotskyist activity in Spain and collaboration with the International Commission of the League of Nations, with Field and the American Intelligence Services.

– Collaboration in France with the French police, the Gestapo, and the American Intelligence Services.

– Repatriation of Trotskyists into Czechoslovakia and the other people's democracies during the war so as to betray the secret organizations of the Party and their leaders to the Gestapo and prepare for the future.

– Sending Mirek Klecan to Czechoslovakia during the occupation so as to betray Fucik and the underground Central Committee to the Gestapo.

– The formation of a Trotskyist network based on an espionage network in all the people's democracies.

– Being the delegate of the Fourth International in the Eastern countries.

– Having had contacts and collaborated with the Rajk and Kostov groups.

– Having been in contact with an important group of spies in Hungary (whose name I have forgotten).

– Being the leader of a Trotskyist network in Czechoslovakia centred round the former volunteers from the International Brigades.

– Being the chief resident leader of an American espionage

network in Czechoslovakia directed by Field, a direct collaborator of Allen Dulles.

– Having been in contact with Tito's men and having prepared
a *coup d'état* in Czechoslovakia.

– Being responsible for the death of hundreds of Jews in
France during the war.

– Collaboration with the Gestapo in Mauthausen . . .

In July Major Kohoutek again threatened to arrest my wife. He
told me that the Security Services had long intended to do so,
and that she wouldn't be the first wife of a defendant to be in
this prison. 'You mustn't think that her French citizenship can
protect her. On the contrary. We can easily say she's an agent of
the Second Bureau, that they'd put her onto you. Believe me,
I can find enough witnesses to say that.'

They also attacked my parents-in-law, simple, honest people
who had devoted their lives to their family, the Party. They
were accused of being anti-Party cosmopolitans. If this term
was usually attributed in Ruzyn to Jews, intellectuals and
comrades who had lived abroad during the war, it was particularly absurd to attribute it to my wife's parents. They had come
from Spain to France at the beginning of the century. They had
fled from the hard regions of Aragon whose earth was so poor
that it could not nourish a peasant's family. My wife's father
became a miner. He had joined the French Communist Party
when it was founded in 1921. He had learned to read by painfully
stumbling through the articles in *L'Humanité*. Lise's mother
was a Catholic, but she managed to conciliate communism
with her religion. Frédéric Ricol, my father-in-law, had brought
up his children with a candid, unconditional faith in the
communist ideal. For the whole family the USSR and Stalin
were the incarnation of goodness, the guarantee of a happy
future which would free man from servitude.

My wife's brother was also accused of being a Second
Bureau spy although he had been a much respected militant
communist since his youth. These continual threats against my

wife affected me deeply. I was well enough acquainted with the methods practised in Ruzyn, and I knew the Security would have no difficulty in getting false evidence and carrying out their threat. I knew there were women in the prison and I had often wondered whether Lise was one of them.

I was all the more affected by this threat because that day I had managed to read a report against my wife on Kohoutek's desk, which began with the words: 'Comrade London told me yesterday . . .' And I deduced that she was surrounded by police spies who provided the Security with continuous reports about her. I was later proved right.

This was a new psychological preparation, a new conditioning. I was only to realize later the nature of the turn my interrogations were taking. For the time being it seemed as though a more serious charge was to be brought against me than 'being responsible for the Fourth International in the Eastern countries', a Fourth International 'led by the Trotskyist group of former volunteers from the International Brigades in Czechoslovakia'.

This trial was no longer mentioned. But now Kohoutek claimed that I had not confessed all. I had omitted some very important facts. Furthermore, my 'confessions' only served to cover the real culprits and to shield them from justice.

This, he said, was because I counted on some of the culprits, who occupied important functions in the Party and the state, to help me. 'Your interrogations,' he concluded, 'will not be over until you have confessed everything.'

And the roundabout continued, the interrogations succeeding each other at an infernal rate.

Towards the end of July Kohoutek came to the room where I was being questioned by one of his interrogators, and took me to his office. There he told me that his superiors had just given him some orders concerning my case. After talking to the Party officials, they had authorized him to speak not only in their name but in the Party's name.

The Party, he said, had discovered the existence of a vast

plot against the state directed by some of its leaders. He then started enumerating the names of all the members of the Political Bureau: 'It's not him ... nor him ...' He mentioned them all except for the Secretary General of the Party. 'Do you see who I mean?' asked Kohoutek.

'You mean Slansky?'

'Yes, that's right, Slansky. You are to be interrogated about all the contacts you and the other volunteers of your group had with him; you must say all you know, and give the smallest details.'

He added: 'You're not the first one the Party told us to interrogate about Slansky. We already have numerous statements against him, some of which were made a long time ago.' To convince me, he read a long statement against Slansky without telling me who made it.

'There are plenty of others,' he went on. 'Besides, you yourself have already implicated Slansky.'

'I have?'

'Yes, of course. Haven't you told us that you had nothing to do with the promotion of your accomplices after their return from France? Haven't you said that Slansky himself ordered them to hurry back to Prague, that he met them personally on their arrival and subsequently gave them important posts in the Party and the State?'

My astonishment increased: 'Then why have you so far always prevented me from using those explanations in my defence, and even from mentioning Slansky's name?'

He replied: 'Because you persisted in denying that you were responsible for the Trotskyist group and that you had spied with Field. Now that you have signed your first confessions, the Party thinks we can go further.'

Finally Kohoutek said sententiously: 'Think about it, Mr London. Who do you think gave the order to arrest you and the other volunteers? We couldn't have done it without Slansky's orders. He sacrificed you because he thought he'd save his own skin by throwing you overboard.'

I was stunned by the turn the situation had taken. I had in fact always thought that Slansky, as Secretary General of the Party, was, together with the other Party leaders, primarily responsible for my arrest and that of the other veterans from Spain. That was why he had systematically refused to see me when I had asked him to help me discuss my dealings with Field with the Party, why I had found myself up against that wall of suspicion for nearly two years, and why he had deliberately handed me over to Security, branding me as an enemy. Because of this he had passed over our pleas, had let us be charged for decisions taken by himself or the Secretariat, and had never denied the monstrous distortions made by the Security officials of our true activities in Spain and France, all of which were known to him.

If Slansky was now under arrest* that meant that the Party was aware of the odious machinations of which my comrades and I had been victims. Had the time for explanations come at last; were we at last to be trusted again? If the Party had recovered, was it now going to reveal the fascist gangsters operating in its ranks, men whom I had encountered here in Ruzyn and who practised methods worthy of the Gestapo?

And yet there was one important flaw in my reasoning. Although Kohoutek suggested we were Slansky's victims, he also led us to understand that we were his accomplices. Weren't Kohoutek and his bosses looking for an alibi for what they had done to us?

But this did not change the fact that Slansky was responsible for what was happening to us and many others. From the

* I was wrong. At this stage Slansky was still Secretary General of the Party. A little later, on 31 July 1951, his fiftieth birthday was officially celebrated, and he received the highest honour of the state from President Gottwald. On 6 September, before the Central Committee, he criticized himself and his work in the Party Secretariat. At Gottwald's instigation the Central Committee decided to appoint him Vice-Premier. He was no longer Secretary General but was kept on as a member of the Political Secretariat of the Central Committee, and was only arrested on the night of 23 November 1951.

questions it transpired that most of the regional Party secretaries, who had to be sanctioned by the Secretary General,
had been arrested together with Svermova, Sverma's widow.
Besides, these first reports which Kohoutek showed me and
which implicated Slansky dated from the time of my arrest.
Did that not confirm the suspicion I had always had: that the
enemy was hidden in the Party leadership itself? The arrest of
the veterans from Spain, the trial they tried to bring against us,
must have served as a diversion and enabled them to continue
under disguise . . .

Furthermore, if our trial had not yet taken place as foreseen,
if their plan of repeating Rajk's trial had failed, was this not
because they had failed to obtain my 'confessions', as leader of
the group, as quickly as they had expected, and as quickly as
they should have done to carry out their plan? All this confirmed
that there was some truth in what Kohoutek had said. I clung
to the idea that if the Party had decided to arrest its Secretary
General it knew there was something rotten in the State of
Denmark! Like every prisoner, cut off from reality, I built
castles in the air out of the most fragile hopes.

After all that I had gone through in the last six months, my
brain was no longer capable of rational thought. I was living in
a world which was inside out, and my thoughts and deductions
were shaped after this world of folly.

Six

It was now Kohoutek himself who interrogated me every day. I
thought I would at last be able to see the problem of the former
volunteers from the Brigades in its true light, and continued to
reply frankly and truthfully. I told of facts and events which I
knew about, because I had experienced them myself or had
been informed about them by people who were directly concerned.

One day Kohoutek gave me a pencil and some paper and ordered me to write all I know about my contacts and those of the other volunteers with Slansky. 'It will all be carefully checked by the Party leaders and Gottwald, ' he added. I described in detail the return of the former volunteers who had fought in the French Resistance in July and August 1945.

It was while I was off duty in a house belonging to the FTPF that Tonda Svoboda had written to me. He said that a telegram signed by Slansky had arrived requesting the immediate return to Prague of the Czech Communist cadres, including Holdos, Svoboda, Zavodsky.

They departed in agreement with the French Communist Party of which they had hitherto been members, and a letter signed by Jacques Duclos was sent to the Secretariat of the Czech Communist Party confirming the fact that they had been members of the French Party during the war.

When I returned to Paris they were all in Prague except for Svoboda, who left a few days later. I myself only came into contact with Slansky in spring 1946. Between two sessions of the Eighth Congress of the Czech Communist Party I acted as interpreter between him and Jacques Duclos. He asked me if I was London. When I said I was, he said he had heard a great deal about me and would like me to call on him at his office before returning to France. I went to see him the day before I left, and he received me with Dolansky, a member of the Political Bureau responsible for the International Department of the Central Committee.

Our meeting lasted almost an hour. We discussed various problems about which the French Communist Party had informed Slansky by letter, and he wanted details about the difference of opinion which had existed, after the Liberation of France in 1944, between the leadership of the French Communist Party and certain Czech comrades.

It was on my return from Germany in 1945 that I became aware of the political disagreement amongst some former volunteers from the Brigades in the leadership of the Czech language group of the French Communist Party. Under the influence of the leaders of the communist emigrants in London, they had started to create organizations of the Czech Communist Party in France, particularly in the Nord and the Pas-de-Calais areas where there were numerous refugees.

The leaders of the French Party had opposed this decision, maintaining that the economic and political refugees in the French Communist Party were submitted to Party discipline and had to carry out its instructions like the French members. Nobody had the right to meddle in the affairs of the French Communist Party, and above all not to create organizations of a foreign Communist Party in France.

The matter remained unsettled. Nevertheless, the Secretariat of the French Communist Party had informed its opposite number in Czechoslovakia and had reiterated its attitude to the problem.

Slansky then spoke to me about three comrades who had been penalized by the French Communist Party for their conduct during the war and who occupied important positions in Czechoslovakia in spite of this. When I showed surprise, Slansky replied that these were all matters of the past, that everyone must be given a fair chance and that today, in the country's new situation, there was a lack of experienced cadres.

With regard to the problem of the veterans from Spain who had returned to Czechoslovakia, Slansky told me that, in his opinion, some of them did not occupy the function which corresponded to their capacities. He hoped that in the future they would be promoted to more important posts where they could be of greater use. He had named, Pavel, Hromadko, Svoboda, Zavodsky, Nekvasil . . .

At the end of our meeting Slansky asked me whether I would agree to return to Prague and work for the Party. I refused, telling him about my family and my bonds with the French Communist Party with which I had worked for many years and of which I now felt part. Slansky insisted, saying that if I returned I could work for the Cadre Department of the Central

Committee as Comrade David's assistant. He added that this would be an excellent change in the department since he and Gottwald considered David to be incompetent and wanted to replace him. In fact I was to be the one to direct this department.

He also told me that a Congress of European Partisans was soon to be held in Prague and he hoped that Prague would be chosen as the centre of the future European Federation of Partisans. This would strengthen the Party's position in the country, he said, in view of the major role it had played in the Resistance. He asked me to mention this plan in Paris and to come back the next day for the letter he was going to write to the Association des FTPF about these problems. So I saw him once more just before my departure.

At this stage I was rather surprised by the casual way in which the cadre problem was treated, and yet, accustomed as I was to the methods of the French Party and having been away from Czechoslovakia for many years, I told myself that I was not in the position to give a correct verdict.

In autumn 1946 I went to Prague to consult the Ministries of Culture and of Foreign Affairs about the weekly review *Parallèle 50* and the Czech Information Bureau in Paris. On this occasion I saw Slansky a third time. During this meeting Slansky asked me about the political situation in France, in the presence of Geminder who now directed the International Department of the Central Committee. Both of them regretted that Prague should be so ill-informed about the situation in France and asked me if I would act as correspondent of the International Political review, *Svetove Rozhledy*, which was edited by the Central Committee. I agreed.

This was what I said about my dealings with Slansky. But when Kohoutek saw what I had written he flew into a rage and left the room, saying he would consult his 'real chiefs'. When he came back an hour later he said his chief had refused my statements and tore up the pages I had written.

'I had appealed to you in the name of the Party and now

you've written a bad novelette. If you continue to behave like this it will be proof that you are still lying to the Party and covering up for men whom we know are guilty, because we have full evidence of a conspiracy against the State. You well know that I alone, a mere captain in State Security, am in no position to interrogate you about the Secretary General of the Party. You well know that I could not do this without special orders from the highest officials in the Party. I have already shown you some of the material against Slansky, part of which is several months old. If the Party has now decided to put an end to this business in spite of Slansky's position that means that it is in possession of irrefutable evidence against him. You must trust the Party and let it guide you. If you refuse to be guided by the Party's interest we shall use methods of which you have never even dreamt. And you might well not leave this place alive.'

During the next days, until the end of August, Kohoutek behaved with me like a fisherman slowly hauling in his fish, inch by inch, despite its jumps, somersaults and desperate attempts to escape.

Slansky's telegram to Paris in 1945, in which he urgently demanded the return of the former volunteers to Prague, my conversation with him in 1946, when he mentioned his intention of promoting some of them to leading posts, now constituted 'proof' of the criminal complicity between myself, the former volunteers and Slansky.

The few articles which I contributed to *Svetove Rozhledy* and the other Party periodicals became 'acts of sabotage and espionage performed on Slansky's order in the progressive French movement.'

The letter I was to give to the Association des FTPF in Paris proposing Prague as the centre of the future European Federation of Partisans constituted proof of my complicity with Slansky in order to strengthen his personal position in Czechoslovakia by exploiting for his benefit the partisan movement 'of which he has considered himself the organizer, ever since his brief visit to Czech territory during the national Slovak rising . . .'

When I was first questioned about my conversation with Slansky in 1946, I said that it had taken place in Dolansky's presence and this circumstance had been noted; but in the same report, later, it was omitted.

As I emphasized the fact that Dolansky witnessed the entire meeting with Slansky, Kohoutek said that on no account was Dolansky's name to be mentioned in the report; that he was not asking me about him but about Slansky. He therefore worded it as follows: 'When Dolansky left the room for a few minutes, Slansky asked me . . .'

In the next reports Dolansky's name was omitted altogether and all that remained was the conversation between 'two accomplices'. Out of a conversation which lasted about an hour, and a five minute farewell meeting, Ruzyn produced 'a conversation which lasted intermittently for two days. . . '

So, thanks to linguistic acrobatics, tendentious interpretations, and pure and simple lies, the report on my 'hostile activities and my complicity with Slansky, materialized. By this sleight of hand the Trotskyist group of the former volunteers from the International Brigades became an integral part of the 'centre of conspiracy against the state'.

Thus 'our group', originally independent, and intended to lead to something like the Rajk trial, was now a mere branch of the 'Centre' and if I, as a group leader, was one of the fourteen leaders of the 'centre of conspiracy against the state led by Rudolf Slansky', 'my accomplices' were integrated and tried for matters which led off from the major trial – with the exception of Pavel who was tried on his own. As for Laco Holdos, he was to be accused first of 'Trotskyism' and then of 'bourgeois Slovak nationalism' and was sentenced for this with the Novomesky–Husak group in 1954.

When I signed my first 'confessions' I was in a terrible state of moral and physical exhaustion. The 'roundabout' had led me to the limits of human resistance. The idea that this miserable existence might continue was unbearable. I was through. I had neither the physical nor moral strength to fight on, to deny and still less to retract my first 'confessions'. And yet something in me still resisted.

Seven

Kohoutek started to draw up the 'partial administrative reports'. Resting on the principle that two precautions were better than one, he claimed not only that the administrative reports were not 'definitive' but that these 'partial' reports had to be co-ordinated. Before coming to the report 'for the court', therefore, the defendant would have every chance of explaining himself, of making the changes which he might deem necessary for his defence. These administrative reports only served to 'facilitate the work in progress'.

Then he felt he had to add subsidiary explanations. He must have thought the matter extremely important and went to infinite pains to obtain the wordings which fitted into the new idea concocted by the Soviet advisers. So this was what he said: 'In your report for the court, there will be two parts: one accusing you, one exonerating you. In this second part you can include everything in your favour or what you consider to be extenuating circumstances. So it's quite normal that we should only write down the negative points here. It's not for us to write your defence. Besides, you'll have a lawyer with whom you can discuss all that.'

This was a monstrous lie. When we got to the report 'for the court' the order was given that on no account were the interrogators' wordings to be diluted; on the contrary, they were to be made harder. And never again was this 'second part' mentioned.

In civilized countries this is known as extortion of signature. But here extortion of signature had been elevated into a theory.

Once months of torture had broken a man's resistance on one point this theory enabled the interrogator to obtain signature after signature, report after report, compiling the mountain of papers which, in this system of criminal bureaucracy, served as truth and facts. Indeed, why should the defendant continue this unequal struggle if he has been told that he will be able to defend himself in court? But at that point only the signatures which had been extorted would count. And how could you then make people believe that not one, but dozens, of signatures had been extorted? How could you fail to be crushed by this mountain of signatures confirming the negative side? To begin with, you had not understood the plan of the Soviet advisers and the interrogators; you had let slightly distorted statements pass because you had no idea what they were leading to. You would have realized, had you been guilty. But since you had nothing to do with this caricature or with the character attributed to you, you couldn't see what was going on. And the interrogator took advantage of your exhaustion, your inattentiveness, your ignorance and good faith.

Sometimes I fought for a whole day over a word, for days and nights over a sentence. But nothing put Kohoutek off. When I tried to go back on what I had said, either because he had attributed tendentious political interpretations to it or because he had skipped entire passages of my explanations, he said, perfectly seriously: 'You're a politician and your statements must be drawn up accordingly. You have been in prison for so long that you know nothing of what is going on outside. There are too many useless things in your statements. But we, who know about the conspiracy against the state, we know what the Party needs.'

There was no more objective truth. No more facts. For them a politician was simply someone who knew how to lie and say what the Party needed, who distorted facts, a man's life, ideas, and deepest convictions, in *their* way, the way which suited *them* one day, one month, one week. And it was always the same magical incantation: 'You must trust the Party, let it guide you. It's in your own interest.' He ended on an almost paternal note: 'I'm talking to you in the name of the Party.' I, Kohoutek, the torturer, the creator of lies and the extortioner of signatures.

He took no pains to hide how little he cared about the heap of statements which he had accumulated when they impeded his new formulation instead of corroborating it. He dropped numerous charges and 'confessions' of my fellow defendants in the 'Trotskyist group' of the former volunteers from the Brigades. But on the other hand he introduced new charges, which were to fit the new character I was to assume in the Slansky conspiracy. He had to 'prove' that 'over a long period, until my arrest, both in Prague and elsewhere:

–'I had concerted successively with the other leaders of the conspiracy (Slansky, Geminder, Frejka, Frank, Clementis, Reicin, Svab, Hajdu, Löbl, Margolius, Fischl, Sling, Simone) or with other persons in an attempt to destroy the independence of the Republic and the people's democratic regime as guaranteed by the Constitution. For this purpose, we had established contact with a foreign power and with foreign authorities. . .

–'I had been in contact with a foreign power or with foreign authorities in order to reveal state secrets; I had committed this act although I had been especially instructed not to impart these secrets and knew that the post I occupied entailed the utmost secrecy; I had betrayed state secrets of particular importance in a particularly dangerous way, on a vast scale, and over a long period of time. . . ' *

My role as leader of the Trotskyist group of former volunteers from Spain now faded away. It was no longer of primary importance. What now came to the fore in my reports was my active participation – as one of the fourteen leaders – in the centre of conspiracy against the state. I was put in the group from the Ministry of Foreign Affairs together with Clementis,

* These were the charges for which I was tried and sentenced. See the book *The trial of the leaders of the conspiracy against the state led by Rudolf Slansky*, Orbis, Prague, 1953.

Geminder and Hajdu. This, under Geminder's leadership, became one of the branches of the centre of conspiracy. Together with Vavro Hajdu and others I was an active member of it and acted as Geminder's liaison agent.

Furthermore, I carried out my enemy activity in the Ministry of Foreign Affairs with the complicity of the bourgeois nationalist Clementis.

I was the intermediary between Slansky and the British member of Parliament, Zilliacus, who was himself accused of espionage.

I was an American spy in direct contact with Noel Field and in the pay of Allen Dulles.

For over three weeks in August Kohoutek tirelessly reshaped the reports. Every time he had written a page or two, he would leave the room to show what he had done to the 'real chiefs', as he called them proudly. When he returned he rewrote the pages in front of me, altering the text according to his orders, or else told me crudely that the text of my 'confessions' would not be final until it had been translated and approved by his superiors.

This eagerness and obstinacy had something confusing about it. I could not imagine that for so long, and so meticulously, someone could work in such detail on the formulations. Kohoutek retyped the text bit by bit, extorting my signature at each change. From change to change, from extract to extract, I felt the original was sliding into the distance although it retained something familiar about it. The intention was to put everything out of my control, to stop the words from being mine, to separate me from my acts and thoughts. But not too much in case I rebelled and interrupted this continuous process of wearing me down.

It took an unforeseen incident, a chance event, to enable me to have a precise image of the mill in which Kohoutek wanted to crush me.

Towards the end of August 1951, when the administrative reports were beginning to form an impressive mass, I was surprised to see Kopriva, the Minister of Security, and Doubek, head of Ruzyn, enter the room where Kohoutek was laboriously writing out his formulations.

'So you've decided to talk at last. It's your only hope,' Doubek said as an opening gambit.

He listened to the interrogation for a moment and then started asking me questions. I still vividly remembered our first meeting, the 'We'll destroy you with or without your confessions' with which it had ended.

As he had refused to believe me then, before I had signed anything, and while I was fighting tooth and nail to show the Party the truth and denounce the persecution of which I was the object, I knew he would not believe anything which went against his preconceived idea.

If, on 3 April, he had rejected my defence as an attempt to trick the Party, my only chance to get a hearing from him was to play his game, but to take advantage of his presence in order to answer his questions as objectively as possible. In other words, not to question my guilt in general, but to give a truthful answer to every single question and prove to him the difference between my authentic answers and the ones which had been 'treated' by Kohoutek and his 'real chiefs'. Kopriva could not be unaware of this, since he had entered the room holding my 'administrative reports', and referred to them when he asked his questions.

He seemed to be checking my reports: he asked me who led the group of former volunteers from Spain, in Czechoslovakia. I replied that it was originally Pavel, but that after my return I had shared the responsibility with him. To his question: 'Who elected or designated Pavel?' I replied: 'Nobody! He was neither elected nor designated. He was regarded as an authority by all the volunteers because he had had the highest military rank in Spain and had always been an officer of the International Brigades.' I added: 'The same applied to me. In Spain and France I had always occupied important political functions, which was why I retained my authority among the former volunteers.'

Kopriva seemed surprised by my answers. He asked me if Pavel had mentioned his collaboration with Slansky to me. I said no. 'Then how do you know he was working with Slansky?' I replied, as everyone knew, that Pavel was on a labour commission directed by Slansky and that in February 1948 Slansky had proposed him as leader of the workers' militia. I also explained that in 1946, when we met, Slansky had spoken well of Pavel to me and had said that he intended to use him for a better purpose, like all the other veterans from Spain. I added that Slansky was well informed about the problems of the former volunteers in France, and had been told about them both by the Party leadership and by me during our meeting in Dolansky's presence.

I saw him leaf through the report, looking for Dolansky's name. But, as I have said, it had disappeared.

Kopriva seemed irritated. He asked me: 'Then why do the former volunteers all stick up for each other?' 'Out of comradeship.' 'Why did you distribute them in every organ of the state, as you did in the Ministry of Foreign Affairs?' 'Because I knew them. Besides, they were good men.' 'Give me their names,' he replied roughly. 'Bieheller, Lastovicka, Farber, Veivoda, Bukacek, Ickovic, Hosek, Ourednicek. . .' but Kopriva interrupted me: 'Ah, because you think they're better than you? You're all the same.'

I saw that his attitude to the volunteers had not changed. He asked again: 'Why and for what purpose did you distribute the former volunteers in the various state offices?' 'I had no purpose,' I said. And since he started insisting, I replied in confusion: 'We had no purpose, but if that is objectively considered as a weakening of the state, and since every weakening of the state is to a certain extent an act of sabotage, and every act of sabotage leads to a definitive weakening of socialism and strengthening of the forces aiming to restore capitalism. . .'

Kopriva listened to me in astonishment. He now spoke about

Hasek, Slansky's brother-in-law, whom I had met in Switzerland where he was the CTK (Czech Press Agency) correspondent. He reminded me of a conversation we had had together after February 1948 about Slansky, a conversation about which Kohoutek had drawn up a report. On his return from Prague Hasek had told me that Ruda (Slansky) was now to assume full responsibility for the Party leadership since the President (Gottwald) was going to concentrate on his functions as a representative, as Dimitrov had done.

Gradually, intrigued by my answers, Kopriva started to argue with me as though we were exchanging views. He said that Hasek was not always to be taken seriously. I replied that that was how Hasek saw the problem and that I was only repeating what he had said years earlier.

Kopriva seemed both dissatisfied and disconcerted by my answers. Despite my apprehension of the consequences of my act, I was satisfied that this time, at least, he had listened to me, and hoped that my replies may have sown the seeds of doubt in his mind as to what was going on here in Ruzyn, especially since, throughout our conversation, Kohoutek, who was standing behind Doubek and Kopriva, continued to make threatening signs to me.

After Kopriva and Doubek had left, Kohoutek took me to task. He said that my attitude towards the Minister had been disgraceful, that the other defendants interrogated by him had answered satisfactorily, and that my attitude could have serious consequences. With these words he sent me back to my cell.

Later on in the evening Kohoutek called me back to his office. He was furious and told me that he had been reprimanded by his superiors because of me; that he hadn't been hard enough with me; that my replies had upset the Minister and had made him doubt the veracity of my 'confessions'. But he added that his 'friends' had spoken to him and managed to convince him, and that they hoped to 'provide the President with a good report despite the bad impression made by your replies'.

Kohoutek then started reproaching me, and told me 'to get it into my skull once and for all that I must sustain "my confessions" in every circumstance and in front of everybody, because otherwise my head, and my family's existence, would be at stake'.

The next days Kohoutek continued to draw up his 'administrative reports'. Before finishing he said that 'the parts of the report which we have so far drawn up with you have been submitted to President Gottwald. He was satisfied and said that we must continue along these lines with London.'

So, whatever I did, I had to yield to this evidence. The Soviet advisers and their henchmen in Ruzyn would always have the last word with Gottwald and the Party leaders.

On several occasions Kohoutek repeated to me that my attitude towards Kopriva was held against me, and that I must take care not to repeat it if another chance ever presented itself, especially after what the President had said.

After the first general manipulation of my 'confessions' Kohoutek told me, at the beginning of September, that he was going on holiday. He warned me once more: 'If you want to stay alive and if you want your wife to be spared don't take advantage of my absence to go back on what you've said. Think of your children.'

I no longer had any reason to doubt Kohoutek's threats. Kopriva's change of face and Gottwald's satisfaction cannot have been inventions. I realized the futility of my resistance and the impossibility of telling the truth to anyone who might believe me, to anyone who was not taking part in the roundabout of the Soviet advisers. I stood before the abyss and never before had I thought it so deep.

Eight

For the first time in over seven months I remained in my cell without being interrogated. For the first time I was given permission to smoke and managed to hide seventy cigarettes. During Major Kohoutek's last interrogation I stole some matches.

I started thinking about Lise, our children and her parents, and I was more worried about them than ever. I wanted this tragedy to end as soon as possible so that my family should be spared, so that they should forget me and go on living. But would they be left in peace?

My letters could contain no messages or hints. When a passage seemed suspect the censor returned my letter and I had to write it again. 'Darling Lise, how boring and monotonous my letters must seem, but I can't help it. I can easily imagine and understand your desire to know what is happening to me, as you ask impatiently in your letters. But I can't write about my case and you will understand that my correspondence must be limited to the most personal things. And what can I write about my present life? My days are so alike. You mustn't ask what is happening to me. Tell me about Michel, Françoise, Gérard. . .'

How hard the life in store for them would be, all the harder because of their faith in me and their hope. How could they guess that we had already said our last farewell? They would believe me to be guilty. But if they were ever to know the truth, they would suffer still more. It was better they keep their illusions and forget me.

A dull roar of thunder and blinding flashes of lightning made me look up at the sky which was now a greyish black, streaked with the green traces of the lightning flashes. The damp wind swept through my cell and large drops drummed on the window panes. The smell of damp meadows gave the air I was breathing a sweetish quality.

It must have been marvellous to feel one's face whipped by the wind, the drops run down one's hair, one's forehead, nose and cheeks. I wanted to be with the people I loved, with Lise and the children. Why did I have to end in such misery, and why did it last so long? I was crying, and in despair I started knocking my head against the wall – I just wanted to get it over with, once and for all.

The cell door opened noisily. The warder burst in and shouted: 'You don't know how to behave in prison! It must be your dirty conscience. But it's too late now.'

He pushed me to the basin, tore my shirt off and held my head and shoulders under the cold tap.

I decided to take advantage of Kohoutek's departure and kill myself. I started by not eating or drinking for four days so as to weaken myself. Lacking the courage to prolong my hunger, I graduated to the second stage of my suicide. I had saved fifty cigarettes which I crumbled into my soup and I added the heads of dozens of matches which I had stolen. I ate it all, hoping that my body, enfeebled by my recent hunger strike and brutal treatment, would not resist nicotine and sulphur poisoning.

I was very ill. I thought I had at last succeeded, and only just managed to hide my condition from the warders. I suffered the most terrible pains, but once again I had failed.

At this point Dr Sommer had me transferred from my cell to the infirmary. Indeed, my physical state was such that he thought I needed treatment if my interrogations were to be continued. I received injections and medicines, but had no idea what they were. I remained in solitary confinement and only left the infirmary to be led to my trial. When the interrogations resumed I was permitted to sit on a corner stool.

Nine

Much later I was to discover that Lise had not abandoned me. Towards the end of September 1951, after she had failed repeatedly to obtain a hearing from the Party and the Security Services in order to clear up my problem, she wrote Klement Gottwald a long letter:

Dear Comrade,

I am appealing to you personally, as President of our Party, to tell you what I know about the case of my husband, Artur London, with whom I have lived for sixteen years and who has been under arrest for eight months.

Before joining my husband in Prague at the beginning of 1949 I was a member of the French Communist Party where I performed important functions. I was elected at the Tenth and re-elected at the Eleventh Congress of the Party Central Control Commission. I have been national secretary of the Union des Femmes françaises since its first congress in 1945, and a communist since 1931. I have never belied the Party's trust in me, or failed to perform any task assigned to me during or after the war. I appeal to you, dear comrade, as a communist conscious of my duties and responsibilities in order to clear up my husband's case.

I read with care and attention the criticisms which you formulated at the last Central Committee meeting about the work of the Central Committee Secretariat. You referred to the choice of cadres and the attention which must be paid to comrades in responsible positions. I would like to inform you briefly of the circumstances in which London was appointed cadre director in the Ministry of Foreign Affairs.

My wife then outlined my *curriculum vitae* starting with my departure for Moscow in 1933, emphasizing that 'in the underground, London worked under the direct control of the French Communist Party in highly responsible posts.' She mentioned that the French Communist Party had wanted me to stay in France and direct the Main d'Oeuvre Immigré, that my health was poor and had necessitated my stay in Switzerland.

When my husband was appointed Under-Secretary of Foreign Affairs the Party Secretariat gave him neither an assistant nor the advice necessary for his work. After his appointment he tried to meet Slansky in order to discuss his job, but was never received by him. As far as I know he was not even allowed to see Kopriva, who then directed the Central Cadre Department.

I gather that at a meeting of the Party organization of the Ministry of Foreign Affairs my husband was accused of sabotaging the training school for the workers' cadres. I can bear witness before the Party and before you, dear comrade, to the enthusiasm with which he prepared this school and the inadequate assistance given by the Secretariat of the Central Committee to his organization, as far as the recruiting of the cadres was concerned. The school was ready, but the pupils were lacking. Since the proposals of the Secretariat of the Central Committee had still not arrived, my husband decided to put into practice Stalin's advice to bureaucrats: 'chairs don't have legs to walk with', and he sent some employees from the Cadre Department to recruit pupils in the various provinces with the help of the regional Party Committees. He then submitted these candidates to the Central Cadre Department of the Central Committee for approval. As far as I can remember Comrade Geminder had agreed to this, and this was how he managed to inaugurate the first school. I know that my husband was subsequently criticized severely during a meeting of the Central Committee's Commission for Foreign Affairs. I believe it was by Slansky himself who had taken up the accusations of Sling, the regional secretary of Brno, and described my husband's methods as 'partisan'. Subsequently it was the Central Committee Cadre Department which recruited the pupils, and my husband complained of the difficulties resulting from the choice of cadres.

She went on:

With regard to the way in which the employees of the Party apparatus meddled in the Ministry's affairs by passing over the heads of Ministers and Under-Secretaries, and giving orders which did not correspond to the line chosen by the Ministers, I must remind you that London had drawn the attention of both Geminder and Siroky to this error a year earlier.

Another question I would like to raise is the intervention of the State Security Services in the life of the Ministry of Foreign Affairs (and I suppose the same applies to the other ministries and offices) – interventions largely concerning the staff. By abusing their privileges as members of State Security these people spoke directly to the employees of the Ministry, passing over the heads of the normal leaders, and asking them for every sort of information. These methods created an atmosphere of uncertainty, distrust and fear among the employees in the Ministries. London complained about it to Zavodsky, and informed Siroky, who said he was right and that he would mention the matter to Kopriva and you, unless it stopped.

There is no doubt that London was depressed by these methods and all the difficulties with which he was faced.

Lise gave a detailed account of my dealings with Field and again expressed her certainty that I was a victim of provocation and that there were hidden enemies in the Party and the Security Services who 'were trying to distract the Party's attention from their own dealings by magnifying the London case'.

She explained to Gottwald that on 26 March, two months after my arrest, she had told Bruno Köhler in person and had then informed Comrade Kopriva in writing about all the matters which might elucidate my case.

I thought, since I have been London's wife for sixteen years and a communist for twenty, that it was logical and normal that I should be interrogated after my husband's arrest. I know all about his life and his work as well as his political ideas. It goes without saying that, as a conscientious communist, I can only act and speak in the Party's interest about all I know, even if it works against my husband. I thought that my statements could help clear up the London case, and wrote to the State Security last June asking to be questioned. The comrade to whom I applied promised that I would be, but I wasn't. In July I wrote to Comrade Köhler, responsible for the Cadre Department, in order to renew my plea to be interrogated and inform the Party about what I know. I also maintained that my husband was innocent and that the Party would end by finding out the truth and clearing up my husband's case. If the truth were against him, I, as a communist, would submit to reality: our sixteen years together, as well as the fact that he is the father of my three children, would not weigh heavy on my conscience.

To this last letter, written frankly and honestly, I was amazed to receive the following reply:

Czech Communist Party
Secretariat of the Central Committee
Ref. IV/Ba/Ka-809

> Prague, 13 July 1951
> Comrade Lise Ricol-Londonova
> Na Dyrince 1
> Prague XIX

Comrade,

With reference to your letter addressed to Comrade Köhler, who is now on holiday, I must reply as follows: you want to tell us all you know about your husband, but from the tone of your letter it is evident that you intend to defend him. This is known as 'acting in favour of the defendant' and we cannot allow it. I advise you to behave like a disciplined Party member and give your views to the court when they are asked for.

> Comradely greetings,
> Baramova.

Let me reply to this as follows, Comrade Gottwald:

1) When I appealed to the Cadre Department of the Central Committee I did so as a Party member, convinced that I was addressing that organ of the Party in charge of helping its members solve their personal and their Party problems. The reply I received does not appear to come from the Cadre Department of the Central Committee but from the public prosecutor addressing a false witness.

I am proud to be a communist and I realize that my whole life and work give me the right to carry my head high, and I cannot allow Comrade Baramova or anyone else to treat me like this.

2) Comrade Baramova's reference to acting in favour of the defendant would mean that a communist is not allowed to express his opinion on the Party if this is not in accordance with the accepted Party line at a certain moment. This would mean no more nor less than gagging criticism and creating an atmosphere which prevents people from adopting personal responsibilities through fear.

3) In my opinion this attitude is directly opposed to WHAT YOU

PREACH; in other words that each member should appeal to the Party confidently and trustfully and submit his thoughts and opinions to it. Such an attitude as that of the Cadre Department towards me means that it is impossible for communists to confide in the Party.

I beg of you, dear comrade, to do whatever is necessary for me to be heard by the Party and tell all I know about my husband.

In the last weeks before his arrest I too suffered because of the life my husband was forced to lead. In spite of this my political confidence in him has not been shaken. This confidence rests on the fact that all his political activity can be checked and that sixteen years in common have made it possible for me to vouch for his total loyalty towards the Party even during the most difficult periods.

I am sure that I have not applied to you in vain and I am confident, now that the Party leadership is in your hands, that the Party will find a just solution to this whole business.

With sincere communist greetings,

Lise Ricol-Londonova.

Lise's last sentence alluded to Slansky's departure from the General Secretariat of the Party and his promotion to Vice-Premier.

It is hard to imagine what Gottwald's reaction must have been when he read this letter. He already knew of the sort of charges which were held against Slansky and Geminder, and this ingenuous, frank appeal should have warned him that something was wrong, if he had been able to read it objectively. It should have proved to him the inanity of the conspiracy in which they were trying to implicate me and which Lise, who knew nothing about it, almost disproved. But Gottwald was too involved in the whole process of repression to hear a word 'in favour of the defendant'.

Some ten days after Lise had personally presented this letter to President Gottwald's secretary in Hradcany Castle, she was summoned to the headquarters of the Central Committee. The signatory of the summons, whose name she had forgotten, met her and showed her into a room where another individual arrived a few minutes later and sat behind a desk. His first gesture had been to light a lamp and turn it full in my wife's face. 'You have asked to be heard. What do you want?'

In spite of her surprise my wife saw a flicker of hope – the man opposite her spoke with a Russian accent; (from her description he sounded like Janousek). She thought that the Soviets, who had heard of the terrible things going on in Czechoslovakia, had decided to lead a counter-investigation, and that thanks to them the truth would come to light. Had she not tried to alert the leadership of the Bolshevik Communist Party a few months before my arrest, by submitting a report, including my *curriculum vitae*, on my various activities in Spain, in France, in the concentration camp and after my return to Prague?

She had mentioned the Field case, putting it in its true light, and had handed this report to a girl who had been brought up in the Soviet Union and worked in a department of the Ministry of Foreign Affairs. Lise had met her through a veteran from Spain, and she claimed to be in direct contact with the Soviet ambassador. Lise was so pleased to have found this thread – which must have led directly to the Soviet advisers.

So now my wife recapitulated the various points of her long letter to Gottwald. She added certain details or facts, and spoke with full conviction: it was so easy to check the sources of my activity. The man sat, impassive and immobile as a statue, without saying a word. When Lise stopped, waiting for him to ask a question, he didn't budge: 'Is that all?'

Lise was disconcerted. She began her explanations all over again, trying to stick to the points which she considered most important for me. But she came up against the same silence, the same motionless face and expressionless eyes which stared at her without blinking. She stopped. Then she asked:

'Can you tell me what's happening to my husband, what he's accused of? He's been under arrest for almost eight months and I know no more about him than I did the first day. The three letters I received from him told me nothing. You must know whether he's guilty or innocent and I have the right to know the truth, both as his wife and as a communist.'

Then the man replied: 'There's no charge against your husband. He's still in detention under suspicion and the investigation isn't over yet. He may well be released. All you can do is to wait patiently, go on writing to him. If things get any worse for him the Party would inform you and help you.'

Lise, ready to clutch at the smallest straw, could hardly contain herself for joy. *After eight months I was not regarded as a culprit. Nothing was lost yet, and the real culprits were soon to be unmasked. Everything would sort itself out.* And then, for the first time, she had been heard.

Lise's last meeting with André Simone, the foreign editor of the communist daily *Rude Pravo*, towards the end of November 1951, illustrates the illusions which countless comrades still cherished. Simone lived with his wife, not far from my family. Lise and her parents used to come across him when they went for a walk, or did their shopping. Instead of avoiding them, as most of our former acquaintances did, he was always kind and said something encouraging. One evening – it was after the news of Slansky's arrest on 23 November 1951 had been publicly announced – my wife found herself in the same tram as Simone in Wenceslas Square. He called her and sat down next to her.

'Your troubles will soon be over,' he told her suddenly. 'With Slansky's arrest everything becomes clear. It is he who was responsible for the arrest of your husband and so many other comrades. If he's been arrested it's because Gottwald has seen through him. I've just written a long report to Klement Gottwald, full of supporting facts which will help reveal the catastrophic policy of Slansky and his men. You know that Gottwald has criticized the cadre policy of the Party Secretariat over the last years. Even I have been persecuted. But now I'm sure that the black period we've been through will soon be over. Keep hoping, Lise, everything will turn out all right.' He then told her about how he had been discriminated against for months on end.

'He was in a very good mood that evening,' my wife later told me, 'optimistic, ten years younger. He seemed like a wrestler just about to enter the ring.'

And yet we were all old Party members, with a rich and varied experience in various sectors of the international communist movement. We wanted to be good Marxists, realists. But we were living outside reality, in our dream world. In the hardest moments we clung to our illusions, hoped for a miracle and stopped short of that truth which frightened us and which we didn't want to know. . .

André Simone was arrested in his turn a few months after this last meeting with Lise. A year later he was one of the fourteen defendants in the trial of the leaders of the centre of conspiracy against the state . . . He appeared with Slansky and as Slansky's accomplice.

Ten

I had been under arrest for nearly nine months now. I had known Koldeje and its cells, the unbearable physical and psychological tortures, Smola's outbursts of rage and Kohoutek's interrogations. And yet, if they had told me that, when Kohoutek came back after his holidays, the questioning would continue every day for another twelve months and that I would have to watch the reports being rewritten an incalculable number of times, I wouldn't have believed them.

I can now see certain keys to these tactics. Slansky's arrest in November was followed by that of Geminder and others. Their interrogations and 'confessions' necessarily entailed new formulations in the administrative reports of the men who, like myself, had to be included in the trial. But when I was interrogated about them and when Kohoutek made them out to have always been traitors to the Party, I thought that they had already been under arrest for some months. I don't believe that any man can imagine the Party leaders capable of letting such charges accumulate against the other Party leaders, without their knowledge and while they remained free, at their posts, for weeks and months on end.

It was not until September that Slansky was promoted from Secretary General of the Party to Vice-Premier – a disgrace, but a gilded disgrace. Indeed, what was happening to us is an excellent illustration of the means of fabricating such a trial. First the charges, the crimes, the framework of the trial were set up and only then were the victims, the designated culprits, arrested.

But at the depths of my isolation in Ruzyn, in spite of what I had already gathered of the mechanism of the reports, the extortion of confessions and signatures, the whole prefabricated side of the case I was involved in, I was incapable of understanding the cause of months of rewriting. Twelve months spent connecting these mendacious and shameful reports – the end of the autumn, a long winter, a whole spring, a summer and another autumn. . .

They inserted fragments, distorted them and redistorted them. They passed from 'administrative reports' to 'preparatory reports' and 'reports for the court'. They lifted passages from the reports of the other defendants with whom I had no connection in order to insert them, out of context, in my reports. They transformed these passages into personal declarations against my fellow defendants, while passages from my reports were treated the same way.

It was called 'the coordination of the material in our possession'.

I can still remember certain changes, maybe the ones I fought hardest against, or the ones that struck and humiliated me most. I remember one interminable battle that went on all night. Perhaps I only retained what I could understand clearly. I understood, for example, that by rewriting something they ended by forging the whole sense of it. The mere suppression of a name led to wonders. I repeated for the umpteenth time: 'In

1940 I was put into contact with Feigl by Siroky. Siroky told me to remain in touch with him, to entrust him with certain tasks for the Party and to cash the cheques he gave the Party every month. Until 1940 Siroky himself kept in touch with him and cashed the money. Siroky then told me that Feigl had been expelled from the Austrian Party in 1937 but that it had been a mistake. He told me that he knew all about the case, and that he was determined to have it revised after the war. And sure enough, in 1945, Feigl was called back to the Czech Communist Party by a decision of the Central Committee.'

This is how these facts were interpreted in my report:

'In 1940 I entered into contact with Feigl although I knew he had previously been revealed as a Party enemy and expelled from the Austrian Party; in spite of that, I told Feigl to perform various tasks for the Party and accepted monthly sums from him at a time when I knew that the money came from American capitalists.'

The way these questions were formulated and the way the answers were written down invariably proved our guilt:

Question: 'When and where did you start your espionage dealings with the American agent Noel Field?'

Answer: 'In 1947, in his office at the Unitarian Service in Geneva.'

They refused to record the facts in their full complexity, on the pretext 'we're not writing your defence.'

Question: 'It is known that the Aid Department for the Czechs in Marseilles was a branch of the American intelligence services and that during the war it supported your Trotskyist group of former volunteers from the International Brigades financially. Name the members of this Trotskyist group who received money.'

Answer: 'Holdos, Zavodsky, Svoboda, etc.'

The interrogators refused to write anything but the names.

The continual repetition of the same word, the same phrase, went on for hours, days, nights, and weeks on end . . . until it penetrated your brain, like the Chinese torture of the water drop.

When the interrogator questioned me about the 'Trotskyist' group of former volunteers in Marseilles, he asked:

'What group, Mr London?'

'The group of former volunteers in Marseilles.'

'The Trotskyist group, Mr London! Let's start again. What group?'

'The group of former . . .'

'No! The Trotskyist group.'

Gradually the interrogator became angrier and more brutal. He interrupted the questioning to have me punished. And then the record continued.

About Noel Field I said:

'My first dealings with Noel Field were in Geneva in 1947. . .'

He interrupted me.

'What dealings, Mr London?'

'Dealings.'

'No! Espionage dealings. Start again, calling things by their proper name.'

And since I refused to qualify innocent contacts with the word espionage, he punished me and on it went. . .

Hearing the same words and expressions repeated for weeks, months, and years on end you finally repeated them automatically yourself, like a machine. No one remained without a label He was a 'Trotskyist', a 'bourgeois nationalist', a 'Zionist', a 'veteran from Spain', a 'spy'. And if they questioned you about your youngest son you reached a point when you said: 'My son, the little Trotskyist Michel, is almost a year old.'

Whenever some positive element appeared in the abject character they made me out to be, whenever I seemed to have been good at my job in the Ministry of Foreign Affairs, for example, the interrogators gave the credit to 'the Cadre organization's, or any other employee.

I had once detected some dubious elements amongst the workers' cadres recruited by the Party regional Committees for our diplomatic school. I had to wage a personal battle to have their dossier re-examined, and they were subsequently expelled.

About this the interrogators wrote: 'X. . ., Y. . ., Z. . ., were discovered, thanks to the vigilance of the Cadre Commission, to be bad elements with a dubious past, and were sent back to their home region by the Ministry.'

The truth gradually disappeared completely. This is what became of it at our trial:

The judge: 'How were the Cadres from the provinces recruited at the Ministry of Foreign Affairs?'

London: '. . . The recruiting policy of the workers' cadres was sabotaged in such a way that recruiting took place in the regions where members of the central conspiracy against the state had a great influence, like the regions of Brno, Ostrava, Pilsen and Usti-nad-Labem. There Slansky's partisans recruited cadres unable to perform any job, either out of ineptitude or because they were elements with a suspicious past. That is why numerous candidates were sent away after a year's training – simply because they were politically unreliable. Among them there were members of fascist organizations, volunteers in the fascist army, participants in the fights against the partisans and so on. Ultimately there was not one working-class cadre who held an important post, either in the leadership of the Ministry of Foreign Affairs or in diplomacy. . .'

At other times you were made to sign reports page by page. You signed without knowing what was on the next page. Even if a detail seemed wrong or distorted to you, you ended up by signing because you could no longer fight over something so unimportant. This could happen several times before you reached the page where all these things were explained. But then it was too late. . .

Facts about Smrkovsky, under whom I had fought in the early thirties in the Youth of the Red Unions, of which he was the national leader, were brought into my report in the following way. When interrogated about my work in the Youth movement I had said, amongst other things, that in 1935, at a KIM congress in Moscow, Smrkovsky had raised certain political problems concerning the Party's relations with the young. The interrogator wrote: 'Smrkovsky's Trotskyist past'. When I protested he replied that it was well known, and that Smrkovsky had himself signed numerous reports on the subject. The interrogator continued: 'We could easily have written that he was a Gestapo agent. Hadn't you heard that? And yet it's well known. You must have forgotten. Besides, he admitted it himself.' And yet this last term was not in the report. Only his 'Trotskyist past' was mentioned.

Their confidence in their absolute power was such that the ringleaders of Ruzyn did not hesitate to get interrogators to describe perfectly normal activities and jobs as crimes.

This was what happened to a business letter sent to me by Kavan, our press attaché in the embassy in London, about Zilliacus's offer to write an article for *Tvorba*, the weekly paper of the Czech Communist Party, and my telegraphic reply.

One day Kohoutek had me brought into his office and insistently questioned me about Kavan's dealings with Koni Zilliacus, a left-wing member of the British Labour Party. I told him I knew nothing about them. He became aggressive and showed me a copy of the letter my friend Pavel Kavan had written me at the beginning of 1949. He told me about Zilliacus's offer to write an article for *Tvorba* and asked whether or not he should accept it. To this was joined a copy of my telegram in which I said that *Tvorba* was not interested in this article.

'I remember this exchange of letters perfectly, but I can't see what's reprehensible about it. It was part of our job.'

This completely legal fact was interpreted as a 'crime' in the indictment. The public prosecutor told the court that 'the copy of the letter dated 5 February 1949 written by Pavel Kavan and London's telegraphic reply prove that London had dealings with Zilliacus hostile to the state.'

The charge against Kavan was actually the result of a forgery. When I spoke to him about it a year later at the Central Prison of Leopoldov he told me that the Ambassador in London, Kratochvil, and not he, had sent this letter and that I had replied to Kratochvil. And yet it was Kavan's name in the copy of the letter shown me by Kohoutek.

But then, at the end of 1951, or at the beginning of 1952, Kohoutek questioned me about Zilliacus.

'Weren't there some letters from Geminder to Zilliacus in the diplomatic pouch bound for London?'

I remembered a letter which Geminder had given me for Zilliacus. The latter's name was spelt wrong, with a K instead of a C. There were two or three other points about Zilliacus, but I couldn't remember them at thet ime.

Kohoutek started to type out a report, which he read aloud:

'I declare that I received three or four letters for Zilliacus.'

I interrupted him and repeated that I could only remember one letter. He snapped at me, saying that this report was for their own information, that it was his business how he formulated it, and that it didn't much matter what I said, since the number of letters sent to Zilliacus would be decided by Geminder.

Two days later Kohoutek questioned me again, and told me that Geminder admitted having sent about ten letters. So the 'papers' I vaguely remembered must have been letters: I must remember them more clearly.

I admitted that they may have been letters but personally I couldn't swear to anything. Some time later, Kohoutek returned to the attack. I repeated my version of the facts. As far as the number of letters was concerned, he said, there was a contradiction between the diplomat Goldstücker, who was also under arrest, Geminder and myself. He read me and then showed me passages from their reports in which they acknowledged the existence of about ten letters.

I told him that the only people who knew about this were Goldstücker, who received the mail at the embassy in London, and Geminder, who gave me all mail from the Party in large sealed envelopes. I never knew what was in them. If there were other letters inside them I knew nothing about them or about whom they were addressed to.

So this time, when Kohoutek wrote in my report 'three or four letters', I didn't protest.

And then I suddenly remembered. The three or four 'papers' I had forgotten were telegrams sent to Paris, to our embassy in 1949 at the time of the first Peace Congress. We asked for the tape of the speech made by Zilliacus at the Peace Congress, to give it to the parallel congress being held in Prague by the delegates unable to obtain visas for France. In a second telegram we asked for a text of the speech for *Rude Pravo* which wanted to publish extracts. But despite what I said the report remained the same.

A few days later an interrogator wrote my report with me. It was two small pages of double-space typing. 'You can sign it another day, first I've got to show it to my chief,' he told me. Four days later, a few minutes to six, the interrogator had me brought to his office and gave me a paper to sign. He told me he had to return it to his chief on the dot of six. I said that the text was longer than what we had originally written and that I didn't know what was in it.

He answered impatiently: 'The spaces are wider, otherwise it's just the same as what you read the first time. Sign it and read it tomorrow. I'm in a hurry and I haven't got any time to lose.'

I went on about the greater number of pages and said there must be some changes.

'No, not about you. There are only a few formulations which describe Zilliacus better. Besides, you'll see when you read it. Sign it, I've got to go. I'm late already.'

I signed it.

A few days later, on my insistence, I was allowed to read the report. I then saw that next to the passages about Zilliacus's political background there were others about myself, including my 'confession' to having transmitted his letters 'knowing perfectly well that it was a secret correspondence against the state'. I protested about the interrogator's dishonesty and he tried to calm me. When he failed he called Kohoutek.

Kohoutek told me that what I regarded as a 'confession' was no such thing, since they had specified that the letters I received were sealed and that I did not know what was in them. I shouldn't worry about such a detail, he told me, there was no danger of my getting a heavier sentence because of it. After all, I only had two charges of espionage against me, Field and Zilliacus, while the other defendants had ten or more, all far more serious than mine. My part had been a minor one, and besides, whether I liked it or not, we had to get the matter over with and my report would stay as it was.

I had two more rows with Kohoutek during the next few days but it was to no avail. After being rewritten again, the report was altered, expanded to include other defendants, Kratochvil and Goldstücker, and was thereby integrated in the report for the trial and included in the bill of indictment.

The true story of my dealings with Zilliacus is as follows:

At the beginning of 1949 I knew that Zilliacus was a member of the left-wing group of the Labour Party and that he played an important part in the international aid campaign for democracy in Greece. He was a Unitarian, and collaborated with the international communist movement. I also knew, since the press had gone into it at length, that in August 1948 he had accepted an invitation to Yugoslavia and that on his return he had continued to fight for the Greek cause. That was all.

In March 1949 Pierre Villon, a member of the Central Committee of the French Communist Party, came to my flat with Darboussier and Jean Lafitte, all campaigning in the Peace Movement. They were then taking part in a preparatory meeting for the First International Congress of the Peace Movement in Prague.

As they discussed the Congress they mentioned Zilliacus as an important figure in Great Britain and added that they counted on his active participation in the Peace Movement. Commenting on his recent visit to Yugoslavia, they said that it was perfectly normal, that, as a socialist, he should have accepted this invitation.

I have already explained the exchange of letters and telegrams with the embassy in London about the article for *Tvorba* and with the Paris embassy about the recording of Zilliacus's speech.

These telegrams were sent through normal channels, and, as with every telegram sent by the Ministry of Foreign Affairs, copies were given to the other Under-Secretaries, to the Premier and to the President.

In order to give an illegal aspect to the telegrams the report said that they were sent in code, although *every* service telegram to the embassies together with its reply was in code and labelled 'secret'.

Thus I became 'a link in the espionage network uniting Slansky and Geminder to the former intelligence service agent Koni Zilliacus. This was an important figure who ensured contacts with the centre of conspiracy against the state and leading circles of western imperialists. . .'

At the trial I was made to say:

'From the beginning I noticed the letters sent by Geminder to London in the diplomatic pouch for Kratochvil and Goldstücker. They were addressed to Koni Zilliacus. I even remember that on the envelope Zilliacus was spelt with a K instead of a C.'

The judge: 'How many of these letters did you send Zilliacus in the diplomatic pouch?'

London: 'I can remember three, perhaps four . . . I kept no record of this correspondence in order to wipe out its traces.'

The prosecutor: 'Did you know what these letters contained?'

London: 'No, but when Geminder told me that it was all part of the conspiracy I realized it was a secret correspondence against the state. Otherwise it wouldn't have been necessary to disguise it.'

The judge: 'You say you remember three or four letters sent in this way. Mightn't there have been more?'

London: 'Perhaps. I admit there may have been ten.'

Over the months I passed imperceptibly from the stage when the interrogators purposely tried to alter what I had said to work on it, reformulate it, transcribe it, deform it, to the stage when they obliged me, purely and simply, to learn their own formulations by heart. It was the rehearsal of the trial in which we would be acting in a play performed against ourselves.

From transcript to transcript the interrogators moved ever farther from the facts. They no longer cared whether the real facts could be checked by anybody, as in the case of my social background. They made me say my family and upbringing were bourgeois. I could not even hope that this would shock people into realizing what I had been reduced to. The same applied to my alleged Trotskyist activity in the French workers' movement. Dozens of militant leaders of the French and Spanish Communist Parties, not to mention the Czechs, knew what I had been up to. But that no longer counted.

After over fifteen years' experience the Soviet advisers reckoned that someone who knew the truth about one point would keep quiet about it. First of all this was because he didn't know the other points of the indictment and because the enormity of them would prevent him from attaching too much importance to detail. But they also agreed with Goebbels that the larger the lie the higher were the chances of its being believed. Finally, they counted on the discipline of communists, on their trust in the Party. How could someone question the Party's appreciations or appear to defend a traitor in the witch hunt which had been created around us?

So, at the beginning of 1952, Kohoutek ordered his interrogators to draw up a clear report of all my criminal 'activities' in order to pass it on to the Party. But, to be on the safe side, Kohoutek ended up by doing it himself. It was seventeen pages long, and formulated in an incredible manner. The charges it held no longer corresponded to any of the 'statements' or 'confessions' which had been previously extorted. They were far worse! Undeterred by my presence he wrote entire pages of questions and answers. When he told me to sign them I protested indignantly about the importance of the charges and their new formulation, although I had signed other 'confessions' in the past.

Kohoutek tried to calm me. He said that the Party leaders needed a very concise report which reflected the whole of my 'enemy' activities, so he had been obliged to compress several reports into one. This made the interpretation of the facts seem worse but I had to resign myself to it because, by writing this, he had only been following the instructions of the Party and the Soviet advisers.

I replied that this report was enough to have me hanged, but he said I shouldn't take things like that. It was just an 'informative' report, not intended for the court, but for use behind the scenes. Besides, he could easily have written it without telling me about it.

In order to convince me once and for all, Kohoutek read me passages from the reports drawn up with Geminder and Clementis, pointing out that certain formulations were much worse than the ones in mine and that I would be wrong if I refused to sign.

Every time I objected, until the day of my conviction, he made the same threats: 'Your sentence will depend on your attitude, not on the degree of your guilt. The Party can have you convicted if it likes – it can get you a heavy sentence with hardly any material against you or a light sentence with a great deal of material against you. Your only chance to save your head is to rely on the mercy of the Party.'

Now, at least, things were clear.

Eleven

In the second fortnight of March 1952 Kohoutek called me to his office and told me that I was to be confronted with Slansky the next day. He then gave me a typewritten sheet of paper containing what Slansky would say at our meeting and what I was to reply. Nothing was left to chance. Kohoutek told me to learn the whole thing by heart, but, as a precaution, the interrogators made me repeat my lines and Kohoutek himself checked on whether I had learned them properly.

One Saturday Kohoutek told me that I was going to be faced with Slansky a few minutes later. 'Above all, Mr London, you must repeat your lines word by word. Your future depends to a large extent on your behaviour at this meeting!'

Once more he made me repeat my part. He told me that Slansky had already been confronted with numerous defendants in order to check on some of the details in his 'confessions'. What was the point of these confrontations? Were they trying to give a semblance of legality to this whole comedy by recording them in the files of the trial? They were all part of thes ystem of confessions, like the transcripts, the successive formulations, and all the rest. This mass of precautions seemed a slight exaggeration to me.

At this point Doubek came into the room. Kohoutek told him that I had learnt my part very well, and Doubek repeated what his colleague had just said: 'Watch out! Your attitude during this meeting will determine your sentence. So try to repeat the text you learned as accurately as possible.'

On the way, Kohoutek, who was leading me to the room where the confrontation would take place, perfected the final details. 'You must look Slansky in the eyes, talk slowly, not get upset, and stick to the text.'

It didn't even occur to me that the author might be doubtful about his play. I was so used to this laboriousness, to this servile apprehension of not obtaining a perfect result for the 'real chiefs', the Soviet advisers, that I hardly paid any attention to what he said.

Here I was in front of Slansky. He looked drawn and seemed very tired. How did I appear to him? He certainly knew that I'd been inside for over fourteen months before meeting him.

In all that time I had never once been able to look in a mirror, but I could guess at my appearance if only by looking at him.

Slansky spoke. He admitted, according to the text, that he had been the leader of a conspiracy against the state in Czechoslovakia, but suddenly, when the part concerning me came up, he said something different. He said that it was impossible that I should have been in this conspiracy since I had been away from Czechoslovakia for so long.

I was dumbfounded. For a minute I hesitated. What should I do? My first instinct was to take advantage of this opportunity to state my innocence. But I was suspicious. What point would there have been in taking advantage of this deviation from the text, since we were alone together, before his interrogators, Doubek and Kohoutek? What would happen if I did so? I had neither the time nor the means to think. I was so well conditioned to what should happen that my reflexes were automatic.

I could no more escape from them than a driver from his reactions to an unexpected situation on the road. My orders were to learn something off by heart and to stick to it whatever happened. The interest and verdict of the Party were at stake.

My future depended on my attitude during this confrontation. The interrogators may well have put the whole thing on to test me. . .

I had signed my 'confessions'. I knew that a heap of 'evidence', 'statements' by former volunteers from the International Brigades and from my new fellow defendants, Geminder, Goldstücker, Dufek, Clementis, and Svab, existed against me. . .

In these circumstances there was no point in going back on my 'confessions'. It would only aggravate my situation.

Besides, why would Slansky want to spare me? And why was he deviating from the text which he had learnt off by heart, just as I had learnt mine? It must have been to defend himself from having been in contact with me, since he knew about my full responsibility in the alleged 'Trotskyist centre' and in 'American espionage'. They were all charges which he had in some way ratified when he was still Secretary General of the Party, and which might bother him now it was too late.

So, like an automaton, I recited my lines: 'I was in the conspiracy against the state led by Slansky.'

I was then led back to Kohoutek's office. A quarter of an hour later he told me: 'You were right to answer as you did. Any other attitude would have had disastrous consequences for you.' And he added that his 'friends' and the President had asked to be informed about the meeting.

Then, as Doubek was to do later, he described Slansky's attitude as an attempt to escape from his own responsibility for acts of espionage which were also attributed to me and my fellow defendants, in order to limit his part to the ideological leadership of the Centre.

About a month later Kohoutek called me to his office once again. He told me that Slansky was going to be faced with Geminder and Goldstücker and questioned about Zilliacus. At the end of this confrontation I would be summoned, and only had to say that I had received letters from Geminder for Zilliacus through Goldstücker.

He gave me a list of Geminder's and Goldstücker's questions and answers. I could thus have some idea of the extent of their 'confessions' about their correspondence with Zilliacus and *their* dealings with him. Kohoutek then left me with one of his interrogators. Almost an hour later the telephone rang and the order was given to lead me to the room where the confrontation was to take place.

When the door opened I saw my three fellow defendants, sitting round a large table, before Doubek, Kohoutek and some other interrogators. Their eyes were dull and listless. Like me, they must have been wondering what this whole business was about. . .

Eduard Goldstücker! We'd seen each other eighteen months earlier when he came to the bernin Palace before returning to Tel Aviv, where he was our Minister Plenipotentiary. He was one of our youngest and most brilliant diplomats. We had met at the Sixth KIM Congress in Moscow in 1935 where he was acting as one of the leaders of the communist students. His wit and talent as a story-teller were highly stimulating. After the war, which he had spent in England, we met again in Paris, where he was attached to the embassy. After being nominated councillor in London, he had been chosen to represent our country in Israel. And here he was. . .

Bedrich Geminder! He stared into space. He cringed, like a whipped dog. I had known him all my life. His father had been a friend of my father's. Despite the difference in our age we had been very close to each other ever since our meeting in Moscow, where he had been working at the Comintern Press Office since 1935. He was one of George Dimitrov's closest collaborators. During the war he directed the foreign language broadcasts on Radio-Moscow.

Although he was from Ostrava, he was a member of the German minority which was almost entirely transferred to Germany after the victory in 1945. At that time he chose to remain in Moscow. It was only on the insistence of his old comrades, Gottwald and Slansky, that he decided to return to Czechoslovakia in 1948. He then became director of the International Department of the Central Committee.

He was a bachelor and lived with Slansky's family, hardly ever venturing outside the circle of his old friends. He was on good terms with Gottwald, a fact which made him seem like the Kremlin's Grey Eminence, especially since he hid his shyness under a brusque exterior which antagonized those who didn't know him well enough to be aware of the kindness, generosity and sensitivity which he had in him. Poor Bedrich! What could he be thinking when he looked back on his life in Moscow and his friendship with Gottwald. . .

Rudolf Slansky, seated between the two of them, was in the same condition as at our first meeting. Of the three men he was the one I knew least, although he had also been active in Ostrava. But that was in the twenties. Before leaving for Moscow in 1933 I met him twice at the office of the Central Committee, but we only said a few words to each other. It was not until after the war that I approached him, at the meetings of one of the Commissions which he directed for the Ministry of Foreign Affairs.

Everybody recognized and appreciated his qualities as a leader, and both feared and respected him. He seemed rather cold and it was difficult to establish contact with him on a human level. A Party leader since the twenties and a close collaborator of Gottwald, he had been in Moscow with Gottwald during the war. To start with he had worked in the Czech Department of the Comintern; then, in 1944, he had become a member of the General Staff of Partisans on the Ukrainian front. Subsequently he was sent to Slovakia with Sverma, where he participated in the leadership of the national Slovak uprising.

His wife and he had had a terrible time in Moscow: during the autumn of 1943 their little daughter had been kidnapped from her pram, where an elder brother had left her in front of the radio building while her mother was broadcasting for occupied Czechoslovakia. The police investigation had led to nothing. . .

There we were, four militant Party members, two veterans, Slansky and Geminder, whose commitment dated back to the birth of the Czech Communist Party, and two younger men, Goldstücker and myself, who had joined the Party in our childhood. Each of us admitted to having conspired against the the Socialist State to whose creation we had devoted our whole existence . . . We were there for this absurd confrontation which was merely a rehearsal for the play that was to be performed a few months later.

Of all the comrades in prison or implicated in the conspiracy, ninety per cent of us had been militant Party members before the war.

In the summer of 1952 Kohoutek told me I was going to see Slansky again. 'It's not a confrontation this time,' he said. 'You simply have to repeat what you told Sverma in Paris in 1939.'

I found myself in Doubek's office – Slansky was already there.

I repeated: 'In Paris in 1939 Sverma told me that Slansky did not like the men in Gottwald's entourage.'

That was all. I was led back to my cell. That was how these meetings took place in Ruzyn, but the ones I had been clamouring for before my 'confessions', with Zavodsky, Field, Svoboda and the others, were refused me. The confrontations for which the accused pleaded were never permitted, because on no account was the truth to appear.

Now, sixteen years after this nightmare, an account is to be published in Prague of Doubek's own interrogations when he was arrested in 1955 for his 'work' in Ruzyn.* I was to discover from this that even if Slansky immediately admitted to having been the leader of the conspiracy against the state, he resisted for as long as he could against accusations of espionage. This accounts for his deviation from the text at our first meeting.

At the beginning of September 1952 Kohoutek told me that he was going to draw up the report for the court. I had virtually no share in it.

I was in the room when the interrogators typed it out, but I was there like a vase. I had nothing to do with what was being written. Kohoutek occasionally arrived with whole pages which had already been typed and which his interrogators copied out and included in their own products. They gave Kohoutek what they had done bit by bit. In the days that followed he brought the sheets back, duly corrected at the demand of 'the Party and my friends', after intensifying some charges or including new facts.

In all the administrative reports drawn up over the months a certain number of charges were retained and others dropped. These were carefully elaborated tactics. To start with the accused was crushed by a pyramid of charges ranging from deviations and political errors to espionage activities and the vilest crimes. But in the end only the ones which fitted in with the part attributed to him at the trial were kept. The interroga-

* *Reporter*, weekly paper of the Union of Journalists, Prague, May 1968.

tors even went so far as to say: 'You see, we don't want to annihilate you. Out of all this heap we've only kept a few charges. You've got away with the rest!'

Sling, for example, had been accused in a speech by Kopecky,* at the Central Committee in 1951, of matricide, a charge allegedly confirmed in the investigation. At the trial, however, there was no mention of the fact.

The accused – I knew it myself – felt genuine relief when charges, which put them in the most appalling light, were omitted from the proceedings.

Who did not prefer a charge of espionage or political crimes to embezzlement, theft, denunciation or murder? The charge I resented most – of having sent Klecan to Czechoslovakia during the war in order to hand over the clandestine Central Committee with Fucik and Cerny to the Gestapo – was withdrawn. You can have no idea of how I hated this charge. When Kohoutek told me it wouldn't be held against me, he added: 'Reicin's taken it on himself!' As for me, I preferred ten charges of espionage with Field, Zilliacus or anyone they liked, to answering for the worst crime in existence: having handed my comrades over to Hitler's butchers. That was a very good way of making the accused sign the reports for the court. In any case it was decisive for me.

And yet, before the trial, Kohoutek showed me the pile of administrative reports bearing my signature and statements by fellow defendants and witnesses, and warned me: 'If you ever think of changing anything in your statement in court, you see what we have in reserve for you and we won't hesitate to use it against you. Act accordingly!'

When this report was ready Kohoutek showed it to the Soviet advisers who formed – as far as I could gather from Kohoutek's indiscretions – a coordinating commission to make sure that there should be no disagreement between the reports on

* Minister of Information and Culture. He played an important political part in the preparation of the trial and tried to justify it ideologically.

the accused and the statements of the witnesses. That was why, in my report, the passages concerning Field were further modified and new names and facts appeared which had never been mentioned in any of the administrative reports. It was essential that, in the bill of indictment and in your statement, your character should fit into the tragic farce about to be performed. All the conspirators had to be dipped in the same slough of crimes.

I still occasionally rebelled and protested when I heard an interrogator read out his new formulations. When Kohoutek was called he said: 'If you don't want your report written like that – and we're the only ones who know how it should be written – you run the risk of not being tried with Slansky's group. Your activities are not as serious as those of the others, so in this trial you're no longer in the first line. You have some chance of saving your head. On the other hand, if we decided to try you as the head of the Trotskyist group of former volunteers in the International Brigades you know what that would mean for you.'

After such convincing arguments I let them write whatever they liked. And, in a new version, the interrogators included my alleged espionage activity in the workers' movement in France 'in favour of Slansky' and other charges which had not been retained.

When I was presented with the new report I could not suppress my indignation. But Kohoutek told me: 'You're not the only one who doesn't like it. But they all give in. Geminder's been crying ever since he signed his report.'

Kohoutek took the new version and submitted it for a last check from above. After this I was given it to sign, and I did so without even reading it.

Then a new stage began. I was told that I had to learn my report for the court by heart. For six weeks, until the day of the trial, I was taken every day to the interrogator who gave me my lessons. He gave me homework: 'For Saturday these ten pages...' 'For Thursday the next fifteen...'

I got better food, black coffee and cigarettes. Every day I was taken for a walk. Suddenly infinite care was taken of my health. Dr Sommer recommended ultraviolet rays and I received calcium injections. I knew this because I recognized the effects: that heat which runs through your body when the piston of the syringe is plunged down.

I felt better, and my face must have become as suntanned as a winter sportsman's. One day, as Kohoutek was looking at me with satisfaction, I asked him if he thought I was taken in by his solicitude: 'It isn't your interest in my health which has earned me this care. You want me to look well in court. You remind me of my grandmother when she stuffed her geese for Christmas.'

He laughed.

Until the trial Kohoutek repeated to me continuously: 'Think yourself lucky to be included in the Slansky trial. It's your only chance to survive.. . . Don't do anything stupid now!'

If I slipped up there were plenty of witnesses against me, he said. My attitude would determine the number of witnesses called. Another day he showed me a thick bundle of papers and said that they were the statements of twenty witnesses ready to stand against me 'if I tried to jump off the train!' And then he read out a number of passages with satisfaction. On yet another day he read me part of the statements of my fellow defendants concerning my complicity with them.

Four or five days before I was taken to court Kohoutek told me that he had just spoken to the public prosecutor who had gone through my file and considered that my hostile activities were not sufficient to warrant my appearing in the trial. He had reckoned that my sentence would be a maximum of fifteen years. 'You see, I told you so! This trial's a piece of luck for you, so you'd better behave!'

When we met a few months after the verdict, Vavro Hajdu told me that Kohoutek had predicted eighteen years for him. That must have been another aspect of Security tactics. And I don't know whether the interrogators were acting in good or in bad faith. Did the interrogators only say that to calm the prisoners and make them more docile? Or did the prisoners really believe that they would save their skins by obeying the Party's instructions?

One morning Kohoutek told me that Doubek would check personally on whether I had learned my report by heart. I was taken into his office. Next to him sat a man I had never seen before and who listened to what I said attentively, without saying a single word. One of the 'real' chiefs? Doubek declared himself satisfied. I had passed my exam with flying colours.

That evening Doubek came into the room where I was sitting with my interrogator. A civilian was with him and he introduced him as Dr Novak, the judge. Novak asked me whether I wanted to read the bill of indictment myself or if I preferred the interrogator to read it to me. I said the interrogator might as well read it to me. I cared so little.

The next day Dr Novak returned, accompanied by an assessor, to ask me questions about my civil status, name, age, etc.

'Have you had any previous convictions?'

'Yes, under the First Republic, between 1931 and 1933, and then during the war in Paris in 1942, by the state tribunal.'

The assessor made a note of my answers.

Dr Novak continued: 'Why were you convicted?'

'For communist activity and participation in the struggle against the Nazis in occupation in France.'

Then he told his assessor: 'No, there's no point in writing that down.'

The same day the interrogator told me I would see my lawyer, Dr Ruzicka. A few days earlier Major Kohoutek had asked me if I wanted to choose a counsel for the defence and I said no. 'Since you've told me so many times that the Party was going to judge me, why should I choose a lawyer?'

He had objected that the law stipulated the presence of a counsel for the defence in court and that one would be appointed by the court. He added: 'Even if you choose him yourself it won't make any difference. There are only about ten lawyers authorized to take a culprit's defence before the state tribunal.'

I was led blindfolded into the room where my lawyer was waiting for me. Our conversation was very brief and in that time the interrogator, that is to say one of the men drawing up the indictment, sat with us. This was an additional violation of the law and the defendant's right to a defence. How could the defendant do anything to change the bill of indictment before such a witness?

The lawyer told me that he had read the changes and emphasized their gravity for me.

'You risk the death penalty. That's what our law has in reserve for the crimes of which you are accused. Your only hope of getting off with a lighter sentence is to plead guilty and behave well in court.'

That was exactly what my interrogators had told me.

I didn't see my lawyer again for some time. When I was taken to Pankrac prison where the trial was to be held for seven days, I was to ask for him in vain. He only came to see me after the verdict.

At the end of our first meeting I begged him to see my wife and prepare her for what was in store for me. I also asked him to tell her not to come to the trial, because if I knew she was in the room I wouldn't have the strength to recite my statement. He promised to see her, but did not do so. When I saw him after my sentence he again promised to go and comfort her, but did not go this time either.

Twelve

What had sustained me for so many months was the thought of being able to denounce the illegality of the methods used against me in court. But now that the day of the trial was approaching I realized that this would be impossible. I also realized why all the victims who had preceded me had not done so either. We were all up to our necks in it. And I was not the only one who reconstructed the Moscow trials to try and discover some means of resistance or some other traps which could still be set. I thought I could now understand Slansky's attitude at our first meeting. It seemed to me that he wanted to defend himself on the same grounds as Zinoviev and Bukharin, who were ready to admit their own political responsibilities in the conspiracy on a purely intellectual level, thereby hoping to evade the practical charges of espionage. But that didn't work. The men who made up the conspiracy invented everything accompanying it, decorated it and dressed it up with espionage, murder, and other crimes. They were fussy authors, who attached importance to the slightest detail because they knew that if one lie was revealed the whole plot would fall through.

I could not help recalling Moscow at the time of the purges and trials.

During the three years I spent there I had friends of every nationality: Germans, Italians, Poles, Bulgarians, Yugoslavs, Frenchmen, Belgians, Englishmen, Spaniards. I also had a number of Soviet friends. The foreigners were either political refugees seeking asylum or representatives of communist parties and the revolutionary movement working in international organizations, pupils of the Lenin School staying in Moscow before returning to their country of origin where they would carry on the fight.

The bonds between us were strong. The word 'comrade' opened the sesame of our hearts and the fact that we did not speak the same language hardly mattered. Besides, we soon got to understand each other with a few words of Russian, a few words of our own and other languages.

Ever since the attempt to kill Kirov the atmosphere had changed. Friends saw little of each other. Our Soviet comrades avoided us. Eminent personalities I had met in the Lux hotel or in the corridors of the Comintern – Bela Kun, Heinz Neumann and so many other well-known leaders of the world communist movement – disappeared one after the other. It was rumoured that something had been discovered about them, something serious which was not to be mentioned for the time being, and that further explanations were needed. But these explanations never came. And other people continued to disappear.

I remembered the first trial against Zinoviev and Kamenev, the shock we had all felt when we saw Lenin's old comrades being disgraced. And then their second trial and their death sentence. In the course of lengthy discussions we tried to explain to ourselves how men with such a past could sink so low, become imperialist agents and commit the most abominable crimes against their country, their people, their fellow soldiers and their Party.

I can still remember my friend Secotine telling me of a meeting he had attended where he heard Yejov speak. He told me how this little man had aroused the enthusiasm of the whole court when he demanded the most implacable punishment for the traitors. Secotine was delighted. Like him we all thought that once the true culprits had been discovered everything would improve and that the comrades who had been unjustly arrested would be released. But things got worse.

Sveridiuk, who had come to Moscow from Prague, where he had lived as a Polish émigré and fought in the Czech Communist Party, visited us at the Czech colony. One day he disappeared with his wife. I heard he had had difficulties because of his brother, one of the leaders of the Polish Communist Party who had been sentenced to death. And then I never heard about him any more.

Marthe, whom I had met in the French colony, also disappeared one day. The people who passed each other in the corridors were afraid to greet each other, and still more frightened of talking. On my floor wives remained alone, for their husbands, or so they said, had been called away from Moscow. After a while they too left with all their luggage, bound for some distant region. Through Secotine I heard that their husbands had in fact been arrested. Secotine, who had known them before in Poland, in the underground, did what he could for them. He wrote letters, took personal steps with the

NKVD, and collected evidence in their favour, convinced that some mistake had been made. He explained to me that a conspiracy directed by the capitalist countries was being organized with the assistance of the oppositionist forces within the Soviet Union. Trotskyists and others were trying to overthrow the regime and, in their attempts to reveal this conspiracy, and liquidate those responsible, it was possible for the Soviet police to make mistakes. But even my friend Secotine disappeared in the confusion, and I never heard of him again.

When I met Lise in Valencia I told her about the atmosphere in Moscow at the end of my stay, and my friends who had disappeared overnight. Why? I spoke of the trials in which Lenin's comrades had been condemned. Lise only knew what she had read in the papers. The accused had betrayed and had admitted their crimes.

And then, a few months later, there had been the trial of the 'Group of right-wingers and anti-Soviet Trotskyists' of which I bought a typed report shortly after my return to Paris. I remember how horrified I had been by Krestinsky's case. When Vyshinsky asked the twenty-one defendants if they pleaded guilty, before the court opened proceedings, they all said yes, except for him:

'I don't consider myself guilty. I'm not a Trotskyist. I was never in the group of right-wingers and Trotskyists, and didn't even know it existed. Nor have I committed any of the crimes I'm accused of. I am not guilty of having had dealings with the German espionage services.'

When Vyshinsky pointed out that he had signed his confessions at the preliminary investigation Krestinsky replied:

'Before you interrogated me, the statements I made at the preliminary investigations were false. Then I stood by them because I realized that I couldn't invalidate them until the court hearing – if there was to be such a hearing. I thought that if I said what I say today – that everything was false – the Party leaders and the government would never hear about it.'

Throughout his interrogation, during the second session of

the trial, he fought over every word, refuting all the charges. And Vyshinsky had then appealed to his fellow defendants to confirm Krestinsky's guilt. The witnesses for the prosecution included his fellow defendant, Bessonov, who claimed to have received instructions from Krestinsky concerning his Trotskyist espionage activities during a meeting in Germany. He smiled, and Vyshinsky asked him why. Bessonov replied:

'I can't help smiling, because if I'm here today it's because Nicolas Nicolayevich Krestinsky designated me as his liaison with Trotsky. Apart from him and Piatakov nobody knew about it. And if Krestinsky had not discussed the matter with me in 1933, I wouldn't be in the dock today.'

The worst of it was that the next day, when he was brought back to court, Krestinsky confirmed all his 'confessions' made at the preliminary investigation. And when Vyshinsky told him that his attitude the day before could only be interpreted as a Trotskyist provocation, Krestinsky replied: 'Yesterday, dominated by a fleeting feeling of false shame, I couldn't tell the truth, I couldn't say I was guilty. I beg the court to record my statement. I admit that I am completely guilty and I take on myself full responsibilty for my crimes and my treason.'

And in his last words to the court a few days later, he had referred to his past as a revolutionary and begged to be allowed to live so that he could atone in some way for his terrible crimes.

In the discussions we had in the Party organizations Krestinsky's attitude was interpreted as that of a bitter enemy who had tried, during the trial, to discredit the leadership of the Bolshevik Party together with Soviet jurisdiction.

I could also remember Bukharin's last words which had upset me at the time, although they had never led me to doubt the authenticity of the trial.

I could now see that the Moscow trials were the precursors of our own. The only difference was that there the main defendants had previously diverged from the official Party line and had represented oppositionist tendencies, and this justified our credulity to some extent.

I recalled the more recent Sofia trials. Kostov, the main defendant in the Bulgarian trial, had also tried to go back on the confessions made during the investigation. His microphone had been cut off, and numerous witnesses for the prosecution had been made to file through the court and confirm the charges against him. Finally he had written a letter to the Party leadership which was reproduced in the book I was reading before my arrest. There was a facsimile of it with his signature, and in it he begged the Party to forgive his attitude of the day before. He repented and hoped that his life would be spared so that one day he would be able to atone. It was all the more poignant now that I knew what it meant and what Kostov must have felt when he wrote it, knowing he was innocent.

I was even more sure that any attempt of this kind was doomed to failure, particularly since my interrogators warned me: 'Don't think that you can go back on your confessions or deviate from your text before the court. If you tried to be clever we'd know exactly what to do with you. You won't get another hearing and all the evidence will be given by the twenty witnesses for the prosecution.'

I later discovered that the repetition of our statements before the trials was recorded on a tape. If one of the defendants deviated from the text during the trial a group of interrogators could order the judge to interrupt the proceedings.

I was sure that if I went back on what I had said there would be the same uproar, the same discussions as the ones at which I had assisted over Krestinsky and Kostov, the same commentaries in the communist press all over the world on my criminal behaviour. I would be the man who spat on the Party and tried to discredit it before world opinion until the last moment, until the gallows.

Two or three days before the trial, I was taken into a room where I found myself before a member of the Party's Political

Bureau, the Minister of Security Karol Bacilek. He wore a general's uniform, and when he spoke to me, not in his own name, but, as he said, 'in the name of the Party and Comrade Gottwald', I knew my number was up.

I heard him explain that the Party appealed to me to stick to my statement as it was written in the report for the court, that I would thereby be doing the Party a great service. He added that the national situation was extremely serious, that there was a threat of war and that the Party expected me to be guided by national and Party interests; if I did so, my conduct would be taken into account.

This confirmed my belief that if I denied anything before the court, if I claimed to be innocent, nobody would believe me and I would be hanged.

And then, although you knew that you were an innocent and powerless victim in the hands of ruthless criminals, whose Machiavellian efforts were solely intended to empty you of any human content, of your conscience as a free man and a communist, you knew that beyond the courtroom, the inter-rogators and the Soviet advisers, there was the Party with its mass of devoted members, the Soviet Union and its people who had performed so many sacrifices for the cause of communism. There was the peace camp, the millions of combatants struggling for the same ideal the world over, the same socialist ideal to which you had devoted your whole life. You knew that the international situation was tense, that the cold war was raging, that everything could be used by the imperialists to spark off another war. As a conscientious communist, therefore, you could not agree to become an 'objective accomplice' of the imperialists.

Then you decided that, since all was lost, you might as well conceal your innocence and plead guilty.

My physical condition had greatly improved over the last weeks. I regretted this because it must be far easier to let the noose go round your neck when you feel wretched.

I thought about this last moment frequently. I dreamed about the gallows. And when my blanket grazed my neck at night I always had the nightmare.

I tried to chase away my thoughts but as the day of the trial approached I was obsessed by them. I was given books to read. But I couldn't read the printed words before my eyes. All I could read was my final farewell between the lines, the appalling conditions in which my family would live and which would mark my children until their adult life. For me it would all be over, but Lise and my children would be stigmatized by it forever. And even if I escaped the gallows I would never be released from prison, particularly after such a trial.

I had been given *Don Quixote*. Although I was reading it for the fourth time I managed to abstract my thoughts. There I was, far from my cell, transported into the world of Cervantes, and I found myself roaring with laughter at Sancho Panza's repartees which made me think of my father-in-law Ricol. The character of Don Quixote had never moved me as much as it did now.

Then came my last night. I couldn't sleep. I felt, rather than heard, the muffled steps in the corridor. The spy-hole stayed open so that I wouldn't know if I was being watched, but at regular intervals the warder's eye appeared in the hole.

What a terrible tragedy Lise and her parents would live through the next day! Only later would the children realize what had happened. Provided they were allowed to survive! They would need immense courage for years and years, maybe for their whole life, in order to face the difficulties which would pursue them beyond my tomb.

Bacilek had promised me that the Party would talk to my wife and prepare her for the trial. When I told him about my fears for the future of my family, already so isolated in a foreign country, he promised me that the Party would make sure they suffered no consequences. I hardly believed these promises, but at least they had been given.

I thought about my own childhood. I had started to develop a political awareness with the Sacco – Vanzetti case, when I clung to my father's hand and tried to sing in unison with the hundreds of men and women surrounding me. It was the 'Internationale' and I was beginning to learn the words. Sacco and Vanzetti had been murdered despite the cry of protest which shook the world, and they were innocent.

A few hours later our trial would begin. How different it would be for us! The memory of those two martyrs marked the dawn of my adult life, of my life as a communist, and had never faded. Should I regret my commitment? I had asked myself that question so frequently in the two years I had spent here, and the answer was always the same: No, I'm proud of my past. The struggle led by our older comrades, our own battles for an international ideal of fraternity, justice and peace, remained valid.

It was the bureaucratic deformation of socialism, dogmatism, the desertion of democratic principles and their replacement by arbitrary methods of command; it was the suppression of criticism, the deification of the Party by the abuse of the formulae 'The Party is always right' and 'The Party needs you', which put us on the wrong track. How unjustly and brutally the Party members had been treated! Suspicion had been systematically cultivated in our ranks. The cadres had been judged by police methods. An atmosphere of distrust, fear, and then terror, developed in the Party and the country. It was produced by this monstrous, all-powerful cancer, which, under cover of state security, ate into the Party and into socialism itself by applying the Stalinist concept of accentuating the class struggle during the construction of socialism.

I had so many things to tell my wife, my children, my friends and comrades. I had never felt so close to them all. And to think that tomorrow they would curse me and think me a traitor. And yet I could only plead guilty! That was what had happened to our predecessors in Moscow, Budapest and Sofia.

Once again I thought of Sacco and Vanzetti. As a child I had wept when I read their last letter, their farewell. Innocent . . .

executed... their memory remained pure.... They were heroes.

The door opened and the warder said: 'Get ready.'

I had a temperature and I asked for something to drink. I recognized my clothes – they were from home. I thought the lawyer must have seen my family and warned them.

I was blindfolded and led out to the yard where the police van was parked. And then there was a void: I fainted. When I came to, I saw the interrogators bending over me. They looked worried. Dr Sommer felt my pulse, listened to my heart and gave me some pills. I got into the police van and off it drove.

Part Four

The Trial at Pankrac

One

It was still dark when we reached Pankrac, the old prison situated in a workers' quarter of Prague, not unlike the Santé in Paris. But Pankrac is self-contained, and in it both investigation and trial take place.

Accompanied by warders and interrogators, my hands chained, I was led along endless corridors into a basement with cells on either side. I was locked into one of them and the spyhole remained open, as in the French death cells. A guard stood permanently outside my door. In one corner of the cell was a mattress, in the other a chair – a warder was to sit in this chair every night I spent there. They were obviously determined to keep us alive until the verdict.

Kohoutek told me that today, 20 November 1952, the public prosecutor was going to read the bill of indictment in the presence of the fourteen defendants. After this the hearings would begin and the first to be heard would be Slansky. At that point I would be taken back to Ruzyn where I would await my turn to be interrogated. After my testimony I would take my place in the dock and remain there until the verdict.

Before the beginning of the trial Dr Sommer, accompanied by a nurse, listened to my chest. He took my blood pressure and gave me some pills. He did the same thing in every cell and this ritual was to take place throughout the trial, sometimes even between sessions.

Shortly before nine o'clock I was taken out of my cell. The doors of the neighbouring cells were opened and my fellow defendants came out into the corridor. We lined up one behind the other, between each of us the same warder we had had in

Ruzyn. This was the first time that we were all together. The only man I did not know personally was Frejka.

Our line moved forward. The first was Slansky, then came Geminder, then myself, Hajdu, André Simone, Frejka, Frank, Löbl, Margolius, Fischl, Svab, Reicin and Sling.

Their faces were closed and drawn, and they had an absent expression in their eyes. None of us looked at each other.

Again the maze of corridors and stairs. Then suddenly we came out into a huge hall, brightly lit, and filled with people. I took care not to look at the spectators because I was afraid of recognizing my wife in the crowd. I hoped my lawyer had seen her, as he had promised, and persuaded her not to be present at the trial.

By chance, as I passed the newspaper reporters, my eyes met those of a man I had known long ago in Ostrava.

We were made to stand in the dock, a warder between each of us, and a few minutes later the Court entered.

I felt that I was on a stage, with my thirteen comrades and the members of the tribunal. Every one of us was ready to perform his part of the spectacle, which had been meticulously produced by the experts in Ruzyn. Not a detail had been omitted. One felt the sureness of touch that these masters of imposture had acquired through experience of numerous trials before ours. There were microphones everywhere, and the lights and electric wires running across the floor heightened the effect of the première.

The judge, Dr Novak, opened the proceedings. Turning to us he asked, perfectly seriously, whether the delay stipulated by law to precede our appearance in court had been respected. We each replied in the affirmative. He then told us to follow the bill of indictment and the proceedings attentively and to benefit from our right to express our opinion about the various pieces of evidence. He even went so far as to tell us that we had the right to defend ourselves as we thought fit. Then he called upon the public prosecutor Urvalek to read the bill of indictment. The accusation ran:

that, as traitors, Trotskyists-Titoists-Zionists, bourgeois nationalists and enemies of the Czech people, of the people's democratic regime and of socialism, they created, in the service of the American imperialists and under the leadership of western intelligence services, a centre of conspiracy against the state; tried to undermine the basis of the people's democratic regime, to impair the construction of socialism, to harm the national economy; indulged in espionage activities, tried to weaken the unity of the Czech people and the Republic's defensive capacity in order to break its firm alliance with the Soviet Union and ruin its friendship with the USSR, in order to liquidate the people's democratic regime in Czechoslovakia, restore capitalism, drag our Republic into the imperialist camp and destroy its sovereignty and national independence.

Not one of the defendants winced as he heard the bill which reproduced numerous 'confessions and admissions' (particularly those of Slansky, Frejka and Frank), as well as the statements of witnesses and extracts from experts' reports on economic and industrial problems. Our crimes ranged from high treason to military treason, passing through espionage and sabotage.

These charges, brought against us by Urvalek in the name of the Czech people, stated that *the conspirators did all they could to prevent the supply of our goods to the Soviet Union and the other people's democratic states, neglecting contracts and asking far higher prices for these goods than the current prices on the world market. In the capitalist states, on the other hand, they sold the same goods at considerably reduced rates in comparison with the prices for the USSR, and far below the level of the prices on the world market.*

Urvalek read some statements by Slansky:

We impeded the development of foreign trade with the Soviet Union by ordering and importing machinery from the capitalist states, although the same machines were made in the USSR where they could be purchased cheaper. A large number of Soviet orders were refused on the pretext that Czech industry was not producing the goods required, while in fact it was producing them.

In other cases trade with the Soviet Union was restricted by deliberately high prices or by orders which were only partially accepted under the pretext that the capacity of the factory was insufficient, while the delivery of the goods was delayed. . . . The same measures were taken against orders from the other people's democracies and trade relations with these countries were thereby reduced accordingly . . .

Urvalek at last reached the end of the list of crimes against the state and the people:

The treachery and perfidious nature of this attack against the liberty, sovereignty and independence of our country, plotted by these criminals, are all the worse since they took advantage of their membership of the Communist Party of Czechoslovakia and the confidence of the Party dear to our workers. They misused the the responsibility of their high posts, in order to ally themselves with our most determined enemies, the American imperialists and their minions, in order to sell our country into capitalist slavery. The conspirators only managed to carry out their criminal activities by feigning agreement with the programme and policy of the Communist Party and hiding their real faces behind a cunning mask. Even when the first members of the centre of conspiracy against the state had been unmasked and put in prison that sly, double-faced Janus, Rudolf Slansky, tried to distract attention from himself as leader of the plot and pretended to be himself a victim of the subversive activities of Sling, Svermova and others.

But although the conspirators led by Slansky succeeded in occupying important posts in the Party and the state they did not manage, as did Tito in Yugoslavia, to subjugate the supreme organs of Party and state, to usurp power and reach their criminal goals.

Thanks to the vigilance, the clear-sightedness and intelligence of Comrade Klement Gottwald, the guide of the Czech people; thanks to the unity of the Central Committee of the Communist Party, firmly united round Comrade Klement Gottwald; thanks to the indefectible loyalty and devotion of the Czech people to the Party, the government and Comrade Klement Gottwald; thanks to the unshakable loyalty of our people to the Soviet Union, the conspiracy has been broken and the criminals' efforts thwarted.... Loyal to the people, the government, the Party and Comrade Klement Gottwald, the organs of State Security stayed the criminal hands of the conspirators in time...

On the basis of the above-mentioned facts:

RUDOLF SLANSKY, *born 31–7–1901, of Jewish origin, of a family of tradesmen ... former Secretary General of the Communist Party of Czechoslovakia, Vice-Premier of the Republic of Czechoslovakia before his arrest*

BEDRICH GEMINDER, *born 19–11–1901, of Jewish origin, son of a tradesman and restaurant owner ... former head of the department of international relations of the Central Committee of the Communist Party of Czechoslovakia*

LUDVIK FREJKA, *born 15–1–1904, of Jewish origin, son of a doctor ... former head of the economic department of the Chancellery of the President of the Republic of Czechoslovakia*

JOSEF FRANK, *born 15–2–1909, Czech, from a worker's family ... former Assistant Secretary General of the Communist Party of Czechoslovakia*

VLADIMIR CLEMENTIS, *born 20–9–1902, Slovak, from a bourgeois family ... former Minister of Foreign Affairs*

BEDRICH REICIN, *born 29–9–1911, of Jewish origin, from a bourgeois family ... former Under-Secretary of National Defence*

KAREL SVAB, *born 13–5–1904, Czech, from a workers' family ... former Under-Secretary of National Security*

ARTUR LONDON, *born 1–2–1915, of Jewish origin, son of a tradesman ... former Under-Secretary of Foreign Affairs*

VAVRO HAJDU, *born 8–8–1913, of Jewish origin, son of the owner of a bathing establishment in Smrdaky ... former Under-Secretary of Foreign Affairs*

EUGEN LÖBL, *born 14–5–1907, of Jewish origin, son of wholesale dealers ... former Under-Secretary of Foreign Trade*

RUDOLF MARGOLIUS, *born 31–8–1913, of Jewish origin, son of wholesale dealers ... former Under-Secretary of Foreign Trade*

OTTO FISCHL, *born 17–8–1902, of Jewish origin, son of a trades-man . . . former Under-Secretary of Finance*

OTTO SLING, *born 24–8–1912, of Jewish origin, son of manu-facturers . . . former secretary of the regional Committee of the Communist Party of Czechoslovakia in Brno*

ANDRÉ SIMONE, *born 27–5–1895, of Jewish origin, son of manu-facturers . . . former editor of the paper* Rude Pravo, *are charged with . . .*

During the three hours which it took to read the bill of indictment there was total silence in the hall. From time to time we were dazzled by the light of the reflectors. We were being filmed, and would soon be shown in dark cinemas before the main feature.

The session was suspended and we were taken back to our cells. In the afternoon I was driven to Ruzyn. I was in a state of complete apathy. I was caught up in a process and I had no more human reactions than a piece of metal on a conveyor belt about to be crushed in a machine.

Two days later, on 12 November, it was my turn to stand witness. In the meantime I had had to repeat my lines again. I also knew the precise moment at which I would be interrupted by the prosecutor and by the judge and what their questions would be.

As I was waiting for my turn in a box in the wings, Kohoutek came to see me. He told me that the Party leaders were following the course of the trial attentively and that they hoped all the defendants would live up to their expectations. He also told me not to forget what Bacilek had said – that my future depended on my behaviour. Then Kohoutek speculated on the sentences. According to him they would be heavy, but there would be no death sentence. Even if, by some chance, there were one or two, they could always appeal. 'I repeat,' he insisted, 'that what the Party needs at the moment is not heads but a large political trial.'

As an example he gave details of the trial of the Industrial Party in Moscow. All the heavy sentences that had been passed.

including the death sentences, had subsequently been commuted to far lighter ones. He spoke of Ramzin, the main defendant, and compared him to Slansky. After being sentenced to death, the Party commuted his sentence to ten years in prison, of which he only served five. He was then released for good conduct. He even added that Ramzin had received one of the highest decorations in the Soviet Union for the work he performed in prison.

His words cheered me considerably, particularly since he spoke with great conviction and seemed to believe what he was saying. I wanted to believe it too, and to convince myself I thought that during the last two years Kohoutek and all the other interrogators had shown a total ignorance of past history. When they tried to talk about it they did so like schoolboys reciting badly learned lines, repeating snatches of conversation heard between the Soviet advisers. If, as he told me, he hadn't made it up, he must have been repeating what the Soviet advisers had said.

Two

I was again led into the hall, and placed before a microphone opposite the Court. Only three defendants were sitting in the dock: Slansky, Geminder and Clementis. They had already stood witness.

When the judge asked me whether I had understood the bill of indictment I said I had. He then asked me if I admitted my guilt. I recited my lines coldly and carefully, as though they did not concern me. I almost felt that I was standing witness at the trial of my double.

'I admit that I am guilty of having actively participated, from 1948 to the day of my arrest, in the centre of conspiracy against the State of Czechoslovakia, formed and led by Rudolf Slansky . . .

' . . . I fully admit my guilt for having ensured and negotiated Slansky's espionage activities with the British agent Zilliacus and, further, as a member of the conspiracy, having used the diplomatic pouch of the Ministry of Foreign Affairs for this purpose. Apart from this I myself had espionage dealings with the American agent Noel Field and gave him information.'

The prosecutor: 'What led you to act as an enemy against the people's democratic Republic of Czechoslovakia?'

'I was brought up in a bourgeois milieu. I have always felt alien to the working classes and I was led by my selfish bourgeois instinct which was to secure my career and personal well-being. But it was above all my eleven-year stay in the West which made me totally alien to Czechoslovakia, so that I really did not know the Czech people, their habits and their struggle for freedom. During my stay in the West I became cosmopolitan and entered the bourgeois camp. This led me into the Trotskyist group from the International Brigades in Spain when I was in France in 1940. The group was centred at Marseilles and financed by the American organization, the YMCA, and its Czech section, the Czech Aid Centre, an organ of the American intelligence services, under the orders of the spy Lowry and the Trotskyist Dubina,'

The prosecutor. 'Give us some details about the Trotskyist group with which you entered into contact in France in 1940.'

'As an émigré in 1940 I worked in the Main d'Oeuvre Immigré. There I found out about the existence of a Trotskyist group in Marseilles composed of former Czech members of the International Brigades. I entered into contact with this group, exerted my influence on it and, thanks to my contacts in France, brought it to Paris.

'Oswald Zavodsky, Laco Holdos, Antonin Svoboda and others were members of this group. All these men came to Czechoslovakia at the end of the Second World War and thanks to Slansky managed to occupy important posts in the Party and the state, as well as in the army.

'Slansky acted as he did because he was a Trotskyist himself, held bourgeois attitudes and attracted people of his own kind, on whom he counted so as to carry out his treacherous plans. It was precisely by assembling such a group of people that Slansky formed his centre of conspiracy . . . '

I then said that it was during the Seventh Party Congress, in 1946, that Slansky, 'after a conversation which lasted intermittently for two days', had told me about his criminal plans and suggested I collaborate with him; that 'to force my hand he had referred to the letter of the Minister of Defence with which his accomplice, Mikse, the military attaché at the embassy in Paris, had threatened me . . .

'Slansky ordered me to undermine and spy on the progressive French movement. Geminder and Zavodsky were working to accomplish the same task . . .

'I came back to Prague after a cure in Switzerland. When Slansky appointed me to the Ministry of Foreign Affairs I had to work there in collaboration with the other accomplices, Clementis, Hajdu . . .

'Dozens of other equally factious accomplices of Slansky received jobs of similar importance . . .

'On Geminder's suggestion I directed my activity towards the important Cadre Department of the Ministry of Foreign Affairs. . . . I used the diplomatic pouch for the purposes of spying against the state. I was a link in the chain of espionage uniting Slansky and Geminder to the former Intelligence Service agent, Koni Zilliacus. The latter was always the Centre's main contact with the leading circles of western imperialists . . . and was aiming to overthrow the regime in Czechoslovakia . . . '

I continued:

'In England, it was the Czech ambassador, Kratochvil, the councillor Goldstücker and Pavel Kavan who were in contact with Zilliacus. They distributed the secret mail which Geminder and Slansky sent Zilliacus in the diplomatic pouch.'

The prosecutor: 'Tell me about your dealings with the American agent Noel Field.'

'I entered into contact with the notorious American agent Noel Field in 1947 in Geneva in Switzerland. . .

'Using the Unitarian Service Committee as a cover, the American intelligence service, with the aid of various individuals in eastern Europe, attempted to penetrate the peoples' democracies and send subversive forces into action. Field, who offered various forms of assistance as well as financial aid to several individuals, made acquaintances and contacts. He attached them to himself and created conditions propitious for enlisting them in his service and making them work for American espionage. This was how Field obtained information of vital importance for espionage against the people's democracies, as was proved in the Rajk trial in Hungary. This network of agents working for American espionage had been set up by Field amongst individuals who reached high posts in the state and Party on their return to their people's democracy . . . '

The judge: 'Did you mention your dealings with Field to anyone?'

'Yes, I mentioned them several times to Slansky, Geminder, and later to Karel Svab. By some subtle hints Svab led me to understand that it was only thanks to Slansky, Geminder and himself that my collaboration with Field had no further consequences.'

The prosecutor: 'That means that Slansky, Geminder and Svab protected you as a collaborator and prevented you from being unmasked.'

'Yes, that's right. This bound me still more closely to Slansky. From then on I carried out his criminal policy against Czechoslovakia still more actively.'

I continued the list of my 'crimes', accomplished as Under-Secretary of Foreign Affairs. Taking advantage of my position in a certain commission I placed 'cadres hostile to the state in the diplomatic service abroad'.

The judge: 'Who were you in direct contact with in the Ministry of Foreign Affairs at the time of your subversive activity?'

'After entering the Ministry of Foreign Affairs I entered into contact with Hajdu, Dufek and Clementis according to Geminder's instructions. With Clementis, and assisted by Geminder, I managed to arrange for the Party Organization Committee to be largely composed of people loyal to us. This would have enabled us to carry out our hostile activity in the Ministry. At the time of the purges, at the end of 1949, we consolidated the positions of our men and placed them in still higher posts, where they replaced those who stood in our way.'

The prosecutor: 'Why were you systematically attempting to gain control of the Party Organization Committee?'

'The activity of the Trotskyist group in the Ministry was determined by the criminal policy of the centre directed against the state. By mastering the Party Organization we ensured and facilitated the performance of a hostile policy and simplified the distribution of our cadres. This was why our Trotskyist group was in close collaboration with Clementis, and could remain hidden. To reach this goal we drew up, in late February 1949, a list of candidates for the Party Committee. It included people who had collaborated with us and were under our influence. But we did not manage to get our candidates in at the next meeting, so Geminder declared the elections null and void. He summoned the conspirators to Clementis's office and said that the list of candidates must be imposed on the Party Committee and headed by the Trotskyist Dufek .. . . We were consequently free to carry out our hostile activity in the Ministry of Foreign Affairs . . .'

The judge: 'So far you have not explained how the Trotskyist group in the Ministry of Foreign Affairs was formed or who composed the crux of it.'

'I was away when the group was formed. Nevertheless . . . I discovered that it had been formed immediately after the events of February 1948 on the orders of Slansky and Geminder. . . . Its members' shady pasts provided Slansky with a guarantee for his plans against the state. To start with Hajdu and Dufek were at the centre of the group . . . and received orders from

Geminder.... After my own appointment in the Ministry in 1949 I became a member of the Trotskyist group.... On Geminder's orders we took advantage of the process of reorganization to retain Benes's followers and Trotskyists favourable to our designs against the state in the central office. We gave them all decisive posts ... '

I went on to say that on Clementis's orders we formed commissions with the same functions as the special departments. This did not require the approval of the government, and enabled us to place in leading posts men designated by Clementis.

I also explained how I had sabotaged the recruitment of the working-class cadres for the Ministry.

The prosecutor: 'Now tell us with which Trotskyists you were in contact during your conspiratorial activity at the Ministry of Foreign Affairs.'

'With the Trotskyists who had fought in the International Brigades, like Josef Pavel, Osvald Zavodsky, Oskar Vales, Antonin Svoboda, Otakar Hromadko, and Hoffman.... They all secured important sections of the Party and the state for Slansky.... We often met in the office or flat of one of the conspirators and during these meetings we discussed the appointment of our men, former members of the International Brigades, in the state offices.'

The prosecutor: 'What happened at your conspiratorial meeting in January 1951?'

'We were afraid. That's why we met early in January 1951. We wondered what we could do to guard ourselves against discovery.... We agreed to ask for Slansky's support. As long as he was in a leading position, he would continue to defend us. We were all the more convinced of this since Slansky had protected us once already.'

The prosecutor: 'How and when did that happen?'

'It was shortly after the Rajk trial, in Hungary, towards the end of summer 1949, at a time when the Party was examining the past of a few former members of the International Brigades in Spain and in France. At that time we had drawn up a list of former volunteers with a shady past at Pavel's instigation, thereby distracting attention from our Trotskyist activity first in Spain and then in France. Thanks to that we managed to hide . . . '

The judge: 'Is that all you have to say about your activity against the state?'

'Yes, I haven't hidden anything, either during the investigation or before the court. I have told you all about my participation in the centre of conspiracy directed against the state and led by Slansky. I have even admitted that, as a conspirator, I led a subversive activity at the Ministry of Foreign Affairs with my accomplices Clementis, Geminder, Hajdu, Dufek and others. I was part of the Trotskyist group in the Ministry of Foreign Affairs and our activity aimed to overthrow the organization of the Ministry. I was also in contact with the American agent Noel Field and in 1947 I transmitted espionage information to him.'

The judge: 'And yet we are informed that you hid something at the beginning of the investigation. What was it?'

'Finally I must draw your attention to the fact that, at the beginning of the investigation, I concealed my principal crime: my participation in the conspiracy. I did that because I knew that the leader of the conspiracy, Rudolf Slansky, was free and that he occupied one of the most important posts in the state. I counted on him and hoped for his assistance. During the investigation I realized that this was pointless, since no help came. That is why I decided to confess everything about my hostile activity against the state and that of my accomplices, including the head of the centre of the conspiracy, Rudolf Slansky himself. I did so in all sincerity.'

In my testimony I referred to my fellow defendants as my 'accomplices' just as they all mentioned me as their 'accomplice'.

My fellow prisoners appeared as witnesses for the prosecution against me: Goldstücker, Kavan, Klinger, Horvath, Dufek,

Hajek, Zavodsky, and a free witness, Borek, Under-Secretary of Foreign Affairs.

Here are some edifying passages about our complicity in crime from the statement of my fellow defendant Svab, Under-Secretary of National Security.

The prosecutor: 'Who were the people who composed the centre of this conspiracy against the state?'

Svab: 'Apart from Rudolf Slansky, who directed this enemy activity, and myself who, as a war criminal and saboteur of national Security, had to see that the activity of the centre of conspiracy was not revealed, the leading group of the centre included Vladimir Clementis, who had undertaken to serve the French espionage service, and who was a bourgeois Slovak nationalist; Bedrich Geminder, a cosmopolitan and bourgeois Jewish nationalist; Bedrich Reicin, the saboteur of the Czech army and a bourgeois Jewish nationalist, and Josef Frank, a black marketeer and Slansky's closest collaborator; the Trotsky-ist Artur London, a Jewish bourgeois nationalist and a spy; Ludvik Frejka, a Jewish bourgeois nationalist, a spy and a collaborator with the American agent Emanuel Voska; Otto Sling, a Jewish bourgeois nationalist; Eugen Löbl, a spy trained in Benes's reactionary group in London; Otto Fischl, a Jewish bourgeois nationalist and agent of the imperialist State of Israel; and André Simone-Katz, a Jewish bourgeois nationalist and a spy ...

'I also covered up in the same way for the other members of the conspiracy, giving the compromising documents to Slansky and individually warning the members of the centre who were in danger.'

The judge: 'Who were they?'

Svab: 'Artur London, whom Slansky and I knew to be a Trotskyist and a collaborator of the American spy Noel Field. In spite of that Slansky gave him an important post in the Ministry of Foreign Affairs in 1948. It was Bedrich Geminder who organized enemy activity in the department of foreign policy. He had the influence to do so as head of the International

Department of the Central Secretariat of the Communist Party of Czechslovakia. It was Slansky who had appointed Geminder to this post.'

The prosecutor: 'How did you and Slansky sabotage the inquiry into the enemy activity in Czechoslovakia of the American spy Noel Field?'

Svab: 'The American spy Noel Field, who was unmasked during the Hungarian trial, said in his statement that he had formed an espionage network in Czechoslovakia and that this network exercised a vast activity.'

The judge: 'How did you hide what you knew about Field?'

Svab: 'When Slansky and I realized that we could not suppress his evidence, Slansky ordered a formal inquiry to be made about the various members of the Centre who were concerned. During the inquiry they were all informed of the content of Field's evidence so as to be able to prepare their defence . . .

'Like Tito, Slansky was mainly supported by the well-organized Trotskyist group of former volunteers from Spain, who covered up for each other. The group was led by the Trotskyist Josef Pavel, Osvald Zavodsky and the spy London. . . . I prevented these groups from being revealed and intentionally distracted the attention of State Security from all the Trotskyist elements by pretending that the Trotskyists were inocuous.

The prosecutor: 'Did Slansky give you instructions about what you had to do in your Security post?'

Svab: 'Yes. I asked Slansky how I should proceed. He advised me to read the book by the former head of the French police, Fouché, and learn something from it. This was before I joined Security. In his book Fouché, who claimed to be a specialist, describes an interminable series of intrigues, frauds and plots. He recommends organizing provocatory groups and staging trials to eliminate or to compromise inconvenient individuals, even going so far as to murder them. Finally he shows how he fell into disgrace despite his loyal services to the king and how he managed to return to favour. I clearly understood that Slansky meant me to act in the same way . . . '

The cynicism of the men who organized our trial was amazing. They put their own ideas into Svab's mouth. It was the same shamelessness with which they persuaded his own sister, Svermova, to testify to his guilt as a member of the conspiracy against the state: 'In Security Slansky used Karel Svab for his enemy activity. The possession of these departments (Foreign Affairs and Security) which were of such importance to the state, was essential in order to prepare a conspiracy . . .'

While I heard Karel Svab's evidence I recalled all he had made me suffer, the months of tension, demoralization, anguish and fear. In the end I regarded him as one of the main causes of my misfortune, one of the men who introduced police and terrorist methods into the Party. His coldness, his way of approaching everyone like a potential suspect, the brutality of all he said and his behaviour towards me, had convinced me of this.

Then, when I heard that he too had been arrested, I started to forget the executioner and think of the victim. The Soviet advisers, in whom he had such blind faith as 'the defenders of proletarian justice', had eliminated him. They had tricked him, manipulated him, used him before arresting him, torturing him and finally including him in the Slansky trial – they needed a representative of enemy forces in State Security.

Karel Svab was a worker, the son of a militant socialist who had also been a worker. In 1918, when he was fourteen, he had provided the Spartacists with ammunition in Germany, where his family was living. In 1929 he spent a year in the USSR as a pupil of the Red Sporting International, and he retained a boundless admiration for the home country of socialism. When the Nazis occupied Prague he was arrested and spent the whole war in prison and concentration camps. He was with Zapotocky and Dolansky in the resistance organization in Sachsenhausen-Oranienburg.

Now, like Frank, he was made to 'confess' that he had been a war criminal working for the Gestapo in the concentration camps. His comrades who fought with him and had been in the camp – Zapotocky, the Premier, and Dolansky, the Vice Premier, both members of the Political Bureau – said nothing.

As I was finishing this book I heard from members of Svab's family. When they saw Svab's dossier, at the time of the legal rehabilitation in 1963, they discovered that, in spite of his absolute confidence in the Soviet advisers, he had refused to rely on the central Control Commission of the Party in November 1950, and had expressed some doubt about the results of its inquiry into the enemies within the Party. As Under-Secretary of Security he had even refused to follow up the proposals of this Commission (which had turned from a political commission into a police commission) to proceed to certain arrests. Some of the members, like my first inquisitor, Smola, went straight into Security and then on to the interrogations, and the whole Commission was entirely in the hands of the Soviet advisers.

By doing this Svab had signed his death warrant. At the beginning of December 1950, at the request of the Soviet advisers and the Control Commission, he was dismissed by his Minister, Kopriva, and on 16 February 1951, he was arrested.

A remark by his sister Anna confirmed my theory about Zavodsky's immediate confessions. Svab was Under-Secretary of Security, and therefore worked on a political level. Zavodsky, a departmental manager, worked on the technical, practical level. Svab's sister wrote: 'Everything points to the fact that if he had known about the real methods of investigation he would not have faced such appalling interrogations or gone back on his "confessions". He would immediately have done whatever they asked.'

This would have changed nothing in the ladder of suffering and martydom between Zavodsky and him. Zavodsky was simply to wait eighteen months longer for the hangman's noose.

Then came Zavodsky's turn to testify against his former chief, Svab, and myself.

The judge: 'What do you know about Karel Svab's activity?'

Zavodsky: 'I knew that Svab was devoted to Rudolf Slansky and that he was among the enemies in his group.

'I myself helped Svab, on Slansky's direct orders, to cover up the activity of Artur London, revealed as an American agent.'

The judge: 'How did this happen?'

Zavodsky: 'In 1949, during an inquiry about the American spy Noel Field, it was incontestably proved that London's dealings with Field amounted to espionage. Slansky knew this prefectly well from what Karel Svab had told him. In spite of this Slansky gave no orders that measures should be taken against London. . . . Slansky had been in contact with London ever since he had brought the group of former volunteers in Spain, demoralized and undermined by Trotskyism, from France to Czechoslovakia and placed them in state offices. London directed this group in France. . . . He told me that Slansky was trying to persuade him to remain in Czechoslovakia and offered him a lucrative position in the Cadre Department of the Central Committee of the Communist Party of Czechoslovakia. He also promised him to look after his family.

'When London returned to Czechoslovakia on a permanent basis, towards the end of 1948, at the time when Slansky and Geminder appointed him Under-Secretary of Foreign Affairs in charge of cadre policy, London, together with Josef Pavel, again resumed the leadership of the enemy group of former volunteers from Spain, and under his leadership the group was again formed into an organized unit of individuals who mutually supported each other . . .

'In 1946, during a conversation I had with London at the central secretariat of the Communist Party, he told me that he was prepared to work in France for Slansky and Geminder and said that, through me, he proposed to provide Slansky and Geminder with secret information.

'London sent me information intended for Geminder until 1947, when he left France for a cure in Switzerland, and spied for the American agent Noel Field, a collaborator of Allen Dulles, head of the American espionage services in Europe. I knew about this extremely serious matter from the information at the disposal of State Security. Rudolf Slansky, who saw all the information of this nature, was also aware of this.'

The text of the statements of all the witnesses for the prosecution was meticulously prepared in Ruzyn, as was all the 'evidence' which I myself was forced to give in other trials.

Everything went off as Kohoutek had explained to me. The public prosecutor and the judge asked their questions at the precise moment indicated in my report. They repeated word for word the questions I had learned in my text, and which had been formulated by the men in Ruzyn. Not a word was changed, nor did they hesitate for a second. They too had learned their lines!

My lawyer did not ask a single question. Our interrogators were right when they said: 'The court will do as we say.'

How was it possible that some of the most responsible jurists, men whose duty it was to respect the law and apply it, could accept with such servility their position as conscious instruments of the illegality and arbitrariness of the proceedings? The rights of the citizen printed in the Constitution, for which the blood of generations had been spilt, are inseparable from democracy and still more from socialism. Those who had sworn to be their champions had agreed to serve our executioners and to give a legal cloak to the witch hunt.

They were not merely docile: they were zealous.

In the case of Geminder, head of the department of International Relations of the Party's Central Committee – I was out of the room when he stood witness – tears came to my eyes when I read of the zeal with which the judge and Urvalek humiliated him.

The judge: 'What nationality are you?'

Geminder: 'Czech.'

The judge: 'Can you speak Czech well?'

Geminder: 'Yes.'

The judge: 'Do you want an interpreter?'

Geminder: 'No.'

The judge: 'Can you understand the questions and will you be able to reply in Czech?'

Geminder: 'Yes.'

The judge: 'Are you fully aware of the crime of which you have been accused in the bill of indictment by the public prosecutor?'

Geminder: 'Yes, I plead guilty to every charge.'

The prosecutor: 'What was your attitude towards the workers of Czechoslovakia?'

Geminder: 'I was indifferent to the interests of the Czech people, and I have never felt any affinities with them. Their national interests have always remained alien to me.'

The prosecutor: 'What school did you go to?'

Geminder: 'I went to the German school of Ostrava. I left Czechoslovakia in 1919 and ended my secondary studies in Berlin where I took my certificate. At the end of my studies I frequented petty-bourgeois, cosmopolitan and Zionist circles, where I met people of German nationality. This all contributed to the fact that I don't really know the Czech language well.'

The prosecutor: 'In all this time you never really learned to speak Czech well, not even in 1946 when you came to Czechoslovakia and occupied important posts in the Communist Party?'

Geminder: 'No, I didn't learn to speak Czech properly.'

The prosecutor: 'What language can you speak perfectly?'

Geminder: 'German.'

The prosecutor: 'Can you really speak German properly?'

Geminder: 'I haven't spoken it for a long time, but I know it well.'

The prosecutor: 'Can you speak German as well as Czech?'

Geminder: 'Yes.'

The prosecutor: 'So you can't really speak any language properly. You are a typical cosmopolitan. As such you sneaked into the Communist Party.'

Geminder: 'I joined the Czech Communist Party in 1921 and remained a member until I was unmasked in 1951.'

So they tried to deny Geminder's right to belong to the Czech community because his parents were Jews from a border region (my border region). Even Masaryk's Republic had recognized the language rights of the German minority. Czechoslovakia was justly proud of being able to include some admirable German-speaking thinkers, historians, writers, artists and journalists in her cultural heritage. It is enough to mention Kafka, R. M. Rilke, Werfel, E. E. Kisch, Max Brod, Weisskopf, Fürnberg.

Gottwald, Kopriva, Bacilek, Siroky, Kopecky, Dolansky, and Köhler ratified all the distortions of the Soviet advisers and their men in Ruzyn. They concealed the fact that we, as militant communists, had acted on their orders and that they controlled those crimes and acts of treason which we were supposed to have committed. We had all had the wild hope that one day they would realize the extravagance of the confessions extorted from us. In reply they sent Bacilek to us to admit, in a roundabout way, that they were aware of the falsity of our confessions and to ask us to stick to them in the Party's name. At the same time we were threatened and blackmailed with the death sentence.

The judges who tried us betrayed their duty by hiding behind the orders received from the Party leadership. In France I had known judges of Pétain who had accepted the emergency jurisdiction under Nazi occupation and the abolition of the rights to a defence. But they were judges in the bourgeois apparatus of repression. And they never became the mere auxiliaries of the police in such a crude way. For form's sake, at least, they continued to presume that the defendant was innocent. They never put into practice Vishinsky's theory that 'the confession alone serves as proof of guilt.' Even the official counsels for the defence tried to help their clients until the last moment. After our arrest in 1942, although we had been deferred to the state tribunal, my wife and I had always had the right to prepare our defence with our lawyer.

Nothing of the sort happened in Pankrac. Prosecutors and judges did not have the excuse that they believed our confessions since they too had learned by heart the script written by the

Soviet advisers and the men of Ruzyn. They knew it was a farce, but they lent themselves to it, not only when they forced us to say that the legal guarantees had been respected when they had violated them themselves, but also when, at every moment, they proved to be the servitors of falsehood.

What else was Novak doing when he deliberately omitted the reasons for my imprisonment in Ostrava in 1931, 1932 and 1933, in Paris in August 1942, my deportation to Mauthausen, as well as all my antifascist activity from my report? He simply had to form my character as a spy and substantiate the idea of a suspicious past.

So there was nothing surprising about the fact that they should believe implicitly in all the material submitted to them by Security, and authenticate it without checking it.

They accepted as proof of my 'baseness' letters and perfectly legal documents taken from the archives of the Ministry of Foreign Affairs or from the International Department of the Party and they produced them as exhibits for the prosecution throughout the trial.

The prosecutor: 'I am showing the court a document which proves the defendant London's activity against the state. It is the photocopy of a letter written in Paris by London on 10 July 1942 to Slansky, and it proves that these two men were writing against the state. I shall then show the original of the letter written by London in Paris on 7 November 1946 to Geminder. It proves his subversive contacts with Geminder. The photocopy of the letter written and sent by Rudolf Slansky to Paris also proves London's subversive dealings with Slansky. I shall also show the photograph of the American spy Noel Field on the back of which London himself has certified his espionage dealings with Field . . .'

Then they produced the documents about Zilliacus sent to and from the embassies in London and Paris, and letters to and from Goldstücker and other employees in the Ministry concerning visa and cadre problems. And finally 'the original of the letter written on 23 March 1950 by Milos Nekvasil to London, which proves London's subversive dealings with the Trotskyist group of former members of the International Brigades'.

Any serious examination of the documents in my file, presented as decisive evidence, would show that my letter to Geminder was merely a friendly greeting accompanying an article for the review *Svetove Rozhledy* to which I had agreed to contribute, and my letter to Goldstücker mere routine. The letter sent to me in Paris by Slansky was an introduction for the new correspondent of the Czech Press Agency (CTK), Jirka Drtina, who had just been appointed to Paris. The last was a personal letter from Nekvasil, in which he ranted against some of our former comrades in the Brigades.

In the case of each defendant the exhibits shown to the jury were all similar. During Vavro Hajdu's statement the following exhibit was provided as 'irrefutable' proof of his anti-Sovietism and his collusion with the Anglo-American imperialists.

The prosecutor: 'I submit to the court the key document, It is one of the speeches broadcast on the BBC on 4 May 1945 in which you (Hajdu) blatantly praise the Anglo-Americans as the instrument of the defeat of Nazi Germany and you don't even mention the part played by the Soviet Union, which was in fact far more important. In your speech you said: "By far the greatest credit for the victory is due to the heroic American and British armies, under the leadership of Field-Marshal Alexander, who fought courageously until the final goal was achieved, the destruction of the enemy and his capitulation." '

This phrase was part of a speech written by Vavro Hajdu to be broadcast to the people of occupied Czechoslovakia, in celebration of the defeat of the Axis forces in Italy and their surrender on 2 May 1945 to the allied armies under the command of Field-Marshal Alexander.

Such a cynical and impudent way of abusing public credulity in broad daylight and of flouting justice suggested the greatest contempt for mankind.

When, during my stay in Moscow, I happened to visit the re-educational colony of the *bezprizornis* in Kuntzevo, in the woods not far from Moscow, the director told us at length about the methods, firm but humane, applied by the apparatus of Soviet justice to help the real men escape from contamination. Like every sincere communist, I had always believed that there could be no true socialist democracy without legality and juridical security, just as there could be no true justice without socialist democracy.

Which of us had not at one point read Makarenko's moving book *The Flags on the Tower*? Who had not wept as he watched the superb film, *The Roads of Life*? That was why my comrades and I could never suspect the Moscow trials.

Like all those who had spent years in prison for their ideas, who had seen the reality of prisons and suffered from the inhumanity of arbitrary bourgeois justice, I too believed that communism would provide a new justice. And now our trial was to be added to the long list of trials which had dishonoured our communist ideal. My thirteen companions and I were victims of this total degeneration. But other comrades would retain their illusions. They would see their worst enemies in me and in those who would follow in our footsteps, while the men who dishonoured us before killing us and shamed our comrades into applauding our murder would remain not only at the head of the Party but at the head of the whole movement.

How did we slip into this alienation of thought? Had I not been the first to fight the men who accused Stalin of imposture? And now I thought of the trials to come, of the hundreds of names in reserve on the administrative reports in Ruzyn. Besides, the words Slansky was to say at the end of his final statement, and which were suppressed in the official documents, substantiated my fears. To our amazement Slansky said: 'Our centre of conspiracy against the state included hundreds of members . . . ' Together with the witnesses no more than seventy or eighty of us had been implicated, so happy days lay ahead for the interrogators of Ruzyn and their ringleaders.

Three

The carefully selected audience consisted mainly of officials from the Ministry of Security in civilian dress, and delegates picked from the factories and ministries. The latter only received tickets for one day of the trial, and they were relayed by other men every day. There were also some Czech journalists and the representatives of the central organs of foreign Communist Parties. Some of them, like Pierre Hentgès, knew me. That was why he was all the harder on me when he reported the proceedings. Had I not entered their camp to murder their wives and daughters?

The families of the defendants were not notified as to the date of the trials. It was by reading the papers or listening to the radio that they heard that their husband, father, brother or son was being tried that day. This was unprecedented.

Between sessions the warders led us into a corridor where there were eight plywood boxes. Opposite there were two open cells, occupied by Slansky and Clementis, and then four more boxes. Our warders from Ruzyn stood before every box to prevent us from talking to each other. I was between Geminder and Hajdu, opposite Clementis's cell. We could see each other perfectly well, and ever since the first day we had exchanged friendly signs of greeting. By looks and gestures, we established a silent dialogue.

We did not all react in the same way. Geminder, for example, stared into space. He seemed deep in thought, walked like an automaton, and sat motionless in his box. He never replied to any smile or sign of friendship. Although he was an old friend of Slansky, who was in the cell opposite him, he never tried to signal to him, but looked away every time he saw him. His eyes were blank. I myself tried in vain to attract his attention. And yet we had known each other since our childhood.

I saw Slansky every time he returned to his cell. He appeared calm, despite his haggard features. He passed before all his fellow defendants, staring at something in front of him, not looking at any of us. From time to time we saw one of his interrogators join him in his cell with a plate concealed between two files. Maybe he required special food for his health.

Between sessions André Simone, who suffered from diarrhoea, used to pass in front of my box to go to the lavatory. He looked very ill. His face had changed completely. He was like an old man. His jaws sagged and his chin receded. I was unable to conceal my astonishment and my interrogator explained that his false teeth had broken in prison, deforming his face, and that he had constant diarrhoea, since he was unable to chew his food. What had they done to him? He had once had such an easy gait and quick wit. When Vilem Novy, with whom he had worked for many years on the editorial board of *Rude Pravo*, came to stand witness against him and the judge asked him to point out André Simone among the defendants, Novy turned to us and looked at us all, without recognizing the man he was looking for. The second time around he looked aghast as he at last recognized André Simone, a caricature of the brilliant journalist he had once known.

As for my friend Hajdu, he sat frowning in the box next to mine, nervously smoking one cigarette after the other. When his interrogator brought him a cup of coffee he replied surlily 'Pass it to London,' as he used to do when we lunched together. He didn't care for coffee much, but he knew that I loved it. During the sessions only a warder stood between me and him. I watched Hajdu. He was tense and scratched the palms of his hands. He, the legal expert, just muttered insults when he heard what was being said in court. When his lawyer was pleading he could hardly contain himself: 'Moron, idiot, bastard!' Several times the warder between us in the dock nudged him to make him keep quiet.

Margolius was very dignified. He managed to dominate his feelings, like Frejka and Frank, whose faces were immobile.

Fischl looked shattered. Löbl was calm, in control of himself. He talked at length to his interrogator between sessions.

Reicin and Svab paid attention to everything around them. Of us all, Sling was the most relaxed, the most energetic. When he saw me he greeted me, and every time he passed me he nodded and smiled. Had he not lost so much weight in these two years of prison he would have been the one who had changed least.

As Sling was giving evidence and gesticulating, his trousers which had become far too big for him fell to his feet. Seeing him in his underpants we all laughed hysterically, and he laughed so much himself that he had difficulty in continuing his statement.

Clementis was one of the ones to laugh most. He tried to calm himself by squeezing his pipe between his teeth to breaking point. Slansky laughed till tears ran down his face, and his whole body shook.

The audience and the members of the court roared with laughter. The prosecutor hid his face behind a newapaper. The members of the court plunged their heads into their files. The warders yelped as they tried to stifle their laughter. The only one not to change expression was Geminder.

But the misfortune which befell our comrade was a mere pretext. The actors of the appalling tragedy were at last allowed some form of relief.

The judge had to suspend the proceedings.

Kohoutek and the interrogators were indignant. During the interval they told us that Sling had made a clown of himself on purpose. By bending down to pick up his trousers he had managed to show his behind to the court. This proved, they said, that Sling was a frightful blackguard who couldn't give a damn about anyone or anything.

During the week of the trial the entire headquarters of Ruzyn, led by Doubek, were mobilized at Pankrac.

We got better food than usual, coffee and cigarettes. When the session was prolonged we were given sandwiches.

There was a constant coming and going in the wings of the

court between sessions and in the subterranean corridor where
we had our cells. The heads of Ruzyn visited the defendants
for whom they were responsible several times a day in order
to keep up the morale of 'their clients'.

As usual Kohoutek was talkative, too talkative. He said that
the Party was satisfied, that our 'friends' had spoken to the
the Party leaders who followed every detail of the trial attentively. His own outlook was still more optimistic than before the
proceedings. I tried to catch what Doubek and the other head
interrogators were saying to my fellow defendants. From what
I could gather they were all discussing the same thing.

When the chiefs left the interrogators again returned to the
subject. They told us that their opinion was based on the conversations they had had with their superiors. According to them
Sling would have one of the heaviest sentences, twenty years;
Hajdu, twelve years; Löbl, twelve years; Clementis and
Geminder, from fifteen to eighteen years; Slansky, twenty or at
most twenty-five years; Margolius, ten years; and me, twelve.

But as the trial proceeded we became increasingly pessimistic.
We feared that the last act of the tragedy would end in a far
more sinister manner than we had been led to imagine.

Dr Sommer diligently visited us and gave us tranquillizers.
At night, in my cell, I could not sleep. I got up, paced round and
from time to time the warder would offer me a cigarette and
try to calm me. The same thing must have happened in the
thirteen other cells, because I heard the sound of steps and
muffled voices.

In the court the hostility was more and more marked. It must
have increased with the proceedings. And then there was the
evidence, the worst of which was Gusta Fucikova's. She accused
Reicin of having handed over her husband to the Gestapo. Her
peroration, which repeated the last words of Fucik in his book
Written under the Gallows, was greeted by frantic applause:

'Whoever has lived for the future and has fallen for its beauty
is a figure hewn in stone. But he who, with the dust of the past,
tries to build a dam against the current of the revolution, is no

more than a puppet of rotten wood, even if his shoulders be decorated with gold braid. To the men whom I loved, I say: be vigilant!'

The day before the prosecutor read his charge, Kohoutek asked me what sentence I thought would be demanded. I replied that we would all be hanged. He then looked at me dully, shaking his head slowly: 'That's not possible. They can't hang you all. They must leave some of you alive. And the chances are that you'll be one of them, since the charges against you are lighter than the others. Even if the sentences are heavy, what counts in all political trials is to remain alive. Don't lose hope.' Even a man like Kohoutek, who was a zealous architect of this trial, seemed overcome by the tragic turn the proceedings were taking in court.

In the evenings, until late into the night, and in the morning, before the sessions, we could hear the tapping of typewriters. From my interrogator I discovered that even here individuals who were still at liberty were being questioned and having reports drawn up on them.

Sometimes, between sessions, a defendant was brought a sheet of paper so that he could make a note of the names he was to add in his evidence. I heard the names of General Svoboda, the Minister Gregor and others. Subsequently, after my release, I managed to look over the papers of this period as well as the typed report of the trial: the more outrageous antisemitic expressions, numerous names and whole passages from our statements were omitted. This reserve material was kept for further trials.

On the morning of 22 November, when he informed me that my statement had been postponed, Kohoutek said: 'After examining Clementis's evidence yesterday, the Party decided to make him appear a second time this morning to make an additional statement about Slovak bourgeois nationalism.'

So it was during the night that the last report had been drawn up with Clementis. He then had to learn his text by heart in order to be ready for the session which opened with his evidence.

The day before the prosecutor's indictment Kohoutek brought me a pencil and paper and asked me to write out my last statement before the verdict. 'You must stick to the line taken in your "confessions" and prove to the Party that you are continuing to do what is expected of you.' A little later I gave him my draft. He left to see his 'chiefs'. Very early the next morning he returned and gave me the corrected text. Three sentences had been crossed out and others had been added. He accused me of not having thought about it enough. 'And now learn it by heart. And don't change anything. Otherwise you'll regret it.'

Fortunately the text was short because I could no longer concentrate. The last days I could hardly follow the proceedings.

I only snatched pieces here and there, from the otherwise dull din. I still felt that my personality was split; I was both actor and spectator in this trial. One thought obsessed me: 'So that was what happened at the trials of Moscow, Budapest and Sofia. How could I and so many other communists, so many honest people, believe in them?'

Four

The seventh day, after the fourteen defendants and the thirty-three witnesses for the prosecution had given evidence without a flaw, Josef Urvalek, the public prosecutor, read the indictment:

'Citizen judges:

'In the memory of man none of our people's democratic courts have had to decide upon the case of criminals such as those sitting in the dock, whom you are to judge today.

'Their moral face has been shown to us in all its horror. We are aware of the peril we have been in. The crimes that have been revealed have made us realize the real causes of the serious defects in numerous sections of our Party, our state and our economy. Like octopi with a thousand tentacles they clutched the body of our Republic to suck its blood and marrow.

'The indignation of our people shows how firmly they have decided to crush any individual who endangers the liberty and independence of our country, who tries to impair our construction of socialism, or who wants to suppress the liberty that the Soviet Union and her glorious army have conquered for us.

'This centre of conspiracy was born in the West during the Second World War to accomplish our subjection by the western imperialists. Only too well do we know that the course and result of the war were different from what the western imperialists intended. They played a bad card when they tried to destroy the Soviet Union with Hitler's help. They did not succeed. Comrade Stalin's brilliant prophecy of 1934 came true. "There can be no doubt that the second war against the Soviet Union will lead to the total defeat of the aggressor, the revolution in certain European and Asiatic countries and the fall of the bourgeois governments and large land-owners in these countries."

'The Soviet Union crushed the "Third Reich" and the Mikado's Japan. With the victory of the USSR and her glorious army of liberation, the bourgeois governments and the large land-owners fell in numerous countries in Europe and Asia.

'The American imperialists, those savage successors of Hitler, tried to prevent their fall and predicted an historical revolution for them.

'As early as the Second World War, the Anglo-American imperialists supported an agency – a whole series of reactionary governments composed of émigrés from Nazi-occupied countries. By assuring them that after the defeat of Nazi Germany they would resume the leading positions they had held before the war they proposed to transform these countries into bases for another war against the USSR.

These bourgeois nationalists and fascist elements of the most reactionary kind were crushed.

'And yet we soon saw that the imperialists, who were playing a game in which the destiny of the nations liberated by the Soviet Army was at stake, had tried to play a false card. The resolutions taken in 1948 and 1949 by the Information Bureau and the Communist and Workers' Parties which unmasked the treachery of the Titoist clique in Yugoslavia have shown, even in the case of Titoist Yugoslavia, what card this was and how dangerous it was. These resolutions have shown that the bourgeoisie remained faithful to the old habit of employing spies and provocateurs in the very heart of the workers' Parties . . . of disrupting these Parties from within and of dominating them themselves. In Yugoslavia they succeeded. But the resolutions of the Information Bureau have not only dealt a deathly blow to Tito's clique but to all the western imperialists. Tito's clique, who turned out to be traitors when the imperialists started fighting the Soviet Union, have been unmasked and their designs have been revealed before the whole world, thanks to the experience the Communist Party of the USSR has gathered in the course of its history.

'Gradually these agencies infiltrated the Communist and Workers' Parties in power in the people's democracies. Thanks to the vigilance of the workers and the Communist Parties, the band of traitors of Laszlo Rajk in Hungary, of Traicho Kostov in Bulgaria, of Kotchi Dzodze in Albania, of Patrascanu in Rumania and of Gomulka in Poland have been revealed and defeated. . .

'Ever since the Second World War the imperialist protectors of the pre-war bourgeois Republic have continued to create their strategic reserves within our Party leadership . . . . Is it mere chance that six of the accused should have come back to our country as spies enlisted in foreign espionage services to accomplish long-term aims: Clementis, Löbl, Sling, Frejka, Hajdu and André Simone? Nor is it by chance that Herman Field, a confirmed spy and close collaborator of Allen Dulles, the head of the American intelligence services in Central and Eastern Europe, recruited his agents through the Trust Fund, a so-called welfare organization which is really an espionage organization and which attracted émigrés at the beginning of the occupation of Poland. Another espionage organization, the USC, functioning in Switzerland under Noel Field, covered up for it . . .

'On the orders of the American imperialists Slansky assembled this whole band of conspirators of which he was the "ataman", that is to say the unquestioned leader . . .

'From the evidence of Oskar Langer, the international Zionist agent, it appears that Slansky was the true leader of all the Jewish bourgeois nationalists and that, in a conversation with him, Slansky emphasized the necessity of giving Zionists and bourgeois Jewish nationalists key posts in economic, political and public life. In his opinion, since these individuals were indispensable to us, there would be no question of objecting to their bourgeois origins. Besides, who were his close friends, from his youth till now? They are here in court, before the people! Geminder, Frejka, Reicin, Sling and company, all old Zionist agents, and with them a whole cohort of other Zionists in leading positions. It was in vain that Slansky tried to hide his Jewish bourgeois nationalist face! He ended his career before the people's tribunal, accused of the worst crimes in our penal code. These odious traitors, having sneaked into the leading sections of the state and Party apparatus thanks to their leader Slansky, proceeded to fill the responsible posts of his section with enemies like himself.

'Who are these men and these groups of men amongst whom Slansky recruited his henchmen for the centre of conspiracy against the state? . . . They are the Trotskyists who were closest to him, even after the liberation of the Republic . . . . After the historical experience of the USSR, from which the whole world drew a lesson, they could never cheat the masses. That was why they pretended to accept the just decisions of the Party and the government. But Slansky sabotaged them . . .

'The third important group from whom Slansky recruited the criminals for his centre were the Zionists. I feel I should examine the movement known as "Zionist" a little more closely. First because, among the accused, there are eight members of Zionist organizations who put themselves at the service of American imperialism. The Zionist organizations have always been involved in the class interests of world capitalism. They are therefore dangerous organizations, which impede the liberation of the working classes.

'The potential danger of these Zionist organizations has ncreased since the foundation of the American protectorate – the so-called State of Israel. Even after its foundation, however, the main base of the Zionist organizations is still in America where the Zionists have numerous adherents among the American monopolists who determine the aggressive policy of the United States. . . . So the Zionist agents of Slansky's centre of conspiracy, by their criminal deeds, were not serving the working people of Israel but rather the American imperialists aiming at world domination and war. Their cosmopolitanism went hand in hand with bourgeois Jewish nationalism. They were two sides to the same coin struck in the Wall Street Mint . . .

'The criminals you see in the dock exploited the natural aversion of the Czech and Slovak peoples to antisemitism, particularly following the Nazis' extensive extermination of the Jews in concentration camps and gas chambers. Profiteers, tradesmen, Jewish bourgeois elements of every description, took advantage of this to sneak into the Party. Refuting all criticism, they could hide their identity as sworn enemies of the nation, by exploiting the sufferings endured by fellow Jews at the hands of the Nazis.

'Our people know perfectly well that our Party will never give up proletarian internationalism and, even in this trial, we are only trying the criminals who endangered the security of the state, the smart Zionist profiteers, the agents of the western imperialists.

"It is evident and logical that Slansky should have chosen to place Zionists in the most important sections of the State economy and the apparatus of the Central Committee of the Communist Party of Czechoslovakia . . .

'The trial shows us the full extent of the Zionist danger

threatening us. But it is also of international importance, because it is not only to our own Communist Party, but also to the other Communist and Workers' Parties that this warning is addressed. They must not let their ranks be invaded by these dangerous agents of the American imperialists . . .

'Zionists, Trotskyists, valets of the bourgeoisie under the First Republic and later lackeys of the American imperialists – Slansky has surrounded himself with men of his own stamp . . . and he knows where to find them: amongst those who, after the war, returned from western countries where they had established friendly contacts with the representatives of the imperialist world, amongst the Zionists, Trotskyists, bourgeois collaborators and other enemies of the Czech people . . .

'The first concern of Slansky and his assistants was to ensure the absolute control of the Party and turn this instrument of the working classes for the construction of socialism into an instrument for the restoration of capitalism. They violated all the basic principles which gave a revolutionary force to our Party, made it capable of acting and of being loved by all the workers. They dominated the men elected to the Party apparatus . . . . Rejecting the methods of patient and systematic persuasion among the masses they preferred to rule with an iron rod. They sabotaged the principles of democratic centralism, of democracy within the Party, criticism and self-criticism. Taking advantage of their position in the Party apparatus they proposed to make the Party turn about and drag it, as Tito had done, into the camp of traitors to socialism – to place the whole Republic under the protection of the American imperialists. The secretaries and leaders of the Party apparatus, in the industrial regions, were Zionist adventurers, foreigners hostile to the Party and people . . .

'But I want to emphasize that the conspirators sought in vain to capture the Party, to change its revolutionary face and prevent it from playing its historical role. They never accomplished their task. The Party, with Klement Gottwald at its head, fought them from the beginning. It gradually managed to unmask various criminal elements and finally discovered them all. Today this gang of criminals in Slansky's service have to justify themselves. The Party has emerged victorious, and it could not be otherwise. The Party and its Bolshevik leaders will continue to lead the people along the triumphant path to socialism . . .

'The proceedings have revealed the common aims of Tito and Slansky. They have also shown clearly that the sabotage of our country's economy was aimed at what the UNRRA mission failed to do. The UNRRA mission was obliged by its failure to introduce the Marshall Plan in the satellite countries. But what it wanted was to create in a poor country the conditions for the restoration of American monopolies. That was how Slansky and his men took part in the great conspiracy against the USSR and the preparations for another war . . .

'The present trial has once again shown up the criminal nature of western imperialist plans which aim to launch a third destructive world war against the USSR and the countries in the peace camp. Faced with these insane plans the Party and the government, like all honest people, have concentrated on our army, an army of peace, destined, like the invincible Soviet army, its great ally and source of inspiration, to crush the modern Crusaders who dare violate our country's sacred frontiers and endanger our liberty. Our army, a true people's army, is the love and pride of our people.

'This is why our people have heard with indignation and anger that the conspirators were directing their criminal efforts against the army, to make it incapable of defending our soil, our independence and happiness.

'The strength of our Party has thwarted these base plans and our army, thanks to its new leaders, has become a formidable force. Our well-shielded people are ready to receive the aggressor, armed from head to foot.

'The conspirators had also got key positions in the Security apparatus in order to be able to conceal their crimes . . . to facilitate the subversive activity of the imperialist intelligence services and the most diverse reactionary elements. . . . Karl Svab, appointed to Security by Slansky, knew all about the posts occupied in the various sections by the centre of conspiracy and about the subversive activities. . . . He transmitted all these reports and denunciations to Slansky, gave him detailed information, but – on Slansky's order – protected these criminals. . . . When we established that the American and Titoist intelligence services had a vast espionage network in Czechoslovakia, Svab was ordered to root it out. He established that Field collaborated with Frejka, Goldmann and Löbl . . . and also discovered some important facts proving Field's collaboration with other traitors of the Czech people. But, on Slansky's orders, he only pursued his investigation so as to prevent the conspirators from being discovered. The spies and traitors retained their posts. So Svab enabled numerous Trotskyists – the Trotskyist group of former volunteers in the International Brigades or the Trotskyists in the Ministry of Foreign Affairs – to indulge in their criminal activity. . . . Those who tried to discredit and cheat our Security apparatus are today in the dock . . .

'Slansky, his group of conspirators and other criminal elements associated with this group . . . were serving and carrying out the instructions of the western imperialists who directed their activity through numerous agents. Of all these agents, Koni Zilliacus is of special importance. He is a master juggler in politics. This apparently "honourable gentleman" travelled all over Europe under the mask of a progressive labourite. He often came to Czechoslovakia. But he will come here no longer. His role is over. . . . We suggest that the English workers should watch this gentleman attentively.

'Slansky knew perfectly well who Koni Zilliacus was. He knew that Zilliacus was a veteran spy . . .

'The first meeting between Slansky and Zilliacus took place in 1946, the second in the autumn of 1947. . . . Ever since the first meeting Slansky and Zilliacus had been on cordial terms, and to contact him Slansky used the diplomatic bag of the Ministry of Foreign Affairs, as well as his accomplices in the apparatus of this Ministry and his accomplices in the Party apparatus like Geminder, Goldstücker, Kratochvil, Kavan and many others . . .

'But Zilliacus was not only "in charge" of Czechoslovakia but also of the people's democracy of Poland, where he was in contact with the imperialist agent Gomulka, and Yugoslavia, where he collaborated with Tito and his accomplices. . . . It was he too who defended Tito tooth and nail when he was revealed to be a traitor by the Information Bureau. And even after Zilliacus had openly defended Tito, neither Slansky nor his centre of conspiracy against the state interrupted their dealings with him. Zilliacus personified the most solid bond between the Slansky group and the western imperialists . . .

'In this trial eleven of the fourteen defendants are charged with espionage. Espionage one of the most loathsome crimes against the state, is almost as loathsome as high treason.

'As far as the real aims of the conspiracy are concerned Slansky himself admitted: "I worked to create favourable conditions for the centre's seizure of power. I hoodwinked Klement Gottwald, tried to isolate him, and tried, as an enemy, to harm him in every way."

'Slansky did not even stop at Klement Gottwald. He had already decided to end the days of our people's beloved leader. He put President Gottwald in the hands of Dr Haskovec, a freemason, collaborator and enemy! If he admits: "I surmised that if we came to power it would be necessary to get rid of Klement Gottwald" it's because he can't deny it. "I could have used Dr Haskovec to get rid of Klement Gottwald and sieze power," Slansky admitted, and there is no doubt that he would have done so . . .

'All the charges have been confirmed by the evidence provided in the course of the trial and by admissions of the accused.

'Before concluding I must answer one more question, How could these saboteurs undermine the bases of the Republic in such a criminal way and still manage to conceal their crimes from the Party, the Security and the people? . . . It has not been easy to unmask them for they occupied leading positions. But they never managed to lay their hands on the heart and brain of our Party. They only penetrated the Central Committee of the Party to a very limited degree. For a certain time they managed to distort the just policy of our Party, falsify reports, figures, cadre files, deviate from Gottwald's Party line and even trick the President himself. But everything has its limits.

'They cheated in the cadre policy, in economic questions, in the formulation of international pacts. And, when necessary, they could also hide behind a smoke screen. When cries of protest against the Zionists arose they clamoured in return against the danger of antisemitism to hide the fact that they were defending the interests of the Jewish bourgeoisie and were tied by world Zionism to American imperialism.

'But that was not all – far from it! They hid behind their Communist Party cards, behind that red booklet sung by one of our poets. They hid in vain. The Party, with President Gottwald at its head, crushed this gang of traitors in time. Our people will never know the gratitude it owes to Comrade Gottwald for having systematically thwarted the criminal efforts of the conspirators plotting against the Republic.

'Czechoslovakia shall not be another Yugoslavia!

'Citizen judges!

'At the nineteenth Congress of the Communist Party of the Soviet Union Comrade Malenkov emphasized the importance of the implacable struggle led by the Communist Party of the USSR against the Trotsky–Bukharin clique, the immense importance of their defeat for the victory of the Soviet army in its great patriotic war. We too are dealing with traitors and mercenaries of this stamp. This gang was also preparing to plunge its dagger into the people's back in the event of our country being attacked by the enemy. It was serving the American imperialists. These criminals are not only the enemies of our country, but of the whole of pacifist humanity. That is why, if they are arrested and rendered inocuous, it will not only be a victory for our country but also another crushing defeat for the American imperialists and another victory for the camp of peace and democracy . . .

'The conspirators have caused losses to our country amounting to millions, and yet we are victoriously accomplishing the aims of the Five Year Plan and constructing a new life, a marvellous life for ourselves and for the generations to follow us. The tireless efforts of millions of workers have thwarted a handful of conspirators. In these last days thousands of indignant letters have arrived in court expressing the firm decision of our workers to repair as soon as possible all the damage done by these imperialist mercenaries . . . . Ever more vigilant, ever firmer and closer to its leaders and Klement Gottwald, our Communist Party is leading its people to a marvellous future.

'Citizen judges!

'In the name of our people, whose liberty and happiness have been endangered by these criminals, in the name of the peace against which they have conspired so infamously, I demand the death penalty for all the accused. May your judgement be pitiless, like a fist of steel. May it be the flame which burns out the roots of this tree sapped by treason! May it be a bell ringing across our country, calling it to new conquests in its march towards socialism!'

Five

While the prosecutor read his charge there was complete silence in the court. I listened with my heart in my mouth. The end was near. I had been under arrest for twenty-two months, torn from my family, my comrades, and prematurely buried in a tomb.

Urvalek spoke with conviction. His voice quavered when he evoked the Party, and the guide of the people, Klement Gottwald. His indignation increased as he denounced the gang of traitors and criminals which he was handing over to the people's vengeance. How can he feign such indignation and act so well,

I wondered. And the same applied to the judges who listened with such composure, and yet knew that they would have no control over the verdict which they would pronounce in the name of the Republic. They waited for orders from the Presidency of the Republic and the Party leadership.

I wanted to vomit. I looked at my companions. They were like myself. Pale and tense, they hung on the prosecutor's lips.

The court was adjourned. The warders led us back to our underground cells where I spent another sleepless night. I even envied the Christians thrown to the wild beasts of the circus. The end came quicker. Tomorrow there would be the counsels' speeches and then each defendant had to make his last statement. I had learned it by heart, Kohoutek had made me repeat it, and I now committed myself to the hands of God, or rather of the Party!

Today, 26 November, the counsel for the defence spoke. Despite my requests I had still not managed to talk to my lawyer, although we were nearing the end of the trial. I was obsessed by this thought: had he seen Lise and prepared her for the shock? Had the Party got into contact with her as Bacilek had promised at the end of his meeting with me?

I was relieved to hear from Kohoutek and the interrogators that Lise was not in the court and that she was at least to be spared this spectacle.

We now assisted at the performance given by our lawyers who, one by one, recited their lines.

Their speeches, which were all the same, would have been an adequate bill of indictment.

Each lawyer defended three of the accused, except for Dr Bartos who defended Slansky and Margolius. Here are some gems from his speech:

Doctor Bartos: 'Neither in the case of the defendant Slansky nor of the defendant Margolius shall I pay attention to the details of their criminal activities since there is no doubt that their guilt, as defined by the Public Prosecutor, has been clearly proved. Their activity cannot be defended and the two defendants have fully acknowledged their guilt.

'And here we come to the greatest difficulty of the defence – from the legal point of view it is impossible to oppose the charge either as far as the crimes are concerned, or as far as their qualification is concerned.

'The exhibits in the file, which have been gathered during the investigation, the evidence of the witnesses, corroborated by the other proofs, confirm the circumstances not only of the charge against my two clients, but of the whole charge . . .'

And this is how Doctor Posmura, the lawyer of Löbl, Svab and Geminder, defended Geminder:

'Slansky soon noticed that Geminder was a weak man who could become a docile instrument in his hands, so he exploited his defects and his bourgeois education. Geminder has admitted to having been in Slansky's power since 1930 and to having been introduced into the heart of the centre of conspiracy in the second half of 1948. So one could say that for some time at least he resisted Slansky's advances and that if he finally yielded it was partly because of his opportunistic ambition and partly because of his personal cowardice. These motives are apparent in all the confessions made by the defendant Geminder.

'I know only too well that these defects do not diminish the guilt of the defendant, which cannot be doubted and has been proved and corroborated. It is only my duty, in accordance with article 19 of the penal code, to draw your attention . . .' My lawyer, Dr Ruzicka, had to defend Ludvik Frejka, André Simone and myself in one speech. This is what he said about me:

'As for the defendant Artur London, his guilt has been proved and he has made a complete confession. I have only to say a few words about the circumstances in which London became a Trotskyist, entered Noel Field's pay, became a member of the centre of conspiracy and performed his criminal activity.

'In 1937, London left for Spain where he enlisted as a volunteer in the International Brigades. It appears from the proceedings that the political situation of the International Brigades was by no means satisfactory. So we can easily understand that London, who came from the petty bourgoisie, and had lived a long time abroad, should at the age of twenty-two, have had dubious friendships with such demoralized "members of the Brigades", as Zavodsky, Holdos, Svoboda, and that he should have come away with Trotskyist opinions.

'After his liberation from the concentration camp of Buchenwald* in 1945, London had a tubercular relapse. He left for a cure in Switzerland and it was there, in the sanatorium, that he was enlisted by Noel Field.

'This is what London said about it: "My personal relations with the American spy Noel Field originate from the aid and subsidies with which he provided me from the funds of the Unitarian Service Committee. After 1947 Field paid for my stay in the Swiss sanatorium and asked me, in exchange, for some secret information."

'London's confession has been confirmed by the results of the Rajk trial . . . the defendant Artur London was the last to collaborate with Slansky. He did so only under strong pressure and because he feared there would be trouble on account of his past activity.

'So I beg of you, citizen judges, not to inflict on the defendant Artur London the supreme penalty demanded by the prosecutor, and to sentence him to prison where he can expiate his faults by working.'

Here they were, these modern knights, the champions of innocence, of the weak, the widows, the orphans! Numerous Czech magistrates and lawyers preferred to become car washers or miners, smelters or hall porters rather than perjure themselves. But there was no difference between those who accepted the new legislation drawn up by the ringleaders of Ruzyn, and the 'magistrates' who passed our sentences.

After the speeches, one by one we were called to the bar to make our last statements.

* I was deported to Mauthausen, not Buchenwald.

308

Having insisted that we present our evidence 'sincerely', the interrogators told us to pronounce our last statement in a tone of sincere repentance. And above all, to show no hesitation, to 'trust in the Party' until the end.

Slansky ended with these words: 'I deserve no other end to my criminal life but that proposed by the Public Prosecutor.' *Geminder:* 'I realize that, however harsh the penalty – and whatever it is it will be just – I will never be able to make up for the damage I have caused.' *Frejka:* 'I have become so guilty that I accept in advance any verdict from the court as a just punishment from the hands of the workers of Czechoslovakia...' *Frank:* 'I beg the state tribunal to judge the extent of my crimes harshly and to pronounce a harsh and vigorous sentence.' *Clementis:* 'That is why the sentence which the National Tribunal must pass on my activity must be a just punishment, however harsh it may be.' *Reicin:* 'I am aware that I deserve the harshest punishment for the crimes of which I am guilty.' *Svab:* 'I therefore beg the state tribunal to appreciate and condemn my treachery with the maximum severity and firmness.' *London:* 'I know that the verdict will be fair.' *Hajdu:* 'I only want to express my regret for these crimes that have been perpetrated.' *Löbl*: 'I sincerely regret all I have done and I know that I deserve a severe and just punishment.' *Margolius:* 'I can only demand the heaviest sentence.' *Fischl:* 'So I request a verdict in accordance with my heavy guilt.' *Sling:* 'I am justly despised and I deserve the heaviest penalty.' *Simone:* 'That's why I beg the state tribunal to pass the strictest sentence on me.'

The judge adjourned the court and said that it would resume the following morning at 9.30 with the proclamation of the verdict.

We at last came to the morning of 27 November 1952, which marked the end of the trial. The warders did not need to wake us, for not one of us had closed an eye all night. The interrogators appeared in our cells shortly before the beginning of the session. Kohoutek and my interrogator avoided conversation. They looked serious and tense. The men who relieved the night warders moved swiftly and quietly, not saying a word.

We were led out into the corridor. We looked shattered. We gazed at each other, our eyes blank, without a spark of life. I had the impression, from what I felt and saw of my comrades, that our bodies had become immense receptacles of anxiety and fear.

We walked like machines. We took our place in the dock, and waited.

The hall was silent. The Court entered. It was exactly 9.30.

The judge, Novak, said: 'The trial is resumed. Stand up and listen to the sentence.'

The warders nudged us and pulled us to our feet.

As I stood I heard, in a sort of dream: 'Sentence. In the name of the Republic.

'The state tribunal of Prague has heard, from 20 November to 27 November 1952, the proceedings concerning the criminal case of the leaders of the centre of conspiracy against the state, RUDOLF SLANSKY AND HIS ACCOMPLICES, for crimes of high treason, espionage, sabotage and military treason.

'As a result of the proceedings the tribunal has decided as follows . . .'

Why at that moment did I identify myself with a comrade in the Resistance I had once heard about? One day he had been summoned to a meeting with the leaders of the FTP in a forest in the Landes, and he suddenly realized that his comrades were there to shoot him; they suspected him of treachery. He knew that nothing would save him. After the bullet had hit him he still had enough strength to cry, as he fell: '*Vive le Parti communiste!*' and in a last murmur he gasped: 'Comrades . . . comrades . . . com . . .'

Was there any hope, other than in the Party, for the millions of human beings who, all over the world, saw in it the end of their troubles and the possibility of producing a just and enlightened society? If we had denounced and revealed the Party's imposture would that not have betrayed our comrades and friends, in this world on the verge of another war? But this question was absurd, since it was impossible for us to do so, both for moral considerations, and because we lacked the opportunity.

I thought of the Soviet Union again. I saw the admirable and courageous Russian people whom I had learned to love, and whom I still loved, who had borne and still bore so many sacrifices; who had given more to the cause of the revolution than any other people – the USSR, the home of the proletarian revolution, the hope of nations, the second home of communists the world over, for which so many had given their lives, and of which Stalin was the greatest grave-digger.

I felt large drops of sweat run down my body, and my shoes were soon drenched. I tried to overcome my dizziness in order to hear and understand what the judge was saying. Several times in the list of crimes, I caught my name, LONDON, together with those of my fellow defendants. But he had not come to the sentence yet. And then I heard numbers of articles of the Penal Code, numbers of paragraphs of laws and then more names, including my own. But it still wasn't the sentence. And then I listened and concentrated with all my might:

'And are condemned for these facts:

'1. The defendants Rudolf Slansky, Bedrich Geminder, Ludvik Frejka, Josef Frank, Vladimir Clementis, Bedrich Reicin, Karel Svab, Rudolf Margolius, Otto Fischl, Otto Sling and André Simone according to article 78, third paragraph of the Penal Code, in consideration of the disposition of article 22, first paragraph of the Penal Code, except for Karel Svab.

TO THE DEATH PENALTY.

'2. The defendants Artur London and Vavro Hajdu, according to article 78, third paragraph of the Penal Code, in consideration of article 22, first paragraph of the Penal Code,

'Eugen Löbl, according to the first article, third paragraph of law No. 231/48 of the law book, in consideration of the dispositions of article 34 of the Penal Code of 1852; for all in consideration of the dispositions of article 29, second paragraph of the Penal Code, for Eugen Löbl, in consideration of the dispositions of article 12 of the Penal Code.

TO LIFE IMPRISONMENT.

'In the case of all the defendants, the loss of nationality is pronounced according to article 42 of the Penal Code and article 78, fourth paragraph of the Penal Code.

'According to the terms of article 23 of the Penal Code, the time that Artur London, Vavro Hajdu and Eugen Löbl have spent in custody because of their criminal acts is deducted from their sentences.'

The silence in the court showed that, however carefully the audience had been selected, they too were overwhelmed by the cruelty of the verdict.

Who could have thought that the Czechs, the members of a nation with an old civilization and democratic tradition, would go still further than the Hungarians, Bulgarians, Poles and Rumanians – eleven death sentences and three life imprisonments!

No applause, no sign of approval. On the contrary, one had the impression that a breath of terror had passed through the room, an icy coldness had overcome the spectators. They craned forwards. Nobody was proud of this ghastly end.

The judge then interrupted the session. We could consult our lawyers before deciding whether or not to accept our sentence. The prosecutor reserved the legal right to specify his point of view.

The spectators stood staring at us. They watched us leave the room, motionless and horrified.

Between our warders we marched to our boxes. We were shattered. We could see nothing. For although we had often thought that death alone would end our trial, we clung to every straw of hope handed us by the only beings we were in contact with, the interrogators, the men who, for us, represented the Party.

We had finally accepted everything, even our own death

sentence. There was no other way out; like Lenin's old comrades before us, like the defendants of Budapest, Sofia and Bucharest we had to accept our part in the trial and confirm the charge.

We no longer found our warders from Ruzyn in the corridor. They had been changed. But the worst of it was that our interrogators were not there either. All through the trial they had been with us. We had been used to finding them in our boxes. They had chatted with us, encouraged us. But now that eleven of us had been sentenced to the gallows, they had disappeared.

Had their final disappearance also been foreseen?

Opposite me, in his cell, I saw Clementis. He had lost all his resilience. André Simone, who had looked sure of himself until the last moment in spite of his deplorable physical condition, was a rag. In the eyes of all my comrades I could see despair at not finding their interrogators, of only having unknown warders next to them. Then, suddenly, we all shouted for our interrogators.

Our interrogators! Over the months and years that we had lived together, victims and executioners, certain bonds had developed between us.

Had the interrogators not promised us, in the name of the Party, that if we agreed to adopt an attitude conforming to the Party's interests we would be spared? When they said that if we relied on the Party it would be taken into account, some of them must have believed it. They weren't all born murderers. Before becoming the docile instruments of the 'ringleaders of Ruzyn' they too had been conditioned.

As I observed them, I had often looked back on my own behaviour.

The corruption of the principle of democratic centralism had gradually led us, in the past, to stop thinking by ourselves and to expect everything from the Party, the supreme guide. We had lost the right to reflect and to protest. Before certain problems we had not always reacted humanly enough. In the case of our interrogators the conditioning had gone so far that they agreed to violate the most sacred rights of man in the name of the Party and the USSR.

But at the same time some of them believed in communist morality, re-education and mercy. They believed firmly that their brutality and constant violence towards us had a sense, a final justification, maybe even that it was proletarian humanism, or at least a way of serving it.

Now they knew everything. Just as we did.

My comrades who had been sentenced to death came out of the boxes and took the unknown warders by the arm: 'Where is my interrogator? Call my interrogator! Tell me where my interrogator is! I want to see my interrogator!' Their last chance of surviving was hidden in these officials who had grilled them hour after hour, day after day, month after month, year after year, but who spoke to them, nourished them with hopes and promises, and acted as an intermediary between them and the outside world, the Party, Gottwald.

And suddenly they no longer had this hope or this resort. No illusion. Nothing. Each man was alone with his death. When he asked for his interrogator he called for his link with the Party and Gottwald – with life. The interrogator represented the agony of the 'confessions', the uninterrupted repetition of the reports, blackmail, infamy and violence. But he also represented power. He was in contact with the anonymous ringleaders who had organized the trial with which he had threatened us, just as he had said they would organize it, making the judges learn the same lines as the victims.

The disappearance of the interrogators meant that all was over. All that remained were the 'confessions', not the men who formulated them; the 'confessions' and the condemnation which they carried with them. No more promises. The condemned men had kept their word to the last, but not the Party.

In retrospect I believe that the last stage of the macabre game which the interrogators of Ruzyn were made to play was beyond their personal responsibility and was entirely the work of the Soviet ringleaders and the Party leaders. Gottwald and the members of the Political Bureau of the time bear the full responsibility for the drama because they agreed to abdicate their right of control, allowed justice to be violated, and finally decided on the life or death of the accused. They blocked their eyes and ears, and surrendered like cowards, heart and soul, to this parallel police force, a state within the state, which acted according to the Satanic wishes of Stalin and Beria.

In defiance of our warders, Hajdu and I looked out of our boxes and spoke to each other: 'What shall we do?' We both agreed: the comedy had lasted long enough, we were going to appeal.

It was at that moment that our lawyers arrived. It was the first contact between the counsels and their clients – after the clients had already been sentenced. I heard phrases which showed that the lawyers were trying to calm the defendants: 'a letter to the President' – 'appeal' – 'don't lose hope.' My lawyer asked me what I intended to do. 'I don't accept the verdict. I want to appeal.' I heard Hajdu say the same thing.

After telling me that he had not had time to see or telephone my wife the lawyer left me, saying that the Court was about to resume.

A few seconds later, Hajdu's lawyer, followed by mine, rushed back breathlessly. They hurriedly told us that after consulting the most competent persons, they advised against an appeal. 'You aren't aware of what's going on. Trucks full of resolutions arrive from all over the Republic. They're from factories, administrations, villages, demanding the death penalty for all fourteen of you. Besides, the international situation is very serious. Eisenhower has just been elected President of the United States. We're on the verge of another war. The prosecutor has decided to take three days to establish his point of view. And if you appeal he'll do so too and you won't have a chance to escape the gallows!'

At this Hajdu and I decided to accept the verdict.

As he was leaving me my lawyer promised again to get in touch with my wife and come and see me in prison. He never came.

The Court resumed; it was the last session. The judge read out our names. One by one we stood up and went to the bar. In a stifled voice we all said the same thing: 'I accept my sentence and renounce my right of appeal.'

The show was over.

The curtain fell.

Kohoutek had once told me: 'The Party needs a trial, not heads!' The Party had had both the trial and the heads.

We were led back to the basement corridor of Pankrac; we waited silently for the warders to open our cells. The first to leave our group was Sling. Before entering his cell he turned to us and smiled. He waved. I didn't know what to think; Sling, my comrade, what did that smile mean?

There was sepulchral silence in the underground corridors. For the two hours that Löbl, Hajdu and I spent in our cells, until the warders came for us to take us back to Ruzyn, I thought about my eleven comrades, and forgot my own fate.

As we left, the three of us marched down the corridor, past the cells where the eleven prisoners awaited execution. When we left Pankrac we really felt we were coming out of a tomb.

The memory of my eleven comrades obsessed me for a long time. I always hoped that Gottwald would grant their appeal. That was the first question I asked my interrogator when he called me to his office for some reason a few weeks later. He didn't answer. Several months went by before I discovered from my wife and my work-mates in Ruzyn that they had all been hanged. When I still refused to believe it, one of my fellow prisoners showed me a newspaper cutting which announced the execution.

Later I heard that all, except for Rudolf Slansky, wrote letters to their families and to Klement Gottwald before they died.*

In this last farewell they all stated their innocence and said that they had agreed to 'confess' solely in the interest of the Party and socialism.

* *Novy Mysl*, political review of the Central Committee of the Czech Communist Party, July 1968.

Otto Sling: 'Before my execution I truthfully declare that I was never a spy.'

Karel Svab: 'I confessed because I considered it my duty and a political necessity.'

Ludvik Frejka: 'I confessed in order to fulfil my duty towards the workers and the Czech Communist Party.'

André Simone: ' I have never been a conspirator, a member of Slansky's centre of conspiracy against the state, a traitor, a spy, or an agent of the western services.'

It was only after the rehabilitation of all these innocent men, early in 1968, that these letters were found in the archives of the Ministry of Security and were at last delivered to the widows and orphans to whom they were written.

As I was writing this book, I also discovered from an article in a Czech paper† how my companions ended:

When the eleven men had been executed the interrogator D. happened to be in the Ruzyn prison in the office of the [Soviet] adviser Galkin. The chauffeur and the two interrogators who were supposed to get rid of the ashes were also there. They said they had put them in a potato sack and had made for the suburbs of Prague, hoping to leave them in a field. Seeing the icy road, however, they decided to throw the ashes on it. The chauffeur laughed. He said it was the first time he had driven fourteen passengers in his Tatra, three alive and eleven in a sack.

† *Reporter,* No. 26, 1968.

Part Five

My Family

One

Here I was in Ruzyn again. I did not return to the infirmary, but was put in a cell in the new building, still in complete isolation. I had the impression that the verdict which had spared our lives was a mere illusion; that Löbl, Hajdu and I would never leave the prison alive. Sooner or later we would be liquidated. Nobody could risk leaving witnesses like ourselves around. Should I spend the rest of my life vegetating between these four walls until I died or was killed?

The immense relief I felt at the verdict, when I realized my life had been saved, gradually gave way to the thought that it might really have been better to get it over with.

Solitary confinement was increasingly oppressive. There was no more questioning. Occasionally an interrogator sent for me to get me to answer a question from some organization of the Ministry of the Interior or the Ministry or Justice. I received no mail from my family. I asked permission to write a letter and was granted it a month later. A month after that I wrote another letter. I subsequently found out that neither of these letters was delivered.

Each time I saw an interrogator I asked him for news of my wife and children. Every morning I asked to see an interrogator to inquire about my family.

I told the interrogator that I was sure that, after hearing me on the radio, my wife had come out against me. He said he knew nothing about it. But I knew Lise too well not to be able to foresee her reactions. She must have made a statement. I was sure, knowing her complete faith in the Party and the USSR, that she did not want to have anything to do with the traitor I now represented for her. In all her letters before the

319

trial, she tried in vain to get me to deny my treachery: 'If you turned out to be a traitor, then, in spite of my love for you, know that every bond between us would be broken!' I pleaded guilty and she heard me do so on the radio.

Lise, if only you knew!

I no longer received medical attention, now that the interrogators didn't need to show me off. My pneumothorax had collapsed some time ago. I was alone with myself, with my thoughts which revolved round Lise, our children and her parents.

I paced round my concrete box like an animal in a cage. As I walked I continually thought about the trial, the endless months of conditioning before I appeared in the dock and 'pleaded guilty' at the bar.

There were fourteen defendants: all of us, apart from Margolius who joined during the war, had been Party members for many years, and some of us ever since the Party was founded.

We were all responsible and conscientious Party members who had given the sincerest proof of our loyalty to the Party. All of us had known hard times, the danger and persecution entailed by our commitment to the fight for communism.

And we had all pleaded guilty to the most terrible deeds, from common-law crimes like theft and murder to war crimes, from the extermination of prisoners in the Nazi camps to espionage and high treason. Ruzyn had conditioned us to such a degree that if we had had to confess to other crimes we would have done so.

There were fourteen of us and each one represented a section of the political or economic life of our country. We provided the basis for other trials. We were scapegoats accused of every sin, victims sacrificed on the altar of socialism.

I felt that our trial went beyond the limits of credulity. Never had there been such violent antisemitism, such coarse lies, such enormous distortions; such contempt for the masses and such disdain for the Party and its members. And these grave-diggers of socialism felt strong enough to defy the good sense of our people and world opinion.

The members of the Communist Parties in the capitalist countries, who condemned us to obloquy in good faith, were far from suspecting that files with evidence of their own treachery were being methodically compiled on some of their best leaders, that the 'ringleaders' were putting this material aside for the day when it might prove useful. How could one let them know?

And here in Prague, those leaders who kept their posts, and the new ones who replaced the scapegoats, were also far from suspecting that there were files on them containing the most crushing 'statements' and 'evidence', some of which had been extorted from the men they sent to the gallows.

A few days before the trial, Kohoutek had questioned me about Antonin Novotny's attitude in the concentration camp of Mauthausen. I had the impression that Kohoutek took pleasure in asking me these questions. At the time I had no idea that Novotny was the new Secretary General of the Party, Slansky's replacement.

In Mauthausen I had hardly had anything to do with Novotny, who had always kept away from the underground resistance organization in the camp – an attitude for which our comrades had severely criticized him. That was all I could say.

Who had started this infernal machine, and who would break it and when? For me it had become clear that the culprit was Stalin along with the monstrous apparatus he had created. After sacrificing the cadres of the Bolshevik Party he started to sabotage the other parties. But it was in vain that I asked why. I could find no answer. I could not find 'an end which justified the means'. To try and explain this phenomenon, as some people had done, by saying that one must accept a revolution in its totality, including the fact that each revolution inevitably devours its children, seemed to me absurd. Indeed, it is a sign of degeneration when a revolution turns the terror directed against its enemies against its own creators.

One day, two days, ten days, a month, two months. I realized that time was passing because, in the corner of my cell, on the darkest wall, I could see a new outline with a new day.

Otherwise there was no way of telling the difference between one day and the next. Never did a ray of sunlight play on the walls. Getting up, chores, reports, food time, going to bed and the endless prison nights. Five cigarettes a day and a few books, most of which I read for the umpteenth time.

It was already three months since the trial, and I still had no idea of what had happened to my family.

And then, early in March 1953, an interrogator came for me. He brought me before two men – a civil magistrate of Prague and his assessor. They told me that my wife had filed a petition for a divorce the day after my evidence in court. They seemed surprised to find that I knew nothing about it, and told the interrogator how astonished they were that none of the letters concerning the petition had reached me. They wanted to know if I objected. No, on the contrary, I said, I agreed. I understood my wife's reasons for making this request, and I knew it was her only hope of living in peace with our children and her parents.

The magistrate was understanding and told me that he would try to get me permission to see my children. I immediately clung to the hope that perhaps, through them, I might see Lise again.

A little later I was taken into an interrogator's office. He had questioned me at Koldeje and had been anything but gentle, and although I hadn't seen him for many months, this was the second time since my sentence and he was no longer the same as he had been two years earlier. He seemed more humane. He had given me some books, saying: 'Here, take these, I know you read a lot.' And later he apologized for his brutality during my first interrogations. 'Our head [Smola] was a brute and whenever he didn't hear shouts and screams in a room where a prisoner was being interrogated he scolded us.'

Today he seemed worried. He offered me a cigarette and told me to sit down. Then he dealt me a blow: 'I've got a letter for you. It's a terrible letter and I don't know whether I should give it to you. Read it first, and then we'll see what we can do for you.'

It was from Lise. She later told me the circumstances in which she had written it. I seized it avidly, although I could tell from what the interrogator said that the news it contained was far from good.

13 March, 1953.

Gérard,

Yesterday I went to the Senate to see about our three children and the divorce. I was told that you had the right to see the children according to the prison regulations. So I signed a document stipulating that 'if the father requests it, I will not object to his seeing the children.' But the more I think about it, the more I find it unjust. It's true that the human aspect is in your favour, and don't think I'm insensitive to it. But there is the other human aspect represented by the children's future; they won't find it easy to obliterate the fact that they are London's children. Don't complicate their existence any further by splitting them between the hatred which a communist must feel for traitors and the love and pity which they must feel for their father.

I know from experience how difficult it is to break bonds of love created over the years, even when you know that they tie you to a man who has failed on every point. I know how hard it is to reject the feelings of pity which oblige you to see him as the man you thought you knew and whom you loved so much. I am an adult and an old communist and yet I need a great deal of strength to dominate my feelings and stick to the path which I know is right. But the children are more fragile.

Life does not stop there, Gérard. If, as I hope, you are fully aware of your faults, and if you have started on the road of your salvation, you must understand that from now on it is in yourself that you must seek the strength and will to become useful to society. The Soviet Union has given us countless examples of this sort. Follow them, and later, if you are worthy, I am sure your children will not refuse to see you.

There, Gérard, that is what I wanted to say and I am sure you agree with me.

Lise.

I thought I had drained the cup to the dregs! I sat on my chair, incapable of any reaction. 'Oh no! Not that! It's too much!' And tears poured down my cheeks.

The interrogator tried to comfort me: 'I understand, Mr London. I shall try to help you. Nobody has the right to prevent you from seeing your children. I shall talk to my superiors. I shall inform them and ask permission to see your wife. I don't know if they'll grant it to me. But I promise to do all I can. And when I see her I shall persuade her to bring your children.'

A few days later he called me again and told me that he had seen my wife and Françoise and that they would visit me with the boys after Easter, a few days later. I made no attempt to reason. It was the first sign of light in the tunnel.

Two

Now that I expected the visit, the days dragged even more than before. I had been in solitary confinement for too long, and there had been no definite goal in my life. And then everything was changed, upset. It was like a heady wine. To my impatience was added the anxiety of what they would be like, how they would greet me, what I should say to Lise since I was forbidden to tell her the truth, under pain of death. And what if this visit made things still worse? We were in such an inextricable, absurd situation. How could I hope to be understood or believed? And, if I succeeded, how could I persuade Lise to divorce me? That week, torn between fear and hope, was one of the worst in my life.

At last, on Wednesday, 8 April 1953, the barber came to shave me in my cell, although it was not his usual day. So the visit was for today. I hadn't seen Lise for over twenty-six months. Twenty-six months of continual torture and degradation.

Early in the afternoon my interrogator came for me. He took me to the wardrobe where I changed my prison clothes for civilian clothes. I was blindfolded and led to a car. In amazement I asked the interrogator where the visit would take place. He replied that we were going to the Bartolomejska, in the heart of Prague, where there were several departments of the Security and the Interior. Before we got there he unbandaged my eyes. We crossed the Bridge of Legions, and opposite me I saw the National Theatre. People were walking in the streets. They passed each other on the pavement, went in and out of shops. Nothing had happened, as far as they were concerned. For them the world still went round; but for me it had stopped long ago.

We had arrived in the little Bartolomejska street. The car drove under a gateway. I went up a floor with my interrogator, and along a high-ceilinged corridor. The interrogator opened a door and let me by. There they were. I looked at Lise. She stood still and I felt she was very moved. In spite of the sadness of her expression I found her more beautiful than ever, with her hair in a bun on her neck. Françoise! She was as tall as her mother, her long, fair, curly hair falling in cascades on her shoulders. She was so pretty with her tender smile as she came to kiss me. Gérard, who was a big boy now, was as mischievous-looking as ever. He stood shyly by his mother. And Michel? He had changed most of all; when I left him he was a baby learning to walk. And now he was over three. He looked at me with amazement in his large black eyes, full of that sadness which he had as a baby and which he was to keep for so long.

Lise pushed the boys towards me. Gérard kissed me: 'Hello, Daddy.' Michel came up, and took two hard coloured eggs out of his pocket. He held them out to me and said: 'They're for you, daddy. It's my Easter present.'

His gesture moved me to tears. I knelt down and hugged him. Lise was standing next to us, and watched us, severely and tenderly. I looked up at her: 'You must find me changed, and aged, don't you?'

She smiled and said: 'If that's all you're worried about, Gérard, it's a good sign.'

I wanted to take her in my arms, embrace her, but I didn't dare. The interrogator told me we had an hour and asked us to speak Czech.

He sat behind a large desk in the corner of the room. At the other end there was a sofa, a round table and two armchairs. Lise pushed me into one of the chairs. I sat with my back to the interrogator. Lise sat opposite me, with Françoise and Gérard on the sofa. Michel never left my side.

As Lise told me about her parents I saw her nudge Françoise. My daughter got up, and so did little Gérard. Taking Michel on his back, he rushed round the room shouting. I heard Françoise talk to the interrogator; she had seen him the week before with her mother, so she knew him and they had an animated conversation of which I caught snatches. She told him about her school, a film she had just seen, and any story that came into her head. I heard him roar with laughter. The whole room resounded with laughter, cries and occasional sobs from Michel when he fell off his horse. Lise told me that she and our daughter had carefully prepared the whole thing so that we should be able to talk to each other in French.

When Lise, who was opposite him, realized that the interrogator was taking an interest in us and trying to listen to our conversation, she immediately reverted to Czech and discussed family problems.

My wife tried to control her expression. She kept smiling, even when she spoke of the most upsetting subjects.

'What did you think of the letter I wrote to Gottwald and the judge during the trial?'

'What letter?'

'Didn't you know? Hadn't you heard about it?'

'No, but I could have guessed. I was sure you'd written. I asked at least a hundred times and they always said no. Another lie! The same applied to the two letters I was allowed to write to you and which were never delivered.'

They'd tricked us till the end. Smola started by making me believe that Lise had rejected me while she was fighting tooth and nail with Slansky, Köhler, Siroky and Gottwald. Then, after my 'confessions', Kohoutek prevented me from writing anything which might inform her of what was about to happen. And why had he not told me about this letter which my wife was the first person to mention? She informed me of what she said in it and it was exactly as I had imagined.

Michel came back to me: 'Daddy, I'm hungry. Could you give me an egg?' Lise couldn't help laughing at the sight of our son, serious as a pope, breaking and peeling his egg, and eating it. He went round in a circle and then came back, to lean on my knees caressingly and ask:' Daddy, will you give me the other one?' Françoise had come back to us too. Her mother whispered to her to make more noise. 'Look after your brothers. I must talk to daddy.'

Lise looked me straight in the eyes and asked me gently: 'Gérard, how could you lie to us like that?'

I thought she meant the incident which I so regretted: 'Are you still thinking about that, Lise? That's got nothing to do with my love for you.'

She interrupted me: 'No, Gérard. That doesn't matter. I mean the trial. You confessed. So you deceived us.'

I stared at her and shook my head, forming a silent NO with my lips.

'But what you said about Field?'

I shook my head again.

She insisted: 'And Zilliacus?'

'No.'

'And sabotaging the French party?'

'No.'

I was frantic, I looked up at the light over our heads, then at the table, and moved my finger round to make Lise understand that there might be hidden microphones.

Lise's questions continued: 'So all the charges against you were false?'

'Yes.'

'Why did you plead guilty?'

I was terrified of the consequences of this conversation for me and my family, but I couldn't lie to Lise. I answered in a whisper: 'Yes, it's all false. I'm completely innocent.'

'Everything? Everything's false?'

'Yes, everything!'

'Why don't you fight then? Why didn't you say anything at your trial?'

'It was impossible.'

The minute I came into the room and Lise first looked at me, I realized that she still loved me. And I now realized that she expected that 'No' to her question about my guilt. She knew it, but she wanted to hear me say it. . .

'If only you knew how I had to fight against myself to believe in your guilt,' she said, 'because you pleaded guilty. At night, in bed, I felt sure you were in the room, you were bending over me and I heard – I really heard your voice murmuring: "Lise, believe me, I'm innocent!" They were hallucinations and I was ashamed of myself. I was always recalling my faith in the Party. And yet my love was stronger than my Party spirit. I was ready to listen to my feelings of pity and love for a man who was guilty. I was so ashamed. But one thought constantly obsessed me: I had to see you, if only for a second. I had to ask you if you were guilty and hear you answer yourself.

'Gérard, you must have faith,' she whispered. 'I've got some good news for you.' In a few words she told me about the Soviet doctors falsely accused of murdering some politicians, and how she heard that the trial being prepared against them was entirely rigged.

'When the Security captain – the interrogator with us now – told us that we'd see you after Easter we were overjoyed,' she continued. 'At last we would know.

'That weekend I went with little Gérard to see our friends the Havels at Luby. It was the best present I could give him for his tenth birthday. You know how he loves the country.

'That evening, at the station of Luby, Tonda Havel was waiting for us in a horse-drawn cart. Gérard was thrilled. At last he could be a real cowboy, pulling on the rains and cracking his whip. I was sitting next to Tonda. The first thing he asked me was whether I had heard the news.

' "No. Why?"

' "Before I came for you the rehabilitation of the Soviet doctors was announced on the radio."

'There had been such a to-do about this plot and to hear that they were rehabilitated raised my hopes. I told Havel that after my return to Prague I would have my first meeting with you. When he heard that, Tonda shouted for joy: "He's innocent! I always knew it. You'll see that they'll release him soon." And he started reminiscing about you, your simplicity, understanding and kindness. "No," he added, "a man like him could never be a liar or a traitor."

'The next day it was the feast of the neighbouring village. Havel wanted to take us there with his daughter Hanka. Taking me to the village dance was a gesture of pride and defiance. The local authorities had persecuted him, taken away his job, and thrown his wife out of the Party, just because he knew several veterans from Spain. They had even gone so far as to say that it was in his farm that the volunteers had practised shooting so as to overthrow the state.

'Havel was proud to waltz with me, to dance the polka and the mazurka. To start with people showed surprise, and then they adopted me. The head forester invited me to waltz. Do you remember him? Without touching on your problem he asked me about my children and parents. Havel was so happy that he gulped down a whole lot of beer mixed with rum.

'And on the way back, with Hanka on one side of him and me on the other, he sang at the top of his voice. The stars shone like suns in the black sky. The weather was marvellous. A light breeze blew and Havel suddenly started reciting poetry. How sorry I was that my Czech wasn't good enough to understand those improvised poems about you. Large tears ran down his face when he spoke of what you must have been through.

'His wife was waiting by the gate of the farm and burst out laughing when she saw her "old man" in such a state. She talked to him gently, like a mother, and took him off to bed.'

So the men condemned in the USSR had been publicly rehabilitated. I could hardly believe it.

Lise insisted: 'Yes, it's official! Not only did the radio announce it this morning, but all the newspapers mentioned it. I even wanted to bring you a press cutting, but Renée, Hajdu's sister, told me it was unwise and might harm both of us.' I couldn't get over this news.

Lise continued: 'So you see, all is not lost, you'll have to fight. You can't remain in a guilty man's skin if you're innocent. And I want to fight with you. I'm going to the Party to talk it over with Siroky and Köhler.'

'Don't do that, Lise, for heaven's sake. If you love me, if you want me to live, don't try anything like that.'

Lise looked at me earnestly: 'But Gérard, don't forget; those who live are those who struggle!'

'In this case it would lead to my death. Please leave the decisions to me for the moment. Above all, believe me when I say that for the time being you can't do a thing for me. We would both be lost if you tried to intervene. You can't understand, but you must believe me. You must leave, go back to France with your parents and the children. You simply *must* leave. After that my hands will be free.'

Lise tried to remain calm, to smile as she talked, but her

expression, which she could not quite control, showed how upset she was by what I said. I repeated again:

'You must take what I say seriously. If you do anything for me it'll be the end, my death sentence.'

Lise's eyes strayed to the large photographs of Stalin and Gottwald hanging on the walls. She suddenly realized that I was living outside the world, outside time. 'Do you know that Stalin's dead?' she asked me.

I could hardly breathe. I looked at her in amazement. 'No, but so much the better.'

Now it was Lise's turn to look at me in astonishment. I can't help laughing when I think of the black look she gave me.

'I hope you're still a communist?'

'Yes, of course. It's because I'm still a communist that I repeat: so much the better.'

Lise continued: 'Gottwald's dead too. Did you know?'

'No, but I'm not going to mourn for him either.'

My wife couldn't understand my reactions, and she gazed at me in silence.

At this point the interrogator came up to us. Lise spoke in Czech about all the difficulties she'd been having since my sentence. She had been fired from her factory and in the new one her work was hard and ill paid. She didn't know how she would survive financially with her miserable salary. Her Party card had also been withdrawn and the letters she had written to the Party Directing Committee remained unanswered.

It was as I had feared. No allowances had been made for my family. I told Lise: 'Write to Bacilek at once. He saw me before the trial and promised you would suffer no consequences. He said the Party would make sure that the families would not be held responsible. So don't let them bully you. Write! And if necessary ask to see him.'

Lise then told me about her parents. 'Mummy was dying to come with us, but daddy didn't want her to. He said: "The Party has condemned him, we must have nothing to do with him. If Lise goes, it's up to her, but you stay here."'

I couldn't help smiling because this was a trait in Ricol which I liked.

My wife then asked the interrogator if she could give me the parcel she had prepared. He consented: it contained sausages, ham, cakes, a loaf and the 'packet of Gauloises which I had always kept with your belongings in the hope that you could smoke them again one day'. She was so pleased to be able to give me those Gauloises.

I didn't want to take the parcel because I knew how difficult life would be for my family. 'I'll take the cigarettes, but you must keep the food for the children.'

Lise got annoyed. 'You'd hurt us if you didn't accept. We'll be happy to know that you're thinking of us when you eat the food we prepared for you.'

The interrogator told us to hurry because we had already been there over an hour. We were near the door. I took my wife in my arms and kissed her. 'I'll withdraw my petition for divorce tomorrow,' she told me. I tried to dissuade her, saying it would be much better for her and the children if she divorced me and reassumed her maiden name. But she answered:

'No, Gérard. I no longer see any point in divorce. I believe in you and I shall stand by you.'

We had to be torn away from each other. I kissed her a last time; and they disappeared behind the door.

Three

Too much news, too many changes all of a sudden. It was impossible to assess them. Was there any connection between Stalin's and Gottwald's deaths and the fact that I had at last been permitted to see my family? And the rehabilitation of the Soviet doctors? And, at the same time, what I heard about my family's life and the persecution they suffered? So what Bacilek had solemnly promised me in his general's uniform was a mere device to trick us once again, to make us stick to our 'confessions'. What interest could the Party have in making a woman with three children and two old parents suffer like this? And how could they justify it?

It was only now that I was to discover how my family had lived since I left them on Sunday, 28 January 1951.

After my arrest my wife had told nobody about what happened. She continued to direct the French department of foreign radio broadcasting. She went to meetings and even to parties: 'The last one was given by the Presidency of the Czech Women's Union in honour of the mother of Zoia Kosmodemianska.* I don't think Anezka Hodinova† ever forgave me this, particularly since I was given a place of honour as former leader of the Union des femmes françaises.'

Gradually, however, the rumour of my arrest spread through Prague. The department where Lise was working was full of informers. Shortly before my arrest Lise had been robbed. Her wallet with her monthly salary, which she had just received, a large quantity of her Darex coupons, and above all her identity papers – including her French identity card – had disappeared from her bag. She had lodged a complaint and had gone to the lost property office to try and get the papers back, for thieves generally got rid of them. But it was no good. In 1956, after my rehabilitation, we were given the papers confiscated from our house when it was searched, and Lise's identity card among them.

A new woman, who collaborated with the general director and owed her assurance and arrogance to the fact that she worked for Security, formulated some serious charges against Lise at a meeting she was unable to attend. Lise had smuggled some attacks against Czecholsovakia to the French anticommunist broadcasting services, she claimed. When my wife

* A young partisan, heroine of the Soviet Union, hanged by the Nazis in 1941.

† Deputy at the National Assembly and president of the Czech Women's Union. Now dead.

heard about this the next day, she went to the meeting, attended by everyone who had been there the day before, and asked for a report to be drawn up on what was about to take place.

She then attacked her slanderer: 'You thought that what with the difficulties I am having at this moment I would let myself be downtrodden by you, that I would let you do what you liked, like a sacrificial lamb. But you were wrong. I won't let anyone slander me. And now provide some proof to substantiate the charges you made against me yesterday when I was away.'

The other woman ate her words. Supported by the other representatives of the foreign departments, Lise insisted that a copy of the report be sent to Bruno Köhler, the secretary of the Central Committee.

Shortly after this she had the conversation with Köhler in which he warned her that she would have to leave the radio and work in a factory.

The official who informed her of her dismissal had seen her before at the meetings of the central staff. As he was very embarrassed at having to tell her of this decision, Lise put him at his ease, saying that Köhler had already told her.

And since she saw an expression of sympathy in this man's face she told him about her difficulties. What was going to become of her? She had to leave her house. Her bank account was blocked. She wasn't allowed to take the furniture. She spoke about her parents and her children, and told him how much she trusted me. She took my letter, my first letter of 1 May, out of her bag, and gave it to him to read, saying: 'Do you think a guilty man would write this?'

The accounts department paid Lise until the end of the month, plus fifteen days' holiday. That was all.

'I got up to leave,' Lise told me. 'The comrade tried to comfort me. He said that I must have the strength to face the difficulties ahead of me. He trusted me. He knew I was a good communist and hoped my present misfortunes would soon be over. I gave him my hand and as he squeezed it I felt him slide an envelope into it. I looked at him in amazement. "No, don't refuse it. I'm delighted to be able to help you. Pay me back when all this is over. It's for the children. Keep your chin up, you're entitled to do so." Then, after a second's hesitation, he added: "Of course, you know the times we're living in. Don't mention it to anyone."

'I had no idea how much he had given me. But I was in such straits that even a hundred crowns would have been welcome. I didn't know how to thank him. At last I had met a real communist.

'In the street I looked at the contents of the envelope: 15,000 crowns.* It must have been his monthly salary which he had just received. It was an enormous sum for us because, apart from the 7,000 crowns I was to receive from the radio after liquidation of my account, we didn't have a penny at home.

'When I told this story to my parents we all wept for joy, not because of the money, but because this humane gesture was the first ray of sunshine in the darkness.'

It was now known that I had been arrested together with other volunteers from Spain. From one day to the next a vacuum formed round my family. Nobody recognized them any more. To avoid greeting Lise our former friends crossed the road and walked on the other side. The sycophants of the day before were the first to cast stones at us.

After a few months' silence Antoinette, a Czech who was born and had lived in France until 1946 and was a great friend of Lise, got in touch with the family. She, in the meantime, had been dismissed from the International Department of the Central Committee where she worked as French editor, and transferred to a state office. She was very unhappy, and couldn't understand what was happening. All her friends from France – Otto, Tonda, Ossik, Laco, Gérard – had been arrested and she refused to believe in their guilt. She remained loyal to Lise, believing that my innocence would eventually be established.

* 15,000 crowns, before the monetary reform in 1953, correspond to 3,000 crowns today.

Two months after my arrest, my friend Vavro Hajdu was also arrested. I thought he had been arrested at the same time as myself, because of our friendship and the tendentious material which had been presented to me in Koldeje and Ruzyn against him, defining us as accomplices in the Ministry of Foreign Affairs. But *they* had preferred to wait two more months. This gave them time to find a charge against him which fitted in with the general plot, and enabled the informers in the Ministry of Foreign Affairs to set up the slanderous campaign against him which had reached its peak at the assembly of the Party organization of the Ministry, at which Siroky himself presided. Vavro had been pilloried with me and excluded from the Party. He was arrested immediately afterwards. The first warning of this was the preparatory meeting of the general assembly of communists intended to take measures against one of Hajdu's collaborators. Certain people attended who shouldn't have been there – a young jurist, F— for example, who, to justify her presence, claimed to be an expert on Jewish questions.

It was after Vavro's arrest that my wife got in touch with the Hajdu family.

'I can't remember exactly when I heard of Hajdu's arrest,' she told me. 'One morning a young woman, small and as dark as a Provençal cricket, with anxious black eyes, appeared at my door. It was Renée, Vavro's sister.

'She told me that her brother had been arrested. Her sister-in-law, Karla, had had such a shock that she had to go to bed. She was now alone with three children.

' "Where can I find out where my brother is?"

'Unfortunately I was unable to help her since, even after two months, I still didn't know where you were. At the time Renée was working at the Ministry of Foreign Trade. She and her brother had followed in their father's footsteps and had studied law. During the war she had escaped the antisemitic persecutions by hiding with her mother in Budapest under a false name. She was very modest, very forthright, and incapable of lying, and she devoted herself body and soul to those she loved. It was impossible not to like her. She told me she was going to resign her job and look for some work in a factory before she was fired. After I left my radio job we decided to look for work together.

'First we went to the local National Committee in charge of labour. They gave us a few addresses. But we thought that if we worked in a large factory we would prove our desire to take an active part in the construction of socialism. The Party would have to take our behaviour into account.

'So we took a tram to CKD – Sokolovo, the largest metal foundry in Prague. We drove for over an hour. and had still not arrived. The distance began to startle us. At that point we saw some notices on the tram windows saying that the CKD–Dukla employment bureau was in Karlin, near the centre of town. So we both decided that we might as well go to Karlin, since it would save us an hour's transport each day. When we got to the address on the notice we saw there were two doors. The one we chose took us to the local management of the Autorenova firm where Renée was surprised to see an old friend in charge of personnel. She explained our situation:

' "It was just as well that you took the wrong door, because Autorenova is far better than CKD. Here's a word for the Sokolovska factory, two steps from here. That's where you have the best chance of earning a high salary."

'Shortly afterwards I found myself talking to Karel Berger, the manager of the factory. We gave him the letter from the staff management. He read my name: "London! are you the wife of Artur, the volunteer in the Brigades?" "Yes, do you know him?" He looked at me compassionately: "I've heard a lot about him."

'I then told him that I was in Prague with three children and my parents. Life was hard for us. I had been dismissed from the radio. I needed to work as soon as possible in order to earn my living, because I had no financial resources.

'He took me to the workshop and introduced me to my future partner, Cara; to the president of the factory committee and the head of the Party organization. We passed a tall, thin man, whom Karel Berger introduced as a veteran from Spain. When he heard my name and I held out my hand I felt him hesitate.

'I started working there on 1 August. I subsequently discovered that Karel Berger had to fight to have me employed and persuade certain members of the factory committee and the Party organization that any other attitude towards me would be reprehensible from the human point of view.'

Renée was taken on by the other Autorenova factory where a friend of hers worked. Later, after being dismissed from the Party School, her husband Lada Krizkovsky was employed at the CKD–Dukla factory, near where his wife was working.

Lise laughed. 'Poor Lada! He was so clumsy with his machine that on our way back from the factory I often saw him with bandages on his fingers, arms, head. But he did his best, and in spite of his wounds he was always smiling and confident that he'd do better in the future.'

When my family moved to the Hanspalka quarter they were almost next door to the house where Renée and her husband lived. They saw each other every day. Renée translated into Czech the letters Lise wrote me as well as all the ones she wrote to the Party organizations and the government. This friendship was a great comfort to them.

Four

Lise had been working for fifteen months in the factory when, on 18 November 1952, she received an anonymous telephone call from Security, asking her to be at home the next day at ten o'clock. A civilian came and told her to prepare a suit, some linen, a shirt and a tie for me. Lise tried to get some news out of him, but he remained evasive, and simply said I was well.

'The fact,' Lise said, 'that they'd come to get some clothes for you filled me with hope. I was sure they were going to release you. At work, as I cleaned and mounted my magnetoes, I sang. I knew we were going to have you back. Antoinette, who was working in my factory too, was as enthusiastic as I: "He may be there when you go home tonight." '

The next day, on Thursday, 20 November, Lise took her usual five o'clock tram. She noticed that instead of drowsing as they usually did, everybody was busy reading the papers. There was a leading article on the front page. Since Lise is short-sighted she went up to a passenger holding the *Rude Pravo* at arm's length, and deciphered 'Trial against the leaders of the centre of conspiracy against the state led by Rudolf Slansky'. That explained it. I couldn't be released before the trial. Then her attention was attracted by a black square. She read the names of the fourteen defendants. That was how she discovered I was condemned. Were it not for the crowd she would have collapsed.

Lise told me:

'When I reached the workshop my companions didn't dare say good morning or even look at me. They had read the news. I'd been working with them for over a year and they had grown fond of me.

'Antoinette arrived. She was pale and distraught. "Have you read the bill of indictment?" she asked me. "No, not yet." "It has terrible charges against Gérard." I borrowed her paper and rushed to the lavatory to decipher the passages where your name was mentioned. I had difficulty in understanding but I gathered that you were accused of espionage with Field and Zilliacus and of complicity with Slansky in sabotage and treason.

'I returned to my stool like an automaton and tried to work. But my eyes were blurred and I could hardly see the object to be filed. Apart from the noise of the machines there was not a voice to be heard in the workshop, which usually resounded with calls from bench to bench, shouts and laughter. Everyone was silent out of respect for my grief.

'A little later the old foreman arrived: "Mrs London, we

realize how hard it must be for you to work today. You ought to be at home, with your family. You can stay away until Monday." I thanked him and left.

'At Prasny-Most, where I had to change trams, I found myself face to face with Françoise who was waiting for the tram to take her to school. She threw herself into my arms and there at last I burst into tears. It was my daughter, accustomed to seeing her mother as a strong woman who never faltered, who consoled me now. She did as she had seen me do so many times to comfort her and her brothers: "No, mummy. You mustn't cry. Of course it's hard for you, for all of us. But you'll see, one day you'll be crying with joy. Everything will turn out all right and daddy will come back. It's only a bad dream. Don't cry, mummy."

'We left each other. Françoise is very proud. She proved this by refusing to change schools after your arrest – and she decided to attend class that day. When I tried to dissuade her, she replied: "Don't worry about me, mummy. I won't let anybody pick a quarrel with me."

'Back home I found my parents in despair. Françoise had told them. My mother was in tears and my father was cursing you. At twelve, when Gérard came back from school for lunch, he asked me candidly: "Tell me, mummy, the London in the trial has nothing to do with our family, has he?" "No, darling." And then, with a sigh of relief, he said: "That's what I told my schoolmates." I lied to him because I still had hope.

'Thursday. . . Friday. . . . All day the proceedings of the trial were being broadcast. On Saturday it would be your turn. I waited for your evidence impatiently, because in my heart of hearts I still hoped you would explain yourself in court and maybe claim to be innocent.

'Huddled round the radio we waited for the fatal moment when we would hear you. Antoinette was there, Hajdu's mother, Renée and her husband, our parents seated side by side as if to support each other. Françoise had a temperature and was lying on the sofa, holding my hand. Michel and Gérard were playing in the other room.

'Suddenly the commentator's voice grew louder: "Now we shall continue the recording of the trial. And here is the evidence of the two witnesses in the Clementis affair, to be followed by the interrogation of Artur London and Vavro Hajdu, both former Under-Secretaries of Foreign Affairs." Françoise squeezed my hand still harder.

'And then your voice! We heard you. Although I have difficulty in understanding when I hear voices on the radio, I understood. To the judge's question: "Do you admit your guilt?" you replied, "I admit my guilt." Guilty! He pleaded guilty. I could only repeat these words. I could hardly understand the rest of of your evidence. Now and again I caught a snatch of it: espionage with Field. . . Zilliacus. . .

'If I had known Czech better, certain turns of phrase, the very way in which your confessions were constructed, all things which I noticed later, would have made me sceptical. But the details escaped me. I just accepted what you said about your guilt. We were all shattered.

'It was atrocious. I thought: if he admits he's guilty it's because he *is* guilty. I knew of your attitude in the war, when we'd been arrested by the Special Anti-terrorist Brigade and interrogated for days and nights on end. Your torturers never got a single detail about your Resistance activity out of you. They never knew that they'd got hold of a good catch: Gérard, the leader of the TA [Travail Allemand], wanted in the whole of France by the Gestapo, who would have paid any price for you.

'How could I think that a man capable of resisting in such conditions would plead guilty if it weren't true?

'How could I imagine that there were methods which could make an innocent man guilty? Such a thought never entered my head. It would have meant suspecting the Party, and that was something I couldn't do.

'Besides, you knew that we would hear your evidence, so I

told myself that out of love for me, for my parents and the children, you would never have agreed to plead guilty if you were innocent. The suffering such a statement caused us would have prevented you from doing so. You would rather have died!

'I remember telling poor Françoise, who was trembling with fever and excitement: "Your father's confessing. You hear his voice? We must never forget that he's betrayed all his duties, he's guilty." And then I had to tell little Gérard the truth. I'll never forget his face. He looked at me, his big eyes filled with tears, and seemed to be begging me: "No, mummy, it's not true, not my daddy!" He started crying and ran out of the room. At home he never mentioned you, but I later discovered that he often fought against boys of his age who hurled your name at him as an insult.

'After hearing you, I did as I said I would in my letters to you and to the Party leaders, when I was fighting for you. I would not remain the wife of a traitor, of a spy. As a communist there could be no question of choosing between you and the Party. However hard that might seem from the human point of view I was going to stick to the Party!

'Still reeling from the shock of hearing you plead guilty I wrote a letter to Gottwald and the judge. It was later shamefully exploited in the press, after being mutilated and expurgated. This is it:

Prague, 22 November 1952.

To President Gottwald.

After my husband's arrest, knowing what I did about his life and activity, I thought he had been the victim of traitors trying to hide their own criminal activity behind the 'London case'.

Until the last minute, that is to say until the day I heard him on the radio, I hoped that if he had committed any mistakes he could make up for them, and that, even if he had to answer for them before the Party and the Court, he would subsequently be able to atone and return to the communist family.

But, after reading the bill of indictment and hearing his confession, my hopes have been shattered: my husband has not been a victim but a traitor to his Party and his country. The blow is hard. A traitor had sneaked into my family. We are all old communists. During the occupation my father said: 'I'm proud to know that my children are in prison for their loyalty to their ideals and the Communist Party. But I'd rather they were dead than traitors.' And now we have seen the father of my three children appear before the people's court as a traitor. I have had the painful task of informing the two older children of the truth. They promised always to behave like true communists.

Although I realize that the bonds between father, brother, husband and child must yield to the interest of the Party and people I am greatly distressed, and this is only human. But, as a communist, and in the interests of the Czech people and world peace, I must applaud the fact that the centre of conspiracy against the state has been revealed. I join all the honest citizens of the country in demanding a just punishment for the traitors you have condemned.

Lise London.

'My second reaction was to file a petition for divorce on Monday morning, while the trial was still being held. I considered it impossible for a communist to continue to be the wife of a traitor to his Party and country.

'That same day, the fifth day of the trial, I went back to the factory. At the end of the day Karel Berger, who was now a plain workman in the factory (he had been fired from the management a few months earlier because he was not of working-class origin and had been in the West during the war), got into the tram. He sat next to me and, after affectionately squeezing my hand, he said: "Lise, don't think I'm reproaching you. I know how sincere you were in writing what your conscience dictated to you. But you shouldn't have done so, because your husband is innocent!"

'I looked at him in amazement: "But you heard him plead guilty on the radio on Saturday as well as I did."

' "Yes, I heard him. But I don't believe in this trial. All the evidence, the bill of indictment, sounds false."

' "But Karel, the Party's behind the trial. It must have checked the charges beforehand. What interest could it have in setting up a trial like this if it weren't true?"

'"That's what I ask myself. The Party isn't always right. You only have to consider its attitude towards you and your family. Had you deserved it? No. I don't believe the Party is what it used to be. It has been dehumanized. You don't understand Czech well enough, otherwise you wouldn't have been taken in. For instance, there are notes of antisemitism in the bill of indictment and the proceedings. And how can you explain that from one day to the other heroes are suddenly treated as spies and traitors? I can't understand and I don't agree. So I have decided to send back my Party card."

'It is remarkable that in this period of mass hysteria one man should have the courage to go against the tide – because it took courage just then. And he left the Party, saying:

'"My brother was one of the leaders of the communist students in Prague before the war. Deported to Auschwitz during the war, he died there. I was very young when he worked for the Party but I admired him and his example taught me to respect communist ideas.

'"I fled to France after the Nazi occupation of Czechoslovakia and joined the Czech army at Agde. I was then eighteen. There, for several months, I lived with the former volunteers from the International Brigades. I learned to respect them, to like them and to trust them. In them I found the purity and courage of my brother. I took them as my model and wanted to follow in their steps.

'"In this trial men were pilloried. I cannot understand why, and since the explanations have not satisfied me I think it would not be honest to remain a member of the Party which condemned them. That's why I must send back my Party card today."*

* In a letter written in June 1968 Karel Berger told us that he had just been elected by 9,000 workers as president of his firm. He ended his letter saying that the Czech spring had returned its full value to socialism and that he was preparing to ask if he could again join the Communist Party.

'I knew what serious consequences this gesture would entail. He had already lost his job as manager. But for him the most important thing was to live in peace with his conscience.

'The more I doubted your guilt, as Renée or Antoinette translated your evidence, the more I tried to keep on the Party's side. I felt like a nun in fear of the devil, who increases her prayers and mortification. I was afraid that my love for you had blinded me. It was not possible for *me* to be right, and the Party wrong.

'And then I grew conscious of my total isolation in a foreign country, and the complete vacuum which the French comrades formed around me. When I saw any of them after your arrest and started to speak in your favour they immediately turned away. I heard that a comrade from the Peace Movement had informed Paris that my attitude was deplorable, that I was taking an anti-Party stand, that I was behaving more like a female defending her mate than a communist. The leaders of the movement asked me not to set foot in their headquarters and ordered the other comrades not to speak to me. The head of the French department of the radio did the same thing. I was a leper. All I needed was a bell.

'By saying that if the Party provided proof of my husband's treason I would know how to behave like a true communist, I tied myself down. I owed it to myself, my parents and the children to stick to one position. When doubts arose, the whole construction was in danger. I thought: Lise, you're in a bad way, or, Look out, Lise, whoever asks himself if he's still a good communist is sliding down the slope to reaction. Oh, these slogans, repeated over and over again, removed all my sense of judgement.

'From morning to evening the loudspeakers blared out the proceedings of the trial in the workshop. The questions of the judge and the prosecutor, the statements of the defendants and witnesses. It was nightmarish! I only caught a few words, and the names I knew. I could hardly stick to my bench in such an atmosphere. And then came the day of the verdict and the defendants' last statements.

'For some time people had been speculating about the penalties. They now said they would be very heavy. But when, the next morning, after reading the sentence, the judge started to list the penalties, everyone was amazed: there were eleven death sentences, and then your name and those of Vavro Hajdu and Eugen Löbl. I was leaning against the bench, my head in my hands. I didn't want to hear. But they shouted to me: "Life!" My neighbours realized what a state I was in. You were to remain alive. I sighed deeply; then I burst into tears. I could hardly get up.

'Antoinette, who worked in the workshop next door, ran in shouting: "He's saved!" She hugged me and cried. The workers said nothing. Two of them, who had known you when they had worked in the Ministry of Foreign Affairs, came to see me and squeezed my hand in silence. Karel Berger came up: "I'm happy for you, for him, for the children."

'My new boss – I had been put in a new workshop, since the beginning of the trial – a strapping, jovial, Schweik-like fifty-year-old told me two or three days later: "The main thing, Mrs London, is that your husband should be alive. You'll be together again one day." When I looked at him in amazement he added: "This whole trial has been nothing but a comedy filled with lies. You can't speak Czech well enough to realize. Remember what I tell you: you'll be together again one day. I'm prepared to make a bet with you."

'On the evening of the verdict, when we were all at home, Françoise hugged me and shouted almost gaily: "He's alive, that's the main thing." Mummy wept for joy and my father hid his feelings with a sulky expression, pulling nervously on his white moustache.

'The only thing my father did not like about the trial was the antisemitism. When he heard that eleven of the defendants were described as being "of Jewish origin" he remained speechless at first. Then he uttered an oath: "My God! What's that got to do with it? Ever since I've been in the Party I always heard that antisemitism was the weapon of reaction to foment discord among the people. So why drag it in now? Jew? So what? What does that mean? Does one say people are of Protestant or Catholic *origin*?" He couldn't get over it. Otherwise, despite your condemnation as a traitor, a spy and everything else, it never entered his head to question a verdict from his Party, even though it concerned his own son-in-law.'

A few days after the trial as Lise, who was on the afternoon shift, was pacing gloomily up and down at the stop at Prasny-Most where she had to change trams, she saw a small, thin figure in evening dress coming towards her, her head in a black shawl. It was Lea, the wife of Fritz Gosse,* the Ambassador of the German Democratic Republic. On her way back from a party, she had recognized Lise and ordered her chauffeur to drop her so she could walk to her villa.

I had known Fritz and Lea ever since they had both been active members of the German Communist Youth. During the war Lea had been arrested by the Nazis, but had managed to escape from a German fortress. She reached the USSR through Poland, with the help of the partisans. She had spent the rest of the war in Russia. As for Fritz, he had been in a secret prison for over ten years, and everyone, including his wife, thought him dead. I was therefore delighted to see him when I arrived at Mauthausen, where he himself had already been held for several months. We were close friends and he took an active part in the underground resistance work in the camp.

After his appointment as German ambassador in Prague we saw a great deal of each other.

Lea asked Lise about the children and her parents. She told her how Fritz and she had suffered from what was going on in Czechoslovakia. The trial. Why all this antisemitism? It was appalling how Geminder had been treated. (During the war she had been a close collaborator of his. He had then been in

* Died in 1957 as the result of his treatment in a Nazi prison.

charge of the broadcasts from Radio Moscow for all occupied countries. Lea worked in the German section.) There were so many false notes in the trial, too. She no longer wanted to remain in Prague. She wanted to go back to Berlin. Her husband had asked to be recalled. She asked for Lise's new address and, before leaving the country, sent her a parcel of food.

Five

The first part of March 1953 was devoted to mourning for Stalin and then to mourning for Gottwald. All one heard on the radio were funeral marches. Gottwald's body was exhibited at the castle and an endless procession of loyal citizens filed past.

Lise found out from the papers that the delegation of the French Communist Party was to be led by Raymond Guyot. For the Ricol parents, who were cut off from everything by their inability to speak Czech, their son-in-law's visit was a godsend. But they hadn't reckoned with the Security precautions; Raymond Guyot never managed to see them, however hard he tried.

When Lise's parents realized this, they were terribly upset. They had looked forward to this visit so much. And when Lise saw them in this state she had a spurt of anger against me: 'Why did he drag us here? It's because of him that my parents are suffering!'

'I was all the angrier,' she later told me, 'because I knew that Hajdu not only wrote to his family, but could also receive visits. But not us. We hadn't heard a single word from you since the trial. This made me assume that you didn't dare write to us now you had pleaded guilty in public.

'So I took my pen and started to write the letter you received. I began it several times, because I lost control of myself and always ended up by writing words of love. On paper my hatred and rage turned into genuine feelings for you, into love. Everything I wrote seemed too kind, prompted only by my love for you. Indeed, I told the men filing our divorce that in no case would I allow them to remove your rights of paternity over your children, that you had paid enough for your mistakes and that socialist humanism did not intend to crush the individual, but to enable him to redeem himself.'

I was now really pleased that Lise had written this letter. It was undoubtedly because of it that we were able to see each other. Until then we had had no news of each other, and neither of the letters I wrote to her had reached her.

I could never fathom the reasons for this cruelty towards me, this device of withholding my letters while my fellow prisoners received theirs. Why was everyone set against me and my family?

The ringleaders of Ruzyn obviously wanted to keep us from getting in touch. Were they afraid that, through Lise, details might reach Raymond Guyot and the Directing Committee of the French Party?

In any case, when Lise's letter about the children entered the hands of the interrogators, and, through them, of the Soviet advisers, its content suggested that Lise was a communist conditioned to such an extent that they had nothing to lose by appearing magnanimous and allowing me and my wife to see each other.

Then there were the recent events in the USSR and Czechoslovakia, the deaths of Stalin and Gottwald, which would have inevitable political consequences. The rehabilitation of the Russian doctors was one of the elements which indicated a new course in the USSR, a course which was to lead to the Twentieth Party Congress in February 1956.

I believe that at this point the Czech Party and the Security leaders began to feel anxious about the trial, of which we were the sole survivors. In the present situation we represented a political factor which went far beyond our own persons.

The course of events showed that my deductions were correct.

For a few months the conditions of our imprisonment were to improve. But the Soviet advisers regained confidence when they realized that the trial was not to be revised and that things would remain as they were. So conditions again deteriorated. Our life in prison became worse than that of the real enemies of the regime or the worst common criminals.

A few days after his departure Raymond Guyot sent an express registered letter from Paris to my family, saying how sorry he was not to have seen them. He said that he had left a food parcel for the children for Easter with a comrade in the International department, and he hoped we had received it.

Lise told me: 'We didn't receive the parcel. I rang the head of this department several times to claim it, but they always found some excuse for making me wait. Only three weeks later did Raymond's present arrive: the hen, the fish and the chocolate egg were in a thousand pieces; the Security men had undoubtedly looked for the secret message which Raymond Guyot had put in the chocolate!'

Since the trial an avalanche of misfortunes had befallen my family. Lise had been transferred during the trial from the workshop where she had repaired magnetoes for military aircraft to another one where she repaired parts for cars and trucks. As a result, her wage packet had been reduced: she was serving a new apprenticeship.

'And then, on the morning of 13 March 1953,' Lise said, 'the loudspeakers announced that comrades Hrbacova [Antoinette] and Londonova were required to go to the manager's office. Karel Berger had also been summoned. We stood before the members of the factory committee, the president of the Party organization and the manager of the factory. They were sitting side by side and looked none too pleased with themselves. What was going to happen now?

'The president of the Party organization started speaking: "After a general discussion about your case it has been decided that you must leave the factory immediately."

'Why had they decided this? Karel Berger was guilty of

having employed me when he was manager, Antoinette of being a friend of mine and I of being London's wife.

'Antoinette started to sob. Karel stood with great dignity and looked his former companions in the eye. I called on the members of the firm committee one by one – my present boss and the workmen with whom I had worked for months in the best spirit of comradeship: "You knew me well. Have you got anything against me? And you . . . and you . . . and you . . . have you anything to criticize about my work or my behaviour in the factory, the union or the Party organization? What right have you to judge me? Even if my husband was guilty towards his country and family, in what way are my family and I guilty? Why should my parents and children suffer? By dismissing me it means they will no longer have anything to eat. Your behaviour is justified neither on a human level nor on the level of the socialist morality to which you always refer. One day you'll regret your attitude at this moment. You'll blush with shame when you look back on it."

'I was simply furious and my Czech vocabulary suddenly improved, as in those dreams in which you hear yourself making a long speech in a foreign language.

'I also spoke about Karel Berger: "He took me on because he knew I had five mouths to feed, I had no money and I was a foreigner in this country. You're dismissing him because he was kind and humane. And what have you got against Antoinette? That she should be a friend of mine and should have remained so when a whole lot of other people turned against me? Admittedly she continued to trust me, because she knew I deserved her trust. That's why you're dismissing her!"

'Our judges were pretty sheepish. Only the president of the Party organization and the manager, Karel Berger's successor, were hostile.

'The factory which Antoinette and I were transferred to was entirely different from the one we left. It produced spare parts. So I had to learn a new job. During the apprenticeship my salary was again to suffer! But I wasn't surprised. Since I was the latest employee and London's wife I was given the most unpleasant, worst-paid jobs, which other workmen refused.

'My first job was to file parts on a machine with no protective screen. The metal splinters from the spherical brush which turned at high speed flew off into my face. Drops of blood ran down my cheeks. I wept with rage and went to see the manager: "You see what a state my face is in? How can you make me work on such a machine? If the work protection department saw the conditions of this factory it would cost you dear!"

'The days passed. I asked to work on another machine. But they still insisted on giving me the jobs nobody wanted. Working like a convict I barely earned a quarter of my previous salary. It was disastrous for my family.

'It was in vain that I complained to the foreman, or the union delegate. They turned a deaf ear. It was practical at last to have found a victim who had to do all the unpleasant jobs which had been set aside.

'One day I decided it had lasted long enough. I checked in as usual and then went to see the foreman. "I've come to the factory because I know that, as the head of a family, it would be reprehensible if I didn't appear at my job. But I've decided to refuse to work until you give me a job which will enable me to feed my three children and my parents."

'I took a stool and sat in the middle of the workshop. The union delegate and the manager's representative asked me to reconsider my attitude: "I'm prepared to work, but I must have a job which will ensure me a decent salary. Put me on a machine at which I can earn my living."

'That afternoon the foreman came to tell me that the next morning a workman would teach me to handle a polisher. I'd won! I soon learned how to handle several machine tools, and my wage packet gradually increased.'

Six

I was no longer alone in my cell. I had the impression that I was shut in a kaleidoscope, and each of its fragments was formed by one of the images or impressions which I brought back from my visits – images and impressions which were constantly changing and giving way to new ones.

One day Kohoutek summoned me to his office to tell me I was entitled to write letters. He stood before me in a major's uniform; the trial had earned him a promotion. A new decoration gleamed on his chest.

As usual he spoke volubly about the political importance of the trial. When I asked, 'Are you going to keep me in solitary confinement, between four walls, for much longer?' he said that nothing had yet been decided about Hajdu, Löbl and me. That other cases had to be examined before ours.

Then, solemnly, he added: 'Never forget how serious your case is. Take care and don't try to be clever. Only when the Party is sure of your behaviour and your attitude will it decide on your future.'

A little later, to my great surprise, I was again interrogated, by Kohoutek himself, and the questions were related exclusively to my wife. The way he formulated these questions, naming people I didn't know and who, he said, were in contact with my wife, frightened me. What was he after?

As I later wrote to Lise, he wanted to hold the threat of arresting my wife over my head so as to keep me under control, and at the same time discredit her in every way in order to obtain permission to arrest her if necessary. The Security also hoped to discredit the other members of my family, notably Lise's sister, Fernande, the wife of the member of a Political Bureau of the French Communist Party, whom they slandered basely. In this way they probably wanted to forestall and shield themselves from any step in my favour, taken by my wife or a member of her family.

Now that all my plans were centred round my family's return to France I was afraid that Ruzyn, by compiling this dossier against Lise, was trying to prevent her from leaving Czechoslovakia. They wanted some guarantee for her.

I was particularly obsessed by the idea that Lise should leave as soon as possible, since, at the end of the interrogation, Kohoutek made the usual threat: 'Think of your family, Mr London!'

After Lise's first visit I was assailed by a sense of anxiety: had they managed to record part of our conversation? Accordingly, in the first letter I was allowed to write to my family, I wrote for the sake of the censor: 'I am deeply moved that you should have explained to the children the Party's generosity towards them in allowing me to see them.'

But, at the same time, since I wanted her to believe in me, I tried to confirm what I had said about the trial, hoping that the censor would miss the sense of my words.

'I spoke and acted during the investigation as the Party told me and expected me to. At the trial I sustained this attitude and continue to do so. I tried to be led solely by the Party's interests, putting personal interests aside. . . . I stick firmly to the declarations I made in court starting with Field and ending with Zilliacus.'

This letter remained in the interrogator's drawer for three weeks. In the end it was passed and Lise received it the day before our second visit. She then told me: 'I was mad with joy when I received your letter through the post. I can use it if needs be. Whoever reads that passage will have no doubt: only an innocent man could write it! This letter is the first written proof of your innocence.'

During her third visit Lise told me how she had been expelled from the Party:

'I was summoned to a meeting of my old factory cell on 20 May 1953. The president of the assembly said that there was only one point on the order of the day: my exclusion, in conformity to the demand formulated by the Central Committee. There was total silence.

'I asked to speak: "According to article 14 of the Party statutes, I demand to know why I am excluded, so as to present my defence."

'Everyone turned to me. I read the letter I had written four days earlier to Comrade Novotny, First Secretary of the Central Committee, about my Party membership. I saw a number of people give signs of approval. And then a hand was raised. It was an enemy of mine, a former veteran from the International Brigades, who asked to speak. He had always held extreme opinions about his comrades from the Brigades under arrest and I had had numerous disagreements with him on the subject. One day he got angry when I said: "As far as I can see, there are only two valid categories of volunteers: yourself and the dead." Since then we had merely nodded to each other. What was he going to say? I listened with curiosity and my surprise was as great as my joy:

' "Comrades, you tell us that you are excluding Comrade London at the request of the Central Committee. But you have given us no justification for this exclusion. We know her to be an excellent worker; indeed, we have often referred to her as the best worker in the factory. We know her to be a good mother and a good comrade. We can only praise her behaviour as a communist. Why should we exclude her? Maybe the Central Committee has reasons which it refuses to impart. But in this case, comrades, the Central Committee itself should pronounce her exclusion, without asking us to do so."

'The president shouted him down: "What you've said proves Londonova's bad influence on our group. It's an attempt to oppose democratic centralization. If the Central Committee asks us to exclude her it must have its reasons and it doesn't need to explain them. We won't tolerate speeches of this kind and measures will be taken against anyone who makes them in the

356

future. And now I want you to vote for Comrade London's exclusion, by raising your hands."

'One after another, hesitantly, they raised their hands and unanimously voted for my exclusion – even the comrade from the Brigades, who was one of the last to comply.

'I then said: "I am going to appeal against this exclusion. I have never been interrogated about the activities of my husband Artur London. My conscience is clean and I have always behaved like a communist."

'The president asked me to leave. I went towards the door. All my old companions at work stood up, one after the other, to shake my hand. I saw sorrow and shame in their eyes. Some of the women I had worked with and of whom I was especially fond were crying. I reassured them: "I don't hold it against you. I still consider you my friends." '

Lise then pulled a sheet of paper out of her bag and said: 'I'm going to read you my letter of protest to the Central Committee (it's dated 27 May 1953):

'I appeal against the decision of the assembly of the Party organization of firm CSAO factory 0104, Prague Karlin, by which I was excluded from the Party on 20 May. This decision, and the way it was taken, is in flagrant contradiction to the statutes of the Party. On Wednesday, 20 May, I was summoned by the Party assembly of the above-mentioned firm. The president read out a letter from the Party Committee of the District of Prague 3, which said that my Party card, removed from me at the time of the trial, was not to be returned to me and that I was excluded by the order of the Central Committee. No justification for this measure was given. I protested, because, in spite of my repeated demands, I have never been heard by the Party. Besides, since no justification for my exclusion was given, it is difficult for me to defend myself, as I am entitled to do according to the Party statutes. I read the Assembly the letter I wrote on 16 May to Comrade Novotny, Secretary of the Central Committee, concerning my Party membership. A comrade at the assembly then suggested that my case be referred to the Central Committee which undoubtedly possesses the necessary information and sufficient knowledge to judge it. The president of the organization rejected this proposal, saying that it was opposed to the principal of democratic centralization, and that if the Central Committee gave the order, the organization could but execute this order, without questioning it. He added that I could always appeal later against this decision.

In my opinion, this procedure is illogical. As the saying goes, it is "putting the cart before the horse!" Article 14 of the Party statutes says: "In the event of exclusion from the Party, care, solicitude and comradeship must be shown and a precise analysis must be made of the reasons for the charges against a Party member." So the procedure used against me cannot be considered valid: someone is excluded and it is only later that he can defend himself by appealing against the decision.

The members of the firm organization present at the assembly only voted for my exclusion because they received an order from the Central Committee. They did so without knowing the reasons for this exclusion.'

The interrogator who had spoken to my wife and Françoise, and whose attitude had changed so radically in the last months, listened in fascination to this conversation. Not once did he interrupt. His confusion showed in his face. Was this the meeting between a traitor condemned by the Party and his wife? It did not correspond to any image he had had. Were the true communists really his bosses, the ringleaders?

Of course I knew that Lise was fighting and would still fight for what she considered 'her' truth, 'her' image of the Party. But I knew it would be no good. Indeed, I was afraid that she would be arrested on the flimsiest excuse.

Françoise attracted the interrogator's attention and I warned Lise: 'Watch out, there are spies who make reports on everything you say and do.'

She looked at me in surprise. 'I saw a report with my own eyes on the interrogator's table. They recently questioned me about you and your friends, including Antoinette. You must leave for France, because they might try and arrest you.'

'Let them try, I'll be ready for them and they don't know what they'll be in for!'

'Don't be silly, you don't know them,' I said.

Before leaving, Lise told me she had had all her papers back from the civil court as well as the confirmation that her petition for a divorce had been cancelled.

Of course I was pleased that Lise had done this, but I feared she might encounter further difficulties, for now she had shown that she was on my side.

Seven

A few days after this third visit I was put in a new cell. The warder who took me there told me, before shutting the door: 'In this cell the water system is controlled by us, from outside. If you want to drink or go to the lavatory you must stand in front of the spy-hole, raise your finger and point to the basin.'

I was surprised by this. This cell was identical to many others I had been in. There were sanitary installations, but they must have been altered in some way. I was so curious that I immediately did as the warder said. I raised my finger and the lavatory flushed automatically. A little later I raised my finger again and pointed to the tap. I wanted to drink. The water started running and stopped automatically.

I was intrigued and examined the cell. It was very clean and freshly painted. Above the lavatory, on the wall and the ceiling, I saw a large spotted surface. That reminded me of something. One day, when I went to see Pavel after he had lost his job as Under-Secretary of the Interior, we started talking about the nepotism which was developing in Czechoslovakia, and of which the best example was presented by Cepicka who had married Gottwald's daughter and had accordingly been promoted to the highest functions in the state and Party. At the time he was Minister of Defence.

As I started discussing the matter Pavel signalled to me to be silent. He took me into the bathroom, opened the bath taps and said: 'I don't know whether my former colleagues are listening in to me. It's better to have conversations like this in the street or in the bathroom with the taps on, because all they hear is running water.'

And everything became still clearer when Kohoutek called me the next day and told me that a first step was being taken to improve the conditions of my imprisonment. My solitary confinement was to end. I was to share my cell with another prisoner.

With my fellow prisoner I would obviously avoid broaching any delicate matter, such as my identity or the reasons for my presence here.

A fortnight later, on a Saturday in June 1953, I was called to Doubek's office. He told me that on the orders of the new President, Zapotocky, there was to be a further improvement for Löbl, Hajdu and myself. We were all going to be transferred to a labour unit in Ruzyn prison; that was to say that from then on we were to be together with the other prisoners.

When I returned to my cell to fetch my belongings I thought that I was right about the microphone in my cell. It was a test to judge my behaviour with other prisoners. A few hours later, when I talked to Löbl and Hajdu, Löbl told me that the same thing had happened to him.

A warder came for me. He blindfolded me and led me along corridors, and staircases, into a lift, to somewhere in the fresh air. When he took my bandage off I saw the entrance gate of the prison where I had spent twenty-eight months. It would be impossible for me to describe the interior of the building because I was always blindfolded except when I was in my own cells and the interrogators' offices. Even later, when Hajdu, Löbl and I were summoned by an interrogator for some reason or other, we were always blindfolded before entering the building, and it remained a mystery to us until the end.

Still escorted by the warder I crossed the yard. We went into an office on the ground floor of another building. It was the headquarters of the small labour unit in the Ruzyn prison. I passed Hajdu as he came out of it. He smiled happily when he saw me and I too was delighted. Now that we were together life would be more bearable.

Half an hour later we found ourselves in the yard with Löbl.

We had been exchanging our first impressions for an hour when the head of Ruzyn himself, Doubek, came in. He made us sit next to him on a bench. We couldn't get over his behaviour. He told us he had been summoned by Zapotocky, who told him to put us in a labour unit and improve the conditions of our imprisonment. We were going to be granted certain privileges. Whenever we had a request to make we were to appeal to him.

Our families could visit us in the gardens of Ruzyn each week, and we were to receive parcels and letters. He even added that part of our possessions which had been confiscated were to be restored to our families. We could hardly believe our ears.

And when he left us, after shaking us by the hand, we were stunned! We, the nobodies, the lepers!

We looked at each other: what was going on? We started speculating on the changes since Stalin's death. Maybe the wheel was going to start turning. But we decided to be careful. We were not to forget that our executioners were there, that we were living within their reach, and that behind them they had the ringleaders, two of whom had just gone by, carrying large brief cases.

Kovic, the former Yugoslav Vice-Consul in Bratislava, whom we had just met, told us that they were Soviet advisers.

When I now compare the date of this change with what was going on in the Soviet Union at the time it coincides strikingly with the change of policy manifested by the replacement of Rakosi by Imre Nagy as head of the Hungarian government. Facts of such importance must have provided food for thought for those in Czechoslovakia who had followed Rakosi's line. Nevertheless, it appeared that these changes did not actually change the system of the trials, since Beria, although he was arrested, was not specifically charged for having been head of Security and Rakosi still remained Secretary General of the Party. At least this was how, looking back on things, I accounted for what happened to us in June and July 1953, starting with our appointment to a labour unit and the end of our solitary confinement.

Our arrival caused a great stir in the labour unit and aroused the curiosity of the other prisoners. There were less than a hundred of them: some were Nazi collaborators, but most of them were common criminals. There were also a few political prisoners.

The prisoners were employed to tend the prison buildings, clean the offices, corridors, and kitchens, do the washing and ironing, gardening, and so on.

A few prisoners came up to us and said that, as they were cleaning the interrogators' offices, they had managed to pinch some of the papers which mentioned our trial and that they would give them to us.

From Kevic, who was condemned to life imprisonment and had already been here several months, we got to know about the unit, its members, the various dangers and forms of provocation which we might expect, and the 'stool pigeons'.

Until Monday we took advantage of every minute to discuss our experiences over the last two years. 'Well, Gérard, what d'you think about it?' said Hajdu. 'One must have gone through it to believe it! When I think that I'd developed a guilt complex about not having believed in the Moscow trials before the war!'

We discovered that we had all followed an identical train of thought since our imprisonment. We resolved always to act together; every time one of us discovered something new he was to tell the others. This solidarity was our only means of defence.

When I came down to the unit I was given the Gauloises which my wife had brought on her first visit and which had remained in the prison office, probably for a closer examination.

I took out a packet and Hajdu's eyes gleamed. Like me, he was a great smoker. But, at the first puff, we both pulled a wry face. Lise told me that she had kept the packets with my belongings in a cupboard full of mothballs.

In our conversations with Löbl, Hajdu and Kevic about the use of drugs as a means of extorting confessions, Kevic told us that he was sure he had been drugged. He asked me if I had ever had boiled potatoes covered with a bitter-tasting oil for dinner. I did indeed remember having had this on several occasions. He said that it contained scopolamin, a drug used on Van der Lubbe who was accused by Hitler and Goering of of having set the Reichstag on fire in 1933, and was tried with Dimitrov in the Leipzig trials. Other prisoners agreed. I knew Kevic to be a wise and realistic man, with none of that mytho-mania which prisoners often had; besides, he was a friend of a nurse who worked with Dr Sommer.

And yet, although I can't be sure, I am not convinced that we were drugged. Admittedly we received medicines without ever knowing what they contained or what their effects were. We had to take them before the nurse and sometimes the warder, who made sure we swallowed them and then checked on whether we had hidden them under our tongues or in a corner of our mouths.

Admittedly I had had injections with mysterious effects. During interrogations I was sometimes in a state of total sottishness and had numerous hallucinations. I went through periods of complete apathy when everything happened as if it didn't concern me, and I couldn't have cared less what the interrogators wrote. But I don't believe it was necessary for our torturers to use drugs, because the system of Ruzyn was far more reliable. Their methods were a practical application of Pavlov's theories of conditioning and psychology.

This system – and practice has proved it – is more effective than any drug. It was tried out in the trials of Moscow, Sofia, Budapest and on hundreds of other occasions, with astonishing results. Their technique, applied for months, or even years, to the same individual, was far more effective than scopolamin. Besides, the purpose of the ringleaders of Ruzyn was to produce at a public trial men whose outward appearance concealed the moral and physical sufferings endured since their arrest, men in control of all their intellectual faculties, behaving normally, and not dazed Van der Lubbes, slobbering at the mouth.

And the ringleaders of Ruzyn were past masters in the art of preparing the defendants in this way.

On Monday and Tuesday Vavro and I had to sort out potatoes in a cellar. Sitting unobserved in the twilight, in spite of the filthy smell and the foul work, these hours alone gave us the opportunity to discuss the conditions in the Party and the country, and to speculate on the reasons for our trial and on the future.

On Wednesday we were attached to the gardening group, where Löbl was already working. Despite the fresh air and the sun, or rather because of them, this day was the worst. We had been so weakened by our imprisonment and diet that I was exhausted. That evening I had a high fever, and was incapable of moving. Two days later Hajdu left the group. By exposing his face to the sun after months in the dark, he suffered second-degree burns. His face was swollen and deformed. Only Löbl, although he had been arrested almost a year before us, resisted tenaciously.

I was sent to the Pankrac prison infirmary for medical visits. When I returned, Kohoutek called me to his office. He asked me how the prisoners in the infirmary reacted when I arrived and how the members of the labour unit reacted when they saw Löbl, Hajdu and me among them. What questions had they asked us and what had we answered?

I said that our arrival had caused a sensation the first day and that the prisoners didn't believe in the trial and our guilt. Kohoutek then told me that we must be assimilated by the mass of prisoners and always stick to the line of the trial. 'Don't forget that you've been sentenced for high treason and that you must live your part.'

Looking at me solemnly, he added that he was not talking in his name. He had been ordered to do so by 'his chiefs'. He asked me to inform Löbl and Hajdu of what he had said when I returned to the unit.

'If you want to leave this prison alive you must always hold the attitude I tell you. Don't ever forget that you must stand by your confessions in all circumstances, before everyone, whether it be the representatives of the state and Party or the courts where you have to bear evidence against your accomplices who stood witness against you. I repeat: whether it be before the public prosecutor, the Party Secretary or even the President of the Republic, you must always stand by your confessions.'

From this conversation with Kohoutek, whom we knew to be the confidential agent of the Soviet advisers, we deduced that the promises made by Doubek on Zapotocky's orders had been cancelled by the ringleaders of Ruzyn. What remained of all the privileges promised us? Letters and visits, at first every month, but then at ever greater intervals. The only advantage was that we weren't separated from our families by a double grid.

To start with Vavro and I were left to ourselves to do the laundry. Later Kohoutek intervened again, forcing us to stay more with the other prisoners. The pressure increased. Kohoutek told us cynically: 'We cannot allow any doubts to arise about the trial. Don't forget that some of the prisoners are serving short sentences and will soon be released. In the Party's interest we must be sure of what they say when they are free.'

A little later we understood that the object of the ringleaders and their confidential agents was to stifle any hope we might have of using the latest developments in the USSR to throw doubt on the validity of the trial. Our treatment deteriorated in the following months.

The head of the labour unit changed. His successor had obviously received orders to discriminate against us: we were dangerous criminals, political enemies of the first order!

Now that we were constantly being scolded, we found that we were provoked, stool pigeons were set on us. Numerous warders had been replaced. The new ones thought it their duty as Party members to be particularly vigilant and hard with us.

We were very worried about this new turn of events, and tried to discover some reason for it.

Hajdu, Löbl and I reckoned that our destiny depended upon the political fluctuations in the USSR. Our trial was a deep wedge in the system and its leadership. The three of us, the only survivors of this trial, had become an important political factor, particularly now that the situation seemed about to change. This led certain leaders of the Party or Security to try and cover their traces by making us helpless, or even by liquidating us, while others hoped to secure their future by improving our conditions. We were tossed from current to current. For the time being the occult force of the Soviet advisers had the last word. Unfortunately we were still in their hands and remained there until May 1954.

To be convinced of this one only had to see how Doubek tried to avoid us when he passed us in the yard.

We had to be prepared for the worst; not give in to any provocation; and try, whatever the price, to gain time.

As the conviction that things wouldn't change in Czechoslovakia, that the trial was 'untouchable' grew among the ringleaders and their men in Ruzyn, the preparation of further trials arising from ours resumed. Over sixty people arrested in connection with the centre of conspiracy against the state were still detained.

In the spring of 1953 the Minister of Security, Bacilek, showed the Political Secretariat of the Central Committee a plan to liquidate these 'remains': the prisoners were to be split into seven groups: the economists, headed by Goldmann; the Grand Council Trotskyist group, with Vlk; the bourgeois Slovak nationalists, with Husak; the Security group, with Zavodsky; the Army, with Drgac; and finally the group of the Ministry of Foreign Affairs, with Goldstücker. There would also be some individual trials, against Smarkovsky, Outrata, Novy, Pavel, etc.

The bills of indictment in all these trials were discussed by the Political Secretariat, who settled the sentences. At that time the members of the Political Secretariat were Antonin Zapotocky, President of the Republic after Gottwald's death; Siroky, who was now Prime Minister; Bacilek; Novotny, now Secretary General of the Party; Cepicka, Gottwald's son-in-law and Minister of Defence; Dolansky, Vice-Premier; and Kopecky, Minister of Information and Culture.

Apart from the trial against the group from the Ministry of Foreign Affairs, which took place in May, after Stalin's and Gottwald's deaths, the others were to take place at the end of 1953 and in 1954, long after Beria had been arrested and condemned to death, at a time when thousands of men had been rehabilitated and were returning home from prison and the Siberian camps.

And Osvald Zavodsky was the last to be executed, after his appeal had been refused in March 1954!

During our long detention, when we had the possibility of getting in touch with each other, we never stopped wondering how such trials could be organized in Czechoslovakia, a country with an old civilization and great democratic traditions.

We recollected our experiences as militant Party members, and in the various sections of the economic, political and social life in which we had worked before our arrest. We recalled our opinions and appreciations of the methods of the Soviet advisers and their executors, the interrogators.

By sticking all these fragments together we also managed to draw a picture close to the one later painted by Party historians.

During the constitutive meeting of the Cominform* the ideologist of the Soviet Communist Party, Jdanov, claimed that the imperialist aggression against the USSR and the people's democracies was accompanied by political and ideological attacks which had to be warded off in every domain of

* Information Bureau of the Communist and Workers' parties, created in September 1947. The members were the Communist and Workers' Parties of USSR, Bulgaria, Czechoslovakia, Hungary, Poland, Rumania, France, Italy and, until 1948, Yugoslavia. Its purpose was to facilitate the exchange of experiences and to coordinate the activity of the member Parties. Its headquarters were in Belgrade until 1948 and then in Bucharest, until it was dissolved in 1956.

political and social life. Hence the necessity of a common ideological front under the leadership of the Soviet Communist Party.

Yugoslavia's decision to reach socialism by her own means clashed with the Stalinist concept of a monolithic socialist camp under the aegis of the Soviet Union in 1948. This difference of opinion between socialist states rapidly infected the world communist movement and the Cominform meeting in June 1948 confirmed the break with Yugoslavia and the banning of the Yugoslav Communist Party. In the resolution it was stated that:

In their policy within the country, the leaders of the Yugoslav Communist Party have abandoned the positions of the working class and the Marxist concept of class and class struggle. They deny the fact that capitalist elements are developing in their country and that the class struggle is therefore increasing in the villages. This denial springs from the opportunistic view that the class struggle never increases at the moment of passing from capitalism to socialism as Marxist-Leninism teaches, but that it disappears, as opportunists like Bukharin claimed, when they spread the idea of a peaceful transition from capitalism to socialism.

The information Bureau judged that a person's attitude towards the Soviet Union indicated his loyalty to socialism. Furthermore, it condemned the policy of independent paths to socialism as a bourgeois nationalist deviation and declared total war on it.

In September 1949, in Hungary, the Rajk trial took place and three of the defendants were sentenced to death. It had been organized by the Soviet advisers with the complicity of the Hungarian Security, to provide glaring proof of Titoist treason, of the infiltration of Tito's agents into all the people's democracies, and to substantiate the Stalinist theory about the accentuation of the class struggle during the construction of socialism.

In the true tradition of the Moscow trials Stalin equated political differences with treason and espionage. The Cominform's resolution of November 1949 described the 'Titoist betrayal in the service of the imperialists' as a conspiracy 'of the Anglo-American war-mongers against the USSR and the people's democracies carried out with the help of Tito's fascist nationalist clique which had become the agent of international imperialist reaction'.

The proof: 'the clique of Belgrade, murderers and spies, were in open agreement with imperialist reaction and, as the Rajk–Brankov trial in Budapest clearly proved, in its service.

'The treachery of Tito's clique was no mere chance, but the result of an order they received from their leaders, the Anglo-American imperialists to whom they had sold themselves. . . . Tito's clique had turned Belgrade into a centre of American espionage and anti-communist propaganda. . . . As a result of the counter-revolutionary Tito–Rankovic policy – the policy of the men who seized power in the Party and the state – an anti-communist fascist-type police state has been instituted in Yugoslavia.'

And the Information Bureau set the cat among the pigeons in the international communist movement by passing its resolution that 'one of the most important tasks of the Communist Parties against the "clique of Tito's spies and murderers" is to strengthen vigilance in their ranks and to uncover the bourgeois and nationalist agents as well as the imperialists, from under whatever banner they may hide.' To seek out the enemy within the Party: that was a fatal blow to the militant members.

A Rajk trial was necessary in all the people's democracies to accentuate the dominant role of the USSR, to call every government and Party to heel, and to abandon national interests, described as nationalist deviation, in the name of the solidarity of the socialist camp and proletarian internationalism.

The preparation of these trials had begun early in 1949 at the same time as the Rajk trial. That was why, on a request presented by Rakosi to Gottwald, Czech Security arrested Noel Field and Pavlik and his wife in May 1949, and handed them over to Hungarian Security. A few months later Rakosi demanded the arrest of dozens of militant communists and high Czech officials including myself, Clementis, Löbl, Frejka, Sling, Goldstücker, Holdos and so on.

On 5 September Rakosi informed Gottwald that in the course of the Rajk trial, which was about to begin, public proof would be given of the ramifications of the plot in Czechoslovakia; two days later he told him, through Svab, who acted as liaison agent with the Hungarian Security, that he was certain that there were spies in high places in Czechoslovakia and that they should be found among the men who had spent the war in London and the former volunteers in the International Brigades. According to Rakosi it was better to arrest innocent men than to risk leaving the culprits at large. The Soviet advisers in Budapest told Svab the same thing.

The leaders of the Polish Party, Bierut and Zambrowski, told Gottwald, in their turn, that they had proceeded to arrest fifty people in Poland who were compromised in the Rajk business, and many of whom were in touch with leading Czech citizens. They insisted that a purge be made in Czechoslovakia as rapidly as possible.

In the course of the Rajk trial two of the defendants, Szöny and Brankov (of Yugoslav nationality), declared that 'in Czechoslovakia the enemies worked better than in Hungary and their group was more efficient and better organized.'

In December 1949, in Bulgaria, Kostov was tried and sentenced to death, while Gomulka was imprisoned in Poland.

But in Czechoslovakia the Party was unwilling to comply with Hungarian and Polish demands and to seek out links in the plot.

I remember a conversation I had with Siroky at about that time. It was before he dropped me. After explaining that the Hungarians were urging us to discover something similar to the Rajk plot, he added: 'Our situation has nothing in common with theirs. We're not emerging from a long period of illegality as they are. Our leadership is united and has been working under Gottwald since 1929. Every member is well known and has proved his worth. We're not going to set up a trial just to please the Hungarians!'

But to sustain this attitude would have required the courage of Tito and the League of Yugoslav Communists, and unfortunately we did not have it.

Strong pressure was exerted on Gottwald. Threatened with having Czechoslovakia coupled with Yugoslavia and being publicly denounced for adopting a hostile attitude to the entire socialist camp, he finally yielded.

It is significant that it was neither the Soviet Party nor Stalin who exerted this pressure directly, but that they did it through the leaders of the other peoples' democracies, and particularly through Rakosi.

In view of the fact that Czech Security was unable to discover any conspirators, Gottwald, to whom Rakosi had sung the praises of the Soviet advisers, applied to Stalin for assistance.

The Soviet advisers started to arrive in 1949. They rapidly constructed an all-powerful apparatus responsible to its chief, Beria, alone. It included Likhachev and Makarov who had already proved themselves in preparing the Rajk trial.

They immediately proceeded to set up a special organization within State Security with the purpose of discovering the enemy within the Party. Later, a special section for the struggle against Zionism was also formed.

Taking advantage of their sanctity and their authority over the Security officials with whom they collaborated, they recruited confidential agents who were wholeheartedly devoted to them, considered them their real chiefs and carried out orders outside official channels and behind the backs of their official superiors.

A parallel police force rapidly developed in every department of State Security, a state within the state whose activity was beyond the control either of the Minister or of the Party leadership. That was how, in absolute secrecy, they managed to prepare for the arrest of former Under-Secretaries, departmental heads and other leaders of key departments of the Ministry of Security – Svab, Zavodsky, Vales and many others –

who, the Soviet advisers feared, might obstruct their future plans.

Even militant Party members and officials in state offices other than Security applied directly to the advisers.

Officially the advisers had no power, but in practice they were more influential than any of the Ministers or Party leaders. They were well-enough informed to know where to get hold of the dubious characters whom they could handle as they wished and whom they could entrust with every task.

At this time, as the cold war raged, the country's internal situation was complicated. Agents from foreign intelligence services entered the country illegally, organized sabotage and distributed enemy propaganda. There had even been some political assassinations.

The national economy was in great difficulty and food was in increasing demand because of the bad harvest. Discontent spread among the population.

In these circumstances the Party's work was influenced by the resolutions of the Information Bureau of 1948 and 1949. The hysteria provoked and sustained by the Yugoslav affair, the trials for treason in Budapest and Sofia, and the repressive measures against leading Party members in East Germany, Poland and Rumania, had given rise to general suspicion.

The very limited system of democracy disappeared increasingly from Party life and gave way to unconditional obedience and blind discipline. Power was concentrated more and more in the hands of a reduced number of leaders, and the Central Committee became a mere tool which passively approved the decisions and political line established by this minority.

This situation enabled the Soviet advisers, supported by their confidential agents and the network of informers and *agents provocateurs* in every section of social and political life, to launch a smear campaign against a number of militant Party members and to collect material against them by encouraging hundreds and thousands of people to write slanderous letters and reports, and provide tendentious information.

The witch hunt was on: the road to the trials was free! Under the pretext of hounding out enemies concealed in the Party, the Control Commission and the Cadre Department of the Central Committee collaborated closely with the Soviet advisers. The Russians were at liberty to consult all the cadre dossiers. The special department within Security, which was itself entirely dominated by the Soviet advisers, escaped all control by the regular Party organizations. They were now free to apply methods, later condemned at the Twentieth Party Congress, which eliminated the best cadres of the Soviet Communist Party, in the army, science, and the arts, and liquidated the most courageous workers and peasants. It was these men and these methods which sullied the socialist standard in the eyes of workers all over the world.

Eight

From their letters and visits I heard about the new measures to which my family was subjected. This time it was my fourteen-year-old daughter who suffered. She was ending the eighth class in her school and had successfully passed her final exams. She then made a request to continue her studies. She was summoned with her mother by the Commission which informed the families of the examination results and any decision taken about the children's future. The president of the Commission told them that Françoise's request to continue her studies had been rejected on the pretext that 'she must first atone for her past', a past of fourteen years; she was only eleven when I was arrested.

It was first suggested that she should serve an apprenticeship as a chimney sweep. Then they tried to make her sign a five-year contract: two years' apprenticeship and three years' work.

This would mean leaving Prague and living in a boarding school at Sumperk, far from the family. For the first time my wife was really disheartened. She went everywhere, to the town hall, to the educational department, to the Ministry of National Education. She pulled what strings she could and tried to get her old acquaintances to help her, but she always came up against a wall of indifference, if not hostility.

My daughter took her future in her own hands. The main thing was to remain in Prague. She came to an agreement with one of her schoolmates who had received an entry form for the apprenticeship school at the CKD-Sokolovo factory in Prague-Liben, filled it in and was taken on in her stead. Once the contract had been signed Françoise told the Commission and the headmaster what she had done. That was how she started to learn the trade of tool fitter.

Françoise was lucky. In her factory her teachers especially the foreman Miroslav Turek, who led her class in the work-room, adored her and she made friends with all her fellow workers.

Francoise had asked to join the youth organization, the CSN, like all her companions. Her card was refused on the pretext that she was French (although she had dual nationality and a Czech identity card). All her classmates and a number of other apprentices were on her side and at a general meeting announced their intention of leaving the movement if she were not admitted. My daughter received her card.

At my family's fourth visit I was accompanied by a young interrogator who appeared to be new on the job, from the questions he asked the chauffeur during the drive.

That day, as well as being excited and pleased about seeing Lise and the chidren, I felt optimistic. For some time I had been with human beings, and above all with my friend Vavro. The day before, the other prisoners had shown us the *Rude Pravo* in an interrorator's wastepaper basket, which contained the 'Resolutions of the Bolshevik Communist Party on its fiftieth anniversary'. Löbl, Vavro and I had all found some extremely important political elements in the article which suggested a turn of the tide and questioned numerous aspects of Stalin's policy and personality.

Lise, too, had noticed these things and spoke about them at the beginning of the visit, assuming that I had not read them. Two or three times the interrogator tried to interrupt us: 'You can only talk about family matters.' But Lise turned to him and said candidly: 'But all these things were printed yesterday in the *Rude Pravo*!' Shy, inexperienced, and obviously inoffensive, the interrogator was confounded by this reply.

At the end of the visit Lise left with the children. Fifteen minutes later the interrogator and I got into the car waiting for us in the yard. As the chauffer stopped at the gate the car was stormed by Lise and the three children. My wife leaned towards the chauffeur and said with her prettiest smile: 'Since you're going to Ruzyn and I live on the way, couldn't you take me and the children to the tram stop?'

The chauffeur, a pleasant young man, didn't even ask the interrogator, who was sitting in the back with me, but opened the door and said: 'Of course! Pile in. There's room for you all.'

Lise got in next to me, with Michel on her knees, and Françoise and Gérard sat next to the chauffeur. Lise pressed herself against me, delighted. We drove on. The interrogator protested shyly. 'Don't worry, comrade,' said the chauffeur, 'they're on our way. We can't let them walk since that's where we're going.'

I was both fascinated and amused by Lise's boldness. She whispered to me: 'He may take us home, so you'll see where we live.'

On the way Françoise spoke gaily to the chauffeur. Instead of staying on the road to Ruzyn which passed the bus stop for Hanspalka, the quarter where my family lived, the chauffeur branched off to the left, drove up the hill and through a maze of side streets to their house.

Lise stayed in the car. She told Françoise: 'Run up and get

mummy and daddy,' and, turning towards the interrogator, said, pointing to me: 'Now that he's here you must let him greet my parents who are too old to move.' With a little more energy the interrogator tried to put an end to this breach of discipline, but the chauffeur calmed him: 'We're already there! It'll only take five minutes!'

Lise's mother had come down. I got out of the car to kiss her. She was weeping with emotion and said: 'I dreamed of you last night. Someone knocked on the door and it was you. And a few minutes ago I was thinking: What if he came? And here you are!'

And then I saw my father-in-law walking slowly towards us. He didn't know why Françoise had called him downstairs. He had been reading the paper. He looked much older, more bent, and his movements were slower. He came up to us with his cap on his head, his spectacles on the end of his nose and a copy of *L'Humanité* in his hand. I was touched to see him and curious about how he would react when he recognized me. Until now he had categorically refused to see me.

When he was standing next to me he looked up in amazement. 'You here?'

We embraced affectionately. 'How are you?' I asked him.

And he answered, as only he could: 'I'm reading the resolutions of the fiftieth anniversary of the Bolshevik Party. Have you read them?'

I said I had, and he added: 'It's because Lise told me this morning there was something wrong with Stalin. That he wasn't mentioned much. And yet I've seen his name twice. That's enough for a document like that. What's wrong with Stalin?'

And, shrugging his shoulders and giving me a nudge of complicity: 'What do you think about it? I'm right, aren't I?'

I was shattered to see him so old and ravaged, but I was disarmed by his candour and purity. I just had time to tell him: 'Trust Lise. She'll explain!' and to embrace my family once again. The frightened interrogator pulled me back into the car, and off we drove. The chauffeur gave me a happy wink.

All the way back the interrogator continued to repeat: 'Don't tell anyone what happened, Mr London. I'd go straight to prison!' The chauffeur turned round and said: 'Don't worry, comrade, nobody'll know.'

When I had returned to the labour unit I looked back on the visit and my unexpected journey to Hanspalka. At the same time I couldn't help laughing and I told Vavro all about it. Vavro laughed till the tears ran down his cheeks when he heard what my father-in-law had said. His son-in-law had been arrested, tried as a traitor and a spy and sentenced to life imprisonment, and yet, when he saw him again for the first time in years, he tried to get him to support Stalin!

Part Six

The Truth will Triumph

One

I knew how dangerous my situation was in the Ruzyn labour unit: if I made one mistake I was sunk. And yet I was determined that the outside world should know the truth. I was going to see to this as soon as my family was safe and I was out of the direct control of the prison ringleaders. I was obsessed by this idea and in every letter, at every visit, I urged Lise to leave the country. It was essential for my family to be out of reach in order to thwart my blackmailers. Only then could I proceed to a new phase of the battle. This gave me a reason for living. I was going to tell people what had been done to us, and how we had been forced to confess.

All I had on my side was my innocence and that of my comrades. But I was sure that the day would come when, in spite of what we were suffering and the prospect of everlasting gloom, justice would be done. For many of us, unfortunately, it would be posthumous justice.

As the months went by my anxiety increased. What if I were executed before the truth got out? During Lise's first visits I managed to explain to her some aspects of the extorted confessions and the very structure of the trial. But what we had been through was so monstrous, so incredible, that I thought I had not said enough. It was far harder to convey than our life in the Nazi concentration camps, and we had not succeeded in conveying it.

Besides, there was no point in Lise's trying to reveal the truth simply by saying that her information came from me. She must be able to use a document written in my hand, with clear, though summary, details about the mechanism of the confessions and the fabrication of the trial, denouncing the true face of State Security and the part played by the Soviet advisers. So, even if I disappeared, the truth would be known! I now had one aim: to write! I managed to get a pencil and some paper, and a blade to sharpen the lead with. But before putting my plan into action I had to find a means of hiding what I had written from the warders who continuously searched us.

I was on very good terms with Kevic. He was a charming comrade, loyal and resourceful. Without telling him my true plan I said I was going to make some notes about the trial which I would have to conceal carefully, since their discovery would get me into apalling trouble. I asked him to persuade one of his friends working in the carpentry shop to make me a little wooden box like the ones the prisoners used for their tobacco and their cigarette stubs. I told him exactly how it should be made. A week later Kevic gave me the box (I still keep it as a precious relic). The lid was hollow, and in it I could keep my papers.

The only man to know my plan and to help me carry it through was my friend Hajdu, from whom I hid nothing.

I could write in my cell, after work and on Sundays, for only a limited period. I was no longer alone. I shared my cell with a criminal sentenced to twenty-three years for attempted murder. He was a ghastly individual, who boasted of having twice eluded justice. He was arrested the third time. 'The first two times they could never prove I was guilty!'

He worked in the kitchen and came back later than I did. On Sunday he was on duty and I had the day off.

We were now under increased surveillance at the labour unit during the day. And when we were locked in our cells the warders frequently looked at us through the spy-hole. I had perfected my technique. I sat down to read – the warders were accustomed to seeing me get through masses of books – and between the pages of my book I placed the sheet of paper, which was about as big as half a sheet of foolscap. Every time I heard steps outside my cell I turned the page. In the meantime I wrote, in a minute but legible hand, in order to say as much as possible in the minimum amount of space. At the end of each line I had to sharpen my pencil.

When my fellow prisoner was about to return I folded the sheet of paper and hid it in the lid of my box. I was searched numerous times but it was never discovered.

When I had covered both sides of a sheet I folded it like the cigarette paper, Rizla, which was sold in the canteen. My box was too small to hold everything I had written, so I started hiding the sheets between the cigarette papers. To make them fit I folded them and put them between the rollers of the mangle while my friend Hajdu conscientiously turned the handle. At the time we worked in the laundry and ironed the linen with a handworked mangle; Vavro manipulated it in order to save me from excessive physical strain, while I put the linen between the rollers.

Lise knew that I was going to give her a message at the first opportunity. The next visit was due in the first fortnight of February 1954. I wrote to my wife asking her to bring me tobacco and a packet of Rizla cigarette paper because I now claimed to prefer rolling my own cigarettes.

So, talking and smoking, I managed to exchange my own Rizla packet for my wife's before the eyes of the interrogator.

The winter of 1953–4 was particularly hard for my family. Despite appearances, their living conditions were appalling. They had been given one floor of a villa. Two other families shared the other flats. The coal ration was insufficient to heat the house. You couldn't even go through the rooms without wearing coats or rugs. Our cousin Mirek Sztogryn managed to get a small stove, around which my family could huddle. When it rained the water ran down the splits in the terrace and had to be gathered in basins.

In these conditions Lise's mother fell ill. The prognosis was alarming and we expected the result to be fatal. Lise rang her sister in Paris and asked her and her brother to come to her mother's bedside. Fernande and Frédo Ricol requested a visa but they were made to wait. Only a month later did Fernande arrive after Jacques Duclos had protested to the Czech Ambassador in Paris about the fact that a visa had not been delivered to the wife of a member of the Political Bureau, Raymond Guyot, who wanted to visit her sick mother. My brother-in-law did not obtain his.

After preventing Raymond Guyot from getting in touch with my family in Prague when he came for Gottwald's funeral, the Security Services now tried to stop my sister-in-law's visa, and refused to grant one to my brother-in-law. They were obviously determined to prevent my wife from seeing her family.

In the second part of my secret message I told Lise:

'You know that since my arrest there has been a continual barrage of insults and accusations against you and the other members of your family. You know what they wanted me to say about Raymond? That he knew about my Trotskyist activity and actively supported it. [I then mentioned the other charges brought by the interrogators against Raymond.]

'Some prisoners said that you knew about my anti-Party activity too, and that you were present at our secret meetings. . . There were also charges against Fernande and Frédo: they claimed that Frédo had been excluded from the Party and that the fact that he had also been evacuated from Mauthausen by the International Red Cross proved he was an American agent.

'All these slanderous statements are an attempt by Security to discredit you all and to shield themselves from any step you might take in my favour.

'You might, for instance, say what really happened between Field and me. But since you have already become suspect, your explanations will never be taken into consideration. They will probably try to use this against you to stop you leaving for France. They will damage you in the eyes of the French Communist Party to such an extent that it will lose all interest in you.'

When Fernande reached Prague my mother-in-law was back at home, in bed with a high fever. She had had a relapse, and the penicillin treatment was resumed. My father-in-law, who, as a former miner, had silicosis, asthma and emphysema, was also in bed with pneumonia. Our three children had diphtheria. Lise had to leave her work to nurse her family. She lived on the money given her by my cousins and the few friends who had remained loyal. Then came a catastrophe: the pipes burst. There was no water in the house for the five invalids. The day before her sister arrived Lise almost had a nervous breakdown. As she was climbing the stairs with two buckets of water which she had gone to fetch at the corner of the street, she fell, and the water ran all over her, to the foot of the stairs. A school teacher, who lived on the ground floor, tried to cheer her up. In the end she too burst into tears and then helped Lise mop up the water.

My wife was desperate because, in Paris, everyone thought that even if I had been rightly condemned as a traitor, my family was treated with respect. Lise had never complained in her letters and had never mentioned the difficulties she was up against. She said nothing about her exclusion from the Party. 'Both because of the censorship in Prague and in France,' she explained. 'In France the enemy would have rejoiced to know that a communist had suffered so much in a socialist country.'

The night Fernande arrived she wept as she sat by her parents. 'How could we imagine that you lived in these conditions?' Then she ranted against me. 'He's responsible for the whole thing! How I hate him!' Lise had not yet explained everything to her sister and she was waiting for the right moment. But it was her mother, lying pale and weak on the pillows, who spoke first: 'Fernande, don't say that about Gérard. The people who have put him in his present situation are responsible; they have turned against your sister. She hasn't told you yet: she's been excluded from the Party, persecuted. And yet she's always been loyal and courageous.'

Fernande was dazed. She looked at her sister: 'You've been thrown out of the Party?'

Then Lise told her what she had been through. She talked about the battles she had fought for me before the trial, and the letter she wrote after the verdict, when she believed I was guilty.

But her faultless behaviour had not saved her, her parents or her children from the attacks of those who pretended to serve socialist humanism.

Lise then said that she and the children had been seeing me every month since April, that she was more convinced than ever of my innocence. She spoke of the letter I wrote after our first meeting and showed Fernande a French translation of the passage in which I said that I had behaved in court as the Party expected, and subordinated my personal interests to those of the Party.

My sister-in-law was quite unprepared for such a situation. She must have experienced a mass of conflicting feelings. One day Lise suddenly asked her, on the tram taking them into town, 'Fernande, look me in the eyes! You know me, don't you? Do you think I could be an enemy of the Party?'

Fernande had hesitated a second and replied: 'No, Lise, I'll never believe it of you!'

That day the visit coincided with my birthday, 1 February. For some months visits had taken place in the guard room in Ruzyn, supervised by an interrogator. Lise had prepared a food parcel for me and before she left the house Fernande pulled two packets of Gauloises out of her bag and said: 'Here, give these to Gérard.' She had shaken her belief in my guilt.

When Lise had told me about her conversations with her sister I insisted that she ask them to help her and the family return to France.

Fernande must already have thought of this as the only way of ending her family's ordeals. When my wife mentioned it, she said that on no account should the children, Lise and their parents continue to live in such conditions, and added that she would discuss it with Raymond as soon as she returned to Paris.

At the end of February Fernande wrote Lise a letter in which she said: 'I am delighted to tell you that Raymond has been to see the Ambassador in Paris to ask officially that all facilities be granted your parents, you and the children for the return to

France. Life will be easier for you here. We are thrilled to know that we shall soon be together again.'

Two

The first part of my message was already in Lise's hands. At the next visit, three months later, I gave her the second part. In all there were seven half-sheets of paper which came to over sixty typewritten pages.

The message began with these words: 'The investigation was not held in order to establish the guilt or innocence of the accused. Guilt was assumed in advance and the Party's decision to proceed with the arrest constitutes proof of it. The interrogations were held in order to confirm the justice of this decision, that is to say the guilt of the accused.'

Then I gave a clear description of the inhuman and illegal methods of the Security Services and the way the trial was constructed. Further on I denounced the ringleaders:

'The Soviet advisers have their confidential agents among the investigators. The man who led my interrogation for so long was one of them [I meant Kohoutek]. In the reports submitted by Security to the Party Directing Committee, the opinion and influence of the Soviet advisers were decisive. They wanted at all costs to see in me a leader of the Fourth International. They were determined to ruin me, and, in their plan, folly went hand in hand with fantasy. I became the victim of all their theories about the plots of the imperialist powers against the USSR and the people's democracies. They wanted to organize a preliminary trial which was to prepare public opinion for the Slansky one. They thought that I had all the qualifications: I was a Jew, a volunteer in the International Brigades, I had spent a long time in the West, I knew Field, and had numerous contacts abroad. The people I knew abroad enabled them, and may still enable them, to apply their theories to other countries and individuals in the West. They may still be saving this possibility up for the future. One day they may hold the very fact that they knew me against my friends.'

I reconstructed the technique of the advisers and their Czech henchmen.

'The prisoners belong to a category of men whom they want to eliminate from political and economic life (Jews, émigrés from London, volunteers in the International Brigades, etc.). They then choose those of them who formed a logical group, against which they could direct the trial. This orientation depended on the political situation at the time and the political aims to be pursued, and they decided to take as the heads of the group those prisoners whose origins and past were best suited to their idea of the moment. . .

'Since our trial both the international situation and the situation in the USSR have changed,' I continued. 'Spectacular trials are no longer required: they are inopportune. That is why the line of our trial has been abandoned. They have renounced the idea of following it up with a succession of other trials as they did in the USSR before the war, since the outcome of our trial has made it difficult to pursue this line. The methods of investigation have changed; the treatment of the prisoners has improved. According to the information that reaches us there are no more uninterrupted interrogations for days on end, no more dark cells, no more physical tortures and humiliations. A semblance of legality has been re-established. At the moment some prisoners are being released without a sentence. Others get lighter sentences than before. Even twenty or twenty-five years are minor sentences for men who would otherwise have gone to the gallows.

'This is not because they refused to sign the confessions but because the Party had not chosen them to play a part in the trials which had been planned. So the Security Services did not devote their maximum efforts to them.

'Once the first wave was over and the repressive measures

had diminished, some prisoners could modify or revoke their former confessions and evidence or actually have the charges and sentence against them reduced at the Party's behest. At the Party conference which took place after our trial, Bacilek declared in his speech: "It is the Party which will decide who is a criminal and who isn't. . . who has collaborated with Slansky for criminal purposes or who has merely been hoodwinked and led astray."

'That is what happened. This new line accounts for the lighter sentences and the releases now taking place.

'It is disgusting of N—, who not only designated me as the leader of the Trotskyist group but also made some other very damaging statements against me and other veterans from Spain. . . to attribute his release to personal merit and to slander us now he is free. . . . I have already said how the other volunteers and I were driven to confess by statements he made against us. Some of them, above all Zavodsky's confession, could have had me hanged five times over. . .

'It is true that I hated them all. But now that I see what was going on I don't hold a grudge against any of them. They were forced to speak, they were mystified, their reports were distorted, just as mine were.

'If I hadn't denied everything for six months we would all have been tried shortly after our arrest. At least three of us would have been hanged and the others would have got heavy sentences.

'For all the months that I refused to talk, he (Zavodsky) persisted in accusing me of every sort of crime. Even later, when he had to bear evidence against me at the trial, he vehemently protested that he was only allowed a six page text instead of the eighteen pages that had originally been planned. His evidence was not published in full in the papers because of a reference to Noel Field's arrest in Prague – an arrest which had been kept secret. His evidence also constituted a public admission of his own guilt.

'When I was later forced to stand witness against him at his trial I heard others declare: "I already knew that London was a spy before our arrest."

'After having forced me, on the basis of my fellow prisoners' evidence, to make my "confessions" which merely confirmed all the lies elaborated against me, the Security Services made me repeat these "confessions" as evidence against the prisoners they had decided to try. . . . I could not refuse to stand witness . . . that would have entailed immense risks, since we were hostages of the men of Ruzyn. . .

'As I gave evidence I tried to minimize the facts by deviating from the text written by Security. On several occasions I attempted to place certain facts in their true light, and when the interrogators scolded me I attributed it to a lapse of memory, fear or nerves before the Court.

'As I have already explained to you the evidence, like all the rest of the trial, was a mere comedy since the decision had been made in advance.'

Ultimately, as I wrote to Lise, we were all the victims of the same inhuman treatment – not only the men who confessed at once but those who confessed last, those who died and those who received heavy prison sentences, those who were tried later and those were able to revoke their previous statements.

'Now I want to write to you about the problem of your departure for France. You will understand what it means for me. I've thought about it a great deal recently and I try to make feeling give way to reason. I want you to leave for France and use every means at your disposal to do so.

'My position is as follows: in two or three months I shall be transferred to another prison, far from here, probably in Leopoldov in Slovakia. Visits are permitted every five months for fifteen minutes. They take place in the worst conditions, behind thick grids, and one can only exchange a few words. If the international tension increases these visits may be cancelled altogether. The price of seeing you in these circumstances (children may not attend the visits) is too high. You, your parents and the children would have to live far from your friends, in hostile surroundings, the objects of continual discrimination and suspicion (the difficulty which Fernande and Frédo had in obtaining visas is proof of that).

'No, Lise, to know of you living in such conditions only makes my moral suffering worse. I now reproach myself for not having insisted strongly enough. But it was because I wanted to cling to the hope which you constantly gave me that something would happen which would change my future, and that, while you were waiting, your life would not be poisoned.

'You must leave, Lise darling. And during our last visit you rightly said that in France you could do something for me. Who knows, you might save me, although this seems more and more unlikely.

'As long as you're here, I'm too frightened of what may happen to you to appeal.

'I don't know how the idea of your return to France has been taken here, after the request of the French Communist Party. I hope all goes well. But they may try to prevent your departure for fear you might lead a campaign against Czechoslovakia. (You aren't well enough acquainted with the neuroses of the Security men and the advisers.) If, for example, the French Communist Party were informed that you can't leave because you yourself are implicated and they should then wash their hands of you – you must fight. Write to Maurice [Thorez] personally. Ask the French Party to repeat its request. Write to Raymond and tell him to intervene personally. Write to the President of the Republic here. Say that to keep you here against your will is illegal; they now set score by legality. You are French, by French and international law, and no one has the right to keep you here if you want to leave.'

I was so full of my memories of the years spent working and fighting with the French Communist Party, of my relations with comrades whose friendship, courage and sincerity I had always appreciated, that I constantly used this past as a source of hope. I never lost faith in the strength and purity of the communist ideal, and never doubted that Lise's account would be questioned.

We supposed that when Maurice was informed, and discovered that militant leaders of the French Party together with a whole section of the political life of the Party under the occupation had been under suspicion, he would automatically demand an explanation.

For me Maurice Thorez's assistance was of primary importance because it was also an assurance that I would not suddenly be liquidated when I demanded a revision of my trial. And even if my executioners liquidated me I would already have sounded the alarm, insisted on my innocence, proved the criminal machinations of Beria and his apparatus under Stalin's aegis with the support of their Czech accomplices. In all events Lise and I would reveal the truth, show up the cancer which had developed in the communist movement and was gradually killing it.

In the course of her various visits, Lise and I prepared a plan by which we would keep in touch after her departure for France. We decided on the words we would use in our letters.

Lise had persuaded my cousin Hanka to remain in official contact with me as my relative. In the letters which Hanka would be allowed to write to me she would transcribe the content of the letters from my wife. She knew our code.

The transmission of my secret message to Raymond and Maurice Thorez became 'We've spoken to his uncle about Michel's adoption.' Lise's first steps in my favour became: 'Michel has been adopted.' 'Home' was Moscow. 'Joseph's friend' was Beria, 'his men' the Soviet advisers, and so on. I was either Gérard, Émile or Michel, since, as far as the prison and Security were concerned, I was officially called Artur.

Three

I was right not to wait any longer before giving Lise my message. She did not receive the whole of it, as I had promised, but she got the most important part.

Two days after the last visit, at the end of May 1954, Vavro Hajdu, Löbl and I were transferred to the Central Prison of Leopoldov in Slovakia. Some forty prisoners piled into the bus. Vavro and I were the only ones to be chained together, according to special orders. After the last stop of the journey, Illava, where we spent the night, Löbl was also chained.

In the morning we reached Leopoldov, a huge, sinister-looking fortress the mere mention of which filled the prisoners acquainted with it with terror. The fortress was built at the end of the seventeenth century by the Austro-Hungarian monarchy as part of the fortifications against the Turks. But it was not completed until the decisive defeat of the Turks. In view of the fact that it was there, and that it had cost a fortune to build, the monarchy decided to put it to some use and so, after 1700, it became a prison. Its first occupants were the political prisoners of the period, the evangelists who were subsequently sold as galley slaves to the Italians.

During the journey Vavro and I congratulated ourselves on having handed over my message, because it was now impossible to have any contact with the outside world.

Leopoldov. Here I had an even greater feeling of isolation. It was impossible to distinguish the surroundings because the walls rose high above the roof of the fortress. The hygiene conditions were appalling and water was scarce. In the work-rooms there were buckets instead of latrines. We were allowed a quick shower bath every six weeks or so. The food was insufficient, and visits, as I told Lise in my message, only took place every five months.

There were eighty men in the first cell we were lodged in. At the far end were two latrines and a dozen taps from which water trickled for about five minutes in the morning, at midday and at night, so that we could drink and wash ourselves and our plates.

Hajdu, Löbl and I were set to work in a room where we had to cut down off feathers. Next to us ropes were being made to tie sheafs of corn.

In our workroom, which was by no means large, there were about seventy prisoners. The windows and doors were kept shut to avoid the draught that would send the down flying. The feathers we received were in their natural state, with little pieces of flesh at the end of them, crawling with maggots.

The prisoners in the smelting department lived in slightly better conditions. The money they earned enabled them to improve their rations by buying lard and bread in the canteens.

The lack of hygiene and the circumstances in which we worked and lived meant that numerous prisoners had eczema, rashes, and purulent conjunctivitis. The doctor treated all these illnesses with mercurochrome and different coloured creams. The first time we walked round the yard, in the dust thrown up by hundreds of boots, what Hajdu and I saw was like something out of Dante: it was a procession of living scarecrows whose faces were covered with red, black, blue and white patches of cream and dressing stuck on with plaster. Their heads were shaven and their beards stubbly.

We stood gaping. Then I exclaimed: 'We've come to a proper freak show!' and Vavro burst out laughing.

We were shaved once a week. In a tiny bowl, a third of which was filled with water, the barber rinsed the two brushes which were used to soap our 140 cheeks. There was no form of disinfectant, and no possibility of washing our faces with clean water after being shaved.

The standards we were expected to fulfil at work were virtually unattainable so we were deprived of the meagre advantages we would otherwise have had. I earned, at the most, six or seven crowns a month. This enabled me to buy a tube of toothpaste, two packets of tobacco of inferior quality, nicknamed 'Stalin's revenge' by the prisoners, some cigarette paper and two rolls of lavatory paper. According to the older prisoners the conditions had been worse before. And yet they were just as bad when I was there as those of the Central Prison of Poissy, dating from the thirteenth century, which I had known during the occupation, reputed to be the worst prison in France.

I was put to work despite my lung infection. I did not receive my extra food ration, which consisted of a glass of milk a day, if I remember rightly, or any form of medicine; and I never received a medical visit.

I managed to remain with Hajdu, first in the cell and then in the workroom. Löbl was working elsewhere, but we kept in touch. We had found a large number of our companions of misfortune, sentenced in the trials which followed ours. The first ones I saw were Otto Hromadko, sentenced to twelve years, Svoboda to fifteen, Vales to twenty-two, Josef Pavel to twenty-five. I heard that Holdos was in another part of the prison and had been sentenced to thirteen years. I also met some colleagues from the Ministry of Foreign Affairs – Pavel, Kavan, Richard Slansky, Eduard Goldstücker and numerous other prisoners. From time to time I saw my friend Kevic who had also been transferred.

The first contacts between fellow defendants were not always very warm. They were marked by the time spent in Ruzyn when the interrogators managed to turn one man against the other and make each one believe he was the other's victim. And then certain prisoners had not yet seen behind the scenes. However incomprehensible it may seem to anyone reading this book today, some prisoners still felt guilty. They spoke to us as if they really had committed crimes which deserved the Party's punishment. It wouldn't have been so bad if they had spoken for themselves, but they had been poisoned to such an extent that they believed the others to be guilty too. One official, high in the political leadership of the army, for instance, considered himself guilty and saw Hromadko as an old Trotskyist who had always been a leader of hostile activity in the army. In his ingenuousness he actually repeated some of Hromadko's remarks which he believed to be against the Party – and our friend Hromadko never minced his words.

On the whole, however, we all resumed our old friendships. Besides, we could now compare and complete our ideas of what we had been through. Our confidence returned. We needed to re-seal our solidarity because we lived in an enemy world. There were common-law criminals in the prison, German war criminals, Czech and Slovak collaborators, spies and western diversionary agents. Then there was a whole mass of fugitives arrested at the border, followers of Benes, social democrats, Catholics, ecclesiastics, some of whom had been forming an opposition and others who had either been provoked by the police or had been implicated in political trials. They all had one thing in common: unduly high sentences and the experience of inhuman methods to extort their confessions.

When these men saw us arrive their first instinct was hostile. For them we were not only communists, and therefore political adversaries, but also the founders of the regime which persecuted them.

There, too, human relations improved the situation. In my second cell I was the only communist among forty prisoners. Every evening, after the curfew, although it was forbidden, we heard a brief sermon and said a prayer. Only two of us, a Yugoslav and myself, took no part in it, and by the third day everyone knew who I was.

For the next two days I couldn't eat anything. As if by chance, every time my bowl was full, someone jogged me and the contents were spilled on the ground. I was ostracized and those who spoke to me were threatened with the same punishment. The only man who stood up to this threat and displayed any sympathy for me was Klima, a former right-wing deputy of the Democratic-National Party who, in 1938, before Munich, had formed part of a delegation, together with Gottwald and Rasin, another right-wing deputy, to tell President Benes of the nation's will to resist Hitler's threats. Although Klima never told me about it, I am sure that my fellow prisoners changed their attitude towards me on the third night because of him. I saw him talking to the young man who normally gave the sermon, and that night he commented on the verse: 'He that is without sin among you, let him first cast a stone. . .'

A little later I was again put in the same cell as Hajdu and my old friend Otto Hromadko. He made us laugh in spite of the sadness and drabness of our existence. The jokes he cracked about his fellow prisoners always hit the mark. He told us anecdotes which changed each time. One day, as he was telling us the third or fourth version of one of his exploits in the Spanish Civil War, Vavro Hajdu interrupted him: 'Hey, that's not what you told us yesterday.' Hromadko burst out laughing and said: 'But it's more interesting like this.'

In defiance of the stool pigeons surrounding us, he joked about the Party leadership. Pavel, who had heard of what he said, was worried about the consequences for Hromadko and the rest of us. One day, when Svoboda, Hromadko, Hajdu and I were in the yard, we saw Pavel at the window of his cell, shaking his finger at Otto. We asked him what Pavel meant, and, without batting an eye, Otto replied: 'I don't know. Maybe he wants to exclude us from the Party.'

Antisemitism was the order of the day. A warder, questioning Eduard Goldstücker about his identity, asked him: "What was your name before?'

'I've always been called Goldstücker."

'You're lying. Your sort of people all had another name before."

Otto Hromadko, a pure Czech, had a large hooked nose like the Jews in antisemitic caricatures. And because of his nose he was the target of the Jew-detectors. Besides, with his irreverent and ironic nature, he was the first to provoke them: 'You see, before calling myself Hromadko, I was called

Kleinberg!' (A pun: in Czech Hromadko means 'little heap' and in German Kleinberg means 'little mountain.')

But one day his nose saved Goldstücker's life, but almost cost Hromadko his. In 1955 they were both transferred from Leopoldov to Jachimov to work in the uranium mines. Here a plot had been hatched by the antisemitic prisoners against Goldstücker, whom they heard was coming. When the convoy arrived they fell onto Hromadko, thinking he was Goldstücker because of his nose, beat him up, and left him lying unconscious in a pool of blood.

In Leopoldov scenes of this description constantly took place against Jews and communists. Hlinka's former fascist guards, collaborators and war criminals attacked every Jew they found. And unfortunately the warders were just as prejudiced. Apart from a few exceptions who confirmed the rule, they and the interrogators believed that Hlinka's guards, the former Nazis, and even the foreign agents, were enemies who had at least fought openly, but that we were worse because we had fought disguised as communists.

Hajdu and I miraculously survived a provocation organized by a warder nicknamed 'Mister Ox' because of his stupidity and brutality. In our cell and workroom there was a foreign legionary who had fought in Indochina, had then joined the American intelligence service and had been sent as a spy and saboteur to Czechoslovakia. Arrested during his second mission, he had been sentenced to serve twenty-five years in Leopoldov. He was violent, tough, and used to fighting hand-to-hand, and he hated Jews and communists. So he had all the qualifications to serve in 'Mister Ox's' plot against us. But the legionary and I had recently entered into conversation, and when he heard that I had fought in the International Brigades he developed a certain respect for me. He asked me lots of questions about Spain and decided to learn Spanish, so I became his teacher. When 'Mister Ox' pointed to Vavro and me and said to him: 'You see those two? If you throw them over the banisters I won't have noticed a thing. It'll be a pleasure to see their bits and pieces being carried off in a sheet,' our legionary put him in his place. From that day on he appeared to be on our side. We had found a champion.

However arduous my imprisonment I was comforted by my old pals from Spain, by being able to wave or talk to Pavel, Vales and Goldstücker, whom we usually saw behind the bars of their cell windows when we were walking round the yard.

I grew thinner. Fortunately the prisoners now received an extra ration of bread. But my state of health deteriorated. I had a fever and I was at last sent to the infirmary for a medical inspection. The doctor took my temperature and simply ordered three days' rest and some aspirin, without saying that I should change work or receive the extra ration of milk to which I was entitled.

I thought a great deal about Lise. Had she at last managed to arrange to leave for France?

We had agreed that if I was to leave Prague she would do all she could to see me before going back. And now I lived in expectation of her visit.

On 30 May 1954, shortly after my arrival in Leopoldov, I had had the right, like all the new arrivals, to write a letter informing my family of my new address and the prison rules: a visit every five months and a letter every three.

'I think you had better ask the Ministry for permission to visit me when you have completed your arrangements to leave. . . . There is no point in your coming before, because I'll only be allowed another visit five months later and I want to talk to you about our personal affairs. I still think that the sooner you and your parents leave the better it will be. . .'

On 29 July I was entitled to write the first regular letter to my family. Again I told Lise:

I hope that all the formalities concerning your move have been settled. Although I agree about Michel's adoption there may be difficulties. But I know how energetic Jeanne and her husband [Maurice Thorez] are, and I am sure that they will manage to overcome the problems at home [Moscow]. When you are discussing the child's adoption you should emphasize the evil influence which Joseph's friend [Beria] had on our son's education and how badly he and his men [the Soviet advisers] behaved towards our Michel [myself]. And since we are now coming to a definite agreement about our family affairs you should also settle Raymond's affairs at home. I was surprised that not only Gérard [myself], but also his colleagues [my fellow defendants] should have had so much trouble about the matter you mentioned.

When you ask permission to visit me, ask for a longer period than usual. [I then added some messages which Vavro always asked me to give Lise for his family.]

I have no news, except that I had bronchitis, but I already feel better. Don't worry. Remember that I think about you the whole time and love you, darling Lise.

Early in October a warder came for me and took me to a cell in the transfer section in the new building of Leopoldov. I had no time to get in touch with Vavro and Otto before leaving. I knew that the other prisoners would tell them that I didn't know where I was going, but I also knew that they would be worrying about me. Every change or move in our present situation was a cause of anxiety. I spent the night alone in a cell. Early the next morning I put on civilian clothes. My arms and legs were chained and I got into a car with opaque windows, and sat between two warders. We left for an unknown destination.

It was only after stopping at Olomouc that the warders told me we were going to Prague. Why? They didn't know. But they told me that they had orders from the Minister of the Interior. I asked them to unchain me but they apologized politely, saying they had special instructions that I should be chained. It was already very cold. I shivered throughout the journey. For some unknown reason the car was unheated, and I felt feverish.

Four

We reached the Pankrac prison in Prague that night. My chains were removed and I was taken to a cell where I spent the night alone with no food. I couldn't sleep and kept on wondering about the reasons for this transfer. Apart from all the pessimistic explanations there was one reason which I hardly dared think of: a visit from my family before they left for France. But I never guessed that this visit would take place in Prague. I always thought Lise would come to Leopoldov to say goodbye.

I walked round my cell all night. As the morning approached nothing happened and I grew more and more nervous. I felt my temperature rising. Finally, after an eternity, a warder came for me. He led me through a maze of underground corridors, from which I thought we would never emerge, until we got to a staircase leading to a narrow landing. He made me stand with my face to the wall: 'Wait there!' Some time later I was led to a cage divided in two by some double bars. This was the visiting room. In front of me I saw Lise, our children, and my parents-in-law.

'Gérard, we're leaving for France the day after tomorrow,' said Lise. 'I asked the Central Committee of the Party to support my request to the Ministry of the Interior to see you in Prague, so that we could all come. But I'm not prepared to see you in these conditions!' and, turning to the warder, she said: 'I'm leaving with my whole family for France. So far we have never seen my husband behind bars, and we are not prepared to do so on this our last visit. I want to see the director.' Then, turning to me again, she said: 'Gérard, don't stand there a minute longer. Leave this cage. We'll see each other, I promise you, but not like this! I'll see you later, Gérard!'

She walked off, pushing the children and her parents in front of her. I asked the astonished warder to take me away too, and left the cage.

I found myself on the landing, at the head of the staircase where a few prisoners were waiting for their visits. Was I going to see my family again? In any case, they were leaving; that was the main thing. I remembered Lise and her dark look when she spoke to the warder. She was obstinate and determined. I knew she would stop at nothing to be able to embrace me and chat with me before they left. So engrossed was I in my thoughts that I didn't even notice that someone was pulling my sleeve. It was only when he nudged me that I realized I was standing next to an old pal from Ostrava, Rudolf Peschl, wearing a prison uniform. He came from Bilovec, an area with a German minority, where he directed the Communist Youth. We had fought together for I had been the regional instructor for his district. We had also been on the district Committee of the Communist Youth. Together we had organized the first strike in the local car factory. What a meeting! He smiled at me and, in answer to my silent question, said: 'Did you think you were the only old communist in Pankrac? Don't you recognize me?'

After leaving Ostrava in 1933 we had met once, by chance, in 1935 or 1936 in the streets of Moscow, and, seated before a plate of red herrings and a bottle of vodka, had discussed his life in the Lenin School. In 1949, at a regional party conference, I saw him again in Ostrava. He then told me about his activity in the war: he thought he was to be parachuted over the Ostrava region where he was to work with the underground Communist Party. He landed safely, but then discovered, to his amazement, that he was several hundred miles away from Ostrava, in a suburb of Warsaw. After a series of extraordinary adventures he arrived at his destination safe and sound.

Why was he here? He told me that he had been arrested, like many other old communists, but had been luckier than I and the defendants in my trial. He only received a light sentence. He couldn't understand what was going on. He told me he had written to Zapotocky about it and that he hoped to see him personally, now that he had almost served his sentence: 'He can't know what's happening here.'

From what he told me about his interrogations I gathered that the methods used were nothing like what we had gone through in Koldeje and Ruzyn. He asked me what had happened to us and about the trial, and I told him it had all been rigged and I was innocent.

Peschl was called to his visit. We embraced, probably thinking the same thing: 'This is where we are after twenty-five years' struggle!'

I was now alone. One after another the prisoners received their visitors and returned to their cells. At last my turn came. I was taken into the visitors' waiting room, where my family and I sat round a table in the presence of two prison officers.

Lise proudly explained that she had seen the director and protested about seeing me behind bars. She had asked to speak to the Minister of the Interior and the Party Secretariat on the telephone. The prison management was in a state of upheaval. This was unprecedented. I knew what she was like when she lost her temper – a real lioness. The director didn't know what to do, as my wife asked for her telephone communications in a mixture of French, Russian and Czech. He left to ask for orders, and returned a little later, telling her to wait. When the visits were over she would be able to see me.

And there we were. Lise was sitting next to me and we were holding hands. The boys were shy, but after a few seconds they kissed me. Françoise told me how sorry she was to leave. I looked at my parents-in-law and wondered what would have become of my wife had it not been for them! Thanks to them my children had had a home in spite of what happened to me and Lise's exhausting work in the factory.

My father-in-law tried to make some jokes, but I could feel that he was on the verge of tears behind his smile. I remembered him at the Special Brigade, after our arrest in Paris in 1942, with his courage and good humour. And then, when we were transferred to the police station, he was put in a cell above mine and we talked to each other through the window. He used to send me cigarettes on the end of a string. And when we were taken for a walk in separate yards I could hear him shout words of encouragement. We called to Lise and she answered us, clinging to the bars of her cell window.

After our arrest in the war, my mother-in-law had been left on her own with Françoise, who was then three. Her husband, her son, her son-in-law and her daughter were all in prison. My brother-in-law, Frédo, in prison since October 1941, had to have a serious operation on his head after the blows he received during his interrogations, and was in the infirmary of Fresnes. Every week my mother-in-law went from prison to prison. with her parcels, while Françoise, weeping with exhaustion, trotted along behind her, clinging to her skirt. They went from the police station where they had seen Pépé, to La Santé where I was; from La Roquette to visit Lise, to Fresnes where Frédo lay in the infirmary. . . . Sometimes she brought us parcels of food and linen, at other times she just came to see us. . . . Not once did she complain. She always had a word of encouragement and the latest news from the front. . . . She tried to help Frédo escape, but the plan failed at the last moment when the organizer was arrested during a police raid.

Sitting before my parents-in-law I thought of all these things. It was they who had stood by Lise and protected her, and it was thanks to them, the parents-in-law of Raymond Guyot, that my wife had not been arrested and my children had not been sent to orphanages.

Lise told me about her plans for departure. Her belongings were to go by train and the whole family would fly to Paris. She confirmed the fact that Hanka Urbanova would remain in touch with me in her stead, visiting me and sending me letters and parcels. Lise had informed the Party Directing Committees, in order to protect our cousins from any unpleasant consequences. She had requested the Ministry of the Interior to draw up a report on the subject so that nobody could hold it against the Urbans.

Lise told me how my physical appearance worried her. I had grown thinner since I left Ruzyn for Leopoldov, five months ago. Yes, I said, I had been ill.

'As soon as I get to Paris, the first thing I shall do will be to persuade Michel's uncle to adopt him. That's the only reason I'm leaving.'

The half hour we had been granted passed all too quickly. I knew every second was counted and I wanted to retain this last image of them. Now the truth would be known. But I had little hope of being able to survive until all had been found out. Lise had difficulty in repressing her tears. 'The main thing for you,' she said, 'is to look after your health. Everything else will be all right. Believe me!'

I hugged them all and held Lise in my arms, whispering: 'The living conditions in Leopoldov would kill me in the long run. I receive no medical attention and I feel worse and worse. I don't think I can last much longer. Do what you can as soon as possible. On my side, I'll start taking action too.'

Lise smiled at me through her tears, and they left. I remained alone in my cell in Pankrac. My family's departure solved my main problem. As soon as I returned to Leopoldov I would be able to fight for the truth.

Two days later I was taken back to the Central Prison in a large convoy of prisoners. I was the only one in chains. I felt much sicker. My temperature must have risen still higher because of the journey to Prague and back, the cold, and my light clothing. In Leopoldov I was put in a new cell with about forty men and I knew nobody. The next day I was to start work. At midday I saw Vavro for a second as he passed in front of my cell and I told him the reasons for my visit to Prague.

My temperature rose. Everything was spinning, and in the afternoon I fainted. A doctor came. I had a temperature of 105.8°F. He gave me some aspirins and put me down for the medical inspection the next morning. I spent a dreadful night, with nightmares brought on by the fever. I sweated, felt hot and cold. I could hardly breathe and thought I was going to die.

The next day I was unable to go to the workroom, from where I would normally have proceeded to the medical inspection. The warder insisted, but I couldn't even put my feet on the ground. Two hours later I was taken to the infirmary on a stretcher.

The prisoner-doctor who directed the infirmary took my temperature. It was as high as ever. He sounded my chest and then inspected me in detail. He established that I had broncho-pneumonia with a bilateral reactivation of the tubercular process. He ordered me straight to the hospital, so I was placed in an infirmary cell where I received treatment, consisting mainly of streptomycin and penicillin injections.

Five

My family left Prague on 6 October 1954. Their departure had been postponed because they had to wait for a French visa for my parents-in-law, whose Nansen passports had expired. It was only after Raymond Guyot had interceded with the Minister of the Interior, who was then François Mitterand, that the visa was granted. As far as my wife and children were concerned, the French Consulate facilitated all the formalities for their departure.

My family had their last dinner in Prague at Antoinette's. 'We drank to your return,' Lise told me when we saw each other later.

In spite of their grief at leaving me behind, my family were relieved that this difficult stage in their life was over. Now that they were facing a new one they were sure that it would end with the triumph of the truth.

Fernande and Raymond, together with Frédo and his young wife Monique, welcomed them at the airport. They all stayed with Raymond, except for Lise, who spent the night with her brother in Ivry. My secret message was in the furniture due to arrive by rail. Lise was right not to take it with her because, at the Prague airport, the customs officers went through all the luggage and handbags and confiscated any written material. They had undoubtedly received orders from Security.

My wife's sister got her a job as secretary to a clothier, and my family's living was assured.

Lise informed Raymond of my situation and explained exactly how the Security worked. She told him of the attacks on the French Party and some of its members. It was a shock for my brother-in-law. Three weeks later Lise fetched my message from the furniture-warehouse where her belongings had to wait many months more before she found a flat in Paris.

Raymond advised her to write to the Directing Committee of the Party and ask for her Party card, which she did at once.

The treatment I received in the infirmary consisted of injections which had to be given every four hours, night and day. In the daytime it was easy: the doctor or the nurse did it. But at night, when they weren't there, my injections could not be interrupted. The warder asked the other inmates of my cell whether anyone could inject me, and one prisoner volunteered. The warders agreed, and every four hours they handed him the syringe through the bars.

He treated me with great solicitude. I still had a temperature of over 104°F. and felt terribly ill. He stood at my bedside and put cold compresses on my wrists and temples. He told me his life history. He came from Spieska Nova Ves, and had been a member of the National Socialist Party. During the war he fought in the SS division, Das Reich, and became a lieutenant. He ended his story saying: 'You see how we've ended up? We're each paying for our belief, I in Hitler, you in Stalin!' And he commented: 'If Hitler hadn't been so stupid, if he hadn't attacked the USSR, if he hadn't performed such massacres in the occupied territory, above all in Russia, and if he hadn't murdered the Jews, we wouldn't have lost the war. That's worse than a mistake. I, and a whole lot of other Germans, will never forgive Hitler for doing that. Not only was it pointless, but all those barbarous acts have made us murderers in the opinion of the world. And that's why we lost the war.'

Another time he told me: 'It's odd that, after being poles apart, we should both be here in the same prison, in the same cell, myself sentenced to thirty years as a war criminal and you to life imprisonment as a communist.'

He really did look after me well until I left the infirmary. I never saw him again. I later heard that he had been released during an exchange of prisoners with West Germany. He always told me that he had no crimes on his conscience. He had been arrested because of a letter which accused him of being a violent Nazi. And indeed he did not deny having been an active member of Hitler's Party.

About a week after I had arrived in the infirmary, towards 20 October, I was taken into a room where a military attorney, whom I had seen at Zavodsky's trial, was sitting.

He introduced himself as an attorney of the supreme military tribunal and started to question me about Pavel. I was amazed, because I knew that Pavel had already been sentenced. To start with I eluded the questions, playing for time so that I could see what he was aiming at. But at the same time I saved up my strength like an athlete, so that I could at last tell him what I thought of the trials.

I made up my mind. I said: 'All the charges against Pavel are false. He's innocent!'

The attorney looked at me in surprise: 'And you're telling me that now?'

He raised his voice and I said: 'Don't shout. I'm telling you now and I've got a number of other things to tell you. If I haven't done so until now it was because I was unable to.' I told him about the threats made to me and my family in Ruzyn if I went back on my confessions.

'Who threatened you?' he asked.

I gave him Kohoutek's name and physical description. I

added: 'Since my family has already left the country and is now out of reach of any repressive measure, and since I'm at last in the presence of somebody who is not from Security, an attorney, I can tell you these things. But you must protect me, because, I repeat, threats have been made to kill me like a rat if I go back on what I said.'

The attorney was pale. He asked: 'And what about the other volunteers from Spain?'

'The same applies to all of them. All the statements and "confessions" extorted from me about them are false, just as their charges against me are false. None of us have ever acted against the Party.'

He paused again. Then he asked: 'And you?'

'I'm innocent like all the others. The whole Slansky trial was rigged!'

The pipe he was smoking dropped out of his mouth. He stood up and called the warder. He was in such a state of nerves that he was literally trembling. He gave orders that I should be taken out and guarded in the corridor.

Half an hour later he called me back. He was pacing up and down nervously. 'What you've just told me, Mr London, is a terrible revelation. It is extremely serious and I shall have to tell my superiors about it.'

'That's why I told you. Please do tell your superiors, tell the President of the Republic and the Party Directing Committee about our conversation. And please allow me to have a normal interrogation at which I can explain myself in detail. But I must again beg you to see to my personal safety.'

Thereupon I was taken back to the infirmary. The next day I asked for special permission to write a letter to the attorney general. I was allowed to write one page. In a few lines I explained that 'confessions' had been extorted from me and the other accused by violent physical and psychological methods.

That was that! The letter was taken away, and all I could do was to wait.

I managed to get a message through to Hajdu and Hromadko

to tell them about my meeting with the attorney and my written demand for a revision of the trial. I told Hajdu that the time had come for him to do the same thing.

At this point, on 24 October 1954, I received a visit from my cousin Hanka. This was an unexpected opportunity to inform the outside world of the step I had just taken.

This visit, three weeks after seeing my family in Prague, was a fortunate coincidence. According to the prison rules I was only entitled to a visit every five months and the permit was automatically sent by the prison administration to my cousin. My journey to Prague, on the orders of the Ministry of Security, did not count as a visit.

Hanka told me that my family had reached France safely and had settled at Raymond Guyot's.

Taking no notice of the warder standing next to me, I decided to tell her about the latest developments, and so, through Hanka, Lise heard of them a few days later.

I told her I had seen the attorney, that I had withdrawn my statements and 'confessions' and had sent a written request to the attorney general to reopen my trial 'because all my statements and confessions were extorted under illegal physical and psychological pressure'.

The warder was so astonished by what I said – he knew who I was and what trial I was referring to – and he was so curious about what I was going to say next, that he did not once interrupt me.

Hanka was delighted. But she was also worried because I told her of my tubercular relapse and my precarious state of health. She promised to write to my wife as soon as she returned to Kolin.

Lise received her letter early in November.

'When I got it,' she told me, 'my first thought was that your illness was going to kill you just after you had asked for a revision of your trial. That was terrible. I realized that we were fighting against time. I remembered what you said when you left me: "Hurry, Lise. Don't lose any time. I won't survive in Leopoldov for long."

'I immediately told Raymond the bad news about your health and of your struggle to prove your innocence. I told him that I was going to write that very day to the highest authorities of the Czech Party to ask that measures be taken to save you, and that you be conditionally released.

'Raymond advised me only to raise the problem of your health, for the time being. He said that it would be unwise to argue or to mention your struggle for rehabilitation, which could perhaps prevent immediate action being taken on account of your health. What he said made sense: "The main problem is to save Gérard!"

'On 9 November 1954, I wrote personally to Novotny, the First Secretary of the Party, to Zapotocky, the President of the Republic, and to the Minister of Justice.

'I telephoned the Czech Ambassador in Paris, Soucek, and asked for an urgent appointment. He saw me the next day and behaved admirably. I gave him the three letters and asked him to post them as quickly as possible since it was a matter of life and death for you. He told me that the pouch left the next day and would be in Prague that evening. That was 11 November 1954, Françoise's sixteenth birthday.'

Six

A few days after I had sent the letter to the attorney general orders were given to dismiss me from the infirmary. The doctor's protests were to no avail. He was even forbidden to give me medicine to take away. I was sent to the new building, and I thought I was to be transferred as a result of my letter. Was I to return to Ruzyn? That was what I feared most. But I soon discovered that this was not the case. Instead of going towards the transfer cells I climbed some stairs and found myself in the isolation section.

For some time it had been rumoured that an isolation section had been set up in the new prison building. Before going to Prague to see my family I had heard that the defendants from the trial of the so-called 'bourgeois Slovak nationalists' were there, together with the regional secretaries of the Svermova group. When I returned I heard that other prisoners had been sent there too – Pavel, Vales, and Kevic. This step had caused everyone great anxiety, since there was no apparent reason for it.

I was now in the same cell as Kostohryz, a well-known intellectual serving a heavy sentence in connection with the trial of the Green International.* He was very friendly and told me about our living conditions. We were cut off from the rest of the prison. Only a very limited number of warders had access to our section. We were also completely cut off from the other floors. Although the prison management had attempted to isolate the cells from each other we still managed to communicate by tapping on the walls. We saw each other during our walks, when several prisoners gathered in the yard at the same time. This was how I managed to see Goldstücker, Kevic, Pavel, Vales, Hasek and some others.

I was amazed to hear that Hajdu had also been transferred to our section, almost at the same time as myself. To our mutual satisfaction he was put in the cell next to mine. Löbl, on the other hand, remained in the old building.

My cellmate told me that Pavel was the fatigue man on our floor. He appeared at soup time. As he pushed the two bowls through the door he managed to slip a pencil, a piece of paper and a note into my hand: 'I must know whether you've already been questioned about me and what happened.'

As I handed him the empty bowls I murmured 'This evening.'

* This trial included all the right-wing political parties, but above all the Agrarian Party.

During the afternoon, while my cellmate peeped through the spy-hole, I wrote a full account of my meeting with the attorney, the revocation of my 'confessions' and statements about myself and the other accused, including him, and my request for a revision of the trial. That evening, when he collected the bowls, Pavel whisked my note away with the skill of a conjurer.

I tried to get in touch with my friend Vavro, but he couldn't understand the old Bolshevik alphabet I used. Thanks to Pavel's pencil I managed to hand him a key to the alphabet the next day, on our walk. That night he told me that he preferred to wait before demanding a revision of his trial.

After my concentrated treatment with antibiotics and other medicines in the infirmary I received no medical attention whatsoever. Every day I asked to see a doctor and get some medicine. But it was no good. All I could get was extra milk. As the days went by my temperature rose again. I felt much worse, I thought that they wanted to kill me like a rat. No doubt the men of Ruzyn were carrying out their threats.

Late one afternoon, after curfew (around 10 December 1954), the head warder personally ordered me to prepare for a transfer. I tried to pass the news on to Vavro but we couldn't understand each other in the rush. As I took leave of my cellmate, with whom I had been on excellent terms, I begged him to tell Vavro what had happened to me.

A few minutes later I found myself in a ground-floor cell on my own. About an hour later the fatigue man scratched on the door and whispered through the spy-hole that Löbl had just been put in a cell in this section. He was to be transferred and wanted to know where I was going. I said that I had no idea and asked what happened to Hajdu. It had suddenly occurred to me, on hearing that Löbl was here, that we were all going to be transferred to Ruzyn because of my letter.

The next morning I was taken out into the corridor but I was kept apart from the other prisoners who were to be transferred. I saw Löbl, but not Vavro. By changing places with one prisoner after the other Löbl gradually managed to edge nearer to me. He asked me what was going on. In a few words I told him of my meeting with the attorney and my letter. He was surprised. Had I thought about the consequences? I said that I had decided to go the whole hog and advised him to do as much: 'It's now or never!'

We were ordered back to our cells. I took the opportunity to enter Löbl's cell, so we had a few precious minutes' conversation. He asked me about conditions in the isolation section. Who was there and what did the other prisoners think about the situation?

I told him what little I had discovered during my stay there and about my insistence that the other defendants should take the same step as I. Löbl was puzzled. 'What did Goldstücker say?' I told him he was thinking the matter over, but I thought he would agree.

We left our cells, but contrary to what I expected I did not leave with Löbl and the others. The others got into a bus while I was put in an ambulance and chained to a stretcher. One warder sat next to me and another one next to the chauffeur. This special treatment worried me.

I had no idea that my wife, who had already received Hanka's letter, had also started to intercede for me.

I soon realized that we were driving towards Prague. Where? To Ruzyn or elsewhere? We arrived at about midnight. We were in Pankrac prison! I was taken to a section where I was ordered to undress. What astonished me was to see that very few of the cells were occupied, and in front of the ones that were the prisoners' clothes lay folded near the doors. It was the first time I had seen anything like that.

The cell I was in was clean and newly painted. There were some inscriptions under the paint but they had been carefully scratched out.

My mattress was placed immediately under the door. When I lay down my head was a yard from the door, facing the window. My clothes had been removed but I was left my tobacco. I couldn't sleep because I was obsessed by what was going to happen to me, and the idea that I was going to be executed.

The light remained on. Unable to sleep, I decided to smoke a cigarette. As I lit it I suddenly noticed that the door was open and that a warder was looking at me. I first thought he was going on his rounds. After a while I got up to light another cigarette and saw that the door was still open and the warder still in the same place. It then occurred to me that normally only prisoners in the death cell were subjected to this constant surveillance. Now I realized why the clothes were in front of the doors, why the cell was so clean, carefully repainted and the inscriptions scratched out: I was in the death cell.

'Where am I?' I asked the warder.

'You ought to know.'

'I know that I'm in Pankrac, but why in this death cell?'

'You ought to know what you've done! You haven't been brought here for nothing.'

'But I was sentenced to life imprisonment, not death!'

'All you need do is ask tomorrow, at the report.'

In the morning I asked to see the prison director or the head warder for an explanation. Nobody came to see me, but I was taken out for a walk. Before letting me out of my cell the warder clapped his hands and said: 'Clear out of the corridor and go back to your cells.' I was alone in a small yard. Before returning to my cell the ceremony was repeated. The warder clapped his hands and ordered: 'Back to your cells!' This time the fatigue men disappeared.

The same thing happened a little later when I was taken to the showers. I was no longer in any doubt: that was how prisoners sentenced to death were treated. And still there was no prison director or head warder to question.

The third day I said I was on a hunger strike. The warders tried to dissuade me. 'I shouldn't be in this section,' I told them. 'I haven't been condemned to death, but to life imprisonment. I want to know what's going on.'

The next day I was taken to see the prison director. He asked me why I had decided to go on a hunger strike. 'I've asked State Security about your case,' he told me. 'They said that one of their representatives would soon be seeing you.' He also told me not to worry; I was in the hands of the management of Pankrac and I must be patient.

I started eating again, waiting for my first interrogation with impatience. But I was still treated as before and nobody came for me. On 24 December I again refused to eat. In the middle of the afternoon a lieutenant came to my cell and told me: 'You're leaving this section. We're taking you somewhere else.' Where? We were now near the infirmary; I knew that because I had come here from Ruzyn once before. But I also knew that behind the infirmary were the gallows. The officer opened a cell, however, and said: 'Go in, we're there.'

I was in the infirmary. I sighed with relief. There were only two men in this cell with a dozen beds: a gypsy and a Yugoslav. I had successfully survived a critical stage. I had revoked my confessions and I was still alive. I later discovered that it was my wife's letter to the Party from Paris which made them decide to look after me.

I spent a happy Christmas, a hopeful Christmas. I had a new lease of life.

Seven

During the second fortnight of December my wife saw a paragraph in *Le Monde* which filled her with joy: Noel Field had been officially rehabilitated by the Hungarian government. Shortly before, his brother Herman had been rehabilitated by the Poles. She told me about her day:

'I read the news in the underground on my way to the funeral of Madeleine Chaumeil [I had known her first husband, Petit-Louis, who died fighting in the International Brigades in

Spain] I couldn't wait to tell Raymond about this new circumstance which permitted me to demand a revision of the trial. The next day I was determined to ask for a visa for Czechoslovakia.

'The ambassador saw me. I told him the facts and asked him to forward my request to Prague.'

Then Christmas and the New Year came. My wife wrote to Prague almost every day, to Hanka, Renée and Antoinette, so that, by putting their letters together, they could understand what she was doing (and elude the censor). Hanka was to keep me informed.

On 26 December, in a long letter, she gave an account of the Christmas party with her sister and Raymond, at the same time giving Hanka to understand that the Field brothers had been rehabilitated and that she had asked the ambassador if she could come to Prague and facilitate the revision of my trial.

She continued: 'Hanka's last letter with news of Émile [me] has worried us very much. On the other hand the fact that he should have left his house [Leopoldov] for his home town [Prague] seems a good sign. It must be in reply to the request made by his family in November. We hope he's receiving the attention he needs and will soon know better days.'

So they knew I'd been transferred to Prague!

On 1 January, Lise wrote again:

In all events I hope to see the doctor [the Czech ambassador] after the holidays and ask him about the result of the request I made a month ago.

I've talked at length to Fernande's husband about adopting the children. He's pleased with Gérard's work [she meant the letter I wrote about the revision of my trial]. He thinks he should continue to study on his own. At the moment there is a good chance that the new version of his thesis might be accepted, and then he'll be able to get his professorship [my rehabilitation].

Jean's father [Maurice Thorez] isn't in Paris. He's spending the winter in Provence because of his health. His wife came to see us twice with her children and was extremely friendly. I know that her husband is taking an interest in the health and morale of my eldest son. He advised an operation [my request for rehabilitation]. An invalid can only recover if he has the will to live. Last week he sent me and my family his love.

At Tonca's [in Czechoslovakia] things take a longer time to sort themselves out than anywhere else, Raymond told me on Sunday. He told Jean [Maurice Thorez] how surprised he was and wonders what the hell they're up to. They're not going to solve their problems at Tonca's; they should do it at home [Moscow]. But that's up to them.

Having received no reply either to her first letter requesting my conditional release or to her demand for a visa, Lise decided to file an official petition with the President, Zapotocky, about the revision of my trial, and she gave it to Soucek, the ambassador, on 22 February 1955.

On 10 November, 1954 I asked you for the conditional release of my husband, Artur London, who has been in prison since January 1951.

Since I made this request a new event has occurred which throws some legal doubt on the verdict pronounced against my husband and gives me the right to demand a revision of his trial. The main charge against him, that he was an agent in the pay of the head of American espionage, Noel Field, is no longer valid. After Herman Field's rehabilitation by the Polish government, his brother Noel, imprisoned in Hungary for five years, was released and rehabilitated by the Hungarian government, who also offered him political asylum. The communiqués informing world opinion emphasize the fact that the idea that the Field brothers were spies was the work of the enemies of democracy, and that the perpetrators of these crimes against truth and human rights should be punished.

These new elements make it the duty of Czech justice to revise the sentence passed on Artur London. (You can imagine what criminal methods were used to force my husband to plead guilty to a crime which he did not commit.)

Since you occupy the highest post in the Republic I am asking you to see to the revision of the A. London case in order to reveal the whole truth and allow an innocent man to return to freedom and his family and to receive necessary medical attention.

I am also sending a long letter to the leadership of the Czech party, enumerating certain points on which I base my conviction that my husband was innocent, even before Field's rehabilitation.

I repeat my proposal to the leadership of the Czech Communist Party: I am ready to come to Prague and help the Party directing Committee and the government throw some light on the London case, by providing all the documents and information I possess. This may be of great use to a new investigation.

In her letter to the Party, addressed to Antonin Novotny, she recapitulated all the lies in the bill of indictment and my evidence at the trial, starting with my 'espionage dealings with Noel Field', my 'Trotskyist activities', my 'sabotage of the French workers' movement'. Then she briefly recalled my true activity in the International Brigades, the Main d'Oeuvre Immigré, during and after the war, and my active participation in the Resistance movements in prison and at Mauthausen. In this last passage she wrote:

In all prisons and concentration camps his comrades always placed him at the head of the clandestine Party and Resistance organizations. In Mauthausen he was one of the organizers and animators of the International Committee of the camp – as the Czech comrades who knew him there can tell you: Antonin Novotny, Jiri Hendrych, both members of the Party Secretariat, Leopold Hoffman from Budejovice, and so many others.

And yet the weeks went by and Lise started to feel impatient. Until then she had kept to herself, avoiding old friends so as not to have to answer their questions about me and the trial. She knew that she had to be careful to prevent the papers from exploiting the matter. That would do me more harm than good.

But now, receiving no reply, my wife decided to ask her friends to support her. On Wednesday, 9 March 1955, she attended the first night of a puppet show. Her appearance in the theatre caused a sensation. Many old comrades and friends greeted her. The Czech ambassador arrived when she was surrounded by people and shook her hand.

'Janine and I had good seats in the stalls. Aragon and Elsa Triolet were in a box and when they saw me they waved and signalled to me to join them. I then went to their box. They embraced me and seemed delighted to see me again. We chatted until the curtain went up and I answered all their questions.'

Later Lise told me that they had asked to see her when they were in Prague in 1954, on their way to Moscow where Aragon was to preside over the Lenin prize. But they never succeeded.

All the time she was in a box with the Aragons, Lise thought: Tomorrow Prague will know of my reception this evening. She accepted every invitation to lunch and dinner which she received.

Eight

On 15 April 1955, my wife took the next step. This time she gave the ambassador a letter addressed to Viliam Siroky, the Premier, asking for a revision of my trial.

My wife's brother, Frédo, of whom I had grown extremely fond not only for family reasons but also because of our work in the Party and the Resistance, our life together in the French prisons and at Mauthausen, suffered greatly when Lise told him of my innocence and what I had been through. He sent a note to Hanka, which she was to read to me when she came to see me in prison:

I am writing to you on little Gérard's birthday, 3 April, 1955. I am delighted to know that you're innocent. Inside myself I never really believed you to be guilty, but it was difficult for me as a communist. Those who weren't in the Party and knew you, Fichez, Souchère and so many others, always refused to believe. If only you knew all the questions we asked each other when we met. I'm so unhappy about not being able to do anything for you. But things are improving. Cheer up, dearest Gérard. If only you knew how many people who love you are behind you. The nightmare will soon be over and we'll look after you when you come home. I embrace you, Gérard, like the time when we left Blois in chains, not knowing that we were going to Compiègne.

Through him Lise got in touch with some former prisoners from Mauthausen, and with the secretary general of the Amicale, Émile Valley, who had been a great friend of mine in the past. When my wife told him I was innocent, he showed no surprise: 'I never really believed he was guilty. I didn't understand what was going on, but I waited. We'll do all we can to help him.'

In a letter dated 3 May Lise wrote to Prague: 'Since the latest news about Gérard's health, confirmed by a letter from my cousin, I can hardly sleep. May Day was a sad day for me. I was at Vincennes, with all the demonstrators, but I could see and hear nobody but him. Ten years ago he had joined in the demonstration, with the first group of prisoners returned from the extermination camps. It was snowing then. . .'

During the procession Émile Valley told my wife that the Amicale was publishing Professor Michel De Bouard's book on Mauthausen in which Leopold Hoffman and I were mentioned as the organizers and members of the first secret international resistance committee in the camp. That was good news. This destroyed the charge of my hostile activities in Mauthausen. Mimile, as the secretary of the organization was called, sent her several copies of the book the next day so that she could include them among the documents for my rehabilitation. A few days later Lise met the ambassador and gave him two copies of the book, asking him to send them to the Party Directing Committee in Prague. Once again she repeated her request for a visa.

Frédo and Mimile informed several comrades from Mauthausen who had known me well and asked them to intercede for me, by recalling the part I played in the camp and my assistance to the French prisoners. Professor De Bouard applied personally to Jacques Duclos to ask him to take steps in my favour. Doctor Fichez, the vice-president of the Amicale, asked for an appointment with the Czech ambassador. He represented my comrades from the Resistance and the camps, and asked for my exemplary behaviour at Mauthausen to be taken into account, for I had saved masses of prisoners. He said that I should be conditionally released on account of my health.

I wrote another letter to the Party leadership from the Pankrac infirmary in January, demanding an interview with one of its representatives, in order to show up the methods used by Security to extort false confessions and statements. Still no reply.

From my cousin's letters I gathered that my wife was continuing to urge my release. During a visit she paid me with her husband, she told me about Field's rehabilitation. This stimulated and encouraged me. I told them that I was doing everything in my power to make the Party revise the trial, that I had already written once since I had been here and that I had just asked special permission to write to the Party leadership once more.

At this visit we talked freely. Far from trying to interrupt us, not only the warder standing next to me but his two colleagues, who had left their prisoners, came to listen to what we were saying. They were so obviously eager to know something about the trials that they even let us remain together longer than the regulations permitted.

The very day that my wife gave the letters for Zapotocky and Novotny requesting the revision of my trial to the Embassy in Paris (22 February) I wrote this other letter to the Central Committee, addressed, this time, to Viliam Siroky. I repeated my request to speak to a Party representative. But I still received no reply.

The only change in my situation was the notification that my sentence had been reduced to twenty-five years, according to the amnesty proclaimed on the tenth anniversary of victory.

My life continued in the infirmary without any changes. I

received the medical attention I required, but my health did not improve. The X-rays showed cavities and a bilateral focus of infection in progressive activity. I also suffered from asthma and emphysema and nervous complaints, acute insomnia and a gastric ulcer.

I heard from a prisoner-doctor that the leading officials had demanded a detailed report on my state of health. At the same time another prisoner said he had been summoned by the officer on duty in the infirmary and questioned in detail about me, my behaviour in the cell, and what I said. He told me he gave the best information. This made me suspect something. But what? It was already May.

During a meal with the Wurmsers, Lise spoke to Ilya Ehrenburg. He told her that he had personally never believed in the trial or my guilt. Lise described all the steps she had taken and her determination to knock at every door to accelerate my rehabilitation. 'If you knew what I've been through. Language fails. You see, if I weren't such a loyal communist, and sure that our cause was just and that nothing must be allowed to harm it, I would a act like any other woman and simply shout that my husband was innocent. I would publicize all the documents and evidence which proved it. . .' Ehrenburg approved of what she said; he thought she was doing the right thing, and advised her to get as many comrades as possible to stand up for me.

A few days later she received a telephone call from Marcel Servin, the secretary of the Party organization. He told her that her Party card would be returned to her in a few days' time. For Lise, Party membership was extremely important because she wanted to return to Prague, where she had been excluded from the Czech Party, as a fully fledged communist.

Lise told me about the meeting of the cell of the République area, when her card was returned to her. The secretary made a speech to the comrades present, saying she was an old member and that her membership of the French Party had been interrupted by a stay abroad. He was now glad to welcome her back to it.

She was very moved, because she remembered the other cell meeting in Prague when she had been excluded. At the time she had said: 'I was, am, and will remain a communist, with or without your card.'

On 2 June 1955 the embassy informed her that her visa for Prague had arrived and she could fetch it when she wanted. The next day she took the aeroplane to Czechoslovakia and was met at the Ruzyn airport by my cousins Urban and Sztogryn, Antoinette and Renée. Her return marked a new stage which we all hoped would be decisive, not only for me but also for Vavro and the others. The first visit she paid was to Hajdu's mother, who hugged her, weeping for joy.

Nine

I now entered my sixth month at the Pankrac infirmary. From fellow prisoners who had been recently arrested or transferred from a labour camp where they were allowed to read the newspapers, I completed my picture of the events which had taken place since I had been cut off from the outside world. I heard new details about the Beria case, which led to trials against Abakumov and Riumin. I heard of the changes in the USSR which followed Stalin's death, that Khrushchev had replaced Malenkov, of the introduction of joint leadership, and the rapprochement with Yugoslavia. This political development was very encouraging. The local papers were full of articles about socialist legality and condemned every infraction of the law. . . . But I still had no reply to my letters.

The news of Lise, given me by Hanka, was comforting. I knew that the French Party had been informed, that Lise had demanded a revision of the trial, that she was now awaiting her visa to come and see me and take further steps to rescue me in Prague itself.

I had no news of Löbl and Hajdu. I didn't know where they were. In Leopoldov? In a labour camp?

I waited. The days dragged on endlessly.

At the end of May a warder took me to a building some distance from the infirmary and showed me into an office. Three men were sitting behind a table. They told me they were part of a special commission from the Central Committee, whose duty it was to verify the violations of socialist law. One of them introduced himself personally. He was Ineman. I had heard about him before my arrest. I knew he was an old Party member and that he had been deported to Buchenwald during the war.

They were there at last! I could hardly hide my excitement. The three men were polite and kind. They asked me about Pavel and Vales. I gave them the best information I could about both of them. I described the illegal methods, the physical and moral violence used at Koldeje and Ruzyn to extort false 'confessions' and 'statements', and the slanderous declarations made by one prisoner about another. And then I referred to all the former volunteers who had been condemned. The representatives of the commission brought me back to the point:

'For the time being we are only studying the cases of Pavel and Vales; you must stick to them!' They were obviously interested in what I said and carefully noted my replies.

When I saw they were about to leave without asking any further questions I said: 'I must remind you that what I have said applies as much to the other volunteers as to Pavel and Vales!'

'We'll see about them later,' they replied. 'The situation isn't as simple as all that. The commission is faced with a series of extremely complicated problems. It'll take time to sort them out.'

They put their papers back in their briefcases, stood up, and were just about to leave when I said: 'And how about me? I've written to the Party Directing Committee several times asking them to examine my case. When are you going to deal with me?'

Ineman told me bluntly: 'As far as the main trial is concerned, there is nothing we can do about it for the time being. I don't want you to have any illusions. It may last a long time. You're one of the fourteen leaders of the centre of conspiracy sentenced during this trial. It was a public trial. All the papers, the world over, wrote about it extensively. Books have even been written about it! So the Political Bureau has decided not to revise that trial.'

When he saw the expression of despair in my face, he added a few words of encouragement: 'Don't give up altogether. Be patient. Everything depends on the internal and international situation. One day we'll have to revise that trial too, but when and how, I don't know!'

I returned to the infirmary overwhelmed by this reply. I then thought about the accuracy of the analysis Hajdu, Löbl and I had made of our prospects in Ruzyn and Leopoldov. We speculated on the conditions for a change in the situation and concluded that one day they would have to revise all the trials except for ours, because they wouldn't want to resuscitate the ghosts of the eleven innocent men condemned to death. To question it would be to raise problems concerning the system and the men. That was why they would try to forget it forever.

I was sunk in despair. There was to be no way out for us – Löbl, Hajdu and me. And yet, two or three days later, I recovered from my depression and started to view the situation from another angle: there must be a way out. When they began examining the trials, whichever case they chose to start with, the whole system was obviously going to be questioned sooner or later. They'd have to come to us one day. As Ineman said, the main thing was to be patient. But, ill as I was, how long would I be able to survive? My condition was still very serious, in spite of the antibiotics and other medicines I was taking. I decided the delay might last a year, and thought about what to do in the meantime.

A few days later, as I was still deep in these thoughts, I was summoned just before the cells were closed for the night. I put on a clean suit, was shaved and went down to an office where I found myself face to face with the Under-Secretary of the Interior, Jindra Kotal, who was in charge of the prisons. I had known him in Mauthausen, a simple, modest, courageous comrade. He had devoted himself singlemindedly to the organization of the clandestine resistance movement in the camp. We had been on the best of terms, and, after my return to Czechoslovakia, I had seen him several times; he was then working on the regional committee of Prague with Antonin Novotny.

Later I saw him at the Leopoldov prison on an inspection tour, wearing an officer's uniform. He walked through the workrooms, accompanied by the commandant and all the prison directors. That was when I realized that he had been promoted. Sitting in front of the pile of feathers which I had to pluck I noticed a bantering expression on his face as he looked at me. He smiled ironically. And I wasn't the only one of his former acquaintances in the workroom. So this man, who had survived Mauthausen, knew of the appalling conditions in Leopoldov. How could he allow people to live like that, in a socialist state, in what were pompously called the Institutions of Re-education through Work? And how could he stand in front of us, his fellow comrades in battle and suffering, without feeling ashamed? That was what the system made of men who had once been humane.

He addressed me politely, coldly, as if he had never seen me before. He inquired about my health. Was there anything I wanted? I was flabbergasted. What was happening to me? I said that my only desire was to have my case cleared up and to be released. I reminded him of my requests to this effect and told him of my recent meeting with the representatives of the special commission of the Central Committee. He replied that these problems were outside his competence. But he wanted to know my other wishes.

'I don't have any others!'

He then made some suggestions. 'Would you like us to get you some books?'

'Of course, I miss reading and I'd always be delighted to have some.'

What else would I like? A better cell, perhaps?

'No, I don't care about that. But you might tell Comrade Ineman to come back and see me as soon as possible so that I can give him a detailed account of the way the charges, the trials and everything to do with the former volunteers in the International Brigades were rigged and the methods used by Security against us!'

He promised to pass on my message and continued: 'What else can I do for you?'

It was then that it occurred to me that Lise was waiting for her visa in Paris.

'Get my wife the visa she has requested.'

'Your wife! Of course! Why do you always write to her about your health? There's nothing she can do for you, and you're worrying her unnecessarily. Why give her more worries than she already has?'

I really didn't expect that. 'So you think I should hide my state of health from my family? I don't agree. I have no right to let them deceive themselves about me.'

When he interrupted me again to ask what I wanted I replied concisely: 'The revision of my case, a visa for my wife, and some books, if you don't mind.'

'We'll see to all that!' he said with a smile, and took his leave of me.

Back in my cell I wondered what the point of this visit had been. Was this measure ordered by the special commission? Did they think that the least they could do was to improve the conditions of my imprisonment in view of the fact that I couldn't be released? I thought about that all night. The next morning I was transferred to a cell where I was on my own. I was brought some books. The warder whom I questioned could give me no explanation. I was far from pleased to be in solitary confinement again.

I spent three days stewing in my own juice. I asked for special permission to write to the Party Directing Committee and the President, and to receive an unlimited quantity of writing paper. I had made up my mind: I was going to write down all that had happened to us, all the inhuman and illegal methods used by the Security men, everything. In my mind I drew up a plan of the report I was going to write in the most convincing and comprehensive way possible. It was an hour after curfew and I was in bed when I heard the key turn in my cell door. It was the director of the infirmary.

'Get up,' he said, 'you're going to be shaved. They'll bring you some clean clothes. But don't lose any time!'

I got up, the barber arrived, shaved me, and whispered in my ear: 'What's happening to you? Where are you going?'

I didn't know.

I was taken to an office in another building, where I was made to wait, facing the wall. A warder sat next to me. Suddenly a door opened behind me and a voice ordered: 'Turn round! Come this way!'

I obeyed. The officer standing in the doorway waved me past him. And I found myself before my wife, radiant, smiling, her eyes gleaming with happiness.

She fell into my arms. 'Here I am at last. Uz jsem tady.'

So my meeting with Kotal was merely to prepare me for this meeting with my wife.

The special commission of the Central Committee had been operating since the beginning of 1955. Evidently the Party leadership already knew about the part played by Security in the fifties. The pressure of external events mounted. In the USSR the prisoners were returning from Siberia, in Poland and Hungary the Field brothers were rehabilitated. Next the Rajk trial had been revised and finally, because of the spectacular change of relations with Yugoslavia, the Party leadership was forced to revise some of the charges made in the trials which contradicted this new political course. The future, however, was still confused and uncertain.

Lise had come for a fortnight. After her arrival she was put up, to her amazement, in the Party hotel. And every day she came to Pankrac to visit me for an hour. This paradoxical situation was typical of the confusion of the times.

The night she arrived Baramova, who was now responsible for the International Section of the Central Committee, rang her to say that an appointment had been made for her on Monday at three o'clock with Barak, the Minister of the Interior, 'who wants to see you'.

On that sunny Sunday before we met, Lise saw, for the first time, the enormous monument to Stalin which had been finished shortly after her departure from Prague. Huge and ugly, it crushed the town from the top of the Letna hill. Through some involuntary slip of the sculptor, Stalin seemed to be at the head of a coffin draped with a flag. As Lise said, it was the burial of communism. And to think that this horror had been inaugurated just when the 'personality cult' was being publicly denounced. That too was typically paradoxical.

On Monday my wife saw Barak, who started to explain the problem of the law violations and to tell her about the special commission which had been set up to deal with these problems. Lise went straight to the point: 'The Security methods used during the investigation were as follows. The "confessions" were extorted in the following manner. The charges were all invented. This was how the reports were drawn up. The evidence at the trial was learnt off by heart by the defendants, the judge, the attorneys and the lawyers.'

Fascinated, the Minister listened to my wife for over an hour. 'But comrade, you know more about it than I do,' he said. 'Where did you find all this out?'

Lise told him how I had given her this information, using our experience of underground work and prison life during the war.

Barak asked where my message was. My wife replied that, after informing her brother-in-law and Maurice Thorez of its contents, she had left it in Paris at my request. At the end of the meeting Barak told her that the special commission of the Central Committee would see her tomorrow and hear what she had to say. 'You see,' he added, making as if to wash his hands of the whole matter, 'I never had anything to do with it. I want the truth to be known about all this.'

My wife then told the Minister that she wanted to visit me that day. Although it was late Barak agreed, so Lise came to Pankrac half an hour later.

Every day Lise brought me a food parcel. It was her dinner, which she put in the refrigerator of the hotel kitchen every evening. Sentenced to life imprisonment for treason, a prisoner in Pankrac, I received my daily bread straight from the Party hotel.

To start with a man from Security, in civilian clothes, sat with my wife and me. He was stubborn, coarse and brutal. He wanted to stop us holding hands and talking about things which he considered taboo. We were determined to take no notice, and continued our conversations unperturbed. He foamed with rage and threatened to interrupt our visits. Subsequently he changed his tactics and listened to us, his eyes half closed.

My wife complained about his presence at our meetings and we had the satisfaction of seeing him replaced by a prison warder who always behaved correctly. Ineman later told me that he was a confidential agent of the advisers, put there to report on us.

Lise was heard on several occasions by the special Commission. She gave further details about the content of my message and what she had done with it. But by refusing to give them the message itself, she thought she would force them to revise my case.

Ineman told her frankly that the same men who had rigged the trial were still in the Security Services. They did everything to prevent the commission from having access to the archives in order to obstruct the revision of the trials. He told my wife to take care when she spoke to people, on the telephone or anywhere else.

What remained of all the charges held against me at the trial? Noel Field had been rehabilitated and the charge of having been an agent in his pay had miscarried. Yugoslavia had been recognized as having always been socialist, so my 'Titoism' was meaningless. Zilliacus had been rehabilitated, so the second charge of espionage fell through. The Rajk trial had been revised, so that most of the charges against me and the veterans from Spain were destroyed. Every day new cracks appeared in the building which had been so carefully erected by the Soviet ringleaders and their men in Ruzyn.

What remained? The decision of the Political Bureau not to question our trial on my account. I saw the time of Lise's visit running out. Then one day, just before my wife was to leave, Ineman and his two colleagues came into the room where we were sitting. 'The commission has been ordered to look into your case!' they told me.

So, despite the initial decision of the Political Bureau, they were now obliged to look into my case. Why? I thought, in addition to the collapse of the main charges, of the steps which Maurice Thorez could not have failed to take; steps which I knew little about, but which his attitude towards Lise and my family proved. Then there was the work done by my comrades from Mauthausen and friends whom my wife had got in touch with during her stay in Paris. And finally there was my manuscript, in a safe place, in France!

The Secretariat of the Czech Party asked Lise to prolong her stay in Prague until the revision of my case was over. She joyfully accepted this decision, which was probably inspired by the Party's desire to avoid indiscretions abroad. So she remained at my side throughout this ordeal.

Ten

All this time it was my sister-in-law and her husband who looked after my family in Paris. My wife now lived in a flat, in an annexe of the Party hotel.

In order to avoid broaching the whole of the trial the commission tried to isolate my own case. They tried to remove a pillar from the construction without letting the whole thing crumble! This was over-optimistic; sooner or later the whole building would collapse, in spite of all the props holding it up. Ineman, who was always frank with me, told me that certain members of the Political Bureau (whom he did not name) were opposed to the revision of my case. As my friend Oskar Vales told me later, when we were discussing the Party leaders, 'They never forgave us their mistakes!', they were trying to find extenuating circumstances at our expense. 'There's no smoke without a fire,' they said. 'They may not have committed all the crimes they were accused of, BUT. . .' They even tried to make us responsible for their own attitude at the time: 'They asked for what they got! They led us astray by pleading guilty and they created difficulties for the Party!'

When the members of the commission produced these arguments one day I replied: 'There you are! The guilty ones are now the victims!' I reminded them of the spectacular rehabilitation of the doctors in the USSR, and the punishment of those responsible, Beria included. And one of the victims, Vinogradov, had even received the Order of Lenin. Why hadn't they sent him back to prison?

They also tried to turn the victims against each other – and some comrades swallowed the bait for a time – by flattering some and slandering others, according to the resistance they put up against their torturers. They even tried to introduce this notion when they publicized our rehabilitation, in order to discredit us.

They were pretty brazen, those men who had supported the trials and voted for the resolutions demanding the supreme penalty for the traitors, now that they argued learnedly about the 'confessions', 'over the walnuts and wine'. Some stupidly declared: 'I'd never have let them force me to sign them.' Others, speaking after the event when they could see through it, turned the whole thing inside out, forgetting that a short time ago they either accepted all the Party's statements at their face value or remained hypocritically silent.

Why not try us again for perjury, to punish us for having succumbed to the most illegal and inhuman methods of State Security, to the mystifications and blackmail in the Party's name? Why didn't they decorate the executioners and the men who organized the trials?*

Before starting to revise my case, the commission told me, they had to sort out the minor cases, the ones tried *in camera*, or the secondary trials which received no publicity. They wanted to clear all the men who were charged for reasons similar to mine: former volunteers from the Brigades and officials in the Ministry of Foreign Affairs. Only later could they really delve into my case.

But they had to be careful. Any false step could be exploited

*Reading the French proofs of this book I saw, in the Czech union newspaper *Prace,* of 5 October 1968, that *Literaturnya Gazeta* of Moscow, of 2 October 1968, made a base attack on Edward Goldstücker, the President of the Czech Writers' Union. A victim of the Stalinist purges, sentenced to life imprisonment in 1953, he was now accused of having been a police spy and one of the main witnesses for the prosecution in the Slansky trial. A little earlier they had accused the former Minister of Foreign Affairs, Jiri Hajek, of being an old social democrat, a Gestapo agent and a Zionist, although he wasn't even a Jew. All this shows that in spite of the Twentieth Party Congress and the rehabilitations, the old Stalinist executioners, assisted by the neo-Stalinists, have not hesitated to pick arguments out of the mud of the trials, or to use these arguments, together with the same base and criminal charges, against the men whom they regard as obstacles to their policy.

by the men in the Political Bureau who opposed the rehabilitations. The commission told us that their work depended on
the decisions of the Party leaders.

Seeing that the investigation of my case might drag on,
my wife immediately made a request for my conditional
release so that I could be looked after in a hospital. She did not
tell me about this in case I should be disappointed by a refusal,
so I was amazed and delighted to find myself in the office of
the Pankrac prison, on 20 July, in the presence of Lise and two
comrades from the commission who had come to attend my
discharge.

I moved to the sanatorium in Ples. Apart from my wife and
my cousins, the Urbans, no one was to know where I was. I was
on a sort of probation.

After four and a half years of the most ghastly imprisonment
I was at last free – if only to a limited extent – but this was
quite something! It was extraordinarily easy to bear! The only
cloud over my happiness was the thought, which obsessed me
and was to obsess me for a long time, of my comrades who were
all as innocent as I and were still in prison. Lise told me that
most of them had left Leopoldov for the uranium mines of
Jachimov or Bribram. I tried to tell myself that life in a labour
camp was better than in Leopoldov, above all for the ones who
were in solitary confinement, but this was a meagre consola-
tion. I didn't forget them for an instant.

One Saturday afternoon in August my wife arrived in the
sanatorium in a terrible state: 'Guess who I met on the bus?
Margolius's widow! I'll never forget what she told me.'

Just after the bus left the station my wife felt that a fair-
haired young woman, part of whose face was hidden by dark
glasses, was staring at her. She looked back at her and after
a second's hesitation they had fallen into each other's arms.
'Londonova? You here? I thought you were in France!'

My wife then told her of the circumstances of her return a
few weeks earlier. Despite the fact that she was forbidden

to talk about it, she told her where I was and about the counter-investigation the special commission of the Central Committee was leading in order to rehabilitate me. Heda Margolius told her how pleased she was – for us at least all had ended well. Lise encouraged her to ask the Central Committee to rehabilitate her husband. 'It won't bring him back to life,' said Heda. 'But I'll do it, for his son's sake.'

The hospital staff welcomed me. The nuns working as nurses were very kind. They turned a blind eye when Lise climbed through a hole in the fence and visited me in the hospital outside visiting hours, and did the same thing later when I joined her in the room she rented in an isolated house on the edge of the woods.

The commission came to see me regularly and asked me to write a report on my activities in the Party and my arrest, imprisonment and condemnation. At the same time they advised me not to refer to the trial itself, for my report would not be accepted if I did. For six weeks, until the end of September, I dictated to my wife over three hundred pages in French. At night Lise returned to Prague with the day's work and dictated it to Renée who translated it straight into Czech so as to submit the instalments of the report as I wrote them. Thanks to this system, I managed to keep a copy of it, and together with the secret message written from Ruzyn, it provided the material for this book.

I ended the report and submitted it to the commission several months before the Twentieth Party Congress. Despite their warnings, I did not limit myself to my personal experiences but tried (although I respected certain taboos) to analyse all the criminal methods employed by the men of Ruzyn under the aegis of their 'real chiefs'.

I wrote about the International Brigades, the true activities of my fellow defendants, the veterans from Spain, and the part they played in the French Resistance. In this section of the report I devoted more space to them than to myself.

Writing about the period I spent in Koldeje and Ruzyn I

recalled my own experiences and those of my comrades. Through my own case the whole mechanism of the trials was revealed, and through my innocence that of all my fellow defendants.

Ineman later told me that my report was of great help in understanding and reconstructing the fabrication of the trials.

I can remember the evening when I hesitated before letting my wife submit the section dealing with the Soviet advisers. She had heard from Vera Hromadkova that a former Security employee (whose name I have forgotten) returned from Leopoldov to Pankrac to have his case revised. He had written to the Party leadership that Likhachev and Makarov, the two Soviet advisers who took an active part in the preparation of his trial, had been condemned in the Abakumov and Riuman group. Shortly after his letter was received he was sent back to Leopoldov and the revision of his case was stopped.

Should I submit my report as it was? I concluded that the truth must be told, whatever happened! The true instigators of all these arrests, of all the trials, had to be denounced, otherwise it would be impossible to understand the whole process.

I ended my report as follows:

I have tried to explain as clearly as possible what seems to me essential for the understanding of my case and the terrorist methods used by Security to force an honest Party member to plead guilty to crimes he never committed.

It is difficult to relate all the complex aspects of my ordeal in a way that makes them accessible to someone who has not experienced it, just as it was difficult to convey some idea of life in German concentration camps to people who had never been deported before 1945.

Many of the details I have given may seem insignificant at first sight. I gave them to enable the comrades who read this report to have a better understanding of the moral and physical tortures inflicted on me, and to enable them to imagine how they would have behaved if they had found themselves in a similar situation for months and years on end.

With the passage of time, I may have forgotten certain important facts which I shall later remember. But I think I have told the main part of the story.

To those comrades who say: 'You should have held your ground!' I must emphasize the fact that I was in the hands of the Party, accused, judged and condemned by the Party. How can one fight if the enemy are the Party and the Soviet advisers, and *every struggle is regarded as a struggle against the Party and the Soviet Union*?

It was only later, after my sentence, that I was informed (partly by my wife who told me about the Russian doctors on her first visit, and partly by reading the Soviet communiqués about Beria, Riumin and Abakumov) of the political events which enabled me to understand what I was going through and spot the enemies who organized this macabre comedy in the name of the Party.

Only when I heard that the Soviet Communist Party had condemned the antisemitic campaign which came out in the doctors' trial did I understand the sources of the antisemitism of which I was both witness and victim in Ruzyn.

When I heard of the condemnation of Beria and his accomplices, the denunciation of the illegal, terrorist methods used by the Soviet Security against honest Party members, I realized that I too had been a victim of Beria and his imitators in Czechoslovakia.

The Soviet Union has given a striking example of political and civic courage when it publicly denounced the infamies committed in the name of communism by enemies camouflaged within the Soviet Communist Party, and when it repaired the damage they caused.

When I understood the problem, my confidence in the Party and the USSR returned. I knew that the truth would soon be revealed.

I hope this honest account will enable the Party to throw all possible light on these problems.

A few months after I had written and submitted these last pages, the speech made by Khrushchev in February 1956 at the Twentieth Soviet Party Congress confirmed the contents of my report.

At that moment I saw the Twentieth Party Congress as the stream which would clean the Augean stables. I never thought that the bureaucratic and reactionary forces in the communist movement would still be strong enough to erect a dam against it, and that in my own country hundreds of men would spend years in prison, some of them dying there even though they were known to be innocent.

In October the commission told me that the Political Bureau was about to reach a decision. But the weeks went by. By December no solution had appeared. I heard that Pavel and Vales had been released; I knew that Dufek, Goldstücker and Kavan were on the way to being rehabilitated and that Vavro Hajdu's case was now going to be examined. This news delighted me and confirmed the fact that the revision of my case entailed that of others.

Every time the members of the commission came to see me I stood up for Hromadko, Svoboda, Holdos, Erwin Polak, Vavro, Hajdu and others. They said that they had received reports about Hromadko's bad conduct in prison. I spoke at length about the conditions in Leopoldov and told them the name of the man who spread these rumours (several of us knew him and mistrusted him). They nodded in silence. I said: 'You know what Hromadko's like. He can't keep quiet. And you can't expect an innocent man sentenced to twelve years, living in the degrading conditions of Leopoldov, knowing about the difficulties his wife and children are up against, to sing the praises of the Party!'

Ineman acknowledged that what I said was true, but added that there were people who were trying to exploit these facts in order to prevent the revision of Hromadko's case.

At the end of December Ineman and the comrades from the commission suddenly turned up in the hospital and told me that, at the last moment, difficulties had been raised by Köhler and Siroky, who maintained that I had deliberately acted against them in France during the war.

So it wasn't enough for them to have taken an active part in the witch hunt, to have had us arrested, accused and condemned; now, to justify themselves, they were trying to distort the truth. They were throwing the last obstacles before my rehabilitation. In view of the general reluctance to revise my case, the maintenance of their charges could influence the Political Bureau and prevent a decision in my favour. Fortunately I knew of witnesses and had no difficulty in proving my honesty to the commission. Ackerman and his wife, who lived in East Germany, and had travelled on the passports refused by Köhler, were two living witnesses. . . . Siroky would not be able to deny, before me and other witnesses of the period, that he himself had asked me to procure another passport for Köhler and his wife because Köhler was so frightened. As for the story about taking the wrong train, it was too stupid for words, unless they were going to use the lies of Ruzyn all over again!

The whole of January went by without any news. On 2 February my wife and I had agreed that I should go to Prague for the weekend (without permission, of course). I had just crossed the hospital fence and was walking along the path through the wood which led to the bus stop, when I saw a figure making its way across the thick snow in the valley, waving to me. I heard shouts and was amazed to recognize Lise's voice. 'Gérard! Gérard!'

I went towards her anxiously. I couldn't catch what she was saying. And then, suddenly, I heard:

'Gérard, you're free! You're free!'

Now she was standing next to me, laughing and crying at the same time. She fell into my arms and hugged me. 'Free! You're free, Gérard!'

And she explained: 'I telephoned the commission this morning to see if there was any news for you, and they told me that they had decided to rehabilitate you two days ago! They'd simply forgotten to tell us!'

Twelve Years Later

Twelve years after the end of my tale came 'the Czech Spring'. In 1968 the dam of reactionary forces, holding back our Party and society from the cleansing waves of the Twentieth Congress of de-Stalinization, burst.

It had taken twelve full years to shake off the past and to announce the rehabilitations, including my own, with due publicity. It had taken twelve years for us to be able to write that Socialism was made for men, with human faces, and for the Czechs and the Slovaks to unite in support of it.

And then, the very day that I arrived in Prague with my wife in order to give my manuscript to the Union of Czech Writers publishing firm, I witnessed the invasion of my country by 600,000 men and 6,000 tanks of the Warsaw Pact armies. I had been five hours in Prague when it began. So my life contained this chapter too, which was possibly the worst from a moral point of view. It was the first time in the history of the workers' movement that the other socialist countries attacked an ally whose only crime was to restore the people's confidence in socialism.

So I could also witness my compatriots' admirable behaviour, the proof of their civic consciousness, their sense of politics and their heroism.

On the morning of 21 August I saw a hundred boys and girls gather before the Ministry of the Interior, surrounded by the Soviet paratroopers and their tanks. I heard them shout: 'Long live Pavel! We're behind you!' I thought that we had not lived in vain. I thought. . . . But they said it louder than I, flying our flag bathed in the blood of the first victim, singing an old revolutionary song to the Soviet soldiers, about the flag red with the workers' blood.

'What are you doing here, brothers?' they asked the soldiers.

'You've been tricked! It is we who are the counter-revolutionaries, our whole country. And yet we are the revolution.' They spoke of life, socialism and liberty, of all I had ever dreamed of, of all *we* had ever dreamed of, and of all that was being practised in our country.

Now, at the end of September, I know that my country won a great victory. If it had yielded, if it had let the invaders fill the prisons, and allowed its children to be tried, if it had let the mill turn again and granted the Russians just one of the men whose heads they clamoured for, what would the consequences have been, not only in Czechoslovakia, but in the five invading countries? How many innocent men would have paid for this new repression?

Even if the hope born in Czechoslovakia in January 1968 had only produced this rehabilitation of the word socialism, this new respect for human values, the Czech and Slovak peoples would have won a decisive battle for the whole workers' movement. But this hope, though in peril, is no longer so fragile. It has spread so far that no force will be able to suppress it, unless it leaves a cemetery in its wake. Jan Huss's people have rehabilitated his slogan, 'The truth will triumph', and have wedded it for ever with the 'Internationale'.

Paris, 30 September 1968.

Epilogue

In December 1954 the *Pravda* announced the trial and execution of Abakumov, Beria's deputy Minister of Security, and of certain leading Soviet advisers who organized the Slansky trial, such as Likhachev.

In 1955 Kohoutek and Doubek were arrested and sent to prison. Owing to the amnesty and reduction of sentences in 1958, they were released. Kohoutek retired and Doubek was given an important job in the official travel agency, Cedok. He was in the Czech delegation at the Brussels World Fair while a number of his victims of the fifties were to spend another two years in prison.

Light administrative sanctions were taken against Smola and the other interrogators.

The public prosecutor, Urvalek, and the judge, Novak, also underwent administrative sanctions, but much later.

Ladislav Kopriva was excluded from the Party in 1963 by the Central Committee, together with Alexander Cepicka, Gottwald's son-in-law and former Defence Minister.

Karol Bacilek lost his post in the Party Praesidium and was replaced as First Secretary of the Slovak Communist Party by Alexander Dubcek. Bruno Köhler was also relieved of his functions as secretary of the Central Committee of the Czech Communist Party.

Bacilek and Köhler were only excluded from the Central Committee and had their Party membership suspended at the Central Committee meeting in May 1968 at the same time as Novotny and Siroky.

The first rehabilitation commission, presided over by Rudolf Barak, who was then Minister of the Interior, presented its report in September 1957. In almost every case it confirmed the verdict. It even considered that the fact that Slansky had been 'unmasked' had 'greatly assisted the Party', and that his sentence was 'just and fair'.

A second commission, presided over by Drahomir Kolder, was created in 1962. It submitted its report the following year, in April. Unlike the first it concluded that the trials rested on false charges. It demanded an annulment of the verdicts and pronounced itself in favour of the juridical rehabilitation of all the accused. The Central Committee refused rehabilitation as Party members to Rudolf Slansky, Otto Sling, Bedrich Reicin, Otto Fischl and Karel Svab.

Only in 1968 was the question of rehabilitation studied in full. On 1 May, the men condemned in the Slansky trial and other similar trials received the highest decorations of the Czech state.

Of the men mentioned in this book, five survivors played an important part in the process of democratization: Josef Smrkovsky, Gustav Husak, Eduard Goldstücker, Josef Pavel, and Leopold Hoffman.